Beginning Lua with World of Warcraft Addons

Paul Emmerich

Beginning Lua with World of Warcraft Addons

Copyright © 2009 by Paul Emmerich

ISBN-13 (pbk): 978-1-4302-2371-9

ISBN-13 (electronic): 978-1-4302-2372-6

Printed and bound in the United States of America 9 8 7 6 5 4 3 2 1

Lead Editors: Joohn Choe, Matthew Moodie
Technical Reviewer: Chris Lindboe
Editorial Board: Clay Andres, Steve Anglin, Mark Beckner, Ewan Buckingham, Tony Campbell, Gary Cornell, Jonathan Gennick, Michelle Lowman, Matthew Moodie, Jeffrey Pepper, Frank Pohlmann, Ben Renow-Clarke, Dominic Shakeshaft, Matt Wade, Tom Welsh
Project Manager: Kylie Johnston
Copy Editor: Jim Compton
Associate Production Director: Kari Brooks-Copony
Production Editor: Kelly Gunther
Compositors: Patrick Cunningham and Dina Quan
Proofreader: Lisa Hamilton
Indexer: Carol Burbo
Artist: April Milne
Cover Designer: Kurt Krames
Manufacturing Director: Tom Debolski

Distributed to the book trade worldwide by Springer-Verlag New York, Inc., 233 Spring Street, 6th Floor, New York, NY 10013. Phone 1-800-SPRINGER, fax 201-348-4505, e-mail orders-ny@springer-sbm.com, or visit http://www.springeronline.com.

For information on translations, please contact Apress directly at 2855 Telegraph Avenue, Suite 600, Berkeley, CA 94705. Phone 510-549-5930, fax 510-549-5939, e-mail info@apress.com, or visit http://www.apress.com.

Apress and friends of ED books may be purchased in bulk for academic, corporate, or promotional use. eBook versions and licenses are also available for most titles. For more information, reference our Special Bulk Sales–eBook Licensing web page at http://www.apress.com/info/bulksales.

The source code for this book is available to readers at http://www.apress.com.

To All World of Warcraft Players

Contents at a Glance

Contents

■CHAPTER 7   Using Advanced Lua to Extend the Texas Hold'em Poker Addon 195

About the Author

PAUL EMMERICH is one of the programmers behind Deadly Boss Mods, one of the most famous World of Warcraft addons ever, with more than 8 million users worldwide. He started programming in 1998 and has worked in Lua since World of Warcraft was released in 2004. He has also created a variety of other projects in Lua, including porting vintage games to Lua. He currently studies computer science at the Technische Universität München in Germany. As Tandanu, level 80 Priest and Chief Coder for the guild Refuge on EU-Aegwynn, Paul enjoys winning raid encounters and adding to his HK count.

Acknowledgments

This book would not have been possible without the help of a lot of people, so I want to say "thank you" to a few people here.

First of all I want to thank Martin "Nitram" Verges, the second developer behind the addon Deadly Boss Mods. The addon would not exist in the form you know it without his help, and I would probably never have had the opportunity to write this book without DBM in my background. Martin also did the majority of the work on Deadly Boss Mods while I was busy with writing this book.

A book like this is not something you write alone; there are many people involved in that process. I want to thank all the people at Apress who worked on this project and made it possible. The first person I want to mention here is Joohn Choe, who started this project and gave me the opportunity to write this book; thanks for that! Also thanks to Kylie Johnston (the project manager for this book), Matthew Moodie (developmental editor), Chris Lindboe (technical reviewer), Jim Compton (copy editor), and Kelly Gunther (production editor).

I also want to thank my friend Tobias Dänzer, who always supported me while writing this book and patiently answered all questions like "Is this understandable?" or "Does this sound good?"

Last but not least, thanks to all users of Deadly Boss Mods. DBM would certainly not be one of the most popular World of Warcraft addons without its strong community supporting it. Thanks for all the feedback, suggestions, and support!

Introduction

Addons are a really exciting topic, as they allow you to modify your game and improve your gaming experience. Only a few online games allow you to modify the user interface to such an extent as World of Warcraft does; you can replace the complete user interface or you can add completely new functionality to it.

There are literally thousands of addons available, and hundreds of helpful macros can be found on the Internet. You are probably already using a lot of addons and macros as a World of Warcraft player, but do you know exactly how your addons and macros work? Virtually all players make use of these tools, but there are only a few people who can write their own or modify existing ones. You will soon be one of them!

Addons can modify almost every aspect of the game's user interface. There are many small addons that make simple but powerful additions to the interface. For example, you can add timestamps to the chat frame with just a few lines of code; you will see how in Chapter 6. Or you can add tooltips to links in the chat; you will try this easy example in Chapter 4. There are also some big addons, however, that consist of tens of thousands of lines of code. So you will also build a big, advanced addon in this book, a fully featured multiplayer Texas Hold'em poker game within the game.

The programming language that is used for World of Warcraft is Lua, a small yet powerful scripting language that is easy to learn. You will know the basics of Lua by the end of Chapter 2. These basics will be sufficient to write your first Hello, World addon in Chapter 3 as you get started with World of Warcraft addons. The real fun starts in Chapter 4 when you are writing your first really useful addons, like the chat frame tooltips just mentioned.

But let's get started now!

CHAPTER 1

∎∎∎

Getting Started

This chapter will discuss a few very basic things about Lua and World of Warcraft addons before we dive into the Lua language in Chapter 2. You are also going to see a few useful tools we will use throughout the book.

What Is Lua?

Lua is a programming language developed in 1993 by Roberto Ierusalimschy, Luiz Henrique de Figueiredo, and Waldemar Celes at the Pontifical Catholic University of Rio de Janeiro in Brazil. Lua is Portuguese for moon; the correct pronunciation is "LOO-ah." Lua is available under an MIT license, a very unrestrictive license that basically allows you to use Lua for anything as long as you keep the copyright notice and license.

The advantages of Lua are its extensibility, simplicity, efficiency, and portability. It is easy to write modules that add functionality, and it's also easy to embed Lua as a scripting language in another program like a game. Scripting languages are programming languages that are used in a specific part of another larger application. So World of Warcraft (written in C++) uses Lua for its user interface (UI). There are actually many games out there that use Lua to script the user interface or for configuration files (for example, Warhammer Online or Far Cry). But it is also possible to write whole programs in Lua, as there are extensions available that allow you to use libraries or frameworks like wxWidgets (wxLua), the .NET Framework (LuaInterface), or 3D engines like OGRE (Lugre) from Lua. These extensions are also called *bindings,* as they bind Lua to a more powerful complex framework or library.

Lua is easy to learn; the syntax is simple and clear. One can read and understand small Lua scripts without knowing anything about the language. So it is possible to use Lua as a language for configuration files that can be edited by people who don't know anything about programming. Lua is a dynamically typed language, which basically means that you will have a lot of freedom and flexibility while programming. You will learn more about this feature in Chapter 2. Despite its simplicity, Lua is a very powerful multiparadigm programming language. It provides imperative, functional, and object-oriented paradigms to write your scripts. I will show what these paradigms mean for you in the following chapters. You also don't need to take care of memory management; Lua provides a very good incremental garbage collector. A *garbage collector* is a program that runs interleaved with your script and frees any unused memory your program had previously used; *incremental* means that it is running all the time, working in small steps.

Even though it is a fully featured powerful multiparadigm language, Lua is still extremely fast. The virtual machine (a program that takes Lua code and executes it) that has been used since Lua 5.1 is one of the fastest such programs for scripting languages out there. There is also a just-in-time compiler (a program that translates Lua to native machine code for your computer on the fly) for x86 architectures available that is even faster

Lua can quickly compile and execute long scripts with thousands of lines of code and easily handle huge amounts of data. It is possible to write Lua scripts that create other Lua scripts consisting only of huge tables with hundreds of thousands of entries, to create persistent data in your script. The Lua compiler can quickly load and compile these data files on demand.

If you think you need to install a few megabytes of software to get Lua running on your computer, think again. The Lua virtual machine is just over 160 KB, and the compiler adds only another 200 KB. (These file sizes are for Lua 5.1.4 on Windows x86.)

Lua is written in plain ANSI C, so it is very portable. It runs on almost every machine and operating system you have ever heard of, and some you haven't; for example, Lua has been successfully compiled on the LEGO MINDSTORMS NXT platform.

A good place to get additional information about Lua in general is its web site, `http://www.lua.org`.

What Are WoW Addons?

The user interface of World of Warcraft can be modified using Lua and XML. XML is a powerful data description language, but you don't need to worry about it until Chapter 5. It is possible to replace the whole default UI with highly customized so-called *addons*. Lua is used as scripting language, while XML can be used as a simple way to create graphical user interface elements.

Blizzard Entertainment, the publisher of WoW, provides a very powerful user interface API (application programming interface, a set of functions that can be used to communicate with the game from a scripting language, in this case Lua) that allows the player to script almost every part of the game. There are addons for almost everything, from unit frame replacements and action bars over chat utilities to in-game mini-games like Bejeweled.

Users quickly developed addons that Blizzard considered too powerful because they were close to bots. Addons like Decursive were able to scan the raid for debuffs and dispel them with one click. Another addon let the user select the best target and healing spell for healers just by pressing a single key. Healers who used these mods could just press the same key over and over again to play perfectly during a fight. Another mod even allowed you to run certain predefined paths, like corpse runs in Molten Core.

So patch 2.0 restricted certain actions to "secure code," which is code from the default UI. The restricted actions are targeting, casting spells, and movement-related functions. However, many functions may still be used under certain circumstances, so it is still possible to create a raid frame mod. But it is no longer possible to create mods like those just mentioned, which automate combat-related tasks during combat.

The default UI provides all functionality a normal user needs to play the game, but addons can provide advanced functions or a different theme. Figure 1-1 shows the default UI that is provided by the game. A heavily modified user interface that replaces almost everything could look like the UI illustrated in Figure 1-2.

Figure 1-1. *The default UI*

Figure 1-2. *A heavily modified UI*

The user interface in Figure 1-2 replaces almost everything. It looks like the UI of a completely different game, replacing even the default font that is used by the game. You can also see the replaced minimap, action bars, and tool tips.

Everyone can go to a web site and download an addon and install it, though only a few of the 11.5 million World of Warcraft players are able to create mods. You will be one of this select few after you've read this book. You probably can't wait to get started, so let's see some useful tools we'll use in the book.

Useful Programs, Tools, and Web Sites

Blizzard provides almost no documentation for its interface API, but you can read the source code of the default UI to figure out how the provided functions work. There are a few web sites that can help you by providing Blizzard's code and documentation for the interface API. And there are a few in-game tools that can aid you while debugging or writing code.

So this section presents some web sites and programs we are going to use throughout the book.

Web Sites

These web sites contain valuable information. You will need them quite often, especially the sites with documentation for API functions.

WoWWiki

http://www.wowwiki.com is a site that you are going to use all the time. It is a wiki that provides a lot of valuable information about the interface API. The most important pages in this wiki, which you are going to need very often, are shown in Table 1-1.

Table 1-1. *Useful WoWWiki Pages*

Page	Description
World_of_Warcraft_API	List of all available API functions
Events_(API)	List of all events
Widget_API	List of API functions that work with GUI elements (*widgets*)

WoW["Compares"]

The web site http://wowcompares.com allows you to browse or download the code of the default user interface. The site also keeps track of changes to the default UI code. You can compare or download *unified diffs* (files that contain all the changes between two versions) of different versions of the World of Warcraft interface.

WowAce / Curse

http://www.wowace.com is the web site of the Ace project, which now belongs to http://www.curse.com. You can find Ace-related mods as well as documentation for the Ace framework there. Curse is the biggest web site for addons, so it is a good idea to publish the addons you are going to write there.

UI & Macros Forum

The official UI & Macros forum at http://forums.worldofwarcraft.com/board.html?forumId=11114&sid=1 is a good place to look for official statements. You can also find interface-related patch notes there.

DeadlyBossMods.com

If you have any questions about this book and its example code, feel free to ask in my forum at http://www.deadlybossmods.com.

Lua.org / Lua-users.org

The official Lua web site is http://www.lua.org. You can download or browse the Lua source code and read the official Lua reference manual there. You can also read the first edition of the book there. The site http://lua-users.org is an unofficial wiki for Lua.

In-Game Tools

In-game tools are World of Warcraft addons that can help you to debug or edit your addons in the game.

DevTools

DevTools is a must-have addon for developers. You can get it on WoWInterface.com: http://www.wowinterface.com/downloads/fileinfo.php?id=3999. It provides you several slash commands, one of which is

```
/dump <expression>
```

This evaluates an expression and shows its value. It is capable of displaying complex data structures in your chat frame, so you can easily debug them.

Another powerful feature of this mod is its event trace frame (see Figure 1-3), which can be shown by using /dtevents.

The mod has a few more useful features; you should read its readme file, which explains everything.

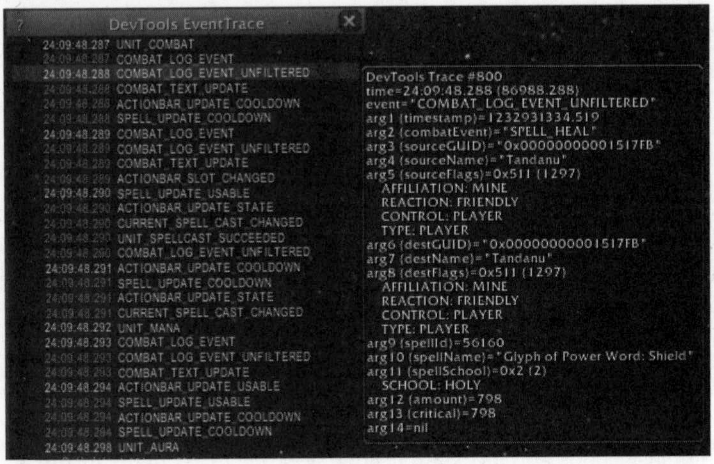

Figure 1-3. *The DevTools event trace window*

Swatter

Swatter provides an improved error frame, which is needed because the default frame that displays Lua errors in World of Warcraft is unusable. Unlike the default error frame, Swatter can handle more than one error message at the same time and it shows a stack trace for debugging. You can see an error message that was caught by Swatter in Figure 1-4.

This addon is included in some addon packages, such as Auctioneer, but a stand-alone version is available at http://zip.norganna.org/libs/!Swatter/.

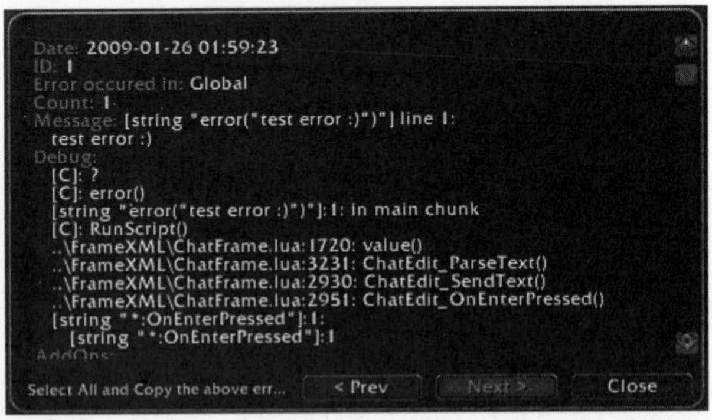

Figure 1-4. *Swatter showing an error message*

WoWLua

WoWLua is an in-game script editor with Lua syntax highlighting. You can write, save, load, and execute Lua scripts in World of Warcraft with this addon. Figure 1-5 shows the editor with a simple Lua script.

Download: http://www.wowinterface.com/downloads/info7366-WowLua.html.

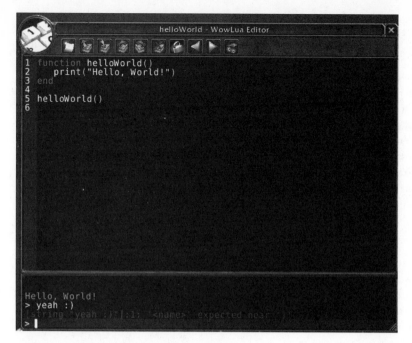

Figure 1-5. *WoWLua with a simple script*

TinyPad

TinyPad is similar to WoWLua. It is an in-game text editor that can execute text as a Lua script. Unlike WoWLua, it does not provide syntax highlighting, but it supports working with item links, so it is useful when you are debugging a mod that uses or creates item links.

Download: http://www.wowinterface.com/downloads/info4417-TinyPad.html.

Programs

There are a few stand-alone programs available that provide useful information.

Interface AddOn Kit

The Interface AddOn Kit is a program that automatically extracts the default UI. Extracting and working with the default UI is covered in Chapter 3.

Download: http://us.blizzard.com/support/article.xml?articleId=21466.

MPQ Editor

The MPQ Editor is a powerful program that allows you to browse and modify the MPQ archives used by World of Warcraft. An MPQ file is an archive format used by Blizzard's games; these archives contain all the data files used by the game. Using this program is also covered in Chapter 3.

Download: http://www.zezula.net/en/mpq/download.html.

IDEs

You don't need a fully featured integrated development environment (IDE) at all to work with Lua, as a normal text editor is sufficient. An IDE usually combines a text editor with a compiler and a debugger. The problem with an IDE when programming for World of Warcraft is that your debugging environment is normally the game. But an external program cannot access the game, so you will spend a lot of time debugging your mod in-game. That is not to say that an IDE is completely useless. A good IDE can help you by providing basic features like syntax highlighting and checking or autocompletion while writing your addon.

I'll provide a customized version of SciTE that I use to write addons. You can find it in the code download package for this book on http: www.apress.com as well as on my site, http://www.deadlybossmods.com. But I will also present some other IDEs here. It is up to you which IDE or editor you use.

LuaEdit

LuaEdit is a fully featured IDE for Lua, but without any support for World of Warcraft. The debugger especially can be very powerful. It allows you to view Lua's internal stack and all local variables, set breakpoints, and execute your script line-by-line.

This IDE is a good choice when you are developing a stand-alone Lua script. Its use for World of Warcraft addons is limited as you won't be able to use most of the debugging features the IDE provides.

Download: http://www.luaedit.org.

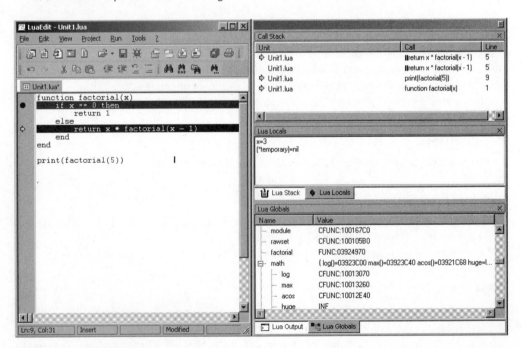

Figure 1-6. *The LuaEdit IDE*

WoW UI Designer

WoW UI Designer is a very powerful IDE that can edit Lua scripts as well as XML files. It even has a GUI designer for World of Warcraft (see Figure 1-7). However, the IDE is still in the beta state and the Lua editing part especially lacks a few features; for example, there is no autocompletion for API functions available.

Its GUI designer is a great tool if you need to create a simple graphical user interface like a configuration menu without digging through large XML files. Its XML editor is also quite good because it can check whether your XML is valid and also whether will be recognized by the game. You will learn more about XML in Chapter 5 when we discuss frames.

Download: `http://www.wowinterface.com/downloads/info4222-WoWUIDesigner.html`.

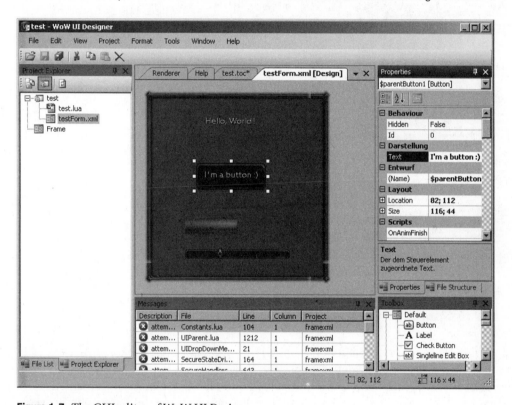

Figure 1-7. *The GUI editor of WoW UI Designer*

AddOn Studio

AddOn Studio is the most powerful IDE available for World of Warcraft. It is based on Microsoft Visual Studio, but it is a stand-alone program with everything you need to run included in the 56 MB download.

This IDE offers everything you might need while developing addons: a basic WYSIWYG GUI designer (see Figure 1-8), Lua syntax highlighting, and even basic IntelliSense support for World of Warcraft API functions. Note that IntelliSense and similar autocompletion features for a dynamically typed language like Lua can never be as powerful as they are for a language with static typing like C++ or Java. The IDE cannot know the type of your variables or the methods of your objects as they are created dynamically when your program runs.

Download: http://www.codeplex.com/WarcraftAddOnStudio.

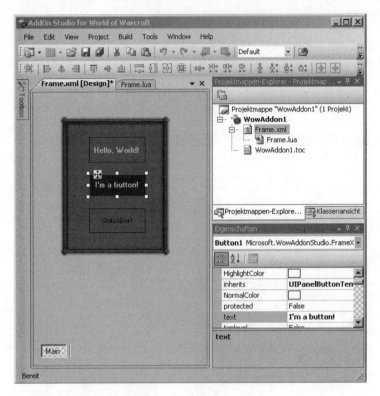

Figure 1-8. *AddOn Studio for World of Warcraft*

SciTE

SciTE (Scintilla-based Text Editor) is the editor I use to develop mods. It does not have fancy features like a GUI designer, but it is simple, fast, extensible, easy to use, and powerful. It supports Lua syntax highlighting, autocompletion, and call-tips for World of Warcraft API functions. SciTE can be fully configured through plain-text files. You can change almost everything with these config files,such as the syntax highlighting, code folding, and the behavior of the editor. Figure 1-9 shows SciTE with a simple Lua script.

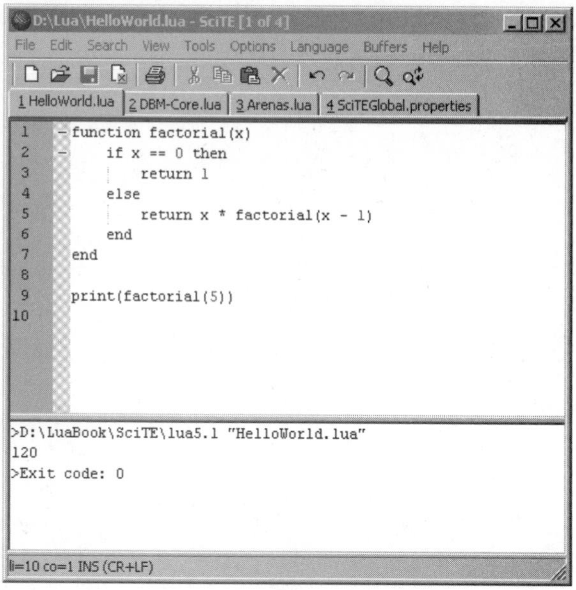

Figure 1-9. *SciTE executing a Lua script*

The editor also embeds Lua as a scripting language, so you can write Lua scripts to add new functionality to your IDE. This can be a very powerful feature; it is covered in the last chapter of this book, where we look at other uses for Lua.

SciTE is available for Windows, Linux, and OS X, unlike the previously mentioned IDEs, which are only available for Windows.

Download: SciTE is included in the source code download for this book, at http://www. apress.com.

CHAPTER 2

■ ■ ■

Lua Basics

This chapter will use Lua as a stand-alone scripting language and will teach you the basics of the language. So you will write simple Lua scripts without using World of Warcraft at all. If you are already familiar with executing Lua scripts in World of Warcraft, it is of course no problem if you use the built-in Lua interpreter (for example with a mod like TinyPad or WoWLua). But I'm assuming that you have never used Lua before, so I'll start with a little tutorial to help you create a working development environment.

Feel free to skip this chapter if you already know Lua.

Using Lua

If you are using an IDE that comes with a Lua interpreter, like the version of SciTE presented in Chapter 1, you are ready to work. Just create a new *.lua file and press the Run key (F5 in SciTE) to execute it.

However, if you choose to use a text editor that has no native support for Lua scripts, you have to set up Lua first. You can download the source code of Lua at http://www.lua.org. Binary versions of Lua are available on http://luabinaries.luaforge.net for Windows, Linux and OS X. Just download the package for your system and extract it to a new folder. It consists of a few files, of which the following two are important to us:

- lua5.1.exe

- luac5.1.exe

lua5.1.exe is the Lua interpreter. If you run it without arguments, it will enter the interactive mode, a command-line interface that allows you to type in and execute Lua scripts line by line. It can also handle uncompiled Lua scripts in text form or compiled byte code files (*.luc). Byte code is a machine-readable form of your program, and loading a byte code version of your script is slightly faster than loading the original source code. World of Warcraft automatically translates your addons into byte code when logging in. You can execute your Lua scripts by executing the following command:

```
lua5.1.exe "YourFile.lua"
```

There are also a few options available:

`-i`	Enters the interactive mode after executing a given file
`-e <statement>`	Executes `<statement>` as Lua code and exits
`-v`	Prints the version number and exits

`luac5.1.exe` is the Lua compiler; it compiles Lua scripts to Lua byte code. You are not going to need it for World of Warcraft, as the game does not accept compiled Lua scripts. Using it is simple; just provide the file name of the script you want to compile and it will produce a `.luc` file.

■**Tip** If you are unsure how to use these command-line-based programs, just use the provided version of SciTE or Lua in World of Warcraft with TinyPad or WoWLua.

Now let's get started with learning Lua. You have a slight advantage if you already know another scripting language, but you should still read this chapter. It is very important that you understand Lua before starting with World of Warcraft programming. However, if you still want to skip the chapter, do so.

Note that some parts of the chapter might be hard going if you have never programmed anything before; if you are feeling lost when reading the sections about functional programming techniques, object-oriented programming, or regular expressions, don't worry. We are going to create some great World of Warcraft addons and you will learn a lot while creating the example mods in the book. If there are sections you don't completely understand this time, you can revisit them when we use these programming techniques in a real addon.

Basics

Lua uses a Pascal-like syntax, which means it's easy to understand for beginners. Pascal is a programming language that is often used for educational purposes. It uses English words where other languages use special characters like curly brackets. Let's start with a "Hello, World" program in Lua:

```
print("Hello, World!")
```

You have already seen this program in Figure 1-8 in Chapter 1. It prints `Hello, World` to the standard output provided by your operating system. If you call the script from a console, it will print it to the console. If you are using an IDE, it will redirect the standard output to a text box in the IDE. `print` is called a *function*, and `"Hello, World"` is an example of a string. A function call in Lua basically looks like this:

```
functionName(argument1, argument2, ..., argumentN)
```

An *argument* is a value (for example a string or a number) that is passed to the function. The function can access all values passed to it and do something with them. So the function print takes an argument and prints it.

Another valid way to call a function is this:

```
print "Hello, World"
```

You don't need the parentheses if the function only takes one argument that can clearly be identified as an argument to that function. Later in this chapter you will see when exactly this feature works and when it is useful.

If you have programmed before, you will have noticed that there is no semicolon to end the line. Most programming languages require semicolons after statements. When programming in Lua, you won't need semicolons at all. However, Lua accepts the use of semicolons, and it can help improving readability if you put several statements into a single line. In some rare situations semicolons are even required to prevent ambiguous syntax. But it is pretty hard to run into a situation where the interpreter tells you that your syntax is ambiguous. If you manage to get that error message, you should rethink your coding style.

Another fact to note is that Lua uses an imperative paradigm, meaning the file is executed line by line. Unlike in other programming languages, like C or Java, you don't need a specific *main* function as an entry point for a program, the point where execution starts. The execution of a Lua script starts in the first line of your file.

Let's look at a more complete example. The following code defines a function that calculates the factorial of a number. It then calls the function for the numbers 1 to 10 and prints the results.

```
function fac(n)
    if n == 0 then
        return 1
    else
        return n * fac(n - 1)
    end
end

for i = 1, 10 do
    print(fac(i)) -- this is executed 10 times
end
```

Let's go through this example line by line. The first line defines a function by using the keyword function with the name fac. It takes one argument, called **n**. It then checks if the argument has a value of 0 by using the equality operator, ==. Note that the equality operator consists of two equal signs. Using one equal sign would give you a syntax error here. If n is 0 the function *returns* the value 1. A function can return by using the keyword return; this means the function has finished its task. The keyword return also takes an argument that will be provided to the code that called the function. If the test fails, meaning that n is not 0, it subtracts 1 from n and calls itself. It then uses the return value of that call and multiplies it by n. The function computes the factorial of n by calling itself, a programming technique called *recursion*. Both the if/else control structure and the function are ended by the keyword end.

The next block is called a for-loop. It counts from 1 to 10 and stores the current value in the variable i. The loop executes its *body* for each value from 1 to 10. The body of a loop consists of all the code until the closing end. The body of this loop is the code print(fac(i)), and it is executed ten times. This means fac(i) is called for all numbers from 1 to 10 and the return value of the function is printed. This script prints the factorials from 1 to 10 to the standard output.

The two hyphen marks begin a comment. Everything after -- in this line is ignored by Lua, so you can include notes to yourself about what particular lines do. Lua also ignores whitespace characters and new lines, so you can use tabs, spaces, and new lines to make your code more readable. It would also be possible to write this script in a single line, stripping all unnecessary spaces. The result would look like this:

```
function fac(n)if n==0 then return 1 else return n*fac(n-1)end end➥
for i=1,10 do print(fac(i))end
```

The Lua interpreter does not care whether you format your code nicely, but anyone who reads the code, including you, will care. Remember that World of Warcraft does not load precompiled addons in binary form. So if you publish your addon, you have to publish your source code, and a lot of people will be able to read it. You should always optimize your code for readability. Lua uses an easy-to-understand syntax that is a bit verbose. It uses English keywords where other programming languages would use curly brackets. This helps to understand what is going on. It is no problem to guess the functionality of simple scripts without knowing anything about Lua.

Variables and Data Types

A *variable* is a named container for a value. So a variable consists of a name and a value. The name is used in the code to identify the variable. The value is the content of the container, and this content is categorized into different data types. In our "Hello, World" example, we had the string data type to store the text "Hello, World!" The factorial example used many values of the type number to represent numbers. You can use different operations on different data types; for example, you can add two numbers, but trying to add two strings will result in an error message.

You have already seen a few variables in the examples. There is no variable that has no value. Even uninitialized variables have a value. The default value for variables is nil, which indicates the absence of a useful value. Valid identifiers consist of letters, digits, and underscores. Identifiers may not start with a digit, and there are some reserved keywords that cannot be used as identifiers:

- and
- break
- do
- else
- elseif
- end
- false

- for
- function
- if
- in
- local
- nil
- not

- or
- repeat
- return
- then
- true
- until
- while

Following are some examples of valid identifiers:

```
myVariable1
_myVariable2
my_variable
_A_
__123
```

Note that identifiers are case-sensitive, so myVar does not identify the same variable as MyVar. Likewise, Else is different from else; the former is a perfectly valid variable, but the latter is a reserved keyword.

Your variables' identifiers should always have meaningful names. This makes reading and understanding your code easier, and it is always important to have understandable code. So the identifiers _A_ and __123 from the example should not be used unless there is a good reason to do so.

You can assign a value of any type to a variable by using a single equality sign; the following example shows the usage of a variable:

```
print(MyVariable) --> nil (the variable doesn't exist yet)
MyVariable = 5
print(MyVariable) --> 5
MyVariable = "Hello!"
print(MyVariable) --> "Hello!"
```

Remember that -- starts a comment, so using an arrow --> after a line of code is no problem. (In discussions of Lua you will often see this kind of commenting used to show the expected result of an operation.)

Now that you've seen how to create variables and assign values to them, we will look at the available data types for values and how to create them.

Data Types

We have a few basic types in Lua: nil, number, string, boolean, table, function, thread, and userdata. You have already seen examples of number and string.

The function type(x) can be used to get the type of a value, as in these examples:

```
print(type("Hello")) --> string
print(type(5)) --> number
print(type(type)) --> function
```

The third example might be confusing. Note that it is not type(type()). It directly passes the variable type to the function type. This variable holds a value of the type function. So a function is just a value like a number or a string, and since variables can hold all kinds of values, they can also hold other functions.

This is a very powerful feature in Lua: anything we can do with normal variables, we can do with functions. In Lua, functions are just variables that hold a value of the type function. We can pass functions as arguments to other functions, and functions can return functions.

Let's have a closer look at these types.

nil

A value of the type nil can only have one value: nil. This type means that something does not have a useful value; for example, a variable that is not initialized is nil. Trying to get the return value of a function that does not return anything also gives you nil.

number

Lua knows only one type of number, while other programming languages distinguish between integers and decimal numbers of different sizes. The most common data types for numbers you might encounter when programming in other languages are double-precision floating point numbers (double), int, unsigned int, long, and unsigned long. The type double uses 64 bits to store a noninteger, with quite good accuracy. There are also single-precision floating point numbers (floats) available; they use only 32 bits, so their accuracy is less good. The other data types can be used to store integers. An int uses 32 bits (4 bytes) of memory and can represent numbers between -2^{31} and $2^{31} - 1$. longs are 64 bits long, so they can store numbers between 2^{63} and $2^{63} - 1$. The unsigned versions of these types can represent numbers from 0 to $2^{32}-1$ (int) and 0 to $2^{64} - 1$ (long).

You don't need to know about these different types for numbers when working in Lua, as you have only one type. But it is good to know that these types exist when you are working with a program in a different language, as the boundaries of these types often limit certain values in a program. Even some values in World of Warcraft are limited by these types. For example, the maximum amount of gold your character can have is 214748 gold, 36 silver, and 46 copper. This is just $2^{63}-2$ copper, one copper less than the maximum value that can be stored in a long.

Lua saves all numbers internally as doubles, which means the type number can represent numbers between approximately -1.79×10^{308} and 1.79×10^{308}. You might wonder how this can be possible. You know that doubles and longs use 64 bits, but longs can only store integers up to $2^{63} - 1$, which is less than the maximum value that can be stored by a double. The answer is that doubles cannot store all values in this range, not even all integers in this range. They can represent all integers from -10^{14} to 10^{14}, so higher or lower integers might be missing. The following code shows what can happen when working with really huge numbers.

```
x = 10^30 -- b^a means b to the power of a
print(x == (x - 1)) --> true
```

It's good to know this when working with huge numbers in Lua. You don't need to worry about these technical details in almost all of your addons. All you need to know is that the type number can store all numbers you are going to need.

Lua has a function that tries to convert a string to a number: tonumber(str). It returns the number represented by that string, or nil if the string is not a number. Examples for strings that can be converted by tonumber are:

```
print(tonumber("5")) --> 5
print(tonumber("-100")) --> -100
print(tonumber("0.5")) --> 0.5
print(tonumber("0xFF")) --> 0xFF (0x indicates a hexadecimal number)
print(tonumber("-3e5")) --> -300000 (XeY translates to X * 10^Y)
```

When writing numbers in code, you can use everything that would be a valid string for tonumber. For example you can write print(0xA1 + 1e2); it is equivalent to print(161 + 100).

string

A string in Lua can contain any characters, even embedded zeros. (Many other programming languages use embedded zeros as control characters to mark the end of a string, so trying to store such a null character in a string will cut it off.) There are no characters that have special meanings, so you can store arbitrary binary data in a string without destroying the string. Think of a compressed chat communication between two addons: no problem to work with strings here.

As you have seen before, strings are written in quotation marks:

```
print("Hello, World!")
```

It is also possible to use single quotation marks; this is especially useful when your string contains double quotation marks:

```
print('"Hello, World!"')
```

This prints "Hello, World" with quotation marks. There is also a third method to mark strings, using square brackets. This allows the use of new lines in a string:

```
print([[Hello,
World!]])
```

This would not be possible with quotation marks. But what if you want to use square brackets inside your string? No problem; you can use any number of equality signs between the brackets to enclose a string:

```
print([==[Hello, World
this is a long multi-line string that can contain quotation marks: " '
as well as box brackets: [[ ]] ]=] [=[
]==])
```

The produced output is this:

```
Hello, World
this is a long multi-line string that can contain quotation marks: " '
as well as box brackets: [[ ]] ]=] [=[
```

If you have programming experience, you might wonder if you can't just use **\n** to embed new line characters. In fact you can. Like most programming languages, Lua provides *escape sequences* (special codes that tell Lua to insert a special character at this position) to insert the usual special characters. Table 2-1 lists these escape sequences:

Table 2-1. *Escape Sequences in Lua*

Code	Character
\a	bell
\b	back space
\f	form feed
\n	new line
\r	carriage return
\t	horizontal tab
\v	vertical tab
\\	a normal backslash
\"	double quotation mark
\'	single quotation mark

So you can rewrite the previous example with these escape codes. The produced output stays the same:

```
print("Hello, World\nthis is a long multi-line string that can contain➥
quotation marks: \" \'\nas well as box brackets: [[ ]] ]=] [=[")
```

The solution with box brackets is much more readable than using the new-line escape code.

Box brackets also have another use; they can be used to start and end multi-line comments:

```
--[[ This is a
multi-line comment]]
```

You can also use the equal sign if you want to use two closing square brackets inside a comment. This is useful when you are commenting out unused or broken code, as code that works with tables may contain lines like a[b[1]] = 5.

Most string operations are defined in the string library, which will be discussed later in this chapter. There are two operators available for strings: the concatenation of two strings: *a..b* and the length operator *#str*. Here's an example of concatenation:

```
print("Hello ".."World!")
```

This concatenates the string "Hello " with the string "World!", resulting in "Hello World!". The concatenation also works with numbers; you can even mix numbers with strings:

```
print("Hello "..10)  --> Hello 10
print(5 .. 0)  --> 50
```

Attempting to concatenate other types generates an error message. Also note that the second line has a space just after the number. Writing `5..0` causes an error message as Lua interprets the point as a decimal point.

The length operator # counts the number of characters in a string:

```
print(#"Hello")
```

This prints 5, as the length of "Hello" is 5.

There is also a function that converts its argument to a string: `tostring(arg)`. It can convert all values to a string representing them. For a value without a useful string representation, like a function or table, it will show the type of the value followed by a memory address.

Strings are stored in Lua's *string pool*. When a new string is created, Lua checks to see if the string already exists and creates it if it does not. A variable never holds the string itself; it only holds a reference to a string. The reference points to the real location of the string in the string pool. So you don't need to worry about memory usage when using a long string in more than one variable:

```
string1 = "a very long string..."
string2 = "a very long string..."
```

The string will be saved only once in your memory. Both variables reference the same string, and this code is equivalent to the following:

```
string1 = "a very long string..."
string2 = string1
```

What happens if a function modifies a string? As both variables `string1` and `string2` reference the same string, the values of both variables would change if you modify the string. This would be an unexpected behavior and could cause strange bugs.

For this reason, strings are immutable values in Lua. There is no operator or function that can modify a string. They can only create a new string and return it. So the concatenation of two strings generates a new string. The two strings that were concatenated are not touched.

So from your point of view, a string is always passed using its value and not as a reference to a string held in Lua's string pool.

boolean

A `boolean` value can only be `false` or `true`. You will learn more about booleans in the next sections when we explore control structures, expressions, and logical operators.

function

As mentioned earlier, functions are normal values just like all other values. There are two ways to create functions; you have already seen the first one:

```
function foo(arg1, arg2)
    print(arg1)
    print(arg2)
end
```

This creates a function called foo that takes two arguments and prints them. foo is now a global variable that holds a value of the type function. There is another way to write this function definition that clarifies this assignment to foo:

```
foo = function(arg1, arg2)
    print(arg1)
    print(arg2)
end
```

This second way to create functions can be used everywhere; for example, as a return value or as an argument to another function. The first version might suggest that the function has the name foo associated with it. But foo is just a variable that holds the function; the function itself has no name. Such functions are called *anonymous functions*, and all functions in Lua are anonymous. Only the variable that holds the function has a name. But it's just a variable. You can assign your function to another variable, and more than one variable can reference the same function.

One important thing to know is that a variable never holds the function itself. It only holds a reference to that function. Functions are stored in a part of your memory called the *heap*, which is basically a huge space where all the data, including other functions or strings, is stored. You don't need to know exactly how the function is stored there. You get a reference that points to the location of that function, and that reference is everything you need. Lua will take care of the rest.

A function is never copied when you pass a function to another function, or when you write code like this:

```
foo = print
foo("Hello, World!") --> Hello, World
```

The first line copies the reference held by print to foo. So it makes no difference if you call foo or print now. Both reference the same function. A new function is only created when Lua executes code like function() ... end.

You will learn more about functions later in this chapter.

Table

Tables are the most powerful data type in Lua. Tables are used to implement all data structures you are going to need. A *data structure* is a smart way to store data so that it can be accessed or modified efficiently. Tables have their own section in this chapter, so this is just a brief overview over them.

The simplest way to use a table is as an *array*, which is basically just a list of values:

```
Table = {"a", 7, "c", -1}
```

This creates a new table containing the values "a", 7, "c", and -1 in this order. Each value can now be read from a table by providing its *index*, the number representing its sequential position in the array. Unlike in many other programming languages, the first value of an array is stored under the index 1 and not 0. The second one is stored under the index 2, and so on. You can now access the values stored in that table by using square brackets:

```
print(Table[1])  --> a
print(Table[3])  --> c
print(Table[5])  --> nil
```

Trying to use an index (or *key*) that is not in the bounds of the array returns **nil**.

Note that you can store all types of values in a table, even other tables.

Tables can be dynamically resized during runtime; to do this you can just assign values to fields that don't exist yet, and Lua will automatically resize the table:

```
Table[5] = "e"
print(Table[5])  --> e
```

However, you cannot use nonconsecutive integers as an index for arrays. But tables are more than arrays, so code like this works perfectly:

```
Table[1000] = "z"
print(Table[1000])  --> z
```

What happened? One could think that Lua created the missing 994 entries and filled them with **nil**. But that would just waste resources. A closer look at tables reveals that they are actually split into two parts. First is the array part of a table; it can only contain consecutive integers as indices. The second part is a so-called associative array: it associates values with other values. Lua uses hash tables to implement associative arrays, so the second part of a table is its hash table. Lua used this part of the table in the previous example and created the new key 1000 in that hash table.

A hash table is a data structure that allows you to store data under a key and access it by providing the key. That means it can be used as an associative array. Hash tables are very efficient when looking up something; it is no problem for Lua to have a hash table with millions of entries. Looking up the value stored under a specific key is still extremely fast because the position of a value stored under a specific key can be calculated. The size of a hash table does not affect the time required to get an entry or to create one at all. It is possible to use any value except for nil as a key.

So a table is not only an array but also an associative array; it associates values with other values. Creating and modifying such tables that implement associative arrays is also easy:

```
Table = { key1 = "a",  ["a key with spaces"] = "b", [5] = "c", [print] = "d" }
```

The new table contains four fields: "key1" with the value "a", "a key with spaces" with the value "b", 5 (the number 5, not the string "5") with the value "c", and a key that is a reference to the function print with the value "d".

If your key is a simple string without spaces, you can just write it like a variable assignment. The same rules for variable names and reserved words apply. But if your key is a string that is not a valid identifier for a variable or any other value, you must enclose it in square brackets. Note that you can use anything except for nil as a key; we just used the function print (or to be more precise: the reference to the function print) as a key. Accessing the entries also works like this:

```
print(Table["key1"])  --> a
print(Table.key1)  --> a
print(Table[print])  --> d
```

key1 is a string index and a valid identifier, and if it's possible to create an entry without using brackets, it is also possible to access it without using brackets by writing Table. *stringKey*. Assigning new values also works like before:

```
Table.newKey = 5
Table["other key"] = 1
print(Table.newKey)   --> 5
print(Table["other key"])   --> 1
```

Again, the table grows dynamically as we add new keys, and we can store all values we want.

Tables only have one primitive operator besides the brackets and periods used to access fields: the length operator #. It returns the value of the array part of a table. Remember, the array part starts at the index 1 and goes to the last set integer index. So an array with holes contains an array part and a hash table, and the length operator use only the array part.

```
print(#Table)   --> 0
```

We don't have the index 1 in our table, so the length of the array part is 0.

```
Table = {"a", "b", "c"}
print(#Table)   --> 3
Table[100] = "d"
print(#Table) --> 3
Table[4] = "e"
print(#Table) --> 4
```

The following line creates a table that is equivalent to the table created in the first line of the example:

```
Table = {[1] = "a", [2] = "b", [3] = "c"}
```

So the length of the array is clearly 3. Now adding a value under the index 100 leaves a hole in our array, so the length of the actual array is still 3. The new index is stored in the hash table part of the table, not in the array. But adding a value under the index 4 extends the array, and it now has the length 4.

A variable cannot hold the table itself; it will just hold a reference to a table. This means that passing a variable to a function or assigning it to a new variable never copies the table. Let's look at a simple example that clarifies this:

```
function foo(t)
    t[1] = 5
end

myTable = {}
print(myTable[1])   --> nil, the field 1 is not set
foo(myTable)
print(myTable[1])   --> 5
```

Note that an empty table is also a valid table; {} creates a new empty table. The function foo modifies the table passed to it because the variable t inside foo holds a reference to the table that was created in line 5. This also works when using assignments:

```
table1 = {}
table2 = table1  -- this copies the reference, not the table
print(table1[1])  --> nil, the field 1 is not set
table2[1] = 5
print(table1[1])  --> 5
```

Line 2 copies the reference to the empty table created in line 1. This is not equivalent to table2 = {}, which would create a new table. To be more specific, Lua creates a new table when executing a table constructor that looks like {}. Now, there is no difference if you use the variable table1 or table2; both point to the same table.

This is very important to understand; you are going to use a lot of functions that take references to tables and manipulate them. You will see the table library later in this chapter; it provides functions to work with tables.

Tables are very flexible and powerful. And these were just the basics you need to know about tables; they can do even more.

Thread

Threads are a more advanced topic and rarely needed in World of Warcraft addons. We will discuss them in Chapter 13.

Userdata

A userdata value is a chunk of data that was created by the Lua interpreter or the program that hosts your Lua script. The host program when you are writing World of Warcraft addons will be the game. If you call a function that is directly provided by the game, it might create such a value for you and return it. You can't do anything with these userdata values; you can't even create them with Lua code, except for passing them to functions provided by the underlying program. Such a function might know what this chunk of data represents.

You will get a table that holds a userdata object when you create graphical user interface elements in World of Warcraft. This table represents a GUI element and provides certain functions to interact with that element. These API functions then read the userdata value from the table to identify the frame that is referenced by the Lua script.

Dynamic Typing

You know now about the available data types in Lua and you might have noticed that a variable is not bound to a type. This means Lua is what is called a *dynamically typed* language. This seems to provide a great flexibility, but it also has some drawbacks.

Let's go back to our example that calculates the factorial of a number. There is no type definition that guarantees that the argument passed to fac(*n*) is a number. The compiler does not complain if you write code like this:

```
fac("A string!")
```

But Lua will generate an error message in line 5 when you try to subtract 1 from n. Subtraction obviously does not work if n is a string. The error message looks like this:

```
HelloWorld.lua:5: attempt to perform arithmetic on local 'n' (a string value)
```

Note that calling fac with a string as an argument does not yield an error. It is perfectly okay to write a function that can take (or return) a value of any type. It is also no problem to test the equality of two values of different types; they will never be equal, but that doesn't generate an error message. But trying to subtract something from a string is not okay.

You will have to make sure that your variables hold values of the types you expect them to. I'll show how to deal with this in Chapter 6 when we discuss error handling.

Expressions

An *expression* uses operators on values and is evaluated to a value. Expressions can be used everywhere Lua expects a value, as in arguments for functions or when assigning a value to a variable. Expressions can evaluate to all values.

You have already seen some simple expressions; recall the second example that defined a function that calculated the factorial of a number:

```
function fac(n)
    if n == 0 then   -- an expression!
        return 1
    else
        return n * fac(n - 1)   -- another expression
    end
end

for i = 1, 10 do
    print(fac(i))
end
```

The first expression is in line 2; it compares the value of the variable n to 0. This expression evaluates to true if n is 0, otherwise to false. This is called a *relational operator*; it compares two values and evaluates to true or false.

The second expression, in line 5, is n * fac(n - 1); this is an arithmetic expression that uses arithmetic operators. It will first evaluate n - 1 and then call fac with this value. The return value of fac then will be multiplied by n.

Arithmetic Operators

Let's take a closer look at arithmetic expressions. All of them operate on numbers and evaluate to numbers. You have already seen a few of these operators in the examples in this chapter. Here are all available operators for numbers:

+-

* (Multiplication)

^ (Exponentiation)

/ (Division)

% (Modulo, the remainder of the division of two numbers)

Actually there is one more operator that is missing in this list: the unary minus. It also uses the minus sign but operates on only one operand:

```
a = 5
print(0 - a)  --> -5, normal minus
print(-a)  --> -5, unary minus
```

This will make a difference when we look at the operator precedence and operator overloading later in this book.

Relational Operators

The second type of operator is the relational operator, like the equality test ==. All of these operators are binary (meaning they operate on two values) and always evaluate to a boolean value, true or false. The available operators are

== (equality test)

~= (negation of the equality test)

< (less than)

<= (less or equal than)

> (greater than)

>= (greater or equal than)

The equality test operator is pretty simple. It first checks whether the provided values have the same type. If they don't, it evaluates to false; otherwise it checks whether they are equal. Note that nil is only equal to itself. The operator ~= does the same, but it tests whether values are unequal. Here are a few examples:

```
print(6 == 5)  --> false
print("5" ~= 5)  --> true, because the first argument is a string
--and the second a number, so they are not equal

print((5 - 4) == 1) --> true
```

As you can see, it is no problem to mix arithmetic expressions with relational expressions. You can use an expression everywhere that Lua expects a value and a relational operator expects two values.

All other relational operators can be used to compare numbers or strings, but not numbers to strings or strings to numbers. With numbers, relational operators work as you would expect; for strings they compare the alphabetical order, as in these examples:

```
print("a" < "b")  --> true
print(1 > 2)  --> false
print("2" < "10")  --> false
```

The last line compares two strings, so it checks the alphabetical order, making "2" greater than "10".

One important thing you should know about the equality test operator ==: if variables hold references to values, it compares the reference, not the content of the referenced data.

The data types that are always references are functions, tables, and strings. You don't need to care about strings as they are unique and immutable. So you can compare two strings without problems.

But let's test this with tables:

```
t1 = {1, 2, 3}
t2 = {1, 2, 3}
print(t1 == t2)  --> false!
```

This simply tests whether t1 and t2 are referencing the same table, and they aren't. It does not check the contents of the tables, only the reference. So it works when you copy the reference:

```
t3 = t2
print(t3 == t2)  --> true
```

The same applies to functions:

```
f1 = function() end
f2 = function() end
print(f1 == f2)  --> false
```

Logical Operations

The third operator type comprises the three logical operators and, or, and not. They can operate over all types, and and and or can evaluate to all types. The not operator always evaluates to a boolean.

These operators consider all values except false and nil as true. That means 0 and the empty string "" are true. (Many other languages consider these values to be false.)

The operator not is the simplest one. It tests whether its argument is nil or false and returns true if it is; otherwise it returns false.

The operator or can be written as a function to demonstrate how it works.

```
function myOr(value1, value2)
    if value1 then
        return value1
    else
        return value2
    end
end
```

We have not discussed this if-then-else-end construct yet. If you are not familiar with it from other languages, here is a short explanation of how it works; the following code shows the syntax.

```
if expression then
    -- body 1
else
    -- body 2
end
```

Lua checks whether expression evaluates to a value that is considered to be true, that is, it is not false or nil. If this is the case it will execute the content of *body 1*, otherwise it will execute *body 2*. The keyword else and the following second body is optional. You will learn more about these *control structures* in the next section. So myOr checks whether its first argument is not false or nil and in this case returns it. If the first argument is false or nil, the expression evaluates to the value of the second argument. So the two following lines of code have the same effect:

```
print(myOr(5, "hello"))  --> 5
print(5 or "hello")  --> 5
```

There is a small, but important difference, however. The operator or is what is called a *short-circuited* operator in Lua. That means it will not evaluate its second argument if doing so is not necessary (that is, when the first argument is true). So the following two lines are not equivalent:

```
print(myOr(5, print("hello")))  --> hello 5
print(5 or print("hello"))  --> 5
```

The first line evaluates both expressions before even calling myOr. The second line causes Lua to look at the first argument (5). The value 5 is considered to be true, so the right part of the expression is not evaluated, and print is never called here.

When Lua calls a function such as print("hello"), it carries out the behavior of the function (in this case printing out hello) and takes the return argument in order to evaluate the expression. In this case, the return value would be nil because print does not return anything.

The and operator can also be written as a function to demonstrate how it works:

```
function myAnd(value1, value2)
    if  not value1 then
        return value1
    else
        return value2
    end
end
```

So and checks whether its first argument evaluates to false or nil; if so, it returns that value. Otherwise, it returns the second value. This operator is also short-circuited like or; if the left expression is false or nil, the right expression is not evaluated.

Precedence

You can combine all of the different operators in one single expression, as you can break a complex expression down into smaller expressions that are arguments to their operators. So it is important to know the operator precedence in Lua. *Precedence* defines the order in which an expression is evaluated. For example, an arithmetic expression like 5 + 3 * 2 follows the usual mathematical rules and starts with the multiplication, reducing the expression to 5 + 6. You can always use explicit parentheses to define the order in which your expression is evaluated. If you are not using explicit parentheses, Lua follows this list, from higher to lower priority:

```
^
# not - (unary)
* / %
+ -
..
== ~= <= => < >
and
or
```

Table 2-2 lists a few examples.

Table 2-2. *Examples of Operator Precedence*

Expression	Parenthesized Expression
5 + 3 * 5	5 + (3 * 5)
a and b or c	(a and b) or c
a == 5 or #c - d / 2 > b	(a == 5) or (((#c) - (d / 2)) > b)
not 5 == 4	(not 5) == 4

If you are unsure about the precedence, use parentheses. Using parentheses in long or unclear expressions also improves the readability of your code.

Expressions are very powerful in Lua, because they can evaluate all types of values and can be used everywhere that a value is expected. So it is very important that you understand how expressions and operators work. Logical operators are especially powerful. For example, you can use the or operator to define default values in functions. A function that expects an argument but is called without an argument sees the missing argument as nil. So we can define a function like this to deal with this situation:

```
function Hello(str)
    str = str or "World"
    print("Hello, "..str)
end

Hello("Lua") --> Hello, Lua
Hello() --> Hello, World
```

The expression str or "World" evaluates to "World" if str is nil or false. It will be nil if we don't provide the argument, so we have just defined a default value.

Tables and Functions as Expressions

In our earlier discussions of tables and functions, there is one important fact I omitted. The code used to create functions:

```
function(<arguments>) <body> end
```

and the code used to create tables:

```
{<contents>}
```

are actually expressions. The value of such an expression is a reference to the created table or function that can be stored in a variable.

This means you can use these constructs in expressions, so it is valid (but useless) to write code like the following variable assignment:

```
x = {1, 5, 9} and function(x) print(x) end
```

You will see why this capability can be useful in the next section, when we look at statements in Lua.

Statements

Statements in Lua, as in many programming languages, can be either assignments, control structures, or function calls.

Function Calls

Function calls are one of the simplest types of statements and you have seen them already in almost all examples. As I mentioned in the first section, the parentheses are not required for certain arguments. This allows you to write

```
print "Hello, World!"
```

instead of

```
print("Hello, World!")
```

This also works for tables:

```
print{1, 2, 3} --> table: 0032A3C8
```

The function print converts its arguments to strings and the string representation looks like this: table: *memory address*. You will learn how to define a function that does the string conversion to produce a useful output later.

Note that this syntax works if you want to pass only one argument and can be confusing to anyone reading your source code. The last example is a bad coding style; this function call can easily be mistaken for

```
print(1, 2, 3)  --> 1 2 3
```

That is something completely different, but it is also a valid call to print, as print can take more than one argument. It tries to convert all of its arguments to strings and prints them separated by tabs. But it is useful if you have a function that takes a huge table as its only argument that contains all other arguments. This syntax can be used to implement named arguments, and a call to such a function could look like the following code snippet:

```
SomeFunction{someArgument = 5, anotherArgument = "test"}
```

It is possible to call expressions that assume the value of a function. But this can lead to sloppy and unreadable code, especially when using functions in expressions (known as *in-line functions*) as in the following example.

```
function myPrint(msg, prefix)
    (prefix and function(x) print(prefix, x) end or print)(msg)
end
```

```
myPrint("Hello", false)  --> Hello
myPrint("Hello", "<My Prefix>")  --> <My Prefix> Hello
```

The whole expression is treated as a function and is called. myPrint calls print if prefix is false or nil; otherwise, it calls the in-line function that takes the argument x and then calls print with your prefix and its argument x. Using an if control structure is much better in this case.

This is perfectly valid, but as you can see, the code is barely readable. The code is also hard to understand, especially if you have never used a functional programming language before. Don't worry if you do not understand how exactly this example works here. There is a better solution using if that is also easy to understand:

```
function myPrint(msg, prefix)
    if prefix then
        print(prefix, msg)
    else
        print(msg)
    end
end
```

The second solution is even more efficient than the first one, as the first function actually creates a new function every time prefix is set.

You have already seen that tables can hold every type of value. So you can insert functions in tables, as in the following example:

```
local t = {}
t.foo = function(x)
    print(x)
end
```

```
t.foo(5) --> 5
```

This works as you would expect it to work. But there is a second way to call this function, by using the colon operator:

```
t:foo(5) --> table: memory address
```

It suddenly tries to print a table. We get the same result when we add the line print(t), so x in foo seems to be t now. The colon operator is just a short way to pass the table as the first argument to the function. The call t:foo(5) translates to t.foo(t, 5). This operator is only available for functions in tables.

Some functions require the table in which they are stored as the first argument. You will see later why a function might want to get this as its first argument (or why we would pass the table as the first argument by hand).

Control Structures

Control structures are used to branch your code and to create loops. Lua provides the control structures if-then-else-end, while-do-end, repeat-until, and two types of for loops: numeric and generic.

if Statements

You have already seen a lot of if statements. They are simple to use and their purpose can be guessed without knowing anything about Lua. An if statement starts with an if-then block followed by code to be executed if *expression* can be evaluated to true:

```
if expression then
    -- do stuff
```

This block can be followed by one or more elseif-then blocks:

```
elseif expression then
    -- do other stuff
```

A final else block can be used; it will be executed if all of the previous expressions were false or nil:

```
else
    -- do more stuff
end
```

An if block is always closed by the keyword end.

while Loops

The second control structure is the while loop. It looks like this:

```
while expression do
    -- code
end
```

It checks whether *expression* can be evaluated to true and executes its body if that is possible. When reaching the end statement, Lua will evaluate the expression again. If it is still true, it jumps back to the body. Otherwise, it leaves the loop. Note that the loop won't be executed at all if the expression is false or nil when starting the loop. It is easy to write loops that do not terminate; here is an example:

```
while true do
end
```

Always make sure that you don't create infinite loops, as they will freeze your program. If an addon goes into an infinite loop, the whole game freezes and must be restarted.

A simple loop that prints the numbers from 1 to 10 and certainly terminates looks like this:

```
i = 1
while i <= 10 do
    print(i)
    i = i + 1
end
```

repeat-until Loops

There is another type of loop available that is very similar to the while loop: the repeat-until loop. As the name suggests, it repeats its body until an expression becomes true:

```
repeat
    code
until expression
```

This loop guarantees that the body is executed at least once, as the first check of the expression is done after the body is executed for the first time. Unlike the while loop, the repeat loop ends if the expression becomes true and continues as long as it is false or nil.

So counting from 1 to 10 with a repeat-until loop looks like this:

```
i = 1
repeat
    print(i)
    i = i + 1
until i > 10
```

for Loops

There are two more types of loops: numeric and generic for loops. Numeric for loops are simple, and they look like this:

```
for var = startValue, endValue, step do
    code
end
```

The startValue argument defines the start value, endValue the end value, and step the increment to use, which can be negative. Here are a few for loops:

```
for i = 1, 10 do
    print(i)
end
```

```
for i = 10, 1, -1 do
    print(i)
end
```

```
for i = 1, 10, 2 do
   print(i)
end
```

The first counts from 1 to 10. Note that step is not provided and Lua assumes it is 1 in this case. The second loops counts from 10 down to 1 by using a negative step, and the third loop prints all odd numbers between 1 and 10.

The fourth loop type is the generic for loop. This is the most powerful type of loop; it takes an *iterator function* and a value to operate on. This iterator function is called every time the loop is executed, and the iterator function (often called simply the *iterator*) can decide whether the loop should be continued. The iterator function's return values will be provided as local variables inside the loop. So a generic for can look like this:

```
for var1, var2, ... varN in iteratorFunc, value do
    code
end
```

An iterator function that is provided by Lua is next, which can be used to traverse over tables. It returns the key and value pairs of a table, so we can use it to print the contents of a table:

```
myTable = {a = 1, ["foo"] = "bar", hello = "world"}
for key, value in next, myTable do
   print(key, value)
end
```

This will print

```
a 1
hello world
foo bar
```

Note that a hash table does not sort its entries. So an element that was just added to a hash table might be the first entry.

The function pairs is a simple function that basically returns the function next and the first argument provided to it. So you can write

```
for key, value in pairs(myTable) do
   print(key, value)
end
```

This is equivalent to the previously used code.

The function ipairs returns an iterator that uses only the array part of a table. You can use it if you have a table that contains both arbitrary values, as keys, and simple consecutive integers:

```
myTable = {"a", "b", "c", "d"}
myTable.foo = "bar"
myTable[10] = "e"
```

```
for key, value in ipairs(myTable) do
    print(key, value)
end
```

It will ignore all nonconsecutive integer indices, so it prints

---

```
1 a
2 b
3 c
4 d
```

You will see another interesting iterator function when working with the string library. There are iterators that can be used to iterate over words or other expressions found in strings.

It is also possible to write your own iterator functions. The function will be called by Lua to get the elements from a data structure until it returns nil. This is an advanced topic and will be covered later in this book.

break

The statement break immediately leaves a for, while, or repeat loop. If you are using a loop to look up a value in a table, you can break the loop prematurely if you find the value you were searching for, as in this example:

```
myTable = {"a", "b", 5, 10, 100}
for k, v in ipairs(myTable) do
    if v == 5 then
        key = k
        break
    end
end

print(key)    --> 3
```

We cancel the loop after finding the value we were looking for; there is no need to look at the remaining elements.

return

The statement return *value* allows us to leave a function and return a result. A function does not necessarily have a result, so you can also just use return. Trying to get the result from such a function that doesn't return anything will provide nil.

Unlike many other programming languages, Lua allows you to return more than one result in a function. Just separate them by commas:

```
function foo()
    return 1, 2, 3, "a", 4
end
print(foo()) --> 1  2  3  a  4
```

The return values can directly be passed to another function, which will see all values. If you want to cut off values, you can use the function select(n,   foo(), which returns all values provided as arguments starting with the *n*th element. So if we still have our function foo(), we can write:

```
print(select(1, foo()))  --> 1  2  3  a  4
print(select(3, foo()))  --> 3  a  4
```

Assignments

Assignments are pretty simple, and you have already seen a few examples of them. They basically consist of a variable, the assignment operator (an equality sign), and a value or expression. The assignment sets the value of a variable to the provided value. You can assign multiple variables to multiple values in one statement using comma-separated lists:

```
var1, var2, var3 = "a", "b", "c"
print(var1, var2, var3)    --> a  b  c
```

It is not an error for an assignment if variables or values are missing:

```
var1, var2 = 1+1, 1+2, 1+3, 1+4
print(var1, var2)  --> 2  3
```

The expressions 1+3 and 1+4 are not saved to a variable, so they will be evaluated but the result is not saved and will be lost. Missing values are also no problem:

```
var1, var2, var3 = "a", "b"
print(var1, var2, var3)  --> a  b nil
```

The variable var3 is nil in this case.

This syntax also allows you to store the results of functions that return more than one value:

```
function foo()
   return 1, 2, 3, 4
end

var1, var2, var3 = foo()
print(var1, var2, var3)  --> 1  2  3
```

It is also possible to use select to cut off arguments you don't need.

```
var3, var4 = select(3, foo())
print(var3, var4) --> 3  4
```

If a function returns an argument you don't need between two required arguments, you will have to create a dummy variable. A commonly used dummy variable is "_".

```
var1, _, _, var2 = foo()  -- we don't need the second and third return values
print(var1, var2)  --> 1, 4
```

It is no problem to use a variable more than once in an assignment. The second assignment will override the first one, but we wouldn't need the value anyway in this case.

There is no difference between initializing a variable and assigning a new value to it. Lua will evaluate all expressions on the right side of the assignment operator before assigning them. This means that it is possible to use this multi-variable assignment to swap the values of two or more variables. Many programming languages require you to write something like this to swap the values of two variables, x and y:

```
b = x
x = y
y = b
```

In Lua it's easier:

```
x, y = y, x
```

Local Variables

We have only created global variables thus far. Global variables are available everywhere. In World of Warcraft, "everywhere" means that a global variable is visible in all addons. So if two addons try to use the same name for a global variable, it might break one or both of them. So when using a global variable, it should be prefixed with your addon's name.

The better solution is to try to use local variables whenever possible. The scope of local variables is limited to the current block. A block can be a function, an if-then-end block, or a loop. A file is internally treated as a function, so you can see a file as a block when looking at the scope of a variable. It is also possible to define your own blocks by using the keywords do and end. Arguments of functions are always local to that function.

You create a local variable by using the keyword local when declaring the variable. The scope of a local variable that is declared or initialized by using local starts after the initializing expression and ends with the current block.

Local variables are a very important part of Lua syntax, so let's look at a few examples:

```
local x = 5
if x == 5 then
    print(x)  --> 5
    local x = 1
    print(x)  --> 1
end
print(x) --> 5
```

The scope of the variable x that is initialized in the first line is the whole file. So it is also valid in all sub-blocks, like if-then-end blocks or functions. The expression x == 5 then evaluates to true and the content of the if statement is executed; the first print accesses the local x we defined before and prints 5. Now we declare a new local variable x inside the if-then-end block. It overwrites the old local x inside this block, so the next print(x) statement prints 1. However, the scope of this new local x ends with our if block's keyword end.

The last line prints 5, which means our new local x only overwrote the x inside its own block. It does not destroy the old local variable of the enclosing block (the file, which is internally actually a function).

The following example shows a common mistake when working with local variables in if statements:

```
if condition then
    local x = 1
else
    local x = 2
end
print(x) --> nil
```

This prints nil because the x we initialize inside the if-then-else-end block is not visible after the block ends. The correct way to write something like this is

```
local x
if condition then
    x = 1
else
    x = 2
end
print(x) --> 2
```

Now we get the expected result. The statement local x declares x as a local variable and initializes it with nil. Then condition evaluates to nil because it references a global variable that is not initialized, so the assignment x = 1 is executed. This assignment sees the previously declared local variable x and sets its value to 2.

But there is a better way to write something like this in Lua. Recall what you learned about expressions in the last section, especially about logical operators. These operators can evaluate to any value, so you can write the following expression instead of the if statement:

```
local x = condition and 1 or 2
print(x) --> 2
```

This looks complicated but is actually not that hard. Lua will first check condition and if it is true will check 1, which is also true. So the and expression will assume the value 1, which will be used for the left part of the or expression. This value is obviously true, so the right side of the or will not be evaluated, and the whole expression evaluates to 1. But condition evaluates to nil in our example, so the left side of the or will also be nil. It will then return its second argument, which is 2.

You might recognize the usefulness of this code fragment if you have used other programming languages that provide the conditional expression condition?value1:value2. This operator is missing in Lua and the idiom condition and value1 or value2 is often used as a replacement. Note that it does not work as expected if value1 is nil or false.

The other control structures, namely while, repeat, and for loops, are also considered to be blocks. Local variables declared inside the bodies of such loops are local to that loop. Note that the expression that checks the loop condition is inside the scope. The variables generated by for loops are also always local to the body of the loop.

It is also possible to create your own blocks by using do end blocks:

```
local x = 5
do
    print(x)  --> 5
    local x = 3
    do
        print(x)  --> 3
        local z = 1
    end  -- the scope of z ends here
    print(z) --> nil
end -- the scope of the second x declaration ends here
print(x) --> 5 so we got our first x back
```

This can be used to limit the scope of local variables, as it is always good to keep the scope as small as possible. You can clearly identify the purpose of a variable that can only be used in a few lines of code. By contrast, it can be hard to figure out what happens with a variable that is used all over your program.

You can also define local functions; this works with both methods of creating functions:

```
local function foo()
end

local foo = function()
end
```

But there is a small difference. The first code translates to:

```
local foo
foo = function() end
```

So when using the first way to define a function, the function is inside the scope of the local variable that holds the function. When using the second way, the scope of this variable starts after the function. Let's go back to our function that calculates the factorial of a number and try to make it local.

```
local function fac(n)
    if n == 0 then
        return 1
    else
        return n * fac(n - 1)
    end
end

print(fac(5)) --> 120
```

It works just fine. But when you change the first line to

```
local fac = function(n)
```

it now generates an error message:

```
attempt to call global 'fac' (a nil value)
```

as it tries to access a global variable fac. So if you want to use the second way to assign a function to a local variable, you have to make sure that this function does not try to call itself or create the variable before assigning the function to it.

The result is the same. You can use both ways to store functions in variables. I use the second way if I want to emphasize that it is an assignment.

There is one more thing we need to know about functions: the *vararg* (variable arguments) parameter, which allows a function to take an indefinite number of arguments.

Variable Arguments

The function print we have been using throughout the chapter accepts a variable number of arguments. It works with one argument or with hundreds of arguments. It prints all arguments it receives, separated by tabs. Let's create a function called printLines that works like print but prints each argument it receives in a new line. We need the vararg parameter for this.

A function head with a vararg parameter looks like this:

```
function printLines(...)
end
```

The three dots are the vararg parameter. They can be used everywhere Lua expects one or more values, as in a function head or a call to a function. We now need to extract all arguments that are contained in these three dots and call tostring and print for each of them. This can be done by using the function select(n, ...). select returns all arguments contained in the vararg starting with the nth, meaning that it omits the first n - 1 arguments. The n argument can also be the string "#", which causes select to return the number of values stored in the vararg.

The following simple for loop iterates over all the arguments passed to printLines and passes them to print:

```
function printLines(...)
   for i = 1, select("#", ...) do
      print(select(i, ...))
   end
end
```

But select only cuts off the first values, so if we call printLines("a", "b", "c"), we get this:

```
a   b   c
b   c
c
```

We only want to print one argument per line. The simplest way to cut the remaining arguments is to parenthesize the call to select. This forces Lua to evaluate it as an expression, and an expression has exactly one value. We have to add the parentheses in line 3 like this:

```
print((select(i, ...)))
```

This produces the result we wanted:

```
a
b
c
```

Note that these three dots can be passed to any function and not only to select. Any other function will receive them like normal arguments and cannot see any difference. That function can, of course, also use a vararg to store these arguments. select is also not restricted to the vararg parameter; you can also just place a list of values or a function call there. For example, you can use select like this:

```
print(select(2, "a", "b", "c")) --> b c
```

You can also place a function call instead of the three strings there. The following code illustrates this:

```
function foo()
    return "a", "b", "c"
end

print(select(2, foo())) --> B C
```

This syntax is useful if you do not care about the first few return values of a function and you just want to get a specific one. But it is more likely that you want to store that return value in a function. This is also no problem:

```
function foo()
    return "a", "b", "c"
end
local x = select(2, foo()) -- we only want the second return value
-- the third return value is dropped
pritn(x) --> b
```

It is also possible to use the vararg directly in variable assignments, like this:

```
function foo(...)
    local a, b, c = ...
    -- code...
end
```

This is roughly equivalent to the following.

```
function foo(a, b, c)
    code...
end
```

The only difference between the last two examples is that all arguments from the fourth on are still stored in the vararg in the first example. Lua drops these arguments in the second example, as the function didn't accept them.

The vararg can be passed on to another function; this allows us to write wrapper functions. A *wrapper* function is one that basically just forwards a function call to another function. It might shift around a few arguments or add them, but the real work is done by the wrapper function. Let's build a wrapper function for print that adds a simple prefix:

```
function prefixedPrint(...)
   print("[My Prefix]", ...)
end

prefixedPrint("a", "b", "c") --> [My Prefix] a b c
```

You will see more examples of wrapper functions in Chapter 6, which goes further into Lua and functional programming.

Another interesting possibility is using the vararg parameter in a table constructor. It can be used everywhere Lua expects a list of values. And it is possible to create an array from a list of values, so the following code stores all values from the vararg in the array part of a new table:

```
local t = {...}
```

Varargs are very common in World of Warcraft; almost all addons make use of them. You will see many examples for varargs in addons and learn more about the function select in Chapter 4.

Lua Standard Libraries

A *library* is a set of functions that can be used by your scripts. Lua comes with seven standard libraries: math, string, table, debug, os, io, and coroutine. However, World of Warcraft does not provide the library io, as this library allows you to write to or read from files. That would allow addons to communicate with other programs. The os library is only partially implemented, for security reasons, as it allows you to execute system commands like deleting files. The debug library is also only partially implemented.

The coroutine library is fully implemented, but is not covered in this chapter as using it is not simple. We will see how it works in Chapter 13.

The Math Library

The math library is fully implemented in World of Warcraft. All functions are available in the table math. World of Warcraft provides aliases in global variables for all of these functions. You can basically omit the prefix math in World of Warcraft; for example, math.sin is the same as sin in WoW. The following math library functions are available.

math.abs(*x*)

Returns *x* if *x* >= 0, otherwise -*x*.

math.acos(*x*)

Calculates the arccosine of *x*.

`math.asin(x)`

Calculates the arcsine of x.

`math.atan(x)`

Calculates the arctangent of x.

`math.atan2(y, x)`

Calculates the arctangent of y/x in the range between –pi and pi.

`math.ceil(x)`

Returns the next integer >= x.

`math.cos(x)`

Calculates the cosine of x.

`math.cosh(x)`

Calculates the hyperbolic cosine of x.

`math.deg(x)`

Converts a radian value to degrees.

`math.exp(x)`

Returns e^x. (e = 2.7182...)

`math.floor(x)`

Returns the next integer <= x.

`math.fmod(x, y)`

Equivalent to the modulo operator x % y.

`math.frexp(x)`

Returns the significand and the exponent of the internal floating-point representation.

`math.huge`

A constant that represents infinity.

`math.ldexp(x, exp)`

Calculates $x * 2^{exp}$. That means `math.ldexp(math.frexp(x))` == x.

`math.log(x)`

Calculates the natural logarithm of x.

`math.log10(x)`

Calculates the decimal logarithm of x.

`math.max(x1, x2, ...)`

Returns the biggest of the provided numbers.

`math.min(x1, x2, ...)`

Returns the smallest of the provided numbers.

`math.modf(x)`

Returns the integral and fractional part of x.

`math.pi`

3.141592...

`math.pow(x, y)`

Equivalent to $x \, ^\wedge \, y$.

`math.rad(x)`

Converts degree to radians.

`math.random(x, y)`

Generates a random integer between x and y. It returns a float between 0 and 1 if x and y are omitted.

`math.randomseed(x)`

Seeds the pseudo-random number generator with x. This is done automatically in World of Warcraft and the function is therefore not available in the game.

All trigonometric functions work on radian values. You can use `math.rad(x)` to convert from degree to radian if you prefer working with degree values.

String Library Basics

The `string` library is also fully implemented in the game. Blizzard has even added a few custom functions that are not available in the standard Lua distribution. Some of these functions are also accessible through global variables in World of Warcraft.

This chapter does not discuss all the functions in the string library, some of which require advanced knowledge of Lua. You will see these functions in Chapter 5.

All string library functions are stored in the table `string`, and some of them are also available in global variables in World of Warcraft.

A useful idiom available when working on strings is to use the colon operator on strings to call these functions. For example, `foo:find(x)` translates to `string.find(foo, x)` if `foo` is a string. It is also possible to use the colon operator directly on strings: `("some string"):find(x)` equals `string.find("some string", x)`.

Some of these functions accept an unspecified number of arguments; this is denoted by using three dots as arguments. Following are the basic string library functions.

string.byte(*str, start, end*)

Returns the numerical representations of the characters between *start* and *end* in the string *str*. The last two arguments are optional; the default value for *start* is 1, and *end* equals *start* by default. So you can call it with two arguments to work with the *n*th character. This function is also available as `strbyte` in WoW.

string.char(*byte1, byte2, ...*)

Converts one or more numbers to a string. So `string.char(string.byte(str, 1, #str))` == *str*. This function is also available as `strchar` in WoW.

string.dump(*func*)

Returns the internally used byte code of the function *func* as a string. You can use the function `loadstring(str)` on this string to get the function back.

string.find(*str, pattern, start, plain*)

Finds the first occurrence of *pattern* in `str`. The next two arguments are optional; *start* is 1 by default and defines the first character the function looks at. If *plain* is provided and `true`, regular expressions and captures in *pattern* are ignored.

The function returns `nil` if it cannot find *pattern*; otherwise, it returns the position of the first and last character of the found occurrence. The function also returns all captures in the found pattern after the two numbers. This function is also available as `strfind` in WoW.

You will learn more about patterns, regular expressions, and captures under "Pattern Basics" later in this section.

string.format(*str, ...*)

Formats the string `str` by replacing certain expressions with the provided arguments. The formatted string is returned. You will learn more about string formatting later in this section. This function is also available as `format` in WoW.

string.join(*separator, str1, str2, ...*)

Concatenates the provided strings. The *separator* character will be used as a separator between the strings. Using this function is more efficient than writing

str1..separator..str2..separator..str3

as this concatenation would create a lot of small strings while evaluating the expression:

separator..str3, str2..separator..str3

and so on. (Concatenation is right-associative in Lua.)

This function is specific to World of Warcraft and is not available in standard Lua. World of Warcraft also provides the alias strjoin in the global namespace.

string.len(*str*)

Returns the length of *str*, equivalent to #*str*. This function is also available as strlen in WoW.

string.lower(*str*)

Returns a lowercase version of the string str .This function is also available as strlower in WoW.

string.match(*str, pattern, start*)

This function works like string.find but doesn't return the indices of the occurrences of *pattern*. It also returns the whole occurrence if *pattern* does not contain captures; otherwise it returns the found captures. This function is also available as strmatch in WoW.

string.rep(*str, n*)

Concatenates the string *str n* times and returns this new string. This function is also available as strrep in WoW.

string.reverse(*str, pattern*)

Returns a reverse version of the string *str*.

string.split(*separator, string*)

Splits a string and returns all substrings delimited by *separator* in **string**. For example, this function:

```
string.split("-", string.join("-", "a", "b", "c"))
```

returns

```
"a", "b", "c"
```

Note that the first argument is the string that is used as the delimiter, not the string to split! So you can't write str:split(*separator*).

This function is specific to World of Warcraft and is not available in the standard Lua distribution. WoW also provides the alias strsplit in the global environment.

string.sub(*str, i, j*)

Returns the substring of str that starts at index *i* and ends at *j*. The last argument is optional and its default value is #*str*. You can use negative indices instead of #*str* - *x*. This function is also available as strsub in WoW.

string.trim(*str*)

Trims leading and trailing spaces from the string *str* and returns the trimmed string.

This function is specific to World of Warcraft and is not available in the standard Lua distribution. It is also accessible in the global environment as strtrim.

string.upper(*str, pattern*)

Returns an uppercase version of the string **str**. This function is also available as strupper in WoW.

Pattern Basics

The string library supports *regular expressions* in patterns. Regular expressions are a very powerful way to describe a pattern in a string you are looking for. Lua has its own syntax for regular expressions; there is no support for Perl Compatible Regular Expressions (PCRE) or POSIX regular expressions. Lua's regular expression system is simpler and slightly less powerful than those systems; for example, there is no support for back references. If you have never heard of regular expressions before, don't worry. They are less complicated than they seem.

We'll use the function string.match to play around with a few patterns. It will look for a pattern in a string and return it if the string contains it.

```
local str = "Hello, World!"
print(str:match("Hello"))  --> Hello
print(str:match("Hello, World"))  --> Hello, World
print(str:match("Hello!"))  --> nil
```

The first call to match looks for the string "Hello", finds it, and returns it. The second one looks for "Hello, World", which is also in our string. The last line prints nil because the string "Hello!" is not part of our text.

So we can check whether a string is part of another string, but this function can do more. There are some characters with special meanings. One of them is ^, which stands for the beginning of the string. The end of the string can be denoted by using $. The following example shows how this works.

```
local str = "Hello, World!"
print(str:match("Hello$"))  --> nil
print(str:match("^Hello"))  --> Hello
print(str:match("World$"))  --> nil
```

The first call to match returns nil because the string doesn't end with "Hello", but the second one works as expected. The last line also prints nil, as the string does not end with the word World (the exclamation mark is missing).

So we can now check to see if a string starts or ends with a specific word. But what do we do if we want to search for the characters $ or ^ in a string? We have to escape them by prefixing them with the character %. But Lua is quite smart and detects when you use one of these characters in the middle of the string. You don't have to escape them there, as it would be pointless to look for the beginning of a string in the middle of it. The following example shows how to escape these characters:

```
local str = "x = e^5"
print(str:match("%^5"))  --> ^5
```

If you want to look for a single percentage sign, you will have to write %%. This method of escaping characters also applies to all other characters that have special meanings we are going to see in the rest of the section.

You might wonder why the function returns the found occurrence. You provided the substring you are looking for as argument, so the return value seems to be unnecessary. But string.match can use more complex patterns than just simple strings. Let's look at character classes. These classes describe a set of characters and they can be used in our patterns. This allows us, for example, to look for a number in a string without knowing which number we are looking for or where exactly in the string it is. Table 2-3 shows all classes that are available.

Table 2-3. *Available Classes for Regular Expressions*

Class	Matches
.	all characters
%a	letters (a, A, b, B, ...)
%c	control characters (\t, \n, ...)
%d	digits (0, 1, 2, ...)
%l	lowercase letters (a, b, c, ...)
%p	punctuation characters (comma, point, etc.)
%s	space characters (space, tab, etc)
%u	uppercase characters (A, B, C, ...)
%w	alphanumeric characters (0, 1, a, A, ...)
%x	hexadecimal digits (0, 1, a, A, f, F, ...)
%z	embedded zeros (\0)

The uppercase versions of these classes (%A, %C, etc.) represent all characters except for those in that class (the *complement* of the class).

You can also combine character classes and characters into character sets that can be used like classes, by putting classes and normal characters in square brackets. So [%w%p] represents all alphanumeric characters, all punctuation characters, and all spaces (not tabs and other whitespace characters like in %s). You can get the complement of a set by prefixing it with a circumflex: [^,] stands for all characters except for commas.

You can use character classes everywhere you can use characters in patterns. Let's look at some examples that demonstrate the usage of character classes.

```
local str = "12 Hello, World! 123"
print(str:match("%l"))  --> e (the first lowercase letter)
print(str:match("%w"))  --> H (the first alphanumeric character)
print(str:match("%p"))  --> , (the first punctuation character)
print(str:match("%d%d%d"))  --> 123 (the first three digits)
print(str:match("%l, %u"))  --> o, W (the first lowercase character➡
that is followed by ", " and an uppercase character)
print(str:match("%W"))  --> , (the first character that is not alphanumeric)
print(str:match("%W%d"))  --> " 1" (the first character that is not➡
alphanumeric and followed by a digit)
```

As you can see, we can now look for a pattern without knowing exactly what it looks like.

But there are four more characters with special meanings: +, -, *, and ?. They determine the repetitions of the preceding character. + will match one or more repetitions, - matches zero or more occurrences, * also matches zero or more repetitions, and ? means zero or one. The difference between - and * is that the former always matches the shortest possible occurrence (that can be the empty string), while the latter returns the longest possible match.

Let's consider a short example that uses these new signs. You will find more examples at the end of this section.

```
local str = "Hello, World! 123"
print(str:match("%w*"))  --> Hello
print(str:match("%w-"))  --> (the empty string)
```

This shows the difference between the two "one or more" modifiers. Both patterns try to find the first occurrence of one or more alphanumeric characters. The first one (which is sometimes described as "greedy") finds the longest possible match, Hello, the second one finds the shortest possible match, which is obviously no character at all.

There is one last element of regular expressions you need to know about: captures. A *capture* is a substring of a regular expression, and you can use it to get specific parts of a string returned by string.match. A regular expression can define up to 32 captures (don't worry; you are not going to need more). Let's look at an example that uses two captures, indicated by the () within the search string:

```
local str = "Hello, World!"
print(str:match("(%w+), *(%w+)"))  --> Hello  World
```

The function string.match now returns two arguments. Without the captures, it would have returned the whole found occurrence, which is "Hello, World". So this allows you to get the first two words of a string. Without captures, you would have to analyze and split the returned string to get the words from it. A special capture is the empty capture (), which returns the current position in the string. This position can then be used for the function string.sub to split the string.

Let's look at some real-world examples from Deadly Boss Mods. The first is from a hook in a Blizzard-defined function that processes raid warning messages. DBM determines whether it is a message from a boss mod and does not call the function to display it if it is one:

```
msg:find("%s*%*%*%* .* %*%*%*%s*")
```

So the pattern is basically looking for messages like *** *text here* *** and ignores leading and trailing spaces. You can clearly see how to escape these special characters here; just using asterisks here would cause an error message. You can test it by defining a (local) variable msg and print the return values of find.

The next example parses the user input from DBM's slash command /dbm timer mm:ss name. It is a great example that shows how to use captures:

```
local min, sec, text = msg:match("^timer (%d+):?(%d*) (.+)$")
```

msg is the whole string after /dbm without leading and trailing spaces. This pattern matches all possible user inputs like timer 15:00 foo, timer 60 some random text, or timer 13:120 pizza. The next few lines of the script do error checking and convert min and sec to a time in seconds.

The next example is taken from the battleground mods. It strips the server from a player's name if their name looks like name-server.

```
name = name:match("([^%-]+)")
```

The set [^%-] stands for all characters except for hyphens, and the pattern looks for one or more occurrences. So the function returns the name of the player without the server. It even works for players with strange special characters in their names, where patterns like %w+ might fail.

Regular expressions can be hard to understand if you are seeing them for the first time. So if you did not understand everything in this section, don't worry. We are going to use these expressions in many example mods throughout the book, so you will get used to them.

More about string.format

The string.format function can be used to format strings by replacing certain expressions. The simplest expression you can use in a format string is %s, which will be replaced by a string or number that is passed to string.format. It might be easier to understand this function by looking at an example:

```
local str = "%s, %d, %f, %x, %X"
print(str:format("a string", 5.123, 5.123, 127, 127))
--> a string, 5, 5.123000, 7f, 7F
```

An expression that is replaced (a *directive*) always starts with % and may be followed by options that define how to format it; it ends with a letter that defines the type of the data to be formatted. In our example there are just a few simple directives without options. Table 2-4 lists the available types.

Table 2-4. *Available Directives for* string.format

Type	Description	Example
c	Character (a number that is interpreted by **string.char**)	a
d or i	Decimal number	123
e (E)	Double in standard notation; E uses E instead of e	1.232340e+002

Continued

Table 2-4. *Continued*

Type	Description	Example
f	Double in normal notation	123.234000
g (G)	Chooses e or f depending on the size of the number and strips trailing zeros	123.234
o	Octal representation of an integer	173
q	Adds escape codes for the Lua interpreter to a string	"\n \' \t"
s	Normal string	"normal String"
u	Unsigned interpretation of an integer	50
x (X)	Hexadecimal representation of an integer; X uses uppercase letters	0x4c7

The directives s and q expect strings or numbers; all other directives take numbers.

Options can be defined before the data type, and all options are optional. There are many options available in format strings; this chapter will only explain the most common ones. Wikipedia has a full list of available options, at http://en.wikipedia.org/wiki/Printf#printf_format_placeholders. However, it is very unlikely that in World of Warcraft you are going to need more than the options I present here.

The first option, the *argument*, is only available in World of Warcraft, not in the standard Lua distribution. It has the format *n*$ where *n* is the argument to use.

```
local str = "%2$s %1$s %1$s"
print(str:format("1st arg", "2nd arg")) --> 2nd arg 1st arg 1st arg
```

It is no problem to use the same argument more than once in a format string. This can be useful when localizing addons, as translated strings might require another order of the inserted text for grammatical reasons. Later in this book we will also see cases where we will need the same argument more than once.

All other options define how to format the output, especially of numbers. One option is the *width* of the inserted text. It is a number that defines the minimum length of the output. string.format will add spaces in front of the string to match the requested width:

```
local str = "%5d"
print(str:format(123))  --> "  123" (two leading spaces)
```

Adding 0 in front of the width causes Lua to use zeros instead of spaces to pad the string. Adding a + forces Lua to show the sign of a number even if it is positive:

```
local str = "%+05d"
print(str:format(123))  --> +0123
```

Another option is the *precision, .n*, which controls the number of digits after the decimal point:

```
local str = "%.3f"
print(str:format(123.456789))  --> 123.457
```

You can also mix these options:

```
local str = "%+010.4f"
print(str:format(123.456))  --> +0123.4560
```

You might know the function printf(*formatstring*, ...) from C. Such a function is not available in Lua by default. But you can write it now by using string.format:

```
function printf(str, ...)
   return print(str:format(...))
end
```

Recall that the three dots are the vararg parameter, which means the function takes a variable number of arguments and forwards them to string.format.

The Table Library

All functions from the table library are available in World of Warcraft. The game even implements an additional function, table.wipe. Some of these functions are also available in global variables in World of Warcraft. The following table functions are available.

table.concat(*tbl, sep, i, j*)

Concatenates all elements in the array part of the table *tbl* to a single string and returns it. *sep* is used as a separator between the elements (default = ""), *i* is the index to start with (the default is 1), and *j* is the last index (the default is #tbl). This function only works for strings and numbers.

This function is more efficient than using a loop to concatenate the strings.

table.insert(*tbl, position, value*)

Inserts a new element at a given position into the array part of the table *tbl*. This function allows you to insert elements at any place in the array and automatically moves other elements to the right place.

Note that the second argument is optional and its default value is #*tbl* + 1. So calling it with just two arguments is equivalent to *tbl*[#*tbl* + 1] = *value*. This can cause problems when you are trying to insert the return value of a function: table.insert(*tbl*, foo()). This causes an error message when foo returns two values and the first is not a number. The safe way to perform such an insertion is table.insert(*tbl*, (*foo*())). The parentheses around foo() cut off the remaining return values. World of Warcraft provides the alias tinsert.

table.maxn(*tbl*)

Returns the biggest numerical index of *tbl*. This also works on the hash table part of a table. The function returns 0 if *tbl* does not have an index that is a number.

table.remove(*tbl, position*)

Removes the element at *position* from the array part of *tbl*. The second argument is optional and its default value is #*tbl*. This function does not leave a "hole" in the array, as it moves elements after the removed element. World of Warcraft provides the alias tremove.

table.sort(*tbl, func*)

This function sorts the array part of *tbl* using the quicksort algorithm. You cannot sort the hash table part of a table by design. The second argument, *func*, is a function that takes two values from the tables and returns true if the first argument should be before the second argument. The *func* argument is optional; the less-than operator < will be used if it is omitted. World of Warcraft provides the alias sort.

table.wipe(*tbl*)

Removes all elements from the table tbl. This is faster than

```
for k in pairs(tbl) do tbl[k] = nil end
```

This function was added by Blizzard in World of Warcraft 3.0.2. It is not part of the standard Lua distribution. It is also available under the alias wipe.

The Debug Library

Only one function from the debug library is available in World of Warcraft: debug.traceback, under the name debugstack. This function returns a string containing the current call stack, which allows you to trace which function initiated the current call to your function. You will see how to use it when we discuss error handling in Chapter 6.

The Operating System Library

The operating system library os allows you to execute system commands or to terminate the host program. So, for obvious reasons, only a few functions are available in World of Warcraft. They are not in the table os in World of Warcraft, but there are global variables available that hold these functions. The name of the global variable is always the same as the table entry; for example os.time is the same as time.

os.date(*format, time*)

Formats a time stamp into a human-readable format. Both arguments are optional: *time* is by default the current time and the format used is mm/dd/yy hh:mm:ss (%c) if *format* is omitted. If format is "*t", the function returns a table with the fields year, month, day, hour, min, sec, wday, yday, and isdst. Otherwise it returns a string formatted as shown in Table 2-5.

Table 2-5. *Available Format Options for os.date*

Code	Effect	Example
%a	Weekday (abbreviated)	Sun
%A	Weekday	Sunday
%b	Month (abbreviated)	Jan
%B	Month	January
%c	Default format	12/29/08 18:15:28
%d	Day of the month	02

Code	Effect	Example
%H	Hour (24h)	18
%I	Hour (12h)	06
%j	Day of the year	004
%m	Month	03
%M	Minute	15
%p	AM/PM	PM
%S	Second	28
%U	Week	14
%w	Weekday (number, Sunday is 0)	6
%W	Week	14
%x	Date	12/29/08
%X	Time	18:15:28
%y	Year	09
%Y	Year	2009
%Z	Timezone	Pacific Standard Time

os.difftime(*time1, time2*)

Returns the time (in seconds) that passed between *time1* and *time2*. This function is equivalent to *time2* - *time1* on all operating systems that run World of Warcraft.

os.time()

Returns the current Unix time (seconds passed since 00:00:00 01/01/1970 UTC).

Summary

In this chapter you have learned the very basics of the programming language Lua. Armed with this information you can work with variables, and you know about the different available data types that can be assigned to variables. You have learned how to create and use tables. You are able to write functions. This chapter also looked at expressions and how to use them. Control structures gave us the possibility to control the flow of our programs. You then learned how to create and use local variables. The last part of this chapter presented the Lua standard libraries, which provide many useful functions we are going to use in the following chapters.

We now need to apply our knowledge in World of Warcraft. In the next chapter we will use what we have learned here to create a simple "Hello, World" addon. You are going to learn how to use the World of Warcraft API from Lua, and you will refine your Lua skills as we go on to write more and more complex and powerful addons.

## CHAPTER 3

Using the WoW API to Create a "Hello, World" Mod

Let's get started. You have already seen some Lua examples in Chapter 2, so writing a "Hello, World!" mod will be no problem for you.

But this first example mod will do a bit more than just displaying "Hello, World." It will provide two slash commands: /hwadd <id> <text> and /hwshow <id>. The former adds text to a table that will be saved, while the latter sends the text that was saved under id to a chat channel. Gold farmers might think that the only possible use of this addon is to spam the trade chat with advertisements, as it allows you to send a lot of text with one macro. Another good use for this mod could be to save long boss or battleground instructions, for example, in a single macro. You can then easily send them to the raid or battleground chat.

Let's start with running Lua code in the game.

Running a "Hello, World" in WoW

To run a script like the one we're going to create, just type the following slash command in World of Warcraft:

```
/script print("Hello, World!")
```

The command /script <text> compiles <text> as a new chunk and executes it.

■**Note** A *chunk* is a block of Lua code with its own scope. So if you define a local variable in a /script command, it will not be visible in the next /script command.

You already know the print function, but here it has one small difference from standard Lua: World of Warcraft writes the output to the default chat frame and not to your standard output. So this will show "Hello, World" in your default chat frame.

That's it? Yes. Basically that is it. But this is more a simple macro-like script, and I promised that you are going to learn how to write addons, so let's create your first real addon. This example was just to show that Lua in World of Warcraft works just like normal Lua. We can now start creating a Lua script that is loaded as an addon by the game.

Our First WoW Addon

Let's create the addon I described at the beginning of the chapter. The first thing we need to decide before we can start creating the mod is where to put our Lua files.

Folder Structure

You might already know that you need to put addons in the World of Warcraft Interface\ AddOns folder to install them. This folder is probably located in C:\Program Files\World of Warcraft\Interface\AddOns on your file system. So let's create the folder HelloWorld inside that folder. This is the place where we will create all the files for our "Hello, World" mod. But have you ever looked in the AddOns folder? There are many different file extensions. Which types of files can be used by an addon?

World of Warcraft provides API functions to handle the following file types: Lua scripts (.lua), XML (a data description language, which you will learn more about in Chapter 5) files (.xml), textures (images that can be used by addons) (.tga and .blp), sounds (.wav and .mp3), fonts (.ttf) and models (3D objects) (.m2). You will be able to use all default files that come with the World of Warcraft client in your addon. This includes the background music, spoken text, textures, models, and much more. And if that is not enough, you can just provide your own sounds, textures, and so on with your addon.

The World of Warcraft API provides a virtual file system, which means you can use remote files as if they were on your local disk. This allows you to access all files in your Interface folder and all files in the MPQ archives.

■**Note** MPQ is the archive format used by all Blizzard games. Think of it as something like a zip file. You will see more about MPQ files later in this chapter.

This virtual file system is built when you start the client, so the game won't recognize new files until you restart it. Whenever you add a new file throughout this book, you'll have to restart the game; simply reloading your interface (by typing /script ReloadUI() or simply /reload if you have the addon DevTools installed) won't work.

These MPQ archives also contain the Lua and XML files that define the default UI. The whole UI is also written like a regular addon in Lua. Later in this chapter you will see how to look at the code of this default UI.

When working with World of Warcraft, all paths to files are relative to your World of Warcraft folder, and files from MPQ archives will be mapped into that root folder. There is no way to access any file outside the installation folder. So a path name of a sound file could look like this:

Interface\AddOns*yourMod*\sounds\something.mp3

or this:

`Sound\Creature\Illidan\BLACK_Illidan_04.wav`

The first example references a file that is included in your addon. The second references a file in the archive `expansion-speech-locale.mpq`. (You will learn how to browse and extract these MPQ archives later in this chapter.)

Playing a sound file is a simple and good example that uses a path, so let's try this first. The game provides a simple function that takes the file name of a sound file and plays it: `PlaySoundFile(file)`. Test it by running this command:

```
/script PlaySoundFile("Sound/Creature/Illidan/BLACK_Illidan_04.wav")
```

You will hear Illidan's famous "You are not prepared!" But Illidan is obviously wrong here; you are prepared.

■Note Since you can play any sound file that is in your `Interface\AddOns`, it is very easy to write an in-game MP3 player. You just need to copy all your MP3s into that folder and provide the addon with a list (for example, as a table) of your files because there is no function that returns a list of files in a directory. For example, if you put all your MP3s in the folder `Interface\AddOns\MyMusic`, you can run the following command to play one in-game:

```
/script PlaySoundFile("Interface/AddOns/MyMusic/MyFavoriteSong.mp3")
```

But the file type we need for our addon is obviously a `.lua` file, as we want to code Lua now. We need to tell the game somehow to execute the Lua script. We also need to provide the game some additional information about our addon, such as its name. The file type we are going to use for this is called a *TOC* file. Let's see what this is.

The TOC File Format

A TOC (table of contents) file contains metadata, or "data about data," describing an addon along with a list of Lua and XML files to load. There are a few basic attributes like the name of the addon and the version of World of Warcraft it was made for. But it is also possible to define custom attributes and store arbitrary data in a TOC file. So let's create a TOC file for our "Hello, World!" mod.

■Note World of Warcraft reads the TOC files only once while starting. So if you change anything in a `.toc` file you will have to restart your game. Remember, reloading your interface won't work.

We have already created the folder `HelloWorld` inside `Interface\AddOns`, so let's create our TOC file here. World of Warcraft tries to load a TOC file with the same name as the folder, so we create `HelloWorld.toc` as shown here:

```
## Interface: 30100
## Title: Hello, World!
## Title-deDE: Hallo, Welt!
## Notes: The best "Hello, World!" addon!
HelloWorld.lua
```

There are two types of commands in this TOC file: lines starting with ## contain metadata. All other lines are files that will be executed to load the addon.

We are defining the following metadata for our addon:

```
Interface = 30100
```

This tells the game that our addon is written for World of Warcraft 3.1.x. If this version number is lower than the current interface version, World of Warcraft will report that the addon is outdated or even incompatible.

```
Title = Hello, World!
```

This defines the name of our addon, so it will show up as "Hello, World!" in the list of installed addons.

```
Title-deDE = Hallo, Welt!
```

An example of localization, this is a special line that will only be executed if you are using a German client. It overwrites the old title we defined before, so our addon will show up as "Hallo, Welt!" in German clients. You can append any locale to any metadata name to localize your addon. A locale consists of a language code followed by a country code, so deDE stands for German-Germany. The locale of English clients is always enUS, even if you have the European version.

```
Notes = The best "Hello, World!" addon!
```

This will be shown in the tooltip of the addon.

There are many metadata attributes that are recognized by World of Warcraft; Table 3-1 shows them.

Table 3-1. *Available Metadata Attributes*

Metadata	Description
Interface	The interface version the addon is written for.
Title	The name of the addon.
Notes	More information about the addon.
RequiredDeps	A comma-separated list of addons that are required for this addon. The addon will load after all dependencies are loaded, and it won't load if one of its dependencies is missing or disabled.
OptionalDeps	A comma-separated list of addons that will be loaded before the addon if they are installed and enabled.
LoadOnDemand	0 (default) or 1. A load-on-demand addon will not be loaded when logging in. You can load the addon by calling LoadAddOn(*addon*) in another addon.

Metadata	Description
LoadWith	Requires LoadOnDemand = 1. A comma-separated list of addons. The addon will be loaded if one of these addons is loaded.
LoadManagers	A comma-separated list of addons. This will set LoadOnDemand to 1 if one of the given addons is enabled.
SavedVariables	A comma-separated list of global variables that will be saved to \WTF\Account\<*account name*>\SavedVariables\<*addon*>.lua when logging out.
SavedVariablesPerCharacter	This does basically the same as SavedVariables, but it will save everything on a per-character basis to \WTF\Account\<*account name*>\<*server*>\<*character*>\SavedVariables\<addon>.lua.
DefaultState	Either enabled or disabled. Determines whether the addon will be enabled or disabled by default.
Secure	1 or 0. Secure addons are digitally signed by Blizzard. There is no way to get such a signature at the moment, so this attribute can only be used by Blizzard's addons.

You can also use your own metadata by using attributes starting with x-. The API function GetAddOnMetadata(*addon, attribute*) can be used to get the metadata. Note that this function also works for addons that are not loaded yet. So the TOC file is the place to define when a load-on-demand should be loaded. You don't have to append the locale when retrieving metadata; this is done automatically.

Let's look at an example. Deadly Boss Mods' module for the instance "The Eye of Eternity" is a TOC file that makes extensive use of custom metadata:

```
## Interface: 30100
## Title: <DBM> Eye of Eternity
## Title-deDE: <DBM> Auge der Ewigkeit
## LoadOnDemand: 1
## RequiredDeps: DBM-Core
## SavedVariables: DBMEyeOfEternity_SavedVars, DBMEyeOfEternity_SavedStats
## X-DBM-Mod: 1
## X-DBM-Mod-Category: WotLK
## X-DBM-Mod-Name: Eye of Eternity
## X-DBM-Mod-Name-deDE: Das Auge der Ewigkeit
## X-DBM-Mod-Sort: 3
## X-DBM-Mod-LoadZone: The Eye of Eternity
## X-DBM-Mod-LoadZone-deDE: Das Auge der Ewigkeit
localization.en.lua
localization.de.lua
Malygos.lua
```

I removed all localized attributes except for the German ones; the real file is longer as each localization requires four additional lines.

The file defines all metadata that is needed by DBM to build the list of available mods without loading them. The most important attribute is X-DBM-Mod-LoadZone, which instructs DBM to load the addon when you enter the specified zone. This is a key part of how DBM's load-on-demand structure works. The real power of metadata is that it is available before the mod is loaded.

We have created a TOC file, but we now need to add Lua code to do cool stuff. World of Warcraft provides us a lot of functions that can be used to work with the interface.

Using the WoW API

You have already seen a few API functions: `print`, `PlaySoundFile`, `LoadAddOn`, and `GetAddOnMetadata`. All API functions are available in global variables, so they are available everywhere: in Lua files, in XML files (they can embed Lua code, which we will learn more about in Chapter 5), as well as in command line scripts. These functions have self-explanatory names and arguments. You can find a complete list of WoW-specific functions on the WoWWiki page, `http://www.wowwiki.com/API`. This book does not contain a list of all available functions for two reasons: it would be comparatively long as there are many functions and it would be outdated after the next patch.. All Lua functions described in Chapter 2 are also available, unless mentioned otherwise.

There are a few different types of functions. Most common are the "real" API functions, so called because they are written in C and made available through Lua's C API. An example of such a function is `PlaySoundFile()`. There is no Lua file in the default UI that defines this function. Instead, it is directly provided by the underlying interface API, and in most cases it's not possible to implement this type of function using Lua.

You can also find a lot of functions in the Lua files of the default UI; most of these functions start with the prefix UI. An example of this second type of function is `UIFrameFadeOut(frame, time)` which fades out a frame by reducing its alpha value (the opacity of a frame) over time.

Remember that you can always use `/script <lua code>` to execute Lua code in-game. Use this to play around with some API functions to see how they work. For example, you can test `UIFrameFadeOut` by calling it with these arguments:

```
/script UIFrameFadeOut(Minimap, 1)
```

This will fade out your minimap to be invisible after 1 second. But how do you get it back? And what is behind the global variable `Minimap`?

This brings us to the next type of API function: the object-oriented part of the interface API. All frames are objects; they can be created by calling `CreateFrame(frameType)` or by using XML files. You will see how to create these frames and the available types in Chapter 5. A frame is basically just a table that holds a `userdata` value and a lot of methods. Recall that you have to use the colon operator to call methods and that methods are basically just functions stored in tables. The thing to remember here is that frames contain many methods. So the third type of API function is a real API function that is stored in a frame and expects to be called with the colon operator. Let's call this type widget or frame functions, as they are closely related to graphical user interface elements.

For now we'll just look at the basics of the object-oriented API. You will learn more about frames and the object-oriented model behind them in the next two chapters. Let's look at a method that is available for all frames: `SetAlpha(value)`. It sets the transparency of a frame (a number between 0 and 1), and all its methods are called by using the colon operator. Try this to get your minimap back:

```
/script Minimap:SetAlpha(1)
```

A `GetAlpha()` method is also available; it returns the current alpha value. You can find a complete list of all available methods and frame types in Appendix A.

But back to our Hello World mod. We have an addon that has the required metadata to be recognized by World of Warcraft, but it's just a TOC file. Now we need to add Lua code to our file to do something with those API functions. We already have the line `HelloWorld.lua` in our TOC file. Whenever you try to load HelloWorld, World of Warcraft tries to find this file in the folder HelloWorld, so let's create this file.

The game will now execute the Lua code in that file when you log in. So writing `print("Hello, World!")` in that file will display "Hello, World!" in your chat frame after logging in. But that's useless to us; we need something interactive. Let's create some slash commands.

RESTARTS AND EDITING EXISTING FILES

I told you earlier that you need to restart the game after adding a new file. It turns out you don't need to restart it after changes to an existing file. Just type

```
/console reloadui
```

to reload all previously loaded files.

Creating Slash Commands

Creating custom slash commands is easy. There is a table that stores all slash command handler functions, available as `SlashCmdList` in the global namespace. The slash command handler is then associated with a specific slash command like `/hwadd`. This function is then called every time the user enters this slash command. The function receives the string after the actual slash command. So typing `/hwadd test string` will call our handler with the argument `"test string"`.

To create the mod I discussed at the start of the chapter, we need two custom slash commands: one that stores a new string and another that retrieves a string and sends it to the chat. There are two steps to creating a slash command. First, we have to choose a unique identifier for our slash command handler that will be used in the next step as a key in the table `SlashCmdList`. Our identifier for `/hwadd` is `HELLO_WORLD_ADD`, and our function will be the value associated with this key. We also need to define the actual slash commands we want to use and associate them with this identifier. This is also done using global variables, `SLASH_identifier1` to `SLASH_identifierN`, to associate more than one slash command with a command handler. In our case we use `SLASH_HELLO_WORLD_ADD1` and `SLASH_HELLO_WORLD_ADD2` to associate two slash commands with our command handler.

The second step is to store the slash command handler in the table `SlashCmdList` by using our identifier as a key. This handler is a function that takes one argument. Remember that the slash commands we want to use are `/hwadd <id> <text>` and `/hwshow <id>`. This means we need two slash command handlers. The code is pretty simple.

If you haven't created the file `HelloWorld.lua` yet, do it now. Then add the following code:

```
HelloWorld_Text = {}
local channel = "SAY"

SLASH_HELLO_WORLD_ADD1 = "/hwadd"
SLASH_HELLO_WORLD_ADD2 = "/helloworldadd" -- an alias for /hwadd
SlashCmdList["HELLO_WORLD_ADD"] = function(msg)
     local id, text = msg:match("(%S+)%s+(.+)")
     if id and text then
           HelloWorldText[id:lower()] = text
     end
end

SLASH_HELLO_WORLD_SHOW1 = "/hwshow"
SLASH_HELLO_WORLD_SHOW2 = "/helloworldshow" -- an alias for /hwshow
SlashCmdList["HELLO_WORLD_SHOW"] = function(msg)
     local text = HelloWorld_Text[msg:lower()]
     if text then
           SendChatMessage(text, channel)
     end
end
```

Let's go through this file line by line. At the beginning we initialize two variables. The global variable `HelloWorld_Text` will hold a table with our strings that are stored when the user types `/hwadd`. The local variable `channel` will contain the chat channel we want to use. Then we create our first slash command with the ID `HELLO_WORLD_ADD`. The function with the key `HELLO_WORLD_ADD` in `SlashCmdList` will be called every time we enter `/hwadd <text>` or `/helloworldadd_<text>` with `msg = <text>`.

The first line of the `HELLO_WORLD_ADD` handler parses the user input. This is done by using regular expressions; if you haven't already read the section about them in Chapter 2, read it now. First, `%S` is the complement of `%s`; since `%s` represents all whitespace characters, `%S` stands for all non-whitespace characters. The code + means "at least one." The brackets around the expression define it as a capture, so the matching string will be the first return value of the `match` method. So `id` will be the substring of `msg` beginning with the first non-whitespace character and ending with the first whitespace. The second expression stands for the separating space between the two arguments, and the third expression (the second capture) is the rest of the string.

This pattern will work for all imaginable user inputs like "   foo   bar". The `match` method returns `nil` if the pattern does not match the given string, so our next task is to test whether `id` and `text` are not `nil`. A valid input will set `id` and `text`, so we can use the lowercase version of `id` as key in `HelloWorld_Text` and set the value of this field to the given text. If the pattern didn't match, the input the function fails silently; but it's easy to add an error message for invalid inputs:

```
if id and text then
     HelloWorld_Text[id:lower()] = text
else
     print("Usage: /hwadd <id> <text>")
end
```

The second slash command handler is quite simple: it takes the user input, converts it to lowercase, and uses it as a key in HelloWorld_Text. If there was some text to use as a key (in other words, if the user provided an ID), we call the function SendChatMessage(*msg, channel, language, target*) to send a chat message with the previously stored text. Only the first argument is required. The *channel* argument can be one of the following values: SAY (default value), YELL, EMOTE, WHISPER, PARTY, RAID, BATTLEGROUND, RAID WARNING, GUILD or OFFICER. The language argument is the language to use; nil will use the character's default language. Finally, target is needed only for channel = WHISPER.

Persistence

One problem remains: the table is not *persistent*, meaning that your texts will be gone when you log out. So we need to save them somewhere. We can use the metadata attribute you've already seen, SavedVariables, to save a value. Just add this line to our TOC file:

```
## SavedVariables: HelloWorld_Text
```

(Don't forget to restart your game after updating the TOC file.) What exactly does this line do?

When you log in, World of Warcraft loads your mod, which then initializes HelloWorld_Text with a new, empty table. After the mod is loaded, the game tries to load the saved variables for this mod. If HelloWorld_Text has not been saved yet, because you are using the mod for the first time, nothing happens. The global variable HelloWorld_Text will not be set to nil in this case. If HelloWorld_Text is saved, it will set the global variable to the saved value, dropping the old empty table. What's important to note here is that the initialization of a saved variable while loading a mod defines a default value. When you log out, the game gets the value of HelloWorld_Text and saves it if it's not nil.

But these default values can also cause problems. Imagine you have an addon that stores its options in a table. The default value could look like this:

```
MyAddOn_Options = {
    Option1 = true,
    Option2 = false,
    Option3 = "a string!"
}
```

Now suppose that after using the addon for a few days, a new version is released. It adds new options, and the initialization of MyAddOn_Options is changed to:

```
MyAddOn_Options = {
    Option1 = true ,
    Option2 = false ,
    Option3 = "a string!",
    Option4 = 7.5,
}
```

If a new user of this addon installs this version, there's no problem. The user has no saved variables, so she gets all four options. But if you update your addon, World of Warcraft overwrites the global variable MyAddOn_Options, dropping the new default option table. Option4 will be `nil` because your old saved value does not have this field. This will cause error messages like "`attempt to perform arithmetic on a nil value`" if the mod assumes that `Option4` is a number and tries to add it to another value. It is always important to keep your mod updatable, as you might want to add additional features in a later version. Future patches also might break your mod if Blizzard decides to change API functions. You will then have to fix your mod and release a new version of it.

There are a few possible solutions for this issue. One is to rename the global variable, but this method has a lot of disadvantages: you have to replace all occurrences of the variable, the users will lose their old settings every time you add a new option, and it is poor coding style if you have to rename all occurrences of this variable. A solution that might be suitable for small addons is to add a simple check whether an option that should be set is `nil`. You can then set the default value in the `if` block. But this can quickly become confusing, and it's also not the best coding style.

The best solution is to keep a separate table with the default values. The saved table will then store only those options that were changed by the user. We will see a smart way to implement this later in this book. This solution also has the benefit that you can always access the default value of an option to reset it. We will be using this solution for all examples that have saved options in this book.

We have created our first World of Warcraft addon, and I have mentioned that the default UI is also written like an addon. So you might wonder how Blizzard wrote their code. To conclude the chapter, let's take a look.

Extracting the Default UI

The default UI is stored in MPQ archives, and there are several ways to get that code. The simplest way is to use Blizzard's Interface AddOn Kit, introduced in Chapter 1, to extract it. It's easy to use and extracts all Lua, XML, and TOC files as well as all textures used by the default UI.

You can also use an MPQ viewer or editor like MPQ Editor, also introduced in Chapter 1, to browse all MPQ archives. These MPQ editors are more powerful than Blizzard's interface tool. Such an editor can be used get the paths of available sound files, models, and textures, and to extract some Lua and XML files that Blizzard's tool does not extract (such as the code used by the login screen).

Using MPQ Editor is like working with a zip utility. You select "Open MPQ Archive" from the File menu and navigate to the `Data` folder inside your World of Warcraft installation folder. Let's open the file `lichking.mpq`, which contains WotLK-related data. If the program asks you for "Open Options," keep the default values. You can now browse through the contents of the archive, open files by double-clicking them, and extract files by using drag-and-drop. As an example, let's look at the `Sounds` folder; it contains the background music and some creature sounds. You can use all of these sounds in your addons.

■**Attention** MPQ Editor is a very powerful tool that also allows you to modify MPQ archives. But don't do this. It can break your game, and it's against the EULA.

You can also use the web site `http://wowcompares.com`, which has detailed *diffs* for all patches.

Note A diff shows all differences between two versions of a file; this allows you to spot changes in patches.

The code from the MPQ archives can be helpful if you are unsure how an API function works or to figure out changes after a patch, since Blizzard provides little or no documentation. You might notice a few strange things; for example, the code uses semicolons everywhere. Most addon authors don't use semicolons at all, as semicolons are not necessary in Lua in most cases.

The code is easily readable and has a few helpful comments. Some comments are definitely worth reading:

```
elseif (status == "error") then
    --  Should never happen haha
end
```

Here's another example:

```
else
    -- Temporary Hack (Temporary meaning 2 yrs, haha)
    mapFileName = "World";
    OutlandButton:Hide();
    AzerothButton:Hide();
end
```

Summary

At this point you know how to work with Lua, you know the basics about the World of Warcraft API, and you can create addons that are recognized and loaded by World of Warcraft. So it's time to create your first useful addon in the next chapter.

CHAPTER 4

■ ■ ■

Working with Game Events

This chapter is about event handlers and how to use them. An *event handler* is a function that is called by the game every time a specific event occurs. World of Warcraft provides a variety of events, ranging from clicks on UI elements to combat-related events. So what we need to do is tell the game that we are interested in an event and provide an event-handler function that should be called when the event occurs. Such a function is also called a *callback function*.

We will build three example mods in this chapter, the first of which will provide mouse-over tooltips for item, quest, and spell links in the chat frame. Figure 4-1 shows the mod we are going to build.

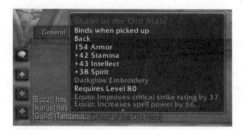

Figure 4-1. *The mod ChatlinkTooltips in action*

The next example mod will be something more abstract, a timing library. However, it provides important functions we are going to need for other examples in the following chapters. This timing library will allow us to schedule a function to be called after a given period of time.

The third mod we will build in this chapter is a fully featured DKP auctioneer that can be used to auction items during your raids. It will make use of the timing library.

For these mods we need to handle certain events, such as the event that occurs when you hover the pointer over a link in a frame. Another event we will need to handle occurs when someone sends you a chat message. However, we need to discuss frames before we can start working with events. What is a frame, and how is it related to events? You need to learn something about frames and events before we start creating our mods.

Using Frames as Event Listeners

A frame is a UI element, such as a button or a text box, but we are not discussing the creation of graphical user interface elements yet. So we will use the very basic frame type that is called simply Frame in the following examples. Such a frame is not visible by default, and we are going to use just one feature of this frame: it can be used as an *event listener*, which means it can register events and corresponding handlers to deal with those events. The following line shows how to create such a frame, by using the API function CreateFrame:

```
local myFrame = CreateFrame("Frame")
```

You've already seen this function in the last chapter; it creates and returns a frame of the requested type. But what can we do with this frame now? The created myFrame table (which is also called an *object*) is basically just an identifier that can be passed to other API functions. These functions (also called *methods*) are always available in the created table, and we must call them with the colon operator.

Different frame types have different methods; a button, for example, has a method that sets the text on the button. A basic frame like we are using here does not have such a method. A list of all available methods for all frame types can be found in Appendix A. We are going to use only a few methods here: SetScript, GetScript, HookScript, and HasScript. These methods deal with event handlers, which are also called *script handlers* in World of Warcraft (events are also called scripts). I will use the term "script" from now on to refer to such an event and "script handler" to refer to the event handler callback functions.

Different frame types may have different scripts. For example, a button has the script OnClick; other kinds of frames don't have this, because it's very common to handle a button click but not a click on a normal frame. There are other ways to interact with the mouse in frames; there is for example the script handler OnDragStart that is invoked when the user tries to drag the frame. We need the following methods.

```
frame:SetScript(script, func)
```

This function registers a script handler that will be called when *script* is called. A script is always identified by a string that starts with On. The second argument can be either a function or nil to remove the script handler. SetScript will overwrite any existing script handler for the given script.

The first argument that is passed to that script handler (which is just a function) when the script occurs is always the frame that is responsible for the script. This allows us to assign a function to more than one frame. All following arguments depend on the script type.

```
frame:GetScript(script)
```

This function can be used to get the function assigned to a specific script. It returns nil if there is no handler for this script.

```
frame:HookScript(script, func)
```

This function works only if the frame already has a script handler for this script. It will add *func* as an additional callback function to *script*. Removing the original script handler will also remove all hooks.

```
frame:HasScript(script)
```

This function returns 1 if *script* is a valid script for the frame's type, nil otherwise. Note that this function cannot be used to check if a script handler for a script is set. You have to use GetScript for this.

Now, what scripts could we use now to play around with? If you look at the list of available scripts for normal frames that can be found in Appendix A, you will notice that almost all of them are related to graphical user interface elements. For example, there are scripts like OnShow, OnHide, OnDragStart, and OnDragStop. These scripts occur when a frame is used as a window and you open, close, or drag it.

But back to the example tooltips mod I promised at the beginning of the chapter. We don't need to create a frame here as we can use the already existing chat frame. The type of chat frame is ScrollingMessageFrame. It provides the script handlers OnHyperlinkEnter and OnHyperlinkLeave, which are invoked when your mouse hovers over or leaves a link in this frame. A link is any clickable chunk of text in a message frame. So, besides obvious links like items, chat channels and names of players in front of a message are also links. So let's get started building this addon.

Creating ChatlinkTooltips

The first thing we need is a folder in Interface\AddOns called ChatlinkTooltips. The second step in creating an addon is always to create its TOC file with the name ChatlinkTooltips.toc. A TOC file for such an addon could look like this:

```
## Interface: 30100
## Title: Chatlink Tooltips
ChatlinkTooltips.lua
```

Feel free to add additional metadata like a description by using the attribute Notes. The next task is to create the file that does the hard work, ChatlinkTooltips.lua.

Chat Frames and Their Script Handlers

We need to get references to all the chat frames we have. We need to work with their script handlers, as we need the scripts that occur when the user hovers the mouse pointer over a link in the chat. We can use the ChatFrame*X* global variables for this. *X* is the number of the chat frame we want, so your first chat frame is ChatFrame1, the second one is ChatFrame2, and so on. Your default chat frame (the one with the edit box to send a message) is also stored in the global variable DEFAULT_CHAT_FRAME. Another useful global variable is NUM_CHAT_WINDOWS, which is the maximum number of chat frames you can have. This is by default seven, but addons or future patches might change it.

For this addon we need to create a loop that iterates over all chat frames and sets functions that show or hide tooltips as script handlers for link-related scripts. One added complication in this example is that we need to access each ChatFrame*X* global variable dynamically and in sequence (in other words, we need to access ChatFrame1 in the first iteration of the loop, ChatFrame2 in the second iteration of the loop, and so on). There is a function provided by World of Warcraft that returns the value of a global variable with a given name: getglobal(*name*). The argument *name* is a string here, so we can build the name dynamically during each iteration.

The following code shows such a loop and two dummy functions (showTooltip and hideTooltip) that are used as script handlers. These functions simply print their arguments to the chat frame, so you can see what's going on there. I also created a helper function that tries to hook a script handler if one already exists; otherwise, it sets a new script handler. It is useful to move this functionality into a small function, as we need to do this task for our two script handlers OnHyperLinkEnter and OnHyperLinkLeave. Here is the code:

```
local function showTooltip(...)
   print(...)
end
local function hideTooltip(...)
   print(...)
end

local function setOrHookHandler(frame, script, func)
   if frame:GetScript(script) then -- check if it already has a script handler...
      frame:HookScript(script, func) -- ...and hook it
   else
      frame:SetScript(script, func) -- set our function as script handler otherwise
   end
end

for i = 1, NUM_CHAT_WINDOWS do
   local frame = getglobal("ChatFrame"..i) -- copy a reference
   if frame then -- make sure that the frame exists
      setOrHookHandler(frame, "OnHyperLinkEnter",  showTooltip)
      setOrHookHandler(frame, "OnHyperLinkLeave",  hideTooltip)
   end
end
```

Let's take a look at the body of the loop. The first line just copies a reference to the frame that this iteration is dealing with into a local variable called frame, so we don't have to write getglobal("ChatFrame"..i) all the time. The code then checks if the frame really exists; this check should actually never fail, but you can never know which addons your users have installed that might mess with the chat frames. It then calls the helper function setOrHookHandler, which sets our script handler if the frame does not have one for this script yet. Otherwise, it hooks our script handler to preserve any existing ones. Note that the default user interface does not use these two script handlers. This check is just to maintain compatibility with chat addons that might already have similar functionality.

Item Links

You can now load this addon in the game, but don't forget to restart the game after creating the files. Then try to hover over a link in your chat frame; you will see a message that looks like the following when your cursor enters or leaves a link:

```
table: 168BAC00 item:40449:3832:3487:3472:0:0:0:0:80 [Valorous Robe of Faith]
```

The first argument is the frame responsible for the script handler:

```
table: 168BAC00
```

You will see what we can do with this frame when we add the tooltip later.

The second argument is the data of the link:

```
item:40449:3832:3487:3472:0:0:0:0:80
```

The data of a link can be any string, and links used by the default UI always consist of separate small strings separated with colons. We will create and use our own links in Chapter 9.

The substring up to the first colon is the type of the link, so this is an item link. The following number is the ID (40449) of the item, and the next number is the ID (3832) of the enchant on the item. The next four numbers (3487, 3472, 0, 0) are the item IDs of the socketed jewels. The next number (0) is the suffix ID of uncommon items. It is followed by the unique ID (0) of an item, but not all items have a unique ID, and you can't get any useful information from such an ID. The last one (80) is the level of the player that sent the link, which is used for items that scale with your level.

The third argument is the whole clickable link as it is displayed in the chat frame.

```
[Valorous Robe of Faith]
```

■**Tip** The item IDs are also used by most item database web sites, like `http://www.wowhead.com`. This allows you to build URLs from item links, for example you can use one of the jewel IDs from the links above to get the link `http://www.wowhead.com/?item=3487`

Using Tooltips

We now have the script and the data we need. The only task that remains is showing the tooltip. We will use the frame GameTooltip for this, because it is the default tooltip used by the game. It provides the method SetHyperlink(*linkData*), which takes the data from a link (the long string with a lot of numbers separated by colons) and sets the content of the tooltip to the corresponding item, spell, or achievement. This method will generate an error message if you provide a link that does not have an associated tooltip, like a player or channel link. Therefore, we need to check the link before passing it to this method. The following code shows the script handlers we need for our mod. These two functions will replace our dummy functions. These functions need to be placed before the loop, as the local variables that hold these functions need to be visible in the loop.

```
local function showTooltip(self, linkData)
    local linkType = string.split(":", linkData)
    if linkType == "item"
    or linkType == "spell"
    or linkType == "enchant"
    or linkType == "quest"
```

```
    or linkType == "talent"
    or linkType == "glyph"
    or linkType == "unit"
    or linkType == "achievement" then
        GameTooltip:SetOwner(self, "ANCHOR_CURSOR")
        GameTooltip:SetHyperlink(linkData)
        GameTooltip:Show()
    end
end

local function hideTooltip()
    GameTooltip:Hide()
end
```

Let's go through this line by line. The function showTooltip uses string.split to get the first part, which indicates the type of the link. The long expression in the if statement checks whether it is a link that can be passed to SetHyperlink. But before we call SetHyperlink, we need to call the method SetOwner. A tooltip is always bound to a frame that owns the tooltip, and hiding the owner will also hide the tooltip. So we set the owner of the tooltip to the current chat frame here. Recall that the first argument that is passed to the script handler (in this case, self) is the frame that initiated the call., so self is the current chat frame. The second argument to this method is the anchor of the tooltip. We use ANCHOR_CURSOR here, which causes the tooltip to stick to your cursor. You will learn more about anchors and frame positioning in the next chapter, when we discuss the creation of frames. The code then calls the Show method, which shows the tooltip. The function to hide the tooltip is pretty simple. It just calls the method Hide on the tooltip.

The mod is now ready to be used. Note that it also works for spells and names in the combat log, as the combat log is also just a chat frame.

You know how to use script handlers now, but all the script handlers we've worked with thus far are somehow related to the graphical part of the user interface. The most interesting script handlers are not related to the GUI but instead handle the OnEvent script. I previously mentioned that scripts are events, so that might sound strange—a script handler for other events? Yes, this script handler has its own events. All events related to gameplaying will invoke the OnEvent script handler and pass an event as a string to it. So this is worth a closer look.

OnEvent

We need to discuss another method of the frame object before we can use the OnEvent script handler: frame:RegisterEvent(event). This method is used to register a gameplay-related event by this frame. Only events registered with this frame are passed to its OnEvent script handler.

In this context I'll use the terms *script* and *script handler* to refer to GUI-related events and event handlers like those we saw in the last section. The terms *event* and *event handler* will refer to the OnEvent script handler. These event handlers deal with gameplay events like chat messages, the casting of spells (by you or other players), or entering instances.

Event Handler Basics

The distinction between GUI-related events and gameplay-related events might be confusing just now, but you will get used to it. Let's look at an example that uses the event CHAT_MSG_WHISPER to demonstrate an event handler. This event occurs every time you receive a whisper message. Note that you can whisper to yourself for testing purposes.

```
local frame = CreateFrame("Frame")

local function myEventHandler(self, event, msg, sender)
   print(event, sender, msg)
end

frame:RegisterEvent("CHAT_MSG_WHISPER")
frame:SetScript("OnEvent", myEventHandler)
```

This will show CHAT_MSG_WHISPER followed by the name of the player who sent the whisper and the text of the message in your chat frame every time you receive a whisper message.

The first argument that is received by an event handler is always the frame the handler is attached to (named self in this case). The second argument is the name of the event that occurred (event here). All following arguments depend on the event.

The event handler receives 13 arguments on CHAT_MSG_WHISPER events. You often refer to the third argument as arg1, or "the first argument of the event," as the actual first two arguments are fixed. The most commonly used arguments of the event are the first one (the message), the second (the sender), and the sixth (sender status, such as "AFK" or "DND"). The last (the 13th) argument is a counter for all received chat messages in this session. The meanings of these four arguments are the same for all chat events, including messages in the raid (CHAT_MSG_RAID) or guild (CHAT_MSG_GUILD) chat.

But what about the other nine arguments? Some of them are used in other chat events like CHAT_MSG_CHANNEL. They refer to the chat channel or to the affected player of a channel action like a kick or a ban. You will rarely need to use arguments other than the player who sent the message and the text of the message, so you do not have to worry about all these arguments.

Some arguments are always an empty string or 0. Their exact purpose is unknown; they might have been used for something in an older version. But removing them from the list would shift down the following arguments, breaking compatibility with existing event handlers. So don't wonder if you encounter arguments that don't seem to make sense. You will see how we can quickly extract one of these arguments by using varargs in the next section.

Event Handlers for Multiple Events

Most addons have only one event handler function and one frame that registers all events and passes them to this callback function. So there is exactly one function that has to take care of all events that your addon needs to be informed about. This function might look like the following example:

```
local function myEventHandler(self, event, ...)
   if event == "CHAT_MSG_WHISPER" then
      -- we received a whisper, do something with it here
      local msg, sender = ...
```

```
        print(sender.." wrote "..msg)
    elseif event == "ZONE_CHANGED_NEW_AREA" then
        -- we are in a new zone, do something different
    elseif event == "PARTY_MEMBERS_CHANGED" then
        -- someone joined or left our group, deal with it
    elseif event == "..." then
        -- to be continued...
    end
end
```

Recall the meaning of the three dots in the head of this function: "there are an unknown number of additional arguments." As discussed in Chapter 2, these three dots are called a vararg, and you can use them everywhere that Lua expects a list of values. We can get normal variables from this vararg by writing code like line 4 in the example:

```
local msg, sender = ...
```

It is also possible to cut off the beginning of the vararg by using select. For example, if you want to get the sixth argument of a CHAT_MSG_WHISPER event (the status of the sender) from the vararg, you don't have to create five dummy variables to get to it. You can just use the following code.

```
local status = select(6, ...)
```

But with that approach, the whole function can quickly become huge and unclear. It is not uncommon to write addons that listen to 20 or more events. So the next step you might take is to split up this function by reducing each part of the if block to a single function call. You then have a lot of small functions, each of them dedicated to one event. It could look like this:

```
local function onWhisper(msg, sender)
    -- deal with whispers
end

local function onNewZone()
    -- we are in a new zone
end
-- ... etc

local function myEventHandler(self, event, ...)
    if event == "CHAT_MSG_WHISPER" then
        onWhisper(...)
    elseif event == "ZONE_CHANGED_NEW_AREA" then
        onNewZone(...)
    elseif event == "..." then
        -- etc
    end
end
```

But there is an even smarter way to do this. You can create a table and use the event as a key and store the related handler under this key. This makes splitting up the events really easy, and you don't need the huge if construct. Our event handler would then look like this:

```
local eventHandlers = {}
function eventHandlers.CHAT_MSG_WHISPER(msg, sender)
end

function eventHandlers.ZONE_CHANGED_NEW_AREA()
end

local function myEventHandler(self, event, ...)
   return eventHandlers[event](...)
end
```

Another advantage of this solution is that registering a new event with a new event handler at any given time is really easy. Just call the RegisterEvent method of your frame and add the function to the table. This solution can also be faster if you have a lot of events. You will see examples of this and more on performance in Chapter 13.

Another script handler that is also worth a closer look is the OnUpdate handler.

Using OnUpdate to Build a Timing Library

The OnUpdate script handler is always executed before the game renders the user interface. This means that if your game runs at 25 frames per second, this script handler will be executed 25 times per second. The function receives one additional argument, the time elapsed since the last call to it. So we are going to use this script handler to build an addon that provides a function that schedules another function to be called after a certain time. Creating the TOC file is up to you this time.

The Scheduler

What we need is a function that takes a time (in seconds), another function, and a list of arguments. The addon will then call the provided function with those arguments after the specified time. This functionality is needed quite often; we will make use of this addon in later examples. The following code shows this schedule function and a table that stores all scheduled tasks:

```
local tasks = {}

function SimpleTimingLib_Schedule(time, func, ...)
   local t = {...}
   t.func = func
   t.time = GetTime() + time
   table.insert(tasks, t)
end
```

You know that the vararg parameter can be used everywhere Lua expects a list of values, so {...} will create a new table and fill its array part with the values stored in vararg. The array part will thus store all arguments that will be passed to the function. The next line stores the function in the hash table part under the key func. The exact time at which the function is executed is stored under the key time. The API function GetTime() returns the current system uptime with millisecond precision. Adding time to this value gives us the moment in which the task should be executed. The OnUpdate handler will then check this entry against the current value of GetTime(). The last line of the function inserts our new task into the table tasks, which stores all tasks.

We now need to write the OnUpdate handler that executes a task when it's due. This function iterates over all tasks and checks if a particular task's time is up. We will use the function unpack to get the arguments from the table. This function returns all values stored in the array part of a table. Here's the handler code:

```
local function onUpdate()
    for i = #tasks, 1, -1 do
        local val = tasks[i]
        if val.time <= GetTime() then
            table.remove(tasks, i)
            val.func(unpack(val))
        end
    end
end

local frame = CreateFrame("Frame")
frame:SetScript("OnUpdate", onUpdate)
```

Note that the code does not use ipairs to traverse the table. Instead it traverses the table backward, by using the numeric for loop with a start value of #tasks, an end value of 1, and a step of –1. We then store the current entry in the table in a local variable in the loop. Traversing the table forward could cause problems here, as we are using table.remove to remove elements while traversing it. This function will move elements after the removed element down by one. So if you remove the current element while traversing over the table with ipairs, the next element will be skipped.

The loop saves a reference to the current element and checks whether it should be executed now. If this is the case, the task is removed from the list and executed. It is important to remove it before executing it, as the execution might cause an error. An error cancels the running Lua script. So if you remove it after you execute it and an error occurs, the next time the OnUpdate handler is invoked this entry will still be in the table. In this case, the script will try again to execute it; it will fail again, and you'll get the same error over and over.

Another question that might come up is what happens if you have a nil value in your arguments? Consider the following call:

```
SimpleTimingLib_Schedule(1, print, 1, nil, 3)
```

You can use /script to execute this in-game. The result you get is that 1 is printed to your chat frame after 1 second. The second and third arguments of the scheduled task are ignored by our code because unpack only works on the array part of the table, and the third entry will be in the hash table part. The operation is actually slightly more complicated than this because the array part can also contain nil values, but only under certain circumstances. But this topic is beyond the scope of this chapter; we will take a closer look at tables in Chapter 13. For now: don't use nil in scheduled functions.

Another function that can be useful for such a library is a function that cancels a task; let's call it SimpleTimingLib_Unschedule.

The Unscheduler

What we have to do now is traverse the table and remove one or more tasks. The function will take the same arguments as the scheduler, except for the time. It will then remove all tasks that match the given criteria:

```
function SimpleTimingLib_Unschedule(func, ...)
   for i = #tasks, 1, -1 do
      local val = tasks[i]
      if val.func == func then
         local matches = true
         for i = 1, select("#", ...) do
            if select(i, ...) ~= val[i] then
               matches = false
               break
            end
         end
         if matches then
            table.remove(tasks, i)
         end
      end
   end
end
```

Recall that select("#", ...) returns the number of arguments stored in the vararg.

The function iterates over the table and uses a second loop to determine if the arguments of the task match our arguments. Note that this loop also matches tasks with additional arguments that were not passed to SimpleTimingLib_Unschedule . This allows us to remove more than one scheduled task at once. Let's test this with the following code:

```
SimpleTimingLib_Schedule(1, print, "Foo", 1, 2, 3)
SimpleTimingLib_Schedule(1, print, "Foo", 4, 5, 6)
SimpleTimingLib_Schedule(1, print, "Bar", 7, 8, 9)
SimpleTimingLib_Unschedule(print, "Foo")
```

This will print "Bar 7 8 9" after one second as the call to the Unschedule function matches the first two calls to the Schedule function.

■**Tip** You can use TinyPad to execute these code fragments in-game.

But this unscheduler comes with a bug in combination with the scheduler. Did you spot it? Look at the following code:

```
local function buggy()
    SimpleTimingLib_Unschedule(print, "Bar")
end

SimpleTimingLib_Schedule(2, print, "Bar")
SimpleTimingLib_Schedule(1, buggy)
```

The table tasks will have two entries after this code is executed; the second one is a task to call buggy. After one second has passed, the scheduler executes buggy and removes the other entry. The table is now empty, as the task that calls buggy has already been removed by the OnUpdate script handler just before the task was executed. Lua now returns into the loop in the OnUpdate handler and the body of the loop will be executed a second time with i = 1. It cannot know that the table is empty by now, and it will execute the line local val = tasks[i], setting val to nil. The next line then tries to get val.time and causes an error message, as trying to index a nil value is not possible.

Fixing this is easy: we just have to change the line that accesses val.time to this:

```
if val and val.time <= GetTime() then
```

This demonstrates how it is important to check that your variables are of the type you expect them to be. We expected val to be a table here, but it was nil in the previous situation because of a tricky call to the Unschedule function.

OnUpdate and Performance

OnUpdate can be a very helpful script, but it can also be a real performance-killer. So you have to always be careful when using it. Always keep in mind that it is executed every single frame.

You also should ask yourself if it is really necessary to execute a certain task every frame. If you think something has to be executed as often as possible, it is often sufficient to execute something every few frames or every 0.5 seconds. A common way to restrict how often an OnUpdate handler is called is to wrap it with the function I'll present next.

As mentioned previously, the second argument that is passed to the OnUpdate script handler is the time that elapsed since the last call to it. We can use this to limit the calls per second.

```
local function onUpdate(self, elapsed)
    -- the update task is here
end

local frame = CreateFrame("Frame")
local e = 0
frame:SetScript("OnUpdate", function(self, elapsed)
    e = e + elapsed
    if e >= 0.5 then
        e = 0
        return onUpdate(self, elapsed)
    end
end)
```

This will invoke the function onUpdate twice per second. If you want to invoke it every few frames, you can use the following wrapper function:

```
local frame = CreateFrame("Frame")
local counter = 0
frame:SetScript("OnUpdate", function(...)
    counter = counter + 1
    if counter % 5 == 0 then
        return onUpdate(self, elapsed)
    end
end
```

This will call the function onUpdate every five frames.

Using the Timing Library for a DKP Mod

The chapter's final example will use the timing library we just built together with event handlers to build a DKP auctioneer. The addon will be controlled through a simple command-line interface (slash commands). Another useful feature is to allow other players in your raid or guild, such as your officers or raid leaders, to start or stop an auction for an item.

The mod will follow the rules of the DKP system that is used by my guild. All bids that are placed during an auction are hidden, and the player with the highest bid will have to pay the second highest bid plus one DKP at the end. If only one player bids on an item, he pays the lowest possible bid as defined by your DKP rules. If more than one player bids the same amount and this amount is the highest bid, they must roll for the item. You can adjust the addon to match your DKP rules.

Variables and Options

After an auction is started, the addon will post the item and the remaining time to a configurable chat channel. The addon will then accept bids via whispers and post the highest bidders to the chat channel when the time is up.

So let's start with this mod. Building the TOC file should be an easy task for you. Note that you should add the following line to your TOC file:

```
## Dependencies: SimpleTimingLib
```

This makes sure that SimpleTimingLib is loaded before the DKP addon is loaded, as we will need this library.

We will start with Lua code to define a few variables that save the current state of the addon as well as the options:

```
local currentItem -- the current item or nil if no auction is running
local bids = {} -- bids on the current item
local prefix = "[SimpleDKP] " -- prefix for chat messages

-- default values for saved variables/options
SimpleDKP_Channel = "GUILD" -- the chat channel to use
SimpleDKP_AuctionTime = 30 -- the time (in seconds) for an auction
```

```
SimpleDKP_MinBid = 15 -- the minimum amount of DKP you have to bid
SimpleDKP_ACL = {} -- the access control list
```

The access control list (ACL) is a list of players who are allowed to control the addon via chat commands. It starts empty, meaning that nobody is allowed to control your addon.

Add the variables SimpleDKP_Channel, SimpleDKP_AuctionTime, SimpleDKP_MinBid, and SimpleDKP_ACL to the saved variables in your TOC file. The next function we are going to write is the function that starts an auction. It takes two arguments: the item and the player who requested the auction.

Local Functions and Their Scope

Let's think about this function before we create it. It is a good idea to store this function in a local variable, as we only need to access it from within this file and never from the outside. But what about the scope of this variable? Its scope starts after the variable is created, which means after the statement containing the keyword local. So if you have a lot of functions in local variables, a situation like the following might come up:

```
local function foo()
    bar()
end

local function bar()
    -- do something
end
```

The function foo tries to call the function bar here, but it does not see the local variable bar, which is created a few lines later. This means it will try to access a global variable called bar and not the local one it should access. So it is a good idea to create all local variables that should be available in the whole file at the beginning of your script. This avoids such problems because the scope of a local variable starts after its declaration; the initialization does not affect it.

If we think about the functions we are going to need, we come up with the following local variables:

```
local startAuction, endAuction, placeBid, cancelAuction, onEvent
```

They have the following meanings:

startAuction starts a new auction.

endAuction is called when the current auction expires and it sends the results to the chat.

cancelAuction can cancel an auction prematurely.

placeBid will be called every time someone wants to place a bid on the currently running auction.

onEvent will be our event handler.

Starting Auctions

We can now start implementing these functions. The following code shows startAuction. Note that all strings used by this function are created outside the function and that the function and its variables are wrapped in a do-end block. So these local variables are only visible where they are needed.

Storing strings in variables allows us to change them easily without searching and changing every occurrence of the string. This is also useful when we want to translate our addon later (a topic we will deal with later in the book).

```
do
local auctionAlreadyRunning = "There is already an auction running! (on %s)"
local startingAuction = prefix.."Starting auction for item %s, please place your➡
 bids by whispering me. Remaining time: %d seconds."
local auctionProgress =  prefix.."Time remaining for %s: %d seconds."

function startAuction(item, starter)
   if currentItem then
      local msg = auctionAlreadyRunning:format(currentItem)
      if starter then
         SendChatMessage(msg, "WHISPER", nil, starter)
      else
         print(msg)
      end
   else
      currentItem = item
      SendChatMessage(startingAuction:format(item, SimpleDKP_AuctionTime),➡
SimpleDKP_Channel)
      if SimpleDKP_AuctionTime > 30 then
         SimpleTimingLib_Schedule(SimpleDKP_AuctionTime - 30,➡
SendChatMessage, auctionProgress:format(item, 30), SimpleDKP_Channel)
      end
      if SimpleDKP_AuctionTime > 15 then
         SimpleTimingLib_Schedule(SimpleDKP_AuctionTime - 15,➡
SendChatMessage, auctionProgress:format(item, 15), SimpleDKP_Channel)
      end
      if SimpleDKP_AuctionTime > 5 then
         SimpleTimingLib_Schedule(SimpleDKP_AuctionTime - 5,➡
SendChatMessage, auctionProgress:format(item, 5), SimpleDKP_Channel)
      end
      SimpleTimingLib_Schedule(SimpleDKP_AuctionTime, endAuction)
   end
end
end
```

■**Caution** Do not use `local function startAuction(item, starter)` here. This would create a new local variable `startAuction`, but we want to use the local variable we created at the beginning of the file.

The function looks long and complicated, but it is pretty simple. It first checks to see if there is an auction running and prints an error message if there is. The error message is whispered to the player who tried to start the auction if it was started remotely. If there is no ongoing auction, it will set the current item to the new item and send a chat message to the configured channel. The next lines are just scheduling status messages to be sent when 30, 15, and 5 seconds remain. The last call in this function schedules `endAuction` to be called at the end.

Ending Auctions

The next function we are going to write is `endAuction`. You will have to adjust this to the DKP system you are using. There are four cases this function has to handle:

- The first three cases are quite simple:
  - There is no bid at all.
  - Only one player bid on the item.
  - More than one player bid and the highest amount is unique.
- The fourth case is that more than one player bid the same amount and it's the highest bid.

The bids will be stored and sorted in the table `bids`, so we have to think of a format for this table before we can write the function to read from it. An entry in the table consists of the player's name and a number representing their bid, so you might be tempted to use the name as the key and the bid as the value. However, this is not a smart approach, because we need sorted tables, and hash tables by design cannot be sorted. If we used a hash table here, we would have to build an array from it and sort the array. So the simpler way to do this is to create a small table with the keys `bid` and `name` for each bid and store these bid tables in the table `bids`. `endAuction` will then sort this table in descending order, so `bids[1].name` will be the winner of the auction.

The following code shows `endAuction` with its helper function to sort the table `bids`:

```
do
local noBids = prefix.."No one wants to have %s :("
local wonItemFor = prefix.."%s won %s for %d DKP."
local pleaseRoll = prefix.."%s bid %d DKP on %s, please roll!"
local highestBidders = prefix.."%d. %s bid %d DKP"

local function sortBids(v1, v2)
    return v1.bid > v2.bid
end
```

```
function endAuction()
   table.sort(bids, sortBids)
   if #bids == 0 then -- case 1: no bid at all
      SendChatMessage(noBids:format(currentItem), SimpleDKP_Channel)
   elseif #bids == 1 then -- case 2: one bid; the bidder pays the minimum bid
      SendChatMessage(wonItemFor:format(bids[1].name, currentItem,➥
SimpleDKP_MinBid), SimpleDKP_Channel)
      SendChatMessage(highestBidders:format(1, bids[1].name, bids[1].bid),➥
SimpleDKP_Channel)
   elseif bids[1].bid ~= bids[2].bid then -- case 3: highest amount is unique
      SendChatMessage(wonItemFor:format(bids[1].name, currentItem, bids[2].bid +
1),➥
SimpleDKP_Channel)
      for i = 1, math.min(#bids, 3) do -- print the three highest bidders
         SendChatMessage(highestBidders:format(i, bids[i].name, bids[i].bid),➥
SimpleDKP_Channel)
      end
   else -- case 4: more than 1 bid and the highest amount is not unique
      local str = "" -- this string holds all players who bid the same amount
      for i = 1, #bids do -- this loop builds the string
         if bids[i].bid ~= bids[1].bid then -- found a player who bid less --> break
            break
         else -- append the player's name to the string
            if bids[i + 2] and bids[i + 2].bid == bid then
               str = str..bids[i].name..", " -- use a comma if this is not the last
            else
               str = str..bids[i].name.." and " -- this is the last player
            end
         end
      end
      str = str:sub(0, -6) -- cut off the end of the string as the loop generates a
      -- string that is too long
      SendChatMessage(pleaseRoll:format(str, bids[1].bid, currentItem),➥
SimpleDKP_Channel)
   end
   currentItem = nil -- set currentItem to nil as there is no longer an
   -- ongoing auction
   table.wipe(bids) -- clear the table that holds the bids
end
end
```

The if blocks clearly show the four cases the function handles. The first three cases are pretty easy. The function just has to format a few strings and pass them to SendChatMessage; nothing special here. The fourth case has to build a string that contains the names of all players who bid the same amount. The resulting string looks like "Player1, Player2 and Player 3" and is built in the loop.

Once it has dealt with the auction, the function sets the variables currentItem to nil and wipes the table bids. The addon is now ready for the next auction. Our next function brings us closer to the topic of this chapter: events. We need a function that allows players to place a bid via whisper on an item.

Placing Bids

This function needs to handle the event CHAT_MSG_WHISPER and check if an auction is currently running and if the whisper message is a number. It then creates or updates an entry in the table bids.

```
do
    local oldBidDetected = prefix.."Your old bid was %d DKP, your new bid is %d DKP."
    local bidPlaced = prefix.."Your bid of %d DKP has been placed!"
    local lowBid = prefix.."The minimum bid is %d DKP."

    function onEvent(self, event, msg, sender)
        if event == "CHAT_MSG_WHISPER" and currentItem and tonumber(msg) then
            local bid = tonumber(msg)
            if bid < SimpleDKP_MinBid then
                SendChatMessage(lowBid:format(SimpleDKP_MinBid), "WHISPER", nil, sender)
                return
            end
            for i, v in ipairs(bids) do -- check if that player has already bid
                if sender == v.name then
                    SendChatMessage(oldBidDetected:format(v.bid, bid), "WHISPER",➡
nil, sender)
                    v.bid = bid
                    return
                end
            end
            -- he hasn't bid yet, so create a new entry in bids
            table.insert(bids, {bid = bid, name = sender})
            SendChatMessage(bidPlaced:format(bid), "WHISPER", nil, sender)
        end
    end
end
```

The event handler checks if currentItem is set, which would mean that an auction is running. It uses tonumber(msg) to determine if the whisper is a number. The function checks whether the player has already placed a bid and updates it if necessary; otherwise it creates a new entry in bids.

We now need to create a frame and use it as event listener for the CHAT_MSG_WHISPER event and set our event handler function onEvent as script handler for the script OnEvent. Recall that a script handler that handles the OnEvent script is called an event handler, so every event handler is a script handler. Place the following code after the do-end block we inserted above:

```
local frame = CreateFrame("Frame")
frame:RegisterEvent("CHAT_MSG_WHISPER")
frame:SetScript("OnEvent", onEvent)
```

But we still can't test the addon in-game, as there is no way to create an auction. So let's build some slash commands to do that.

Creating Slash Commands

We will register the slash commands /simpledkp and /sdkp. Table 4-1 shows the commands we are going to build.

Table 4-1. *SimpleDKP slash commands*

Command	Description
/sdkp start <item>	Starts an auction for <item>.
/sdkp stop	Stops the current auction.
/sdkp channel <channel>	Sets the chat channel to <channel> if <channel> is provided. Otherwise it will print the current channel.
/sdkp time <time>	Sets the time to <time>. If <time> is omitted it prints the current setting.
/sdkp minbid <minbid>	Sets the lowest bid to <minbid>. If <minbid> is omitted it prints the current setting.
/sdkp acl	Prints the list of players who are allowed to control the addon remotely.
/sdkp acl add <names>	Adds <names> to the ACL.
/sdkp acl remove <names>	Removes <names> from the ACL.

The slash command handler is quite long as we have eight commands to deal with. The commands acl add and acl remove are capable of taking a list of names separated by spaces. We can get the names from this string by using string.split, but we don't know how many results we will get. So one possible solution to this is the following code:

```
for i = 1, select("#", string.split(" ", names)) do
   local name = select(i, string.split(" ", names))
   -- do something with the name
end
```

But this will execute string.split every time it enters the loop. So the better way is to create a helper function with a vararg. This function can then operate on the vararg, and the splitting will be done only once, when calling the function. So our slash command handler looks like this:

```
SLASH_SimpleDKP1 = "/simpledkp"
SLASH_SimpleDKP2 = "/sdkp"

do
   local setChannel = "Channel is now \"%s\""
   local setTime = "Time is now %s"
   local setMinBid = "Lowest bid is now %s"
   local addedToACL = "Added %s player(s) to the ACL"
```

```
local removedFromACL = "Removed %s player(s) from the ACL"
local currChannel = "Channel is currently set to \"%s\""
local currTime = "Time is currently set to %s"
local currMinBid = "Lowest bid is currently set to %s"
local ACL = "Access Control List:"

local function addToACL(...) -- adds multiple players to the ACL
   for i = 1, select("#", ...) do -- iterate over the arguments
      SimpleDKP_ACL[select(i, ...)] = true -- and add all players
   end
   print(addedToACL:format(select("#", ...))) -- print an info message
end

local function removeFromACL(...) -- removes player(s) from the ACL
   for i = 1, select("#", ...) do -- iterate over the vararg
      SimpleDKP_ACL[select(i, ...)] = nil -- remove the players from the ACL
   end
   print(removedFromACL:format(select("#", ...))) -- print an info message
end

SlashCmdList["SimpleDKP"] = function(msg)
   local cmd, arg = string.split(" ", msg) -- split the string
   cmd = cmd:lower() -- the command should not be case-sensitive
   if cmd == "start" and arg then -- /sdkp start item
      startAuction(msg:match("^start%s+(.+)")) -- extract the item link
   elseif cmd == "stop" then -- /sdkp stop
      cancelAuction()
   elseif cmd == "channel" then -- /sdkp channel arg
      if arg then -- a new channel was provided
         SimpleDKP_Channel = arg:upper() -- set it to arg
         print(setChannel:format(SimpleDKP_Channel))
      else -- no channel was provided
         print(currChannel:format(SimpleDKP_Channel)) -- print the current one
      end
   elseif cmd == "time" then -- /sdkp time arg
      if arg and tonumber(arg) then -- arg is provided and it is a number
         SimpleDKP_AuctionTime = tonumber(arg) -- set it
         print(setTime:format(SimpleDKP_AuctionTime))
      else -- arg was not provided or it wasn't a number
         print(currTime:format(SimpleDKP_AuctionTime)) -- print error message
      end
   elseif cmd == "minbid" then -- /sdkp minbid arg
      if arg and tonumber(arg) then -- arg is set and a number
         SimpleDKP_MinBid = tonumber(arg) -- set the option
         print(setMinBid:format(SimpleDKP_MinBid))
      else -- arg is not set or not a number
         print(currMinBid:format(SimpleDKP_MinBid)) -- print error message
```

```
                end
          elseif cmd == "acl" then -- /sdkp acl add/remove player1, player2, ...
              if not arg then -- add/remove not passed
                  print(ACL) -- output header
                  for k, v in pairs(SimpleDKP_ACL) do -- loop over the ACL
                      print(k) -- print all entries
                  end
              elseif arg:lower() == "add" then -- /sdkp add player1, player2, ...
                  -- split the string and pass all players to our helper function
                  addToACL(select(3, string.split(" ", msg)))
              elseif arg:lower() == "remove" then -- /sdkp remove player1, player2, ...
                  removeFromACL(select(3, string.split(" ", msg))) -- split & remove
              end
          end
      end
  end
end
```

The code is long but simple. It basically just deals with setting and retrieving options and is a long if-then-else block that processes the different commands. The only part that is slightly more difficult is the part that deals with the ACL. This part splits the string and passes everything except the first two substrings to the helper function that adds or removes the names from the table.

We can now test the mod in-game. It is working pretty well, but there are a few issues left: the stop command does not work, as we haven't implement the cancelAuction function yet; the ACL is pointless as we haven't implemented remote control yet; and we can see outgoing whispers and placed bids in our chat frames. We don't want to see them. Let's fix these problems.

Canceling Auctions

Canceling auctions is pretty easy. We just need to set the variable currentItem to nil, wipe the table bids, and unschedule all scheduled tasks. Here's the code:

```
do
    local cancelled = "Auction cancelled by %s"
    function cancelAuction(sender)
        currentItem = nil
        table.wipe(bids)
        SimpleTimingLib_Unschedule(SendChatMessage)
        SimpleTimingLib_Unschedule(endAuction)
        SendChatMessage(cancelled:format(sender or UnitName("player")),➥
SimpleDKP_Channel)
    end
end
```

The API function UnitName(*unitId*) returns the name of a unit as it appears in the game. The name "player" always refers to you, so UnitName("player") returns the name of your character.

> **■Tip** A unit ID is used to identify a unit, for example `target` is your target, `pet` is your pet, and `party1` is the first member of your party. You can find all available unit IDs in Appendix B.

Our cancel function exposes an issue with our timing library: we are unscheduling all calls to `SendChatMessage` here, but other addons that use this library might also have scheduled a call to this function. Therefore, we do not want to unschedule this one. You will see how to fix this issue in Chapter 7 when we update the library.

Remote Control

We want to allow players on your ACL list to create and cancel auctions via chat commands. You can add your guild's officers and raid leaders to this list, so they can start auctions when you are not the master looter in your raid. We want to listen for chat commands in the raid, as well as guild, whisper, and officer chat, so we need to add those events. Go to the line in your code where you registered the event `CHAT_MSG_WHISPER` and add the following lines of code there:

```
frame:RegisterEvent("CHAT_MSG_WHISPER") -- look for this line...
frame:RegisterEvent("CHAT_MSG_RAID") -- ...and insert these four new lines after it
frame:RegisterEvent("CHAT_MSG_RAID_LEADER")
frame:RegisterEvent("CHAT_MSG_GUILD")
frame:RegisterEvent("CHAT_MSG_OFFICER")
```

Our event handler will now also be called for these events. Their first two arguments are the same as they are for whisper messages. So we can just change the code in our event handler to the following code:

```
function onEvent(self, event, msg, sender)
    if event == "CHAT_MSG_WHISPER" and currentItem and tonumber(msg) then
        -- old code here
    elseif SimpleDKP_ACL[sender] then
        -- not a whisper or a whisper that is not a bid
        -- and the sender has the permission to send commands
        local cmd, arg = msg:match("^!(%w+)%s*(.*)")
        if cmd and cmd:lower() == "auction" and arg then
            startAuction(arg, sender)
        elseif cmd and cmd:lower() == "cancel" then
            cancelAuction(sender)
        end
    end
end
```

A player on the access control list can now create an auction by writing `!auction <item>` in the chat. To cancel an auction they must enter `!cancel`. The pattern that allows this might look complicated if you are still getting accustomed to regular expressions, so let's analyze it.

The first character, `^`, tells us that it looks for the beginning of the string. This is useful because we don't want to trigger the code if someone writes text like "...!cancel ..." to the chat.

The next character is !, which has no special meaning. It is followed by a capture that matches %w+, one or more alphanumeric characters. This is the first capture, so the found string will be returned as the first argument and stored in the local variable cmd. The next expression is %s*, which means we are looking for whitespace, and * means that it matches zero or more. The next expression is our second capture; it matches .*, an arbitrary number of arbitrary characters, which matches the rest of the line.

This means we are looking for an exclamation mark at the beginning of the string, followed by a word. This can optionally be followed by whitespace and any other text. The first word is the first return value (cmd) and the optional text after the optional whitespace is the second return value (arg).

One issue remains: we do not want to see outgoing whispers and incoming bids.

Hiding Chat Messages

Blizzard provides the function ChatFrame_AddMessageEventFilter(*event*, *func*), which allows us to set up filters for chat messages. The function takes an event and a function as arguments; *func* is called every time before a chat message of the type *event* is displayed. This function receives the same arguments as the event handler of the corresponding event. The first return value of the function is a boolean that determines if the chat frame should cancel processing of this event. So setting this to true will filter the message. The function also has to return all arguments of the event (arg1 - arg11 for chat messages) that are also passed to it. This allows you to modify these arguments to change incoming chat messages.

But we only need the simple part of this chat filter API here as we just want to hide certain messages but not modify them. We need to set up filters for the events CHAT_MSG_WHISPER and CHAT_MSG_WHISPER_INFORM; the former will filter incoming bids, the latter is responsible for outgoing whisper messages. Suitable filter functions look like the following; you can just insert them anywhere in your DKP auctioneer file (preferably at the end):

```
local function filterIncoming(self, event, ...)
    local msg = ... -- get the message from the vararg
    -- return true if there is an ongoing auction and the whisper is a number
    -- followed by all event handler arguments
    return currentItem and tonumber(msg), ...
end

local function filterOutgoing(self, event, ...)
    local msg = ... -- extract the message
    return msg:sub(0, prefix:len()) == prefix, ...
end

ChatFrame_AddMessageEventFilter("CHAT_MSG_WHISPER", filterIncoming)
ChatFrame_AddMessageEventFilter("CHAT_MSG_WHISPER_INFORM", filterOutgoing)
```

The function filterIncoming does the same check that is also done by the event handler to determine if an incoming whisper is a bid and does not display the message if it is a bid. The function filterOutgoing checks if the message starts with the prefix that was defined at the beginning of our script and swallows the message if it does. Both functions also have to return all arguments of the event handler, even if we didn't change them.

The mod is now ready to be used. It is a fully featured DKP auctioneer that you can easily adjust to match the rules of your DKP system if you use a different one.

Summary

In this chapter you learned how to use frames to listen to scripts and events. This allows us to write addons that respond to events from the game. Virtually every addon makes use of script handlers and event handlers, so this is a very important part of the World of Warcraft API. We have written three powerful example mods in this chapter: The first one added mouse-over tooltips for links in chat frames, the second was a library that allowed us to schedule functions to be called after a certain time has passed, and the third example was a fully featured DKP auctioneer.

All of these addons made extensive use of script handlers and events. We worked with a lot of events, but only a few script handlers. That's because most script handlers are related to the graphical user interface. This leads to our next topic, creating graphical user interface elements in World of Warcraft.

CHAPTER 5

■■■

Using XML and Frames

This chapter is about creating graphical user interfaces. There are two ways to do this in World of Warcraft. You saw one method in Chapter 4, using Lua to create frames. This chapter's approach is to use XML (Extensible Markup Language), a language that can be used to describe data. The data we are going to describe here will represent frames in World of Warcraft. You will see that using XML for this purpose is very powerful.

Both ways have their advantages and drawbacks. While the main focus in this chapter is on XML, there are some things that can only be done by Lua, so you will also learn more about CreateFrame and frame methods here. One of the biggest advantages of XML is that you get a clear separation of your UI design and your code. This allows you to change the look of an addon later without having to modify any code. It is also easy to implement different skins for your addon just by using a different XML file without even touching Lua code.

The advantage of Lua is that it can create frames dynamically while your script is running. You will see later how to combine XML and Lua to obtain the advantages of both.

The example mod we are going to write will be a fully featured in-game Texas Hold'em poker game. This is quite a long example, so this chapter does not cover the whole mod. The following chapters will continue creating this addon. We will have created only a small part of this addon by the end of the chapter, but it covers many particularly interesting frame types. You will learn how to create configuration frames here and then build the part that deals with the poker game in Chapters 7 and 8.

You should always try to split up a comprehensive program like this into several smaller parts. This can reduce a big problem (creating a poker addon), by breaking it into a number of smaller problems that can then be reduced into even smaller tasks, which can be as simple as a single Lua function.

We are going to need a server that hosts a poker table and a client that can join a table and play on it. The server then may be split into a part that provides auxiliary functions, such as comparing two hands to determine the winner, and a part that communicates with the clients on your table. The client can also be split into a part that allows you to select a table from a list of tables hosted in your guild or raid and the GUI that displays the table you are currently playing on.

We will design and create the basics of the graphical user interface in this chapter. But to do that, we first need to discuss XML.

XML Basics

Let's start with an example, so you can see what an XML file in World of Warcraft looks like. The following XML creates a frame with the script handlers OnLoad and OnEvent. If you want to test the example, store the following code in a file called firstUI.xml and add this file to your TOC file. Adding an XML file to the TOC file works like an addon to a Lua file; you just add a line that says firstUI.xml to your TOC file.

```
<Ui xmlns="http://www.blizzard.com/wow/ui/"➥
xmlns:xsi="http://www.w3.org/2001/XMLSchema-instance"➥
xsi:schemaLocation="http://www.blizzard.com/wow/ui/ ..\FrameXML\UI.xsd">
   <Frame name="MyTestFrame">
      <Scripts> <!-- this is a comment -->
         <OnLoad>
            self:RegisterEvent("CHAT_MSG_WHISPER")
         </OnLoad>
         <OnEvent>
            local msg, sender = ...
            print(event, sender, msg)
         </OnEvent>
      </Scripts>
   </Frame>
</Ui>
```

I need to introduce a few terms before explaining what this example does, so let's look at the terminology.

XML Terminology

An XML *element* is something in the form <*elementName*> contents </*elementName*>. There is a short way to define an element that has no contents: <*elementName*/>. The contents of an element can be other XML elements or text, such as Lua code. An XML document has always exactly one *root element*, which contains all other elements. Elements can also have *attributes*, which look like this: <*elementName* attribute="*value*"/>. The value of an attribute must always be enclosed in quotes, even if it is just a number.

The *opening tag* of an element is the code <ele *attr1*="x" *attr2*="y"> that starts the element; the *closing tag* </ele> marks the end of an element. A comment in XML starts with <!-- and ends with -->.

Elements in World of Warcraft XML

The root element in World of Warcraft is always the element <Ui>, which you can see in the first three lines of the example. The closing tag is in the last line. Its attributes are also always the same, so you can just copy and paste this into every new XML file you create. The opening tag of this element can also be written in just one line as you can insert new lines and spaces wherever you want to.

The attributes of the <Ui> element are xmlns, xmlns:xsi, and xsi:schemaLocation. Their values here contain metadata that identify this XML file as a World of Warcraft UI file to the program that reads it.

Creating Frames

The `<Ui>` root element contains an element of the type `<Frame>` with the attribute `name=`
`"MyTestFrame"`. World of Warcraft will create a frame when it loads this XML file. The name of
the frame can be retrieved by calling the method `frame:GetName()`. The name is also used as
the identifier of the global variable that will be used to store a reference to the frame. So you
can access your frame from Lua code. You can also create named frames from Lua; just pass
the name as second argument to `CreateFrame(type, name)`.

The content of this element is the element `<Scripts>`, which contains all the script handlers of the frame. All script handlers that can be set with `frame:SetScript` are also available
here. Our example frame has the script handlers `OnLoad` and `OnEvent`. The script handler
`OnLoad` is invoked when World of Warcraft has finished loading the frame. Adding this handler
from Lua with `SetScript("OnLoad", func)` is pointless, as the script handler would already
be invoked after the call to `CreateFrame(frame)`. If your frame was created in XML without an
`OnLoad` handler, it is also pointless to add one afterwards. This handler is executed exactly once
when the frame is created. An `OnLoad` handler that is added later will never be executed.

The content of the script handler elements is Lua code that will be put in a function.
But the head of the function is missing here, so how do we know which arguments will be
passed to them? The function head for `OnLoad` is `function(self)`, as this script handler does
not receive an additional argument. `OnEvent` looks like this: `function(self, event, ...)`.
Appendix A lists the arguments that are available for all script handlers in XML.

Including External Lua and XML Files

An XML file can also contain Lua code outside of script handlers and frames. You can use the
element `<Script>` for this. It can either contain Lua code directly or use the attribute `file` to
load a file containing a Lua script. The code will be executed when the XML file is loaded. The
`<Script>` element needs to be placed outside all of your `<Frame>` elements but inside the root
element `<Ui>`.

The element `<Include>` allows you to include another XML file. This file is specified by
using the attribute *file* of this element. This element must also be placed outside of all other
elements but inside the root element `<Ui>`.

You don't need to add Lua or XML files that are included via `<Script>`/`<Include>` elements
to your TOC file. This allows you to include files without using the TOC file, which comes in
handy if you have to add a lot of files that belong together and you want to separate them from
the rest of your files. This is often the case when you work extensively with what are called
embedded libraries, a feature you will learn more about in Chapter 10.

The following XML shows a file that includes a Lua file and an XML file from a sub-folder
called `libs` in your addon. Such files are commonly used when creating Ace addons. Ace is also
covered in Chapter 10.

```
<Ui xmlns="http://www.blizzard.com/wow/ui/"➥
xmlns:xsi="http://www.w3.org/2001/XMLSchema-instance"➥
xsi:schemaLocation="http://www.blizzard.com/wow/ui/ ..\FrameXML\UI.xsd">
    <Script file="libs\LibStub\LibStub.lua"/>
    <Include file="libs\AceAddon-3.0\AceAddon-3.0.xml"/>
    <!-- even more Lua and XML files can be placed here -->
</Ui>
```

As you can see, XML is quite easy. You can create frames of all types by describing them in XML. Appendix A has the full documentation of all attributes and elements that are available for all frame types.

But what happens if you make a mistake in an XML file? And how can you tell whether a file is valid without testing it in World of Warcraft?

Validating and Debugging XML

If you are using one of the more complete IDEs, like WoW AddOn Studio, which I presented in Chapter 1, you already have a good syntax checker with autocompletion support.

But if you are using SciTE, you have only basic support for XML syntax highlighting and code folding. To supplement that, I've included the command-line utility MSV (Sun Multi-Schema Validator) in my distribution of SciTE. This program can validate an XML file against an XML Schema. A schema defines which elements, attributes, and possible values for those attributes are allowed in an XML file that uses the schema. Schemas are also written in XML.

The XML Schema Document that describes how a World of Warcraft XML file should look is the file Interface\FrameXML\UI.xsd, from the default user interface. Even if you are not familiar with XML, you might still find this file interesting. If you are familiar with working with XML, you might want to work with your own favorite XML editor and this file.

Validating XML in SciTE

Press F5 in SciTE to check the currently open XML file. Figure 5-1 shows SciTE with an open XML file that contains an error. The file looks like the example shown earlier, but it has an additional script handler, OnInvalid. This script handler does not exist, and MSV detects that. It also lists all possible elements that could be used there instead.

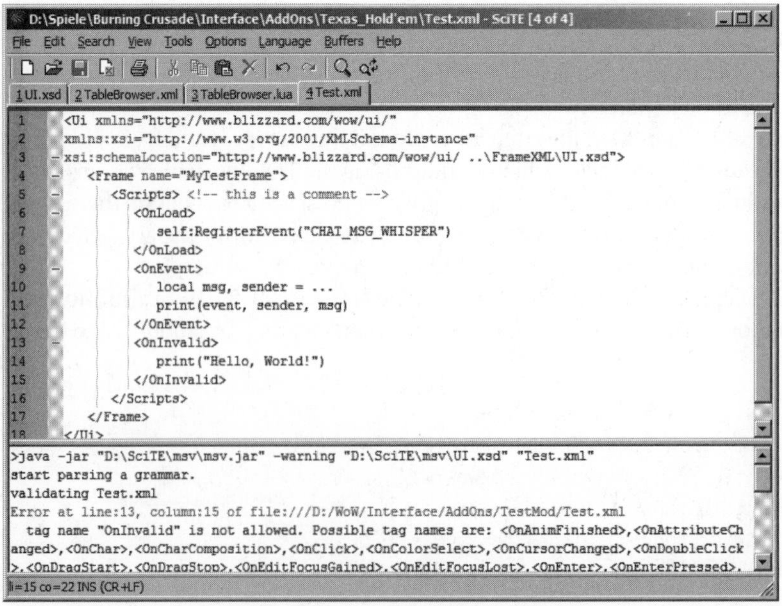

Figure 5-1. *MSV validating an XML file opened in SciTE*

This tool is built upon the free (Apache License) XML library Xerces. MSV itself is licensed under the BSD License. You can find the full texts of these licenses in the SciTE installation folder. These licenses are very free and essentially allow you to do whatever you want with a tool as long as you keep their copyright notice.

■**Note** You also need to have Java installed to use this tool. You can get Java on `http://www.java.com` if you don't have it already installed.

Debugging XML

You will certainly make a mistake or typo when creating XML files. So you should know what happens when World of Warcraft encounters an invalid XML document.

The simplest mistake is actually not related to XML at all—errors in embedded Lua code. The same rules as for Lua files apply here. If your script is syntactically invalid, the game will show an error message when the file is loaded, and the affected XML element is then ignored. Other errors will produce an error message when the code is called, just like normal Lua files.

Mistakes in XML, like using unknown elements or attributes, do not produce an error message in World of Warcraft. The affected element or attribute will be ignored by the game and the rest of the XML will be loaded.

Syntax errors like a missing closing tag also do not produce an error message, but the whole file will be ignored by the game. However, there is a way to get useful information about possible bugs in your XML files.

The function `FrameXML_Debug` allows you to create a very detailed log of everything that is going on while the game loads your XML file. Execute the following command to enable debugging for the current session:

```
/run FrameXML_Debug(1)
```

After reloading your interface, you will have the file `World of Warcraft\Logs\FrameXML.log`. It contains detailed information about every XML file the game loaded, including XML files provided by Blizzard. So you should search for the name of your addon to find the part of the log that is relevant for you. For example, if you try to add the element `OnInvalid` to your script handlers you get the following log:

```
Loading add-on XMLTests
** Loading table of contents Interface\AddOns\XMLTests\XMLTests.toc
++ Loading file Interface\AddOns\XMLTests\Test.xml
-- Creating Frame named MyTestFrame
Frame MyTestFrame: Unknown script element OnInvalid
```

However, if your code contains a syntax error, the only message you will get will be the following:

```
Couldn't parse XML in Interface\AddOns\XMLTests\Test.xml
```

In this case, you will have to check your XML file for mistakes. SciTE with MSV will help you with that.

It is always a good idea to check the XML log of your addon, as it contains more than just error messages. It also contains valuable information about the loading process of your addon, which can help you to spot possible errors.

Frame Basics

This section looks at basic frames and how to make them appear on your screen. A *frame* is the base element of a graphical user interface and will contain all other elements of your GUI. A frame or any other widget (a user interface element like a button) that is contained in another frame is called the *child* of that frame. The containing frame is called the *parent*. Frames can have any number of children but only one or no parent. Changing certain attributes of frames also affects their children; for example if you hide a frame, its children will also be hidden. Setting the transparency or scale of a frame also affects the children.

We will create the first part of the poker addon here: the frame that allows you to browse the list of available tables and join one of them. Start by creating a folder and a TOC file for your new addon, and then add the files localization.en.lua, TableBrowser.xml, and TableBrowser.lua to the TOC file. The order of files in the TOC files defines the order in which they will be loaded. A suitable TOC file for our addon could look like the following. Feel free to add additional metadata like your name by using the Author attribute or a short description in the attribute Notes.

```
## Interface: 30100
localization.en.lua
TableBrowser.xml
TableBrowser.lua
```

The first thing we want to load is the localization file, in which we will put all the strings we are going to use (they need to be available before loading anything else). The next file we want to load is the XML file, as we want to have the frame created and available before our Lua code is executed.

The name of the addon is up to you; I named mine Texas_Hold'em. Fill your XML file with the following code:

```
<Ui xmlns="http://www.blizzard.com/wow/ui/"➥
xmlns:xsi="http://www.w3.org/2001/XMLSchema-instance"➥
xsi:schemaLocation="http://www.blizzard.com/wow/ui/ ..\FrameXML\UI.xsd">
    <Frame name="Poker_TableBrowser">
    </Frame>
</Ui>
```

It defines a frame with the name Poker_TableBrowser that we are going to extend in the rest of this chapter.

Making It Visible

We are going to need a frame that is visible on our screen. Our frame requires certain attributes before it can be seen. We need to provide at least one *point* to which it will be anchored. If we provide just one point, we will also need to set a size. And ultimately we need content for our frame so that we can actually see something.

UIParent

This frame is defined by the game and should be the parent of all other frames. A frame does not need to be the direct child of `UIParent`; it is sufficient if its parent or the parent's parent (or the parent's parent's parent,and so on) is a child of `UIParent`. This allows you to change certain attributes of all frames just by modifying a single frame. For example, if you look at the code that is behind pressing Alt-Z to hide the UI, it basically just says `UIParent:Hide()`. Changing the scale of your UI just calls `UIParent:SetScale(scale)`. So if your frame is not a child of `UIParent`, setting UI scale or hiding it with Alt-Z won't work.

We add the attribute `parent="UIParent"` to our `<Frame>` element in the XML file. The new opening tag of our frame should then look like this:

```
<Frame name="Poker_TableBrowser" parent="UIParent">
```

You can change the parent of a frame from Lua by calling the method `frame:SetParent(parent)`. You can also define the parent while creating the frame from Lua; just pass the parent as the third argument to `CreateFrame(type, name, parent)`.

Anchors

An *anchor* defines the position of your frame within the game's UI. Your frame can have multiple anchors, but we will start with just one anchor to keep it simple. An `<Anchor>` element must be put in the `<Anchors>` element in the `<Frame>` element. That means you have to insert the following highlighted code:

```
<Frame name="Poker_TableBrowser" parent="UIParent">
    <Anchors>
        <Anchor point="LEFT" relativePoint="CENTER">
            <Offset>
                <AbsDimension x="200" y="0"/>
            </Offset>
        </Anchor>
    </Anchors>
</Frame>
```

This code anchors the left side of your frame to the center of its parent. The offset defines the space between the parent frame and the child. A positive x value means that the frame is moved to the right; a negative would move it left. Positive y values move the frame up; negative values move it down. `<AbsDimension>` means that the value is an absolute offset; it is also possible to use `<RelDimension>`, which takes values between 0 and 1 for x and y. The value will then be interpreted as a percentage of the whole screen. The offset is optional, and the default values for x and y are 0. The attribute `relativePoint` is also optional and is by default equal to *point*. This means we can quickly anchor a frame to the inside of its parent by just providing the attribute *point*.

The frame our frame will be anchored to is by default the parent. If a frame does not have a parent it will be anchored to the whole screen. You can also use the attribute relativeTo= "*frame*" in the element <Anchor> to define the frame your frame will be anchored to.

Points

The top diagram below shows all points that are available. The bottom diagram illustrates an example in which the point BOTTOMLEFT of the frame child is anchored to the point BOTTOM of the frame parent with an *X* offset of 15 and a *Y* offset of –10.

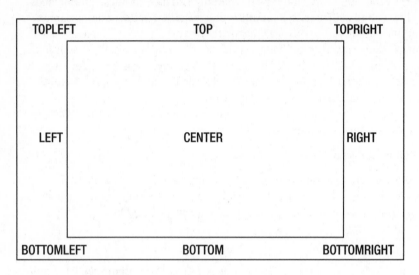

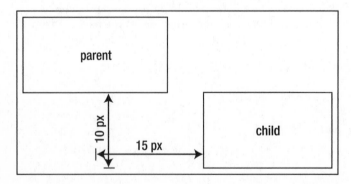

It is also possible to set, get, and delete anchors by using Lua code. The method frame: SetPoint(*point, relativeTo, relativePoint, x, y*) creates a new anchor. All arguments except for point are optional. The default value for *relativeTo* is the parent of the frame, the default value for *relativePoint* is the value that was passed as first argument (*point*), and the offsets x and y are 0 by default. The value *relativeTo* can be either a frame or the name of a frame. It is possible to pass x and y as the second and third arguments when you want to omit *relativeTo* and *relativePoint*.

The method frame:GetPoint(*n*) returns the *n*th point of a frame. The return values are the same as the arguments to SetPoint.

You can delete all points by calling `frame:ClearAllPoints()`. The position of a frame on the screen will not change after calling this method. It will keep its old position until you set a new point by calling the method `SetPoint`. Note that you must always call `ClearAllPoints` if you want to move a frame by changing the anchor. Not clearing the points may produce unexpected results, as you end up with multiple points. You will see how multiple points can affect a frame's position and size later in this chapter.

You still cannot see any effect when you load our XML file, because the frame still has no contents. But we can use another frame, like the frame `MinimapCluster` from the default UI, to test the effects of the methods `SetPoint` and `ClearAllPoints`. The following code can be executed in-game to move the minimap with all elements that belong to it:

```
MinimapCluster:ClearAllPoints()
MinimapCluster:SetPoint("CENTER", 100, -50)
```

You can now test the effects of setting different points. Don't forget to call `ClearAllPoints` before setting a new one.

Caution It is not possible to omit just one of the offsets when calling `SetPoint`. If you pass only one of them, it will be ignored.

Sizes

When you define a size or an offset, you always have two possibilities: using a relative or an absolute value. The relative value is always a percentage of the whole screen. So a frame with the relative height and width of 0.5 will take a quarter of your screen. The absolute value is in pixels, but an absolute value does not depend on the resolution of the game, just on the UI scale setting. The height of the screen is always 768 pixels divided by the UI scale setting, which you can retrieve with `UIParent:GetScale()`. For example, I have my UI scale set to 0.75, so the height of the screen (from an addon's point of view) is 1024. The width depends on the aspect ratio of your screen. For example, I have a 16:10 wide-screen monitor, so the width of my virtual screen is 1024 × 1.6 = 1638.4.

So when we define sizes, or offsets as we did in the last section, we always use a virtual resolution that is then mapped on your real screen by the game. Using fractional values for pixels is no problem. The advantage of this system is that the position and size of a frame do not depend on the resolution. This is especially important when you are playing the game in window mode, as it allows you to resize your window without having to reposition frames.

We can use the element `<Size>` to set the size of a frame. A good size for our table browser is 384 × 350, as 384 is the width of default UI dialogs like the character frame. Add the following code to the element `<Frame>` in the file `TableBrowser.xml`. Adding an element to another element means that you must add it between the opening and closing tag of that other element:

```
<Size>
    <AbsDimension x="384" y="350"/>
</Size>
```

Again, you can also use <RelDimension> here. If you want to set the size from Lua, you can use the methods frame:SetWidth(width) and frame:SetHeight(height). You can retrieve the size by calling GetWidth and GetHeight. Our frame would now be visible if it had any contents. Let's start with a simple border and background for our frame.

Backdrops

A *backdrop* is a combination of a border and a background for our frame. Add the following <Backdrop> element to the element <Frame>:

```
<Backdrop bgFile="Interface\DialogFrame\UI-DialogBox-Background" tile="true"
edgeFile="Interface\DialogFrame\UI-DialogBox-Border">
    <TileSize>
        <AbsValue val="32"/>
    </TileSize>
    <EdgeSize>
        <AbsValue val="32"/>
    </EdgeSize>
    <BackgroundInsets>
        <AbsInset left="11" right="12" top="12" bottom="11"/>
    </BackgroundInsets>
</Backdrop>
```

Let's go through the attributes and elements of a backdrop. The first attribute you can see is bgFile, which sets the path of a texture that will be used as the background texture. If tile is true, the texture will be repeated to fill the whole frame. Setting tile to false will stretch the texture to fill the frame.

The attribute edgeFile is also a texture that is used for the borders of the frame. Figure 5-2 shows the texture that is used in our example. The image contains all parts of the borders of our frame.

Figure 5-2. *The file Interface\DialogFrame\UI-DialogBox-Border*

The element <TileSize> defines the width of the part of the texture that is used as a border. The height is always the height of the texture file. The element <EdgeSize> then defines the size of the texture's parts that will be used for the edges. The borders are the four straight lines you can see in the left half of Figure 5-2, while the edges are the corners in the right half.

The last element in our backdrop is <BackgroundInsets>, which defines how far the background will be drawn. Use lower values if your edgeFile has smaller borders.

For most addons, it is sufficient to copy and paste one of the existing backdrop elements from Blizzard's UI. This ensures that your addon comes with a native look, and you do not have to design your own backdrop.

You can now load the addon containing the XML file and you will see a nice frame in the right part of your screen. But you don't want to show that frame by default, so we will create a slash command and a nice minimap button for displaying this later. Add the attribute hidden="true" to hide the frame by default. You can then show it by calling the method

`Poker_TableBrowser:Show()`. You might want to keep `hidden` at its default value `false` while working on this frame.

Multiple Points

You can also define multiple points, and the frame will then take the space between those points. This overwrites the size setting. Load the poker addon so that you can see the frame, and execute the following code:

```
Poker_TableBrowser:ClearAllPoints()
Poker_TableBrowser:SetPoint("TOP")
Poker_TableBrowser:SetPoint("BOTTOM")
```

This will position your frame in the middle of your screen and stretch it from the top to the bottom. The width is not changed by this code. Now try the following code:

```
Poker_TableBrowser:ClearAllPoints()
Poker_TableBrowser:SetPoint("BOTTOMLEFT", UIParent, "LEFT")
Poker_TableBrowser:SetPoint("TOPRIGHT", UIParent, "TOP")
```

The frame will now take the upper-left quarter of your screen. The width and height from the `<Size>` element will both be ignored.

If you want to fit a frame into another frame, you can either anchor points `TOPLEFT` and `BOTTOMRIGHT` to that frame or use the attribute `setAllPoints` of a frame. If `setAllPoints` is true, it will be fit into its parent and fill it completely. The method `frame:SetAllPoints(otherFrame)` can be used to anchor those points to any other frame.

Layers and Textures

We now have a visible frame with a backdrop, but it is still empty. Next you will see what layers are and how to add artwork to a frame.

Frame Strata

The attribute `frameStrata` of a frame defines the order of a frame. A frame with a higher strata than another frame will appear before that frame. If you do not define the strata of a frame, it will have the same strata as its parent. The following list shows all valid values for the frame strata, from higher to lower order:

- `TOOLTIP`
- `FULLSCREEN_DIALOG`
- `FULLSCREEN`
- `DIALOG`
- `HIGH`
- `MEDIUM`
- `LOW`
- `BACKGROUND`

The strata that should be used by dialogs like the one we are creating is DIALOG. Using this strata means that our frame will be placed above all other UI elements that do not use the whole screen. DIALOG is also used by all dialogs in the default UI, such as the game options menu. You can set the strata from Lua by calling the method frame:SetFrameStrata(*strata*).

■**Note** Frame methods and XML attributes always refer to the strata of a frame or the "FrameStrata"; the singular *stratum* is not used in any documentation or method/attribute name. I'll therefore use the plural strata to be consistent with other documentation or tutorials you find on the Internet.

Layers

A *layer* can hold textures or text and is contained in a frame. The level of a layer defines whether the artwork is in front of or behind other artwork from other layers with a different level. The following example uses layers and textures to add a title region to our frame. Add this to your <Frame> element:

```
<Layers>
    <Layer level="ARTWORK">
        <Texture name="$parentTitle" file="Interface\DialogFrame\UI-DialogBox-Header">
            <Size>
                <AbsDimension x="375" y="64"/>
            </Size>
            <Anchors>
                <Anchor point="TOP">
                    <Offset>
                        <AbsDimension x="0" y="12"/>
                    </Offset>
                </Anchor>
            </Anchors>
        </Texture>
        <FontString inherits="GameFontNormal" text="POKER_BROWSER_TITLE">
            <Anchors>
                <Anchor point="TOP" relativeTo="$parentTitle">
                    <Offset>
                        <AbsDimension x="0" y="-14"/>
                    </Offset>
                </Anchor>
            </Anchors>
        </FontString>
    </Layer>
</Layers>
```

The element `<Layers>` acts as a container for all layers. A `<Layer>` can hold textures (`<Texture>`) or text blocks (`<FontString>`). The only attribute of the element `<Layer>` is its `level`. The following list shows all valid values for this attribute, from higher to lower:

- HIGHLIGHT
- OVERLAY
- ARTWORK (default value)
- BORDER
- BACKGROUND

The level HIGHLIGHT is special, as elements placed in this layer are only visible when you move your mouse over them. So you can place fancy glow effects here.

The layer from our examples holds two elements: a texture and a text. Let's take a closer look at the texture.

Textures

A texture in a layer is basically similar to a frame, in that it needs anchors and a size in order to be displayed. The texture has the name $parentTitle, where $parent will be replaced by the name of the parent. So the name of this texture will be Poker_TableBrowserTitle. A reference to it will be available under the global variable with this name. The attribute `file` sets the texture that will be displayed. Again, to get an overview over all elements and attributes a texture can have, consult Appendix A, which lists all the attributes, elements, and methods of all frame types.

Font Strings

The element `<FontString>` can also have a name, but we don't need one here as we do not intend to change the text later. Note that although we also don't plan to make any later changes to the texture we previously created, we still gave it a name. That is because the name of the texture, $parentTitle, is used as the value for the `relativeTo` attribute in the anchor of this font string. This allows us to anchor the text on the title to its background to ensure that it is displayed at the correct position. It is not possible to anchor a frame to a nameless frame via XML; you would have to use the method SetPoint from Lua and pass a reference to that nameless frame as a second attribute in order to use it as an anchor.

The attribute `inherits` tells the game to use the *font object* GameFontNormal. A font object defines attributes of text such as its size, color, and font. You can find all available font objects in the file FrameXML\Fonts.xml of the default UI. Although it is rarely needed, you can also create your own font object. Appendix A contains the full documentation of the XML element used for that.

Note that this element does not necessarily require a size. The text will take the size it needs. However, you can set a size to limit the size of a font string. If the text exceeds the width, it will be wrapped around. If it also exceeds the height, it will be truncated.

You might have wondered why the attribute `text` is set to POKER_BROWSER_TITLE. The game checks whether there is a global variable with this name when loading a font string. If there is, it will take the value from that variable as text; otherwise it uses this text.

So loading this XML file results in a frame with a nice title region that shows the text POKER_BROWSER_TITLE. We can change the title to more appropriate text by adding the following line to the file localization.en.lua. Remember, this file will be used to store all the strings we are going to use:

```
POKER_BROWSER_TITLE = "Texas Hold'em Table Browser"
```

Our next task is to make the frame movable so it can be dragged around.

Movable Frames

We can make our frame movable by adding the attribute movable="true" to our <Frame> element. We also need to be able to respond to mouse events. You might have noticed that it is currently possible to "click through" the frame. We set the attribute enableMouse="true" to be able to receive mouse clicks.

The script handlers OnDragStart and OnDragEnd can be used to detect when you try to drag the frame. But before we can use these handlers, we have to tell the frame which mouse button we will use to drag it. We have to call the method frame:RegisterForDrag(*button*) for this. The *button* argument can be LeftButton, MiddleButton, RightButton, MouseButton4, or MouseButton5. A good place to call this method is the OnLoad handler of our frame.

In the OnDragStart script handler, we call the method frame:StartMoving() which attaches the frame to the mouse cursor when the user tries to drag the frame. When the user releases the frame we have to call frame:StopMovingOrSizing().

Adding the following <Scripts> element to our frame allows us to drag it around:

```
<Scripts>
    <OnLoad>
        self:RegisterForDrag("LeftButton")
    </OnLoad>
    <OnDragStart>
        self:StartMoving()
    </OnDragStart>
    <OnDragStop>
        self:StopMovingOrSizing()
    </OnDragStop>
</Scripts>
```

One thing you might notice is that we can now drag our frame off the screen. This is certainly not a behavior we intended. We can fix it by adding the attribute clampedToScreen="true" to our frame.

The next thing that is missing is that the frame does not save its position when reloading the UI. We can tell the game to save the position of the frame for us; we just have to call the method frame:SetUserPlaced(*userPlaced*). The saved position will then be restored the next time the frame is created. Note that the saved position overwrites any anchors defined in the XML file. Add the following line to the OnLoad handler of your frame to save the position:

```
self:SetUserPlaced(1)
```

We now have a nice-looking frame; let's add the contents.

Inheritance

The concept of *inheritance* means that a frame derives or inherits attributes and elements from an abstract *template*. Like a regular frame, a template is designed in XML, but it has the attribute virtual="true". Such a template will not be visible and there won't be any reference to this virtual frame visible in Lua. When you create a frame from such a template, the new frame basically copies everything from the template. The frame can then add additional attributes and elements or overwrite those inherited from the template. The attribute inherits="*templateName*" is used to tell the game that you want to inherit from a template called *templateName*. When creating frames from Lua, we can pass the template as the fourth argument to CreateFrame(*type, name, parent, template*). There is no way to create a template from Lua.

This mechanism allows us to define some basics about a frame in a template. All other similar frames then inherit from this template. The most obvious advantage of this is that when there are common attributes or elements, you don't have to write them for every frame. And if you want to change one of the values, you only need to change it in the template. All frames created from this template will also be changed. This is a very powerful feature of frames in World of Warcraft.

It is also possible to inherit from multiple templates, a feature called *multiple inheritance*. Just provide all templates you want to inherit from as a comma-separated list: inherits= "*template1,template2*". The game will copy everything from *template1* and then from *template2*, overwriting any old values. However, it is very unlikely that you are ever going to need this feature, as normal inheritance is sufficient for almost every frame you are going to need.

Let's continue working on our frame now. We need to add some elements like buttons.

The Frame Type Button

Buttons are frames that can respond to mouse clicks. They provide the script handler OnClick, which is invoked when the button is clicked. Buttons also have a texture, a text block that is displayed on them, and a font object that defines the font style of the text. The texture and the font style can change with the state of the button. There is a default combination of a texture and a font, a combination that appears when you place your cursor over the button, another one when you click it, and a fourth combination of texture and font will be used when the button is disabled. A disabled button cannot be clicked.

Buttons in XML

Buttons can have all the elements and attributes that frames can. So setting the position and size of a button also works with anchors and the <Size> element. Again, consult Appendix A to get an overview of everything you can do with a button.

The following XML defines a button that looks like a standard button:

```
<Button name="Poker_Button">
    <ButtonText>
        <Anchors>
            <Anchor point="CENTER">
                <Offset>
                    <AbsDimension x="0" y="1"/>
                </Offset>
```

```
                </Anchor>
            </Anchors>
        </ButtonText>
        <NormalFont style="GameFontNormal"/>
        <HighlightFont style="GameFontHighlight"/>
        <DisabledFont style="GameFontDisable"/>
        <NormalTexture inherits="UIPanelButtonUpTexture"/>
        <PushedTexture inherits="UIPanelButtonDownTexture"/>
        <DisabledTexture inherits="UIPanelButtonDisabledTexture"/>
        <HighlightTexture inherits="UIPanelButtonHighlightTexture"/>
</Button>
```

The size and the anchors are missing here, so you need to add them if you want to use this button. The text of the button is defined with the element <ButtonText>, which in this case is placed in the middle of the button. The elements <NormalFont>, <HighlightFont>, and <DisabledFont> set the font used for the different states. A pushed button always uses <HighlightFont>, as you must have your mouse over the button in order to push it. The four <XTexture> elements define the textures used for the different states of our button.

The interesting part is that the textures use the attribute inherits. The value of this attribute is a template from which all other attributes and elements are copied. So we have to look at these templates to get an idea of what is going on. The following code shows the template UIPanelButtonUpTexture, which can be found in the file Interface/FrameXML/UIPanelTemplates. xml of the default UI.

```
<Texture name="UIPanelButtonUpTexture"➥
file="Interface\Buttons\UI-Panel-Button-Up" virtual="true">
    <TexCoords left="0" right="0.625" top="0" bottom="0.6875"/>
</Texture>
```

This texture uses the attribute virtual="true", so it is a template and not a real texture in the game. The global variable UIPanelButtonUpTexture is also not set to any frame. The element <TexCoords> can be used to transform a texture; you will learn more about this capability when we explore textures in Chapter 8 as we build the client part of the poker addon.

Using a Button Template

It is no problem to use the XML construct just shown, every time you need a button. But what if you want to change the appearance of your buttons? You will have to change every occurrence of this XML construct. Copying and pasting a code fragment to multiple parts of your file produces duplicate code, which you always want to avoid. Your XML will be much clearer if you define this code once as a template, so that all occurrences can then be created from this template.

So you should add the attribute virtual="true" to the button that is defined in the previous code. Every time you need a button you can then use inherits="Poker_Button". But you don't even have to do this, as there is already such a template defined by Blizzard. The advantage of using a template that is provided by the game is that if Blizzard decides to change the style of their buttons, your addon will also receive the updated style. A disadvantage is that the template could receive a change that is not compatible with your addon; for example, deleting an attribute or child you needed. But this is very unlikely for a simple object like a button.

■Tip You should always look through Blizzard's XML files before creating your own templates. All XML files with the word `Template` in their name are a potential resource for templates that can be used by your addon.

The name of this template is `UIPanelButtonTemplate`, and it is also defined in the file `Interface/FrameXML/UIPanelTemplates.xml`. Always look in that file before creating your own template, as it already contains a few good templates. The following code can then be used to create a button from this template. The button should be a child of our frame `Poker_TableBrowser`. All children of a frame must be placed in the element `<Frames>` of a frame, so add the following code to your `<Frame>` element to create the button as a child:

```
<Frames>
  <Button name="$parentTestButton" text="Test :)" inherits="UIPanelButtonTemplate">
    <Size>
      <AbsDimension x="96" y="32"/>
    </Size>
    <Anchors>
      <Anchor point="CENTER"/>
    </Anchors>
    <Scripts>
      <OnLoad>
        self:RegisterForClicks(
          "LeftButtonUp",
          "RightButtonUp",
          "MiddleButtonDown"
        )
      </OnLoad>
      <OnClick> -- the function header is function(self, button)
        print("Clicked with", button)
      </OnClick>
    </Scripts>
  </Button>
</Frames>
```

The method `RegisterForClicks` takes a list of mouse events. Such a mouse event consists of a button (`LeftButton`, `RightButton`, `MiddleButton`, `Button4`, `Button5`, or `Any`) and the moment when the `OnClick` handler will be called. This moment can either be `Down` or `Up`. A second call to this method overwrites the last call. If you do not call this method at all, it will listen to `LeftButtonUp` by default.

Loading this XML will add a button in the middle of your `Poker_TableBrowser` frame; clicking it calls the `OnClick` script handler with the button as the second argument (the first is, as always, the frame itself). This function then produces a message in your chat.

Now that we've successfully created some test buttons, we need to move on to useful buttons. What should our frame look like? Which buttons do we need? Where do we need to place these buttons?

Designing the Table Browser

Before you write any XML, you should always sketch out the frame you are going to create, or at least imagine how the finished frame will look. Figure 5-3 shows a sketch of the frame we are going to create.

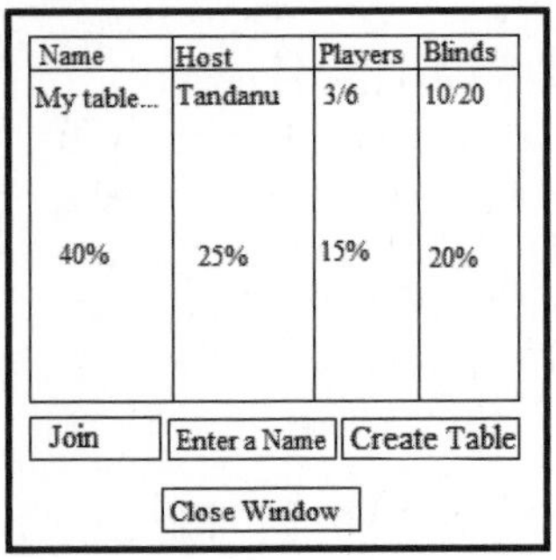

Figure 5-3. *A sketch of the Table Browser*

As you can see, the frame presents a list of all available tables in your guild or group. The user can select a table from this list by clicking on it, so the entries in this list will also be buttons. The Join button under the list can be used to join the selected table. The button Enter a Name can be used to manually enter the name of a player who hosts a poker table, in case that player is not in your group or guild. The button Create Table will bring up a dialog that allows you to host a table. The last button in this sketch is Close Window, as we need a way to close the frame. Let's start creating these buttons.

Simple Buttons

If you added the example button from the last section to your frame, delete it before continuing. The Close button should also be a child of the frame, so we need to place it in the element `<Frames>` of our frame. The following code shows the `<Frames>` element of our frame, which contains one button that is anchored at the bottom of its parent (the frame).

```
<Frames>
   <Button name="$parentClose" text="POKER_BROWSER_CLOSE"➥
inherits="UIPanelButtonTemplate">
      <Size>
         <AbsDimension x="64" y="24"/>
      </Size>
      <Anchors>
         <Anchor point="BOTTOM">
            <Offset>
               <AbsDimension x="0" y="15"/>
            </Offset>
         </Anchor>
      </Anchors>
```

```
        <Scripts>
            <OnClick>
                self:GetParent():Hide()
            </OnClick>
        </Scripts>
    </Button>
</Frames>
```

You also have to add the following line to the file localization.en.lua:

```
POKER_BROWSER_CLOSE = "Close"
```

The OnClick handler calls self:GetParent() to get the parent of the button, which is the frame Poker_TableBrowser. The code then calls this frame's Hide()method.

We could continue adding the simple command buttons, but which anchor would you choose for them? A good anchor is the list of tables that is just above them, so we should create it first.

Building a List Element

We need a list with clickable elements and a header. The header must also be clickable, as we want to be able to sort the list by various criteria. The frame type we are going to use for these elements is, as you might have guessed, a button.

Creating a Border

But the first thing we need is a border around all those buttons. We can use a backdrop to draw a nice border. A backdrop is always part of a frame; you cannot just add a backdrop as a child to another frame. But we can add an empty frame with an appropriate size and a backdrop as a child. The following code shows a frame with a backdrop that does not have a background, only a border. It uses the tooltip border, so we get an unobtrusive border around the part of the UI that will later be a list of all tables.

```
<Frame name="$parentTableList">
    <Size>
        <AbsDimension x="354" y="225"/>
    </Size>
    <Anchors>
        <Anchor point="TOP">
            <Offset>
                <AbsDimension x="0" y="-26"/>
            </Offset>
        </Anchor>
    </Anchors>
    <Backdrop edgeFile="Interface\Tooltips\UI-Tooltip-Border" tile="true">
        <EdgeSize>
            <AbsValue val="16"/>
        </EdgeSize>
```

```
        <TileSize>
            <AbsValue val="16"/>
        </TileSize>
    </Backdrop>
</Frame>
```

Remember, we want this to be a child of the frame `Poker_TableBrowser`, so you have to put this frame in the `Poker_TableBrowser`'s `<Frames>` element. There is nothing wrong with having a frame as a child of a frame, and the child can even have its own `<Frames>` element with its children.

One question that might come up is why we are using `<AbsDimension>` here. After all, I added approximate sizes in percent to the sketch in Figure 5-3. So can't we use `<RelDimension>` here? It would be better to use dimensions relative to the parent frame, but `<RelDimension>` does not work like this. It is always relative to the whole screen and not to the parent frame. This renders `<RelDimension>` useless for our purposes. So we must use absolute values here.

Tip When trying to get a good value for a size or offset, you can always access the frame in /script commands by using its name as a global variable (here: `Poker_TableBrowserTableList`). You can then call the methods `SetHeight(height)`, `SetWidth(width)`, and `SetPoint(point, relativeTo, relPoint, x, y)` on this frame to test a few settings.

We can now start building the list; the first thing we need is the list header.

Creating a Template for the Headers

Each column requires its own head, which is a button. Clicking this button calls a function that sorts the list. We have four columns, so we need four headers. It is a good idea to create a template for these buttons, as this saves a lot of duplicate code. The following XML shows a template that can be used for the header buttons. A template is not a real frame, so you cannot place this inside the `<Frames>` element of a frame. It has to be outside the frame we created previously, but inside the root element `<Ui>`. As we are going to reference this template in our frame later, it must be at the beginning of the file.

```
<Button name="Poker_TableBrowserHeader" virtual="true">
    <Scripts>
        <OnClick>
            Poker_TableBrowser.SortTables(this:GetID())
            PlaySound("igMainMenuOptionCheckBoxOn")
        </OnClick>
        <OnEnter>
            getglobal(self:GetName().."BG"):SetVertexColor(1, 1, 1, 1)
        </OnEnter>
        <OnLeave>
            getglobal(self:GetName().."BG"):SetVertexColor(0.7, 0.7, 0.7, 0.7)
        </OnLeave>
```

```
      <OnLoad>
         self:GetScript("OnLeave")(self)
      </OnLoad>
   </Scripts>
   <ButtonText>
      <Anchors>
         <Anchor point="LEFT">
            <Offset>
               <AbsDimension x="4" y="0"/>
            </Offset>
         </Anchor>
      </Anchors>
   </ButtonText>
   <NormalFont style="GameFontHighlight"/>
   <HighlightFont style="GameFontNormal"/>
   <NormalTexture name="$parentBG">
      <Color r="0.4" g="0.4" b="0.4" a="0.4"/>
   </NormalTexture>
</Button>
```

The code for the anchor and the text and font of the button should be pretty clear. Note that <NormalTexture> does not reference a file; instead it uses the element <Color>, creating a texture with a solid color. We don't use the element <HighlightTexture> here, instead we use the method frame:SetVertexColor(*red, green, blue, alpha*) in the script handlers OnEnter and OnLeave to modify the *vertex color* of our <NormalTexture>. Vertex color is just a fancy term from 3D graphics; you will see more about textures and colors in Chapter 8. All you need to know for now is that a vertex color can be used to modify the colors of a texture. Basically, we are highlighting the background texture of the button by setting the vertex color to 1, 1, 1, 1 when the mouse cursor is over it.

We can't set the vertex color of a frame from XML, so we need to call the OnLeave handler when loading the frame, because the OnLeave handler sets the default vertex color and we don't want to repeat this bit of code. We are using the method frame:GetScript("*handler*") here to retrieve the OnLeave handler. Remember that this handler expects its first argument to be the frame itself, so we need to pass it here.

The handler OnClick defines the action we want to take when we click the button. We call the function Poker_TableBrowser.SortTables, which we will create later. This function needs to know which button was clicked, and to provide that information, we pass the ID of the button that was clicked. The simplest way to do this is to give each button a different ID when creating them from the template and then obtain that ID when the button is clicked. You can set the ID of a frame by using the attribute id="number". The default value for id is 0. It would also be possible to pass self to the function and then call the method frame:GetName() on it; we could use this name to identify which header was clicked. But using IDs is smarter here, as they are just small numbers, while names can be long strings. It's just easier to work with a number.

We will create a few buttons from this template later, and all of them will have the same OnClick handler function.

■**Note** World of Warcraft does not care about the order of the elements inside a button (or any other frame). But XML validation tools will complain if you use an element that belongs to the general frame type after one that is a button-specific element. In the header template, this means that we have to put the element `<Scripts>` (which comes from the type `<Frame>`) before the button-specific elements like `<ButtonText>`.

Using the Template

Let's create actual buttons from this template now. Add the following code to the frame `$parentTableList` to create the four headers used by our list as children of `$parentTableList`:

```
<Frames>
    <Button inherits="Poker_TableBrowserHeader" name="$parentHeaderName" id="1"➥
text="POKER_BROWSER_NAME">
        <Size>
            <AbsDimension x="138" y="24"/>
        </Size>
        <Anchors>
            <Anchor point="TOPLEFT">
                <Offset>
                    <AbsDimension x="4" y="-4"/>
                </Offset>
            </Anchor>
        </Anchors>
    </Button>
    <Button inherits="Poker_TableBrowserHeader" name="$parentHeaderHost" id="2"➥
text="POKER_BROWSER_HOST">
        <Size>
            <AbsDimension x="90" y="24"/>
        </Size>
        <Anchors>
            <Anchor point="LEFT" relativePoint="RIGHT" relativeTo="$parentHeaderName"/>
        </Anchors>
    </Button>
    <Button inherits="Poker_TableBrowserHeader" name="$parentHeaderPlayers" id="3"➥
text="POKER_BROWSER_PLAYERS">
        <Size>
            <AbsDimension x="50" y="24"/>
        </Size>
        <Anchors>
            <Anchor point="LEFT" relativePoint="RIGHT" relativeTo="$parentHeaderHost"/>
        </Anchors>
    </Button>
```

```
<Button inherits="Poker_TableBrowserHeader" name="$parentHeaderBlinds" id="5"➥
text="POKER_BROWSER_BLINDS">
     <Size>
        <AbsDimension x="50" y="24"/>
     </Size>
     <Anchors>
        <Anchor point="LEFT" relativePoint="RIGHT"➥
relativeTo="$parentHeaderPlayers"/>
     </Anchors>
   </Button>
</Frames>
```

This creates four headers in our list and leaves a small space at the right side. We will add a scroll bar there later in this chapter. The buttons all have an ID that will be passed to the sort function when the button is clicked. We are using the IDs 1, 2, 3, and 5 here. We skip ID 4 because the third column actually stores two values: the current players and the maximum number of players for that table.

We need to add the following lines to our localization file to get the correct text on our buttons:

```
POKER_BROWSER_NAME = "Table Name"
POKER_BROWSER_HOST = "Host"
POKER_BROWSER_PLAYERS = "Players"
POKER_BROWSER_BLINDS = "Blinds"
```

A Short Overview of Our XML

The whole file should now have the following structure, as our header buttons are children of the frame that was used for the backdrop:

```
<Ui...>
   <Button name="Poker_TableBrowserHeader"...>
      ...
   </Button>
   <Frame name="Poker_TableBrowser"...>
      ...
      <Frames>
         <Button name="$parentClose"...>
            ...
         </Button>
         <Frame name="$parentTableList">
            ...
            <Frames>
               <Button name="$parentHeaderName"...>
                  ...
               </Button>
               <Button name="$parentHeaderHost"...>
                  ...
               </Button>
```

```
              <Button name="$parentHeaderPlayers"...>
                 ...
              </Button>
              <Button name="$parentHeaderBlinds"...>
                 ...
              </Button>
           </Frames>
        </Frame>
     </Frames>
  </Frame>
</Ui>
```

It is important to keep in mind an overview of the structure of your XML as it grows larger and larger as you add new frames. We'll see a final summary of this file at the end of the chapter as well.

We now need to fill the list of tables with entries. The entries are also buttons.

Creating a Template for the Entries

We need a template for a button that represents an entry in the list. We cannot use the element `<ButtonText>` here as we need one text element for each column (and each button spans all four columns). But this is no problem, because buttons can have layers. So what we need is a button that contains four `<FontString>` elements in one layer. We will use the default layer here, which is ARTWORK.

An entry button calls the function `Poker_TableBrowser.SelectEntry` when it is clicked and the function `Poker_TableBrowser.JoinSelectedTable` when we double-click it. We also use the `OnEnter` and `OnLeave` handlers to get nice mouse-over effects. The following code must be added at the beginning of our XML file (but after the `<Ui>` element), as it shows a suitable template for our entry.

```
<Button name="Poker_TableBrowserEntry" hidden="true" virtual="true">
   <Size>
      <AbsDimension x="328" y="24"/>
   </Size>
   <Layers>
      <Layer>
         <FontString name="$parentName" justifyH="LEFT"➥
inherits="GameFontNormalSmall">
            <Size>
               <AbsDimension x="138" y="24"/>
            </Size>
            <Anchors>
               <Anchor point="LEFT">
                  <Offset>
                     <AbsDimension x="4" y="0"/>
                  </Offset>
               </Anchor>
            </Anchors>
         </FontString>
```

```xml
            <FontString name="$parentHost" justifyH="LEFT"➥
inherits="GameFontNormalSmall">
                <Size>
                    <AbsDimension x="80" y="24"/>
                </Size>
                <Anchors>
                    <Anchor point="LEFT" relativePoint="RIGHT" relativeTo="$parentName"/>
                </Anchors>
            </FontString>
            <FontString name="$parentPlayers" justifyH="LEFT"➥
inherits="GameFontNormalSmall">
                <Size>
                    <AbsDimension x="50" y="24"/>
                </Size>
                <Anchors>
                    <Anchor point="LEFT" relativePoint="RIGHT" relativeTo="$parentHost"/>
                </Anchors>
            </FontString>
            <FontString name="$parentBlinds" justifyH="LEFT"➥
inherits="GameFontNormalSmall">
                <Size>
                    <AbsDimension x="60" y="24"/>
                </Size>
                <Anchors>
                    <Anchor point="LEFT" relativePoint="RIGHT"➥
relativeTo="$parentPlayers"/>
                </Anchors>
            </FontString>
        </Layer>
    </Layers>
    <Scripts>
        <OnLoad>
            getglobal(self:GetName().."BG"):Hide()
        </OnLoad>
        <OnClick>
            if not Poker_TableBrowser.IsSelected(self:GetID()) then
                Poker_TableBrowser.SelectEntry(self:GetID())
            end
        </OnClick>
        <OnDoubleClick>
            Poker_TableBrowser.JoinSelectedTable()
        </OnDoubleClick>
        <OnEnter>
            getglobal(self:GetName().."BG"):Show()
        </OnEnter>
```

```
        <OnLeave>
            if not Poker_TableBrowser.IsSelected(self:GetID()) then
                getglobal(self:GetName().."BG"):Hide()
            end
        </OnLeave>
    </Scripts>
    <NormalTexture name="$parentBG">
        <Color r="0" g="0" b="0.5" a="0.25"/>
    </NormalTexture>
</Button>
```

Despite its length, this code is not as complicated as it might look. It defines a size, a blue background texture, and a layer. The background texture will be shown only if the element is selected or hovered over. The layer contains four font strings of sizes that match the headers, and the font strings use the attribute justifyH. This attribute controls the horizontal alignment of the font string; it can be LEFT, RIGHT, or CENTER (the default).

We also have a few script handlers. The OnLoad handler might look strange because it hides the background texture when loading. This texture is used as a highlight effect, so it should only be shown if the element is selected or hovered over. This means the default state is hidden. It should also be possible to use the attribute hidden="true" in the definition of the <NormalTexture>. However, the attribute hidden is valid there but it has no effect. I don't know if this is a bug or a feature, but it doesn't work. So we have to use this OnLoad handler.

The OnClick handler calls a function that selects the current entry if it is not already selected. Double-clicking the button calls a function that joins the currently selected table. As double-clicking always involves a single click first, it will always call the OnClick handler before calling the OnDoubleClick handler. This means that the entry belonging to the button is always selected here.

The OnEnter handler shows the texture used for highlighting, while the OnLeave handler hides it if the button is not the selected button.

We can now use this template and create the actual buttons from it. By doing a little math, we can calculate that our frame has space for eight such buttons. With that many frames created from the same template, it will be better to create them with Lua.

Creating the Buttons

As mentioned earlier, the fourth argument to CreateFrame is a template from which the frame will be created. So we need to create a frame, set its ID by calling the method frame:SetID(id), and set its position. The ID will later be used by the script handlers to identify the frame.

Using Lua to Create Frames

The following code creates the buttons and should be placed in the file TableBrowser.lua:

```
local MAX_TABLES = 8 -- maximum number of entries that can be displayed

do
    local entry = CreateFrame("Button", "$parentEntry1",➥
Poker_TableBrowserTableList, "Poker_TableBrowserEntry")
    entry:SetID(1)
```

```
    entry:SetPoint("TOPLEFT", 4, -28)
    for i = 2, MAX_TABLES do
        local entry = CreateFrame("Button", "$parentEntry"..i,➥
Poker_TableBrowserTableList, "Poker_TableBrowserEntry")
        entry:SetID(i)
        entry:SetPoint("TOP", "$parentEntry"..(i - 1), "BOTTOM")
    end
end
```

The first line creates a local variable that will be available in the whole file and holds the maximum number of entries that can be displayed in our frame. The do-end block then creates the first button with the ID 1. It is anchored to the top left of its parent (that is, the frame around our list). All following buttons are created in a loop and are anchored to the previous button. Note that frames are just tables, so instead of using frame:SetID(*id*) and frame:GetID(*id*), we could simply use a field in that table. So we could also use the following code to set an identifier:

```
entry.id = i
```

Every occurrence of self:GetID() in the previous script handlers would then need to be replaced by self.id. The advantage of using the frame as a table and storing the information there is that we can place any value there, such as another table containing extensive information. An ID defined via XML (or SetID) can only be a number. The big advantage of XML-IDs is that they can be defined by using an XML attribute; that's why we used them in the headers.

Even though we are not using XML here to create these buttons, we still use SetID and GetID. Why? It does not matter which way of identifying our frames we choose, as we are simply storing a number. I prefer to use SetID and GetID if I have to store numbers and the frame is mainly created by XML code.

Create Contents for Our Buttons

Our buttons are still empty. We have to fill them with contents to get a visible result. We need a table that stores all available poker rooms, where each entry is also represented by a table. A good structure for such a table representing a poker table looks like the following code snippet (this code is not meant to be placed in the file; it just shows what an entry in the table will look like):

```
local testEntry = {
    [1] = name,
    [2] = host,
    [3] = players,
    [4] = maxPlayers,
    [5] = smallBlind,
    [6] = bigBlind
}
```

The index in this table is the ID of the header, which is useful for the function that sorts the list. The entries will be created and put in the table by the communication module of the client. This part of our code will then call an update function every time it changes something in that table. This update function then updates the GUI.

Filling the Buttons

The next thing we need is the update function that reads the entries from the poker room table. The following code shows a basic update function that reads the first `MAX_TABLES` entries from the table. It then shows the corresponding button and sets its font strings if the entry exists. Otherwise the button is hidden.

```
Poker_TableBrowser = {} -- this table stores all functions
Poker_TableBrowser.Tables = {} -- all available poker tables

function Poker_TableBrowser.Update()
    for i = 1, MAX_TABLES do
        local entry = Poker_TableBrowser.Tables[i]
        local frame = getglobal("Poker_TableBrowserTableListEntry"..i)
        if entry then
            frame:Show()
            getglobal(frame:GetName().."Name"):SetText(entry[1])
            getglobal(frame:GetName().."Host"):SetText(entry[2])
            getglobal(frame:GetName().."Players"):SetText(entry[3].."/"..entry[4])
            getglobal(frame:GetName().."Blinds"):SetText(entry[5].."-"..entry[6])
            if entry.isSelected then
                getglobal(frame:GetName().."BG"):Show()
            else
                getglobal(frame:GetName().."BG"):Hide()
            end
        else
            frame:Hide()
        end
    end
end
```

Later you will see what we can do if there are more tables available than `MAX_TABLES`. The function goes over all the buttons and sets their contents to the values from the entries in the table. If the entry has the field `isSelected` set, it will be highlighted.

But the table is still empty, as we don't have addon communication yet, so let's fill it with some test values. The following code generates a few dummy entries and then calls the update function. Place it at the end of your file; we will later remove it when we build the communication module.

```
for i = 1, MAX_TABLES do
    table.insert(Poker_TableBrowser.Tables, {
        "Test Table "..i,
        "Host "..(MAX_TABLES - i),
        i % 3 + 1, -- just dummy values
        10,
        i * 10,
        i * 20
    })
end

Poker_TableBrowser.Update()
```

If you now load the addon in-game, you will see a list of tables. But moving your mouse over the buttons or even clicking on any button produces an error message, as we haven't implemented many of the functions yet. Let's start with the function `Poker_TableBrowser.SortTables(id)`.

Sorting the List

We need to store the current state (the column the list is sorted by and the order of the sort) in two local variables outside of the `SortTables` function:

```
do
    local currSort = 1
    local currOrder = "asc"

    function Poker_TableBrowser.SortTables(id)
        if currSort == id then
            if currOrder == "desc" then
                currOrder = "asc"
            else
                currOrder = "desc"
            end
        elseif id then
            currSort = id
            currOrder = "asc"
        end
        table.sort(Poker_TableBrowser.Tables, function(v1, v2)
            if currOrder == "desc" then
                return v1[currSort] > v2[currSort]
            else
                return v1[currSort] < v2[currSort]
            end
        end)
        Poker_TableBrowser.Update()
    end
end
```

We want to sort by name in an ascending order by default (1 is the ID of the name column, so we set `currSort` to 1 to indicate that the name column should be used for sorting). Clicking one of the headers calls the function with an ID. If the list is already sorted by this ID, the function will change the order the list is sorted by. Otherwise it sorts the list ascending by the new criteria. If no ID is provided, it just re-sorts the whole table. Thus, any time we add a new entry to the table, we can just call this function with no value to put the new entry in the correct position.

The function that does the actual sorting (`function(v1, v2)`) can then access this ID and use it as a key in the table representing an entry. The `SortTables` function then calls `Poker_TableBrowser.Update()` to update the buttons.

You can now load the addon and click the headers. This will sort the list with the test entries. The next functions we are going to implement are Poker_TableBrowser.SelectEntry and Poker_TableBrowser.IsSelected.

Selecting Elements in the List

SelectEntry and IsSelected need to share a local variable that saves the current selection. SelectEntry unselects the old selection if it is not nil and then sets the new one. IsSelected just compares the current selection to the provided button ID.

```
do
    local selection = nil
    function Poker_TableBrowser.SelectEntry(id)
        if selection then
            for i = 1, MAX_TABLES do
                getglobal("Poker_TableBrowserTableListEntry"..i.."BG"):Hide()
            end
            selection.isSelected = nil
        end
        selection = Poker_TableBrowser.Tables[id]
        selection.isSelected = true
    end

    function Poker_TableBrowser.IsSelected(id)
        return Poker_TableBrowser.Tables[id] == selection
    end
end
```

You might wonder why SelectEntry goes over all the buttons and tries to hide the highlight effect. It does this because there is currently no way to get the button that is associated with an entry in the table Poker_TableBrowser.Tables without iterating over all the buttons. We could implement that capability, but it would be quite an effort just to save two lines of code and would require iterating over eight frames. We would have to keep a reference to the button in the entry that describes a poker table. We would need to update this every time we sort the tables, which would result in more code than we have now.

Another possible solution might be to store the button or the button's ID in the variable selection. But this also causes trouble when sorting the table. Note that you can currently sort the table without problems. The highlight effect of the currently selected button moves correctly to the new button after the table is sorted.

■**Note** Calls to frame:Hide(), frame:Show(), or any other method that modifies how a GUI object looks do not take effect immediately. These methods just set an internal attribute of the frame, and the changes are applied when the game renders the next frame. So you don't need to worry about flickering frames if you make several calls to such methods.

The next function we need to implement is `Poker_TableBrowser.JoinSelectedTable()`. We have to put this into the do-end block that we just created, placing it around the functions that handle the selection as we need to access the currently selected object. A good place to add it is after the line `local selection = nil` and before the function `SelectEntry`. But how can we join a game? We haven't created this part of the addon yet, so we'll just add a dummy function that prints a message to the chat:

```
function Poker_TableBrowser.JoinSelectedTable()
    if not selection then
        return
    end
    print(string.format("Joining %s's table %s", selection[2], selection[1]))
end
```

We now get a message in our chat frame if we double-click an element in the list. We will update this function later so that it will actually join the selected table, but this function stub is sufficient for now.

Our next task is to create a scroll bar so that we can handle more than eight open tables.

Scroll Frames for Lists

We need a scroll bar at the right side of our frame, but we do not need additional buttons as our scroll frame won't move the buttons. It will keep the eight buttons we have already created and modify their contents according to the current scroll position. Most scroll frames that can be found in the default UI work like that as you often only scroll through lists of buttons (think of your friends list or guild list). It would be a waste of resources to create buttons for every entry when you can simply create a fixed amount of buttons and change their contents according to the scroll position.

Templates for Scroll Frames

The default UI provides good templates and Lua functions that can be used for scroll frames of this type. The file `UIPanelTemplates.xml` defines the frame template `FauxScrollFrameTemplate` we are going to use. We can find auxiliary functions in the file `UIPanelTemplates.lua`. These templates and functions make creating a scroll bar really easy. We can just insert the following code into the `<Frames>` element of the frame containing the table list, so the scroll frame will be, like the headers and list entries, a child of $TableList.

```
<ScrollFrame name="$parentScrollFrame" inherits="FauxScrollFrameTemplate">
    <Size>
        <AbsDimension x="16" y="216"/>
    </Size>
    <Anchors>
        <Anchor point="TOPRIGHT">
            <Offset>
                <AbsDimension x="-27" y="-5"/>
            </Offset>
        </Anchor>
    </Anchors>
```

```
    <Scripts>
       <OnVerticalScroll>
          FauxScrollFrame_OnVerticalScroll(self, offset, 24,➥
Poker_TableBrowser.Update)
       </OnVerticalScroll>
    </Scripts>
</ScrollFrame>
```

The template FauxScrollFrameTemplate inherits from the template UIPanelScrollFrameTemplate, which contains children like the scroll buttons at the top and bottom of the scroll frame. It also takes care of disabling these buttons if we scroll to the very top or bottom. The only thing we need to do is to place it at the right position with a fitting size and set the script handler OnVerticalScroll.

Scrolling in a Scroll Frame

The OnVerticalScroll script handler is invoked every time you scroll the frame. It receives two arguments: the frame itself and the offset that tells you how far the scroll frame is currently scrolled down. We now need to call one of the auxiliary functions provided by Blizzard that I mentioned earlier: FauxScrollFrame_OnVerticalScroll. The function takes four arguments: the scroll frame itself, the value that tells it how far we scrolled, the height of the items in our list (24 here because our buttons are 24 pixels tall), and an update function. The following code can be found in the file UIPanelTemplates.lua and shows this relatively short, easy function:

```
function FauxScrollFrame_OnVerticalScroll(self, value, itemHeight, updateFunction)
    local scrollbar = getglobal(self:GetName().."ScrollBar");
    scrollbar:SetValue(value);
    self.offset = floor((value / itemHeight) + 0.5);
    updateFunction(self);
end
```

The function gets one of the children of the scroll frame that is created in the scroll frame template. This child is the small square in the scroll bar that indicates the current position. It then calls the method SetValue on this frame to update it to the new position.

The fourth line is the most important one; it sets the field offset in the scroll frame, which is just a table, so we can create fields here. The offset field indicates how many elements at the top are currently hidden because we have scrolled down.

To calculate the offset, the function divides how far we scrolled (value) by the height (in pixels) of the items in our list. It then rounds the result of this division to see how many whole elements we've scrolled by. Note that there is no function like math.round by default, which means that if you want to round a value, you must add 0.5 to it and then cut it off by calling math.floor.

The last line calls an update function that is provided by us; we're going to use Poker_TableBrowser.Update. The scroll frame is passed to this function, which then has to update the list. We need to update this function now or the scroll frame won't work, as it currently does not take the offset into account.

Updating the Update Function

The first thing we might want to update in this function is its head. Blizzard's auxiliary `FauxScrollFrame_OnVerticalScroll` function calls our update function with one argument, the scroll frame. But this comes with a few problems: if we use this argument we'll have to update all calls to `Update` because currently it uses no arguments. Recall that Lua does not care how many arguments a function expects when trying to call it. Missing arguments will be `nil` and additional arguments in the call are just dropped. And we actually don't need the argument, as we know the name of our scroll frame: `Poker_TableBrowserTableListScrollFrame`. The name is quite long because it is the grandchild of our original frame, but we can cope with that.

Using the Offset

What we really need to update is the following line of code, which gets an entry from the table that contains all entries:

```
local entry = Poker_TableBrowser.Tables[i]
```

We just need to add the offset here by making the following change:

```
local entry = Poker_TableBrowser.Tables[i + ➥
Poker_TableBrowserTableListScrollFrame.offset]
```

But our scroll frame still doesn't work, as it cannot know how many elements we want to have in our list. It also does not know how many elements our list can display. So we need to provide that information. The auxiliary function `FauxScrollFrame_Update` can be used for this purpose.

Calling FauxScrollFrame_Update

`FauxScrollFrame_Update` takes quite a lot of arguments, as you will see when you look up the function in the file `UIPanelTemplates.lua`. The following code shows the head of this function:

```
FauxScrollFrame_Update(
    frame, numItems, numToDisplay, valueStep,
    button, smallWidth, bigWidth,
    highlightFrame, smallHighlightWidth, bigHighlightWidth,
    alwaysShowScrollBar
)
```

The first argument is the scroll bar we are working with, the second one is the number of elements we currently have, and the third is the maximum number of elements we can display at a time. The fourth argument is the height of an element in pixels (24 for our elements). The function hides the scroll bar if it is not needed, which means if `numItems <= numToDisplay`.

The next line of the head is used to change the width of the entries in our list if the scroll bar is hidden. The argument `button` is the name of the buttons used in our list without the trailing number. It then sets all buttons to `smallWidth` if the scroll bar is shown; otherwise, it sets them to `bigWidth`. The following code excerpt illustrates this:

```
for i=1, numToDisplay do
    getglobal(button..i):SetWidth(smallWidth);
end
```

The next line of the head works like the last line but it modifies the size of only one frame here. The function does not expect the name of a frame here but the actual frame. We will use this to resize the right header, which shows the blinds of the table.

The last argument, alwaysShowScrollBar, can be set to true to prevent the bar from being hidden.

I'll omit the remaining 70 lines of this function; reading this code would be pretty boring, as it simply changes the width of a few frames and disables or enables the buttons at the scroll bar, and you would learn nothing from it.

But Blizzard does not provide any documentation for their API and templates, which means that if you are going to use another template with other auxiliary functions that are not covered in this book, you will have to read those functions in order to understand what they are doing and which arguments they expect.

So the last update to our Update function is the following call to FauxScrollFrame_Update in the first line of our function.

```
FauxScrollFrame_Update(
Poker_TableBrowserTableListScrollFrame, #Poker_TableBrowser.Tables, MAX_TABLES, 24,
"Poker_TableBrowserTableListEntry", 328, 344,
Poker_TableBrowserTableListHeaderBlinds, 60, 76
)
```

The first argument is our scroll frame, the second is the number of entries we currently have, the third is the maximum number we can display at a time, and the fourth is the height of each entry.

With the second line of arguments we tell the function the name of our buttons and their appropriate sizes. The last line tells the function to change the size of the Blinds column to an appropriate size if the scroll bar is hidden.

Creating More Dummy Entries

If we now load the addon with these modifications into World of Warcraft, we don't see any scroll frame at all, because we have only the MAX_TABLES dummy entries in our list. But we can see that the buttons have been properly resized by the update function. The code in our file that generates the dummy entries we use for testing currently looks like this:

```
for i = 1, MAX_TABLES do
    table.insert(Poker_TableBrowser.Tables, {
        "Test Table "..i,
        "Host "..(MAX_TABLES - i),
        i % 3 + 1, -- just dummy values
        10,
        i * 10,
        i * 20
    })
end
```

We can generate more dummy entries by modifying the upper bound of the for loop that generates them like this:

```
for i = 1, 2 * MAX_TABLES do
```

Loading the addon now results in a nice scrollable list. But we still need to click buttons or drag the bar to scroll it. There is a cooler way to do this.

Scrolling with the Mouse Wheel

We can also use our mouse wheel to scroll. We need the script handler OnMouseWheel, which is available for all frame types, for this. It is always called when the user scrolls the mouse wheel while the mouse is over a frame. This means we need to add this handler to our frame that contains the whole list: Poker_TableBrowserTableList. Search for $parentTableList in your XML to find this frame; we will now add the script handler OnMouseWheel to it.

This script handler receives two arguments: the frame (*self*) and *delta*, a number that determines the direction the user scrolled and how far. If this value is positive it means that the user scrolled upward; negative means downward.

The following code shows such a script handler, which uses the auxiliary function ScrollFrameTemplate_OnMouseWheel to do the actual work of scrolling. Add the following <Scripts> element to the frame $parentTableList:

```
<Scripts>
    <OnMouseWheel>
        ScrollFrameTemplate_OnMouseWheel(Poker_TableBrowserTableListScrollFrame, delta)
    </OnMouseWheel>
</Scripts>
```

The code behind that function is pretty simple:

```
function ScrollFrameTemplate_OnMouseWheel(self, value, scrollBar)
    scrollBar = scrollBar or getglobal(self:GetName() .. "ScrollBar");
    if ( value > 0 ) then
        scrollBar:SetValue(scrollBar:GetValue() - (scrollBar:GetHeight() / 2));
    else
        scrollBar:SetValue(scrollBar:GetValue() + (scrollBar:GetHeight() / 2));
    end
end
```

It scrolls down if we move the mouse wheel down and up if we move it up. The third argument of this auxiliary function, scrollBar, is optional and represents the scrollbar that should be used. The default value for this is self:GetName()..ScrollBar which is fine for us as our scroll frame template's scroll bar name is called $parentScrollBar, so we don't need this third argument. It is only required if your scroll bar is not anchored to your scroll frame or if the name of that scroll bar is not ScrollBar.

While adding the scroll, however, we broke the code that selects items. This code doesn't take the offset into account. We need to fix that.

Fixing the Selection

We need to change the functions Poker_TableBrowser.SelectEntry(*id*) and Poker_TableBrowser.IsSelected(*id*). In the former function we have to change the line that currently just says selection = Poker_TableBrowser.Tables[id] to the following by adding the offset:

```
selection = Poker_TableBrowser.Tables[id + ➡
Poker_TableBrowserTableListScrollFrame.offset]
```

The IsSelected function needs the same change; we can do this by updating the return statement to the following:

```
return Poker_TableBrowser.Tables[id + Poker_TableBrowserTableListScrollFrame.offset]➡
== selection
```

The selection now also works while scrolling, and we now have a nice scrollable list that works exactly as we expect. The first part of the table browser is finished. The next part is creating the three buttons under this list.

More Buttons and Static Popup Dialogs

The first button under the list can be used to join the currently selected game, which is fairly easy. The next one shows a popup that asks you to enter a name. This is slightly more complicated, but the default UI provides us with some functions that can create these *static* popup dialogs, so-called because their contents are defined at load time and usually not changed afterward. The third button can be used to host a poker table, which needs to show a frame with a few check boxes and sliders that allow us to set some options for our game.

We need to create these three buttons. They will be anchored to the frame containing the table list, so these buttons must come after this frame in the XML. The end of your XML file should look like this at the moment:

```
        </Frames> <!--closing tag for children of Poker_TableBrowserTableList-->
      </Frame> <!--closing tag for Poker_TableBrowserTableList-->
      <!-- new buttons will be placed here -->
    </Frames> <!--closing tag for children of Poker_TableBrowser -->
  </Frame> <!--frame Poker_TableBrowser-->
</Ui> <!--closing tag for the root element-->
```

Our buttons will be children of the frame Poker_TableBrowser, so they have to be placed in its <Frames> element. They will be anchored to Poker_TableBrowserTableList, so they have to be placed at the marked position after the closing tag of that frame in the code just shown.

More Buttons

Creating those buttons is easy. We have a good template that can be used, so we just need to set each button's anchor, size, and OnClick handler. The following XML code creates three buttons right under our table list:

```
<Button name="$parentJoin" text="POKER_BROWSER_JOIN"➡
inherits="UIPanelButtonTemplate">
   <Size>
      <AbsDimension x="100" y="24"/>
   </Size>
   <Anchors>
      <Anchor point="TOPLEFT" relativePoint="BOTTOMLEFT"➡
relativeTo="$parentTableList">
```

```
            <Offset>
                <AbsDimension x="4" y="-8"/>
            </Offset>
        </Anchor>
    </Anchors>
    <Scripts>
        <OnClick>
            Poker_TableBrowser.JoinSelectedTable()
        </OnClick>
    </Scripts>
</Button>
<Button name="$parentEnterName" text="POKER_BROWSER_ENTER_NAME"➥
inherits="UIPanelButtonTemplate">
    <Size>
        <AbsDimension x="100" y="24"/>
    </Size>
    <Anchors>
        <Anchor point="LEFT" relativePoint="RIGHT" relativeTo="$parentJoin">
            <Offset>
                <AbsDimension x="23" y="0"/>
            </Offset>
        </Anchor>
    </Anchors>
    <Scripts>
        <OnClick>
            Poker_TableBrowser.ShowEnterNameDialog()
        </OnClick>
    </Scripts>
</Button>
<Button name="$parentCreateTable" text="POKER_BROWSER_CREATE_TABLE"➥
inherits="UIPanelButtonTemplate">
    <Size>
        <AbsDimension x="100" y="24"/>
    </Size>
    <Anchors>
        <Anchor point="LEFT" relativePoint="RIGHT" relativeTo="$parentEnterName">
            <Offset>
                <AbsDimension x="23" y="0"/>
            </Offset>
        </Anchor>
    </Anchors>
    <Scripts>
        <OnClick>
            Poker_TableBrowser.ShowCreateTableDialog()
        </OnClick>
    </Scripts>
</Button>
```

The first button is anchored to the top left of the table list. The second button is then anchored to the first, and the third to the second. The first button just calls `Poker_TableBrowser.JoinSelectedTable()` when you click it. The second button calls the function `Poker_TableBrowser.ShowEnterNameDialog()`, and the third calls `Poker_TableBrowser.ShowCreateTableDialog()`.

You will also need the following lines in your localization file to add text to these buttons:

```
POKER_BROWSER_JOIN = "Join Table"
POKER_BROWSER_ENTER_NAME = "Enter a Name"
POKER_BROWSER_CREATE_TABLE = "Create Table"
```

We have already written the function for the first button, `JoinSelectedTable`. Let's continue with the second button, which shows a simple dialog that asks you to enter a name. It then calls another function with this name, which will later try to contact the host of this game and join it.

Static Popup Dialogs

Static popup dialogs are used by the default UI almost everywhere. For example, the dialog you see when you die is one of them. When someone tries to resurrect you, you get a static popup dialog that asks if you want to accept this resurrection. So these dialogs can be used for simple yes/no questions or information boxes with just an OK button. You can choose the text that is displayed on these buttons.

But what we need is a dialog where the user can enter text and then click an OK or a Cancel button. Such dialogs can also be created with static popups; for example, the friends frame uses such a dialog when you try to add a new friend.

Digging Through the Default UI

It is always a good idea to look at the source code of the default UI when you are trying to create something that looks and works like that UI. So let's examine the file `Interface\FrameXML\FriendsFrame.xml`. The interesting part of this quite long file is the button `FriendsFrameAddFriendButton` and its `OnClick` handler, shown in the following code:

```
if ( UnitIsPlayer("target") and UnitCanCooperate("player", "target") ) then
    AddFriend(UnitName("target"));
else
    StaticPopup_Show("ADD_FRIEND");
end
```

It checks whether your current target is a player by calling `UnitIsPlayer(unitId)`. If this player is a member of your faction, it then directly adds him or her to your friend list. But the interesting part is the `else` block. The code here calls the function `StaticPopup_Show` and provides the argument `"ADD_FRIEND"`.

We can find this function in the file `Interface\FrameXML\StaticPopup.lua`. The function is quite long, so I'm not going to print the whole thing here. Here are the first few lines of the function:

```
function StaticPopup_Show(which, text_arg1, text_arg2, data)
   local info = StaticPopupDialogs[which];
   if ( not info ) then
     return nil;
   end
   -- ...
```

The function takes four arguments: the first one identifies the dialog that will be shown and the next three arguments are additional information that will be included in this dialog. This function is useful for confirmation dialogs like "Do you really want to destroy *<item>*?"

The code then uses the provided string as a key in a table that is stored in the global variable StaticPopupDialogs. The rest of the function creates the dialog from the entry in this table. So we need to create an entry in this table that describes a popup with an edit box.

Creating Simple Popups

An entry in StaticPopupDialogs is always a table. It can contain various fields that describe how the popup looks. Some fields may contain functions that are executed on certain events, for example when the user clicks on a button. Let's start with a very simple example that shows a simple popup saying "Hello, World" with an OK button. The following code creates an entry in StaticPopupDialogs and calls StaticPopup_Show to show that entry. It can be directly executed in-game with a mod like TinyPad.

```
StaticPopupDialogs["TEST"] = {
   text = "Hello, World!",
   button1 = "Okay",
   timeout = 0 -- required element, 0 means no timeout
}
StaticPopup_Show("TEST")
```

This code creates and displays a popup saying "Hello, World" with an OK button. The field timeout must be set either to 0 or to a time in seconds after which the frame is automatically closed. The game uses string.format on the value of the field text. The second and third arguments passed to the show functions are used to format the string. So if you change the field text to "Hello, %s!" and the call to the show function to StaticPopup_Show("TEST", "someone") you get a popup saying "Hello, someone!".

If we also want a Cancel button, we can just add the following line to the table:

```
button2 = "Cancel"
```

This creates a second button in the frame, with the text "Cancel". It is also possible to add a third button, by using the field button3. The third button will be placed between the first and second. It is not possible to create a fourth button. We don't need to worry about creating those buttons or positioning them, as that is all done by the default UI. If we click one of these buttons, the frame closes. But we don't know which button is pressed at the moment. We need event handlers to determine that.

The function stored in the field OnAccept is executed when button1 is pressed, OnCancel is executed when the user clicks button2, and the event handler for the third button is OnAlt. These event handler functions receive two arguments: the frame that is used by the dialog and the data that was passed as the fourth argument to StaticPopup_Show when the frame was created. This data can be anything—for example, a table with additional information about the displayed popup.

The return value of each of these three event handlers controls whether the frame will be hidden when the user clicks the corresponding button. The frame will stay open if the function returns a true value.

Creating More Advanced Popups

We need more options and script handlers to create a frame with an edit box. Table 5-1 lists all available options and event handlers for static popup dialogs.

Table 5-1. *Attributes and Event Handlers for Popups*

Name	Type	Description
DisplayButton2	function	Called when the frame is shown. If the function returns true, the second (Cancel) button will be shown; otherwise, it is hidden. Note that this function is only available for the second button; there is no entry for DisplayButton3.
EditBoxOnEnterPressed	function	Called when the user presses Enter while in the edit box.
EditBoxOnEscapePressed	function	Called when the user presses Esc while in the edit box.
EditBoxOnTextChanged	function	Called every time the user changes the text in the edit box.
OnAccept	function	Called when the user clicks the first button.
OnAlt	function	Called when the third button is clicked.
OnCancel	function	Called when the second button is clicked.
OnHide	function	Called when the frame is hidden.
OnShow	function	Called when the frame is shown.
OnUpdate	function	Called every frame while the frame is visible.
StartDelay	function	A function that returns the time (in seconds) before the first (OK) button will be enabled.
button1	string	The text for the OK button.
button2	string	The text for the Cancel button.
button3	string	The text for the Alt button.
cancels	string	The ID of another popup. The other popup will be closed when this popup is opened.

Name	Type	Description
delayText	string	The text used for the OK button while the start delay is active. The string is processed by `string.format` before it is shown. The first argument is the second argument passed to the show function, the second argument is the remaining time in minutes or seconds. The third argument is "Minutes" or "Seconds". It uses minutes if the remaining time is longer than 60 seconds, seconds otherwise.
exclusive	Boolean	Hides all other frames with this attribute when the dialog is shown.
hasEditBox	Boolean	Creates an edit box in the popup.
hasItemFrame	Boolean	Creates a frame that shows an item. The fourth argument (*data*) that is provided to `StaticPopup_Show` must be a table with the fields `link` and `texture`. `link` contains an item link and `texture` the path to the texture of this item.
hasMoneyFrame	Boolean	Creates a frame that can display a money value.
hasMoneyInputFrame	Boolean	Creates a frame that allows the user to input a money value.
hasWideEditBox	Boolean	Creates a wider edit box than `hasEditBox`.
hideOnEscape	Boolean	Hides the popup if the user presses escape.
interruptCinematic	Boolean	Interrupts cinematic sequences when the popup is shown.
maxLetters	Boolean	Maximum number of characters that can be entered in the edit box.
multiple	Boolean	Allows you to have more than one instance of the popup open at the same time.
noCancelOnReuse	Boolean	Prevents the call to the `OnCancel` function if `StaticPopup_Show` is called while the popup is already shown and `multiple` is not set.
notClosableByLogout	Boolean	The frame stays visible when you start to log out.
showAlert	Boolean	Shows a warning icon in the popup.
sound	string	A sound that is played when the popup is shown.
text	string	The displayed text.
timeout	number	A time in seconds after which the dialog is automatically closed. 0 means that the frame is never closed. This value must be set or you will get an error message.
whileDead	Boolean	Allows the popup to be open while the player is dead.

As you can see, there are enough options to build almost every popup that you are going to need for your addon. Let's create the popup we need for our poker mod now.

Creating Our Popup

I previously mentioned the ADD_FRIEND popup dialog, which is very similar to the one we need. Like all static popups used by the game, it can be found in the file Interface\FrameXML\ StaticPopup.lua. The following code shows a slightly modified version of this popup that can be used by our poker mod. The edit box frame is stored under the key editBox of the frame representing the dialog. This frame is passed as the first argument (self) to most event handlers. Event handlers that are related to the edit box, like EditBoxOnEnterPressed, directly receive this edit box frame as first argument. As always, refer to Appendix A for additional information about edit boxes and their methods. Place the following code at the end of the file TableBrowser.lua:

```
StaticPopupDialogs["POKER_JOIN_TABLE"] = {
    text = POKER_ENTER_NAME_DIALOG,
    button1 = ACCEPT,
    button2 = CANCEL,
    hasEditBox = 1,
    maxLetters = 12,
    OnAccept = function(self)
        Poker_TableBrowser.JoinTableByName(self.editBox:GetText())
    end,
    OnShow = function(self)
        self.editBox:SetFocus()
    end,
    OnHide = function(self)
        if (ChatFrameEditBox:IsShown()) then
            ChatFrameEditBox:SetFocus()
        end
        self.editBox:SetText("")
    end,
    EditBoxOnEnterPressed = function(self)
        Poker_TableBrowser.JoinTableByName(self:GetText())
        self:GetParent():Hide()
    end,
    EditBoxOnEscapePressed = function(self)
        self:GetParent():Hide()
    end,
    timeout = 0,
    whileDead = 1,
    hideOnEscape = 1
}

function Poker_TableBrowser.ShowEnterNameDialog()
    StaticPopup_Show("POKER_JOIN_TABLE")
end

function Poker_TableBrowser.JoinTableByName(name)
    print(string.format("Trying to join %s's table.", name))
end
```

You will have to add the following line to your localization file to get the correct text in the dialog:

```
POKER_ENTER_NAME_DIALOG = "Please enter the host's name of the table ➥
you want to join"
```

The global variables `ACCEPT` and `CANCEL` are provided by the game and contain localized texts for Accept and Cancel. The game already defines many localized strings; you can find them in the file `Interface\FrameXML\GlobalStrings.lua`.

This code creates a dialog with an edit box that takes up to 12 characters (the maximum length of a name) with two buttons. Clicking Accept or pressing Enter while in the edit box calls `Poker_TableBrowser.JoinTableByName(name)`; clicking Cancel or pressing Escape hides the frame. Note that pressing Escape while the edit box is selected does not trigger the default escape handler, which hides the dialog, so we need the `EditBoxOnEscapePressed` handler.

The focus is automatically set to the edit box when this dialog is shown. Only one text box in the UI can have the focus at a given time. The edit box that has the focus is the one that receives all key presses. The `OnHide` handler makes sure that the focus is transferred back to the chat frame's edit box if it is shown.

Let's move to the third button, which allows us to host our own table. We need more frame types like sliders and check boxes for this.

More Frame Types

What we need is a frame with a few options. We need to set the following options for a new poker game:

- The name of the table

- The maximum number of players

- The blinds

- Whether to allow/disallow certain player groups (your guild, the current group, friend list, and so on) to join your game

So we need frames of the following types: an edit box to set the name, a few sliders to set the numeric values like the blinds, and check boxes to set the permissions. But we need another normal frame to hold all these other frames before we can start creating these new frame types.

Another Normal Frame

We already know how to create such a frame, so we can basically just copy and paste the old frame that we already created. Let's start with the opening tag. Place the following code at the end (but before `</Ui>`) of `TableBrowser.xml`:

```
<Frame name="Poker_CreateTable" parent="UIParent" frameStrata="DIALOG"➥
hidden="true" movable="true" enableMouse="true" clampedToScreen="true"➥
toplevel="true">
</Frame>
```

Our new frame has the name `Poker_CreateTable` and an additional attribute: `toplevel`. This attribute makes sure that our frame is always above all other frames with the same strata that do not have this attribute.

A Size and an Anchor

The next thing we need is a size and an anchor. The following XML creates a frame in the middle of the screen that is big enough for our options. Note that this position is just our default position, as we will use `frame:SetUserPlaced(1)` later.

```
<Size>
    <AbsDimension x="250" y="320"/>
</Size>
<Anchors>
    <Anchor point="CENTER"/>
</Anchors>
```

A Backdrop

We also need a standard backdrop. The following code creates one for us:

```
<Backdrop bgFile="Interface\DialogFrame\UI-DialogBox-Background"
          edgeFile="Interface\DialogFrame\UI-DialogBox-Border" tile="true">
    <BackgroundInsets>
        <AbsInset left="11" right="12" top="12" bottom="11"/>
    </BackgroundInsets>
    <TileSize>
        <AbsValue val="32"/>
    </TileSize>
    <EdgeSize>
        <AbsValue val="32"/>
    </EdgeSize>
</Backdrop>
```

We now have a frame that can be shown when we call the method `Poker_CreateTable:Show()`.

Showing the Frame

We add the capability to display the frame into the Create Game button by adding the following function to our Lua file:

```
function Poker_TableBrowser.ShowCreateTableDialog()
    Poker_CreateTable:Show()
end
```

Layers

We now need to add the element `<Layers>` to create a title for our frame. This element is filled with the different layers, which contain the actual textures and font strings:

```
<Layers>
    <Layer level="ARTWORK">
        <Texture name="$parentTitle" file="Interface\DialogFrame\UI-DialogBox-Header">
            <Size>
                <AbsDimension x="275" y="64"/>
            </Size>
            <Anchors>
                <Anchor point="TOP">
                    <Offset>
                        <AbsDimension x="0" y="12"/>
                    </Offset>
                </Anchor>
            </Anchors>
        </Texture>
        <FontString inherits="GameFontNormal" text="POKER_CREATE_TITLE">
            <Anchors>
                <Anchor point="TOP" relativeTo="$parentTitle">
                    <Offset>
                        <AbsDimension x="0" y="-14"/>
                    </Offset>
                </Anchor>
            </Anchors>
        </FontString>
    </Layer>
</Layers>
```

We also need to add the following line to our localization file to get the correct title:

```
POKER_CREATE_TITLE = "Host Game"
```

Script Handlers

The next thing we need is the `<Scripts>` element, to make our frame draggable and to save its position:

```
<Scripts>
    <OnLoad>
        self:RegisterForDrag("LeftButton")
        self:SetUserPlaced(1)
    </OnLoad>
    <OnDragStart>
        self:StartMoving()
    </OnDragStart>
```

```
<OnDragStop>
    self:StopMovingOrSizing()
</OnDragStop>
</Scripts>
```

We now have an empty, draggable frame with a backdrop and a title. But isn't this duplicate code? We already wrote the same code for the last frame we created. Well, yes it is. We could also have created a template that defines the backdrop, title region, and script handlers. I didn't take that approach because starting the chapter by creating a template for such a frame would have been confusing. We would have worked on this template without seeing anything in the game, as a template it not visible.

Exercise: Templates

You can see this as an exercise: create a template for a frame like the one we just created and rewrite our frames to use this template.

Here's a tip to get you started: use the name attribute of the <FontString> element that holds the title. For example, if you choose the name TitleText, you can use the following code in the OnLoad handler to set the title of the frame:

```
getglobal(self:GetName().."TitleText"):SetText("some title")
```

Edit Boxes

We saw edit boxes earlier, in our static popup dialog. Let's take a closer look at them and create one for our frame. The name of the edit box frame type is EditBox. So let's create a simple edit box in our frame.

Simple Edit Boxes

We could also create a template for the edit box, but it is very unlikely that we are going to need another edit box in this addon. Blizzard does not provide a simple template that could be used here, so we will have to create everything by hand. The following code shows a very simple edit box and should be placed in the <Frames> element of the frame Poker_CreateTable:

```
<EditBox name="$parentTableName" letters="25">
    <Size>
        <AbsDimension x="180" y="20"/>
    </Size>
    <Anchors>
        <Anchor point="TOPLEFT">
            <Offset>
                <AbsDimension x="30" y="-40"/>
            </Offset>
        </Anchor>
    </Anchors>
    <FontString inherits="GameFontHighlight"/>
</EditBox>
```

We use the attribute `letters` with a value of 25 here. This limits the maximum number of characters the user can enter in the edit box to 25. Edit boxes have many attributes; for example, it is possible to create edit boxes that accept only numbers. You can find all available attributes and elements in Appendix A.

The next few lines set the size and position of our edit box. The element `<FontString>` sets the font that is used by the edit box; we are using `GameFontHighlight` to get a white text.

You can load this XML in the game and open the frame, but you won't see an edit box. You will just see a blinking cursor in your frame, and you can enter text there.

▆Caution The edit box will take the focus away from your chat frame, and we don't have a Close button yet. If you want to reload your interface, you must click on a player or channel in the chat to the get the chat edit box back. You can also create a macro that reloads your user interface.

Textures and Font Strings for Edit Boxes

Like all frames, an edit box begins without any texture. You have to add every texture by hand by using the `<Layers>` element. Create this element and add the following `<Layer>` element to it to get a border around the edit box:

```
<Layer level="BACKGROUND">
    <Texture name="$parentLeft" file="Interface\ChatFrame\UI-ChatInputBorder-Left">
        <Size>
            <AbsDimension x="32" y="32"/>
        </Size>
        <Anchors>
            <Anchor point="LEFT">
                <Offset>
                    <AbsDimension x="-14" y="0"/>
                </Offset>
            </Anchor>
        </Anchors>
        <TexCoords left="0" right="0.125" top="0" bottom="1.0"/>
    </Texture>
    <Texture name="$parentRight" file="Interface\ChatFrame\UI-ChatInputBorder-Right">
        <Size>
            <AbsDimension x="32" y="32"/>
        </Size>
        <Anchors>
            <Anchor point="RIGHT">
                <Offset>
                    <AbsDimension x="6" y="0" />
                </Offset>
            </Anchor>
        </Anchors>
```

```
        <TexCoords left="0.875" right="1.0" top="0" bottom="1.0"/>
    </Texture>
    <Texture name="$parentMiddle" file="Interface\ChatFrame\UI-ChatInputBorder-Right">
        <Size>
            <AbsDimension x="1" y="32"/>
        </Size>
        <Anchors>
            <Anchor point="LEFT" relativeTo="$parentLeft" relativePoint="RIGHT"/>
            <Anchor point="RIGHT" relativeTo="$parentRight" relativePoint="LEFT"/>
        </Anchors>
        <TexCoords left="0" right="0.9375" top="0" bottom="1.0"/>
    </Texture>
</Layer>
```

Quite a lot of XML code just to get a border for an edit box. Sadly, there is no template provided by the default UI for a simple edit box, so we have to create everything by hand. If you are writing an addon that needs more than one edit box, you should definitely create a template for this.

Let's look at the code. It defines three textures: one for the right border, one for the left border, and a third one anchored to the left and right borders, filling the space between them. The TexCoords elements in the textures are used to transform to the texture; you will learn more about this in Chapter 8 when we take a closer look at textures.

The next thing we need is text to the left of our edit box that says "Table Name". We can put this in the same layer as the textures:

```
<FontString name="$parentText" inherits="GameFontNormalSmall"➥
text="POKER_CREATE_TABLE_NAME">
    <Anchors>
        <Anchor point="TOPLEFT" relativeTo="$parent" relativePoint="TOPLEFT">
            <Offset>
                <AbsDimension x="-4" y="13"/>
            </Offset>
        </Anchor>
    </Anchors>
</FontString>
```

You will also have to add the following line to your localization file:

```
POKER_CREATE_TABLE_NAME = "Table Name"
```

We have a nice edit box now. Next we need sliders to set the blinds and the maximum number of players.

Sliders

A *slider* is a UI element that can be used to set a numeric value. The name of this frame type is Slider.

Slider Basics

We'll use the following slider to set the maximum number of players. Place this code in the `<Frames>` element of the frame `Poker_CreateTable` right after the closing tag of the `<EditBox>` element:

```
<Slider name="$parentPlayers" minValue="2" maxValue="10" defaultValue="10"➡
valueStep="1" inherits="OptionsSliderTemplate">
   <Anchors>
      <Anchor point="TOPLEFT">
         <Offset>
            <AbsDimension x="20" y="-90"/>
         </Offset>
      </Anchor>
   </Anchors>
   <Scripts>
      <OnLoad>
         getglobal(self:GetName().."Low"):SetText("2")
         getglobal(self:GetName().."High"):SetText("10")
      </OnLoad>
      <OnValueChanged>
         getglobal(self:GetName().."Text"):SetFormattedText(POKER_CREATE_MAXPLAYERS,➡
value)
      </OnValueChanged>
   </Scripts>
</Slider>
```

We are using the template `OptionsSliderTemplate` here, which basically defines all textures used by the slider, as well as three font strings and the default size. You can find this template in the file `Interface\FrameXML\OptionsFrame.xml`. The code is not very interesting, so I'll omit it here.

The attribute `minValue` sets the minimum value for the slider, `maxValue` the maximum value, `defaultValue` the start value, and `valueStep` the step. The `OnLoad` script handler sets the font strings `Low` and `High`, which are defined by the template, to 2 and 10. These font strings are placed at the left and right borders of the slider.

You will also need the following line in your localization file for the `OnValueChanged` handler:

```
POKER_CREATE_MAXPLAYERS = "Max Players: %d"
```

But what does the method `SetFormattedText` in the `OnValueChanged` handler do?

The OnValueChanged Handler

The `OnValueChanged` handler is invoked every time the user changes the value and when the frame is created with a default value. It receives the arguments *self* and *value*, where *value* is the new value of the slider. The method `fontString:SetFormattedText(string, ...)` is basically equivalent to `fontString:SetText(string:format(...))`. The only difference is the performance, and we will take a closer look at performance later in this book. For now, use `SetFormattedText` instead of an additional `string.format`.

Caution The OnValueChanged handler is invoked before the OnLoad handler if your slider has a default value. So you can't rely on anything set in the OnLoad handler there.

More Sliders

We need sliders for the small and big blind settings. The code also makes sure that the big blind value is always greater than twice the small blind. Place these sliders right after the old slider in the XML:

```
<Slider name="$parentSmallBlind" minValue="1" maxValue="250" defaultValue="10"➥
valueStep="1" inherits="OptionsSliderTemplate">
    <Anchors>
        <Anchor point="TOP" relativePoint="BOTTOM" relativeTo="$parentPlayers">
            <Offset>
                <AbsDimension x="0" y="-12"/>
            </Offset>
        </Anchor>
    </Anchors>
    <Scripts>
        <OnLoad>
            getglobal(self:GetName().."Low"):SetText("1")
            getglobal(self:GetName().."High"):SetText("250")
        </OnLoad>
        <OnValueChanged>
            getglobal(self:GetName().."Text"):SetFormattedText(POKER_CREATE_SMALLBLIND,➥
value)
            local bigBlindSlider = getglobal(self:GetParent():GetName().."BigBlind")
            if not bigBlindSlider then
                return
            end
            local bigBlind = bigBlindSlider:GetValue()
            if 2 * value > bigBlind then
                bigBlindSlider:SetValue(2 * value)
            end
        </OnValueChanged>
    </Scripts>
</Slider>

<Slider name="$parentBigBlind" minValue="2" maxValue="500" defaultValue="20"➥
valueStep="1" inherits="OptionsSliderTemplate">
    <Anchors>
        <Anchor point="TOP" relativePoint="BOTTOM" relativeTo="$parentSmallBlind">
            <Offset>
                <AbsDimension x="0" y="-12"/>
            </Offset>
```

```
            </Anchor>
        </Anchors>
        <Scripts>
            <OnLoad>
                getglobal(self:GetName().."Low"):SetText("2")
                getglobal(self:GetName().."High"):SetText("500")
            </OnLoad>
            <OnValueChanged>
                getglobal(self:GetName().."Text"):SetFormattedText(POKER_CREATE_BIGBLIND,➥
value)
                local smallBlindSlider = getglobal(self:GetParent():GetName().."SmallBlind")
                local smallBlind = smallBlindSlider:GetValue()
                if 2 * smallBlind > value then
                    smallBlindSlider:SetValue(math.floor(value/2))
                end
            </OnValueChanged>
        </Scripts>
</Slider>
```

Each slider's `OnValueChanged` handler changes the value of the other slider to the appropriate value if it is too small/big. Note that the `OnValueChanged` handler of the small blind handler is invoked for the first time when the slider is created. This is before the second slider exists. The code needs to return in this case as the second slider does not exist yet.

We also need to add the variables that are used in our `OnLoad` and `OnValueChanged` handlers to our localization file, or we will get an error message and no text:

```
POKER_CREATE_SMALLBLIND = "Small Blind: %d"
POKER_CREATE_BIGBLIND = "Big Blind: %d"
```

The other options we need are check boxes to set the permissions. Check boxes are called *check buttons* in World of Warcraft.

Check Buttons

A check button is another quite simple UI element, and Blizzard provides a good template that can be used here: `OptionsCheckButtonTemplate`. So we don't need to worry about textures here.

The following XML code creates four buttons that can be used to set the permissions. It needs to be placed right after the sliders in the `<Frames>` element as it anchors to the sliders.

```
<CheckButton name="$parentAllowEveryone" inherits="OptionsCheckButtonTemplate">
    <Anchors>
        <Anchor point="TOPLEFT" relativePoint="BOTTOMLEFT"➥
relativeTo="$parentBigBlind">
            <Offset>
                <AbsDimension x="0" y="-5"/>
            </Offset>
        </Anchor>
    </Anchors>
    <Scripts>
```

```
      <OnLoad>
         getglobal(self:GetName().."Text"):SetText(POKER_CREATE_EVERYONE)
      </OnLoad>
   </Scripts>
</CheckButton>
<CheckButton name="$parentAllowGuild" inherits="OptionsCheckButtonTemplate">
   <Anchors>
      <Anchor point="TOPLEFT" relativePoint="BOTTOMLEFT"➡
relativeTo="$parentAllowEveryone"/>
   </Anchors>
   <Scripts>
      <OnLoad>
         getglobal(self:GetName().."Text"):SetText(POKER_CREATE_GUILD)
      </OnLoad>
   </Scripts>
</CheckButton>
<CheckButton name="$parentAllowGroup" inherits="OptionsCheckButtonTemplate">
   <Anchors>
      <Anchor point="TOPLEFT" relativePoint="BOTTOMLEFT"➡
relativeTo="$parentAllowGuild"/>
   </Anchors>
   <Scripts>
      <OnLoad>
         getglobal(self:GetName().."Text"):SetText(POKER_CREATE_GROUP)
      </OnLoad>
   </Scripts>
</CheckButton>
<CheckButton name="$parentAllowFriends" inherits="OptionsCheckButtonTemplate">
   <Anchors>
      <Anchor point="TOPLEFT" relativePoint="BOTTOMLEFT"➡
relativeTo="$parentAllowGroup"/>
   </Anchors>
   <Scripts>
      <OnLoad>
         getglobal(self:GetName().."Text"):SetText(POKER_CREATE_FRIENDS)
      </OnLoad>
   </Scripts>
</CheckButton>
```

The code creates four buttons that are anchored to the previous element. Note that the text is just a font string in a layer that is defined in the template. So we have to use SetText in the OnLoad handler to set its text. There is no attribute for this, as it is a part of the template, not a part of the frame type CheckButton. You will need the following lines in your localization file to get the correct texts displayed:

```
POKER_CREATE_EVERYONE = "Allow Everyone to Join"
POKER_CREATE_GROUP = "Allow Group Members to Join"
POKER_CREATE_GUILD = "Allow Guild Members to Join"
POKER_CREATE_FRIENDS = "Allow Friends to Join"
```

We now need to add an OK and a Cancel button.

OK and Cancel Buttons

The Cancel or Close button is quite simple; it just hides its parent. As with all the controls we have added here, the following code needs to be added to the <Frames> element of the frame Poker_CreateTable:

```
<Button name="$parentClose" text="POKER_BROWSER_CLOSE"➥
inherits="UIPanelButtonTemplate">
   <Size>
      <AbsDimension x="100" y="24"/>
   </Size>
   <Anchors>
      <Anchor point="BOTTOMLEFT">
         <Offset>
            <AbsDimension x="20" y="15"/>
         </Offset>
      </Anchor>
   </Anchors>
   <Scripts>
      <OnClick>
         self:GetParent():Hide()
      </OnClick>
   </Scripts>
</Button>
```

This button is anchored to the bottom right of our frame and just calls the Hide method of its parent. The OK/Create button is slightly more complicated, as it needs to retrieve the value from all the sliders. The following code creates this button:

```
<Button name="$parentCreate" text="POKER_BROWSER_CREATE_TABLE"➥
inherits="UIPanelButtonTemplate">
   <Size>
      <AbsDimension x="100" y="24"/>
   </Size>
   <Anchors>
      <Anchor point="BOTTOMRIGHT">
         <Offset>
            <AbsDimension x="-20" y="15"/>
         </Offset>
      </Anchor>
   </Anchors>
```

```
    <Scripts>
      <OnClick>
        local parent = self:GetParent():GetName()
        Poker_TableBrowser.CreateGame(
           getglobal(parent.."TableName"):GetText(),
           getglobal(parent.."Players"):GetValue(),
           getglobal(parent.."SmallBlind"):GetValue(),
           getglobal(parent.."BigBlind"):GetValue(),
           getglobal(parent.."AllowEveryone"):GetChecked(),
           getglobal(parent.."AllowGuild"):GetChecked(),
           getglobal(parent.."AllowGroup"):GetChecked(),
           getglobal(parent.."AllowFriends"):GetChecked()
        )
        self:GetParent():Hide()
      </OnClick>
    </Scripts>
  </Button>
```

The method `editBox:GetText()` retrieves the text of an edit box, `slider:GetValue()` can be used to return the value of a slider, and the method `checkButton:GetChecked()` returns 1 if the check box is checked, or `nil` otherwise. You can write the following dummy function to test whether our frame is working:

```
function Poker_TableBrowser.CreateGame(...)
   print("Creating game...")
   print(...)
end
```

It will just print all the arguments provided to it. We will build the function that creates the actual game in Chapter 7 after we learn about some advanced programming techniques in the next chapter.

An Overview of the Whole XML File

At this point we have created quite a big XML file that might look extremely complicated. But it is actually pretty easy, so let's examine its structure. The following code shows the whole XML file without unnecessary information; that is, it shows only the frames with their names and children:

```
<Ui xmlns="http://www.blizzard.com/wow/ui/"
xmlns:xsi="http://www.w3.org/2001/XMLSchema-instance"
xsi:schemaLocation="http://www.blizzard.com/wow/ui/ ..\FrameXML\UI.xsd">
   <!-- List header template -->
   <Button name="Poker_TableBrowserHeader" virtual="true">
      ...
   </Button>
```

```
<!-- List entry template --->
<Button name="Poker_TableBrowserEntry" virtual="true" ...>
   ...
</Button>

<!-- the main frame --->
<Frame name="Poker_TableBrowser" ...>
   ...
   <Frames>
      <Button name="$parentClose" ...>
         ...
      </Button>
      <Frame name="$parentTableList"> <!-- the list --->
         ...
         <Frames>
            <Button name="$parentHeaderName" ...>
               ...
            </Button>
            <Button name="$parentHeaderHost" ...>
               ...
            </Button>
            <Button name="$parentHeaderPlayers" ...>
               ...
            </Button>
            <Button name="$parentHeaderBlinds" ...>
               ...
            </Button>
            <ScrollFrame name="$parentScrollFrame" ...>
               ...
            </ScrollFrame>
         </Frames>
      </Frame>
      <Button name="$parentJoin" ...>
         ...
      </Button>
      <Button name="$parentEnterName" ...>
         ...
      </Button>
      <Button name="$parentCreateTable" ...>
         ...
      </Button>
   </Frames>
</Frame>
```

```
<!-- Create table dialog --->
<Frame name="Poker_CreateTable" ...>
    ...
    <Frames> <!-- all available options for the new game --->
        <EditBox name="$parentTableName" ...>
            ...
        </EditBox>
        <Slider name="$parentPlayers" ...>
            ...
        </Slider>
        <Slider name="$parentSmallBlind" ...>
            ...
        </Slider>
        <Slider name="$parentBigBlind" ...>
            ...
        </Slider>
        <CheckButton name="$parentAllowEveryone" ...>
            ...
        </CheckButton>
        <CheckButton name="$parentAllowGuild" ...>
            ...
        </CheckButton>
        <CheckButton name="$parentAllowGroup" ...>
            ...
        </CheckButton>
        <CheckButton name="$parentAllowFriends" ...>
            ...
        </CheckButton>
        <Button name="$parentCreate" ...>
            ...
        </Button>
        <Button name="$parentClose" ...>
            ...
        </Button>
    </Frames>
  </Frame>
</Ui>
```

The whole file is about 600 lines long; quite a lot for just a simple menu. We will see a few ways that allow us to build simple configuration menus without touching a single line of XML in Chapter 10, when we discuss libraries. But a handcrafted configuration menu is often more powerful and looks better than an automatically created one.

Summary

In this chapter you learned how to use XML to create frames and saw various different frame types with their different attributes and elements. This book does not present examples of all the frame types that are available, but Appendix A lists all of them with all attributes, elements, script handlers, and methods. The focus here was on creating configuration menus, as such a menu is needed in almost every addon.

You also learned about inheritance and creating frame templates with XML. This knowledge helped us when we created the first frame of our poker mod by using XML with a few lines of Lua code.

You need to learn more about Lua before we can continue working on our poker addon. The next chapter will again work with Lua without World of Warcraft at all. It will focus on advanced programming techniques and provide more details about Lua.

CHAPTER 6

■ ■ ■

Advanced Lua

You've already used a lot of Lua code in the example mods in the last two chapters. The basic Lua knowledge you acquired in Chapter 2 was sufficient to write some cool mods. But Lua can do even more, and you can write even more powerful mods like the still missing parts of our poker addon.

You can execute all the examples in this chapter in a standard Lua interpreter. But you are now familiar with executing Lua in World of Warcraft, so feel free to use the built-in Lua engine in the game.

This chapter deals with functional and object-oriented programming in Lua, and it shows implementations of common data structures like linked lists in Lua. We'll use the programming techniques in this chapter to complete our poker addon in the next chapters, so make sure to read this chapter carefully before moving on to Chapter 7.

More About Functions

We've already discussed the basics, but functions can do a lot more than you've seen. Lua is a great functional language, so functions play an important role in Lua programming. You will see how local variables are related to functions and how we can use this relationship.

Static Scoping

As you have worked with local variables, you might have wondered what happens if you have a construct like this:

```
do
    local x = 5
    function foo()
        print(x)
    end
end -- the scope of x ends here
x = 1 -- sets the global variable x to 1
foo() --> 5
```

It prints 5, because Lua uses *lexical* (also known as *static*) scoping. This means that the function foo in our example does not care about the global x. A function always refers to the context in which it was created, and never to the context it is called in. So even changing the line 8 statement x = 1 to local x = 1 does not change the result. The function still refers to its local x.

Closures

Functions are, like all other values, first-class values. This means that functions can take functions as arguments or even return other functions. All functions in Lua can do this, and such functions are called *higher-order functions.*

So let's look at a function that creates another function and returns it. And we'll add another interesting thing, by creating a local variable before returning the function. Because of Lua's lexical scoping, this local variable is then visible in the returned function. The following code snippets belong together and should be placed in one Lua file:

```
function createCounter()
    local x = 0
    return function()
        x = x + 1
        print(x)
    end
end
```

The createCounter function creates a local variable, initializes it with x, and returns a function that prints the local variable and increments it. We can call createCounter and save the return value (a reference to a function) in a local variable. I'll again indicate the output of each function with a --> comment.

```
c1 = createCounter()
c1() --> 1
c1() --> 2
c1() --> 3
```

This works as we expected. The local variable x is visible in the returned function, so c1 is a simple counter. But what happens if we try to create a second counter?

```
c2 = createCounter()
print(c1 == c2)  --> false
```

The first thing we notice is that c1 and c2 are not referencing the same function, because executing the function() ... end part creates a new function. So let's test whether our new counter also works:

```
c2() --> 1
c2() --> 2
c2() --> 3
```

The second counter also works correctly. But what happened to our old counter? The second call to `createCounter` obviously set the local variable x to 1 again. So let's test c1:

```
c1() --> 4
c1() --> 5
c2() --> 4
```

This time, Lua created a new local variable x for our second counter. Both counters are completely independent of each other, even though both are referencing a local variable that seems to be the same.

The first counter function saved the local variable that existed when it was created. Only the created function knows that this variable even exists; it is not possible to access or modify this local variable from another function.

It is also possible that such a variable can be referenced by more than one function. Our function `createCounter` could return more than one function; for example. it could also return a function to decrement the counter or one that returns the current value of x.

A function that preserves the context it was created in is called a *closure*. The conserved variables that can be accessed by closures are called *upvalues* in Lua. So a closure is a function bound to its scope, conserving local variables accessed by the function. Executing a `function() ... end` expression generates a new closure of that function; the original function acts as a *prototype* for that closure. Note that all functions created in Lua are actually closures. But in many cases only one closure of a given prototype exists, because the block (for example, a file) that creates the closure is executed only once.

More than one function can be bound to the same context. Let's expand our previous counter example:

```
function createCounter(start)
    local x = start or 0

    return {
        incrementAndPrint = function()
            x = x + 1
            print(x)
        end,

        decrementAndPrint = function()
            x = x - 1
            print(x)
        end,

        getCurrentValue = function()
            return x
        end
    }
end
```

Recall what you have learned about tables: They can store any values. So of course they can store functions. Our `createCounter` now creates three closures bound to the same context. They are packed into a table and returned by the function. Because functions can return more than one result, it would also be possible just to return all three functions. But putting them in a table clearly indicates that these three functions belong together. So we can now create our new and improved counter:

```
c1 = createCounter()  --> uses the default value 0
c1.incrementAndPrint() --> 1
c1.decrementAndPrint() --> 0
print(c1.getCurrentValue())  --> 0


c2= createCounter(5)  --> a new counter starting with 5
c2.incrementAndPrint()  --> 6
print(c2.getCurrentValue())  --> 6


c1.incrementAndPrint() --> 1 the first one still works
```

All three functions are bound to the same scope (which consists of the variable x), and it is still no problem to have more than one counter. All counters work independently of each other, and only the three functions from the same counter are sharing the same upvalue.

Closures are a very powerful concept in functional programming languages. And Lua is a great functional programming language.

Recursion, Part 1: Tail Calls

When Lua calls a function, it always needs to store the place from which the function was called somewhere, as it needs to jump back there when the function returns. It stores this location in a place called the call *stack*. We will discuss what stacks are later in this chapter; but for now, it's important to know that this stack has a limited size. So if you have a massive recursive function, it might fill the stack. It will then *overflow* if you try to do an additional function call. This overflow generates an error message, and your program terminates. You can test it by writing a simple never-ending function:

```
function foo()
   foo()
   return -- not required, Lua also returns when encountering the end of a function
end

foo()
```

You will get the error message `stack overflow`, because when calling `foo` Lua saves the point where execution should resume after `foo` returns. For the first call to `foo`, this would be the line directly after `foo`. Now `foo` calls itself and Lua stores the line after `foo` as the point to return to after this call. But this return point is the statement `return`. So it is somewhat pointless to store this. It could instead just keep the old return point to which the following `return` statement would jump. You can do this in Lua with the technique known as *tail calls*:

```
function foo()
    return foo()
end

foo()
```

■**Caution** Do not test this example as it freezes your Lua interpreter! That means if you try this in World of Warcraft, it will freeze your game.

This results in an infinite loop, as additional calls to foo do not require additional space on the stack. Tail calls are all direct function calls in return statements. So anything in the form return f(...) is a tail call. Any code that performs additional operations on the return value of the called function is not a tail call. For example, recall our function to calculate the factorial of a number from Chapter 2; the recursive call return n * fac(n - 1) is not a tail call. Note that a tail call can call any other function, not only itself. You will see some tail calls in the examples in this chapter and the next.

Recursion, Part 2: Recursive Table Functions

You have already seen many imperative programs with some elements from functional languages in this book. One of our first functions was the function to calculate the factorial of a number. It was a special function, as it called itself. Such functions are called *recursive* functions and can be very powerful.

Let's look at another recursive function, one that allows us to copy a table. Note that you cannot copy a table with an assignment, as it copies only a reference. When copying a table, we have to iterate over it and call the same function again if we encounter another table in that table.

What happens if your table contains these *shared subtables*? Consider the following table:

```
local tbl = {
    {1}
}
tbl[2] = tbl[1]
```

A simple copy function would produce a table with the same structure. But the entries 1 and 2 in the copied table would not reference the same table. So our function needs to keep track of tables already copied.

Or imagine you have a table with *cyclic references*, as in the following example where the table stores a reference to itself:

```
local tbl = {}
tbl[1] = tbl
```

The simple copy function would call itself until the stack overflows. We won't get an infinite loop, as we cannot use a tail call here.

We need to write a function that uses an additional table to track the tables it has already copied to create an appropriate copy. The following code illustrates such a function:

```lua
function copyTable(tbl, copied)
    copied = copied or {}
    local copy = {}
    copied[tbl] = copy
    for i, v in pairs(tbl) do
        if type(v) == "table" then
            if copied[v] then
                copy[i] = copied[v]
            else
                copy[i] = copyTable(v, copied)
            end
        else
            copy[i] = v
        end
    end
    return copy
end
```

The function takes two arguments: the table to copy (*tbl*) and the helper table (*copied*), which contains already copied tables. This second argument is optional, so you don't need to call it with an additional empty table. The local variable copy is initialized with a new table and this new copy is stored in the table copies under the key tbl (which is the original table).

A for loop then goes over all entries in the table to copy and checks whether the type of an entry is table or another type. If it finds a table, it checks whether it has already copied this table. If that is the case, it stores a reference to the already copied table. Otherwise, it recursively calls itself to copy the table, providing the table copied as its second argument. If the value is not a table, it is just copied.

We can now test our function with test cases like the following table, which contains shared subtables and a cyclic reference:

```lua
local t = {1, 2, {3}}
t[4] = t[3]
t[5] = t
local t2 = copyTable(t)

print(t2[4] == t2[3]) --> true
print(t2[5] == t2) --> true
print(t2[5][4][1]) --> 3
```

The last test might look strange. Note that t2[5] references the same table as t2 does, so this reference is equal to t2[4][1]. Also, t2[4] is a reference to t2[3], and this table contains one entry with the value 3.

Many other programming languages come with a function that provides this functionality. It is often called *deep copy*, as it goes deep into the array using recursion. Normal copy functions would just copy references to subtables.

Hooking

Hooking is a technique that allows you to create a function (called the *hook*) that is called every time Lua calls a given other function (the *hooked* function). You can define a function that is called before or after the original function is called. Your function can alter the arguments passed to the original function or even prevent a call to the original function if it is called before that function. If it is called after the original function, it can modify its return values. Hooking is especially common in World of Warcraft development, as it allows you to modify the behavior of another addon or the default user interface.

Let's look at simple code that hooks the function print to add a time stamp. We are going to use the functions os.time(), which returns the current Unix time (seconds elapsed since January 1, 1970), and os.date(format, time), which turns a Unix time stamp into a human-readable format. The first argument to os.date is a string that specifies the format to use. We use the format "%H:%M:%S", in which %H is replaced with the current hour, %M with the minute, and %S the current second.

```
do
    local old = print --> Assign a new reference
    print = function(...) --> Redefine the print command
        return old(os.date("%H:%M:%S", os.time()), ...) --> new print command
    end
end

print("Hello, World!")  --> 05:41:19  Hello, World!
```

As you can see, hooking is pretty simple in Lua. You just save a reference to the function you want to hook and overwrite the old global variable that references the function. The do… end block is used only to limit the scope of the local variable old, which holds the reference to the old function. We need to store that reference, as we are going to overwrite the real print function. Our new function then makes a tail call to the original print function, but it injects the current time as the first argument.

The tail call is not only a better coding style than simply calling old here; it also ensures that the return values of the old function are not lost, as they would be if we didn't store them anywhere. The print function doesn't return anything, but imagine you are in an environment where many Lua scripts have access to the global variables, as in World of Warcraft. No one can guarantee that you are still accessing the original print. Another addon might have already hooked into it and tried to add a return value. This addon would then expect a return value that you had removed, which might break the other addon.

It is also easy to modify the return values or to prevent the call to the original function:

```
function foo(arg)
    print("foo was called with the argument", arg)
    return arg
end

print(foo("Hello")) --> foo was called with the argument Hello
--> Hello
```

```
do
    local old = foo
    foo = function(arg)
        if arg == "Hello" then
            return
        else
            return old(arg).."!"
        end
    end
end

print(foo("Hello")) --> nothing happens
print(foo("Hi")) --> foo was called with the argument Hi
--> Hi!
```

Note that the third return is no longer a tail call, as it modifies the result of old before returning. The hook prevents calling foo with the argument "Hello" and attaches an exclamation mark to the result of the old foo if the argument is not "Hello". Such a hook could also be used to prevent print from printing certain messages.

A SIMPLE ADDON THAT DISPLAYS CHAT TIME STAMPS BY USING A HOOK

Creating a mod that displays time stamps in the chat frame works just like the example that displayed time stamps in print. We need to hook the function ChatFrame1.AddMessage.

The function ChatFrame1.AddMessage expects to be called with the colon operator. Remember that the colon operator silently adds the table the function is stored in as first argument to the call. So we need to pass this first argument to the old function. The second argument is the message to be displayed, which we will modify by adding the current time. The function also takes a few additional arguments (for example, the color of the message), but we don't need to care about them. We'll simply use the vararg parameter to represent them. So the following code should do the trick.

```
do
    local old = ChatFrame1.AddMessage
    ChatFrame1.AddMessage = function(self, msg, ...)
        return old(self, date("%H:%M:%S ", time())..msg, ...)
    end
end
```

Keep in mind that the functions date and time from the os library are not in the table os in World of Warcraft. You can copy this code into a Lua file and create an appropriate TOC file to load your mod.

But the code is so simple and short that if you just want to test that it works, you can simply enter the code via /script <code> or through your favorite in-game editor.

More About the Generic for Loop

So far whenever we have used the `pairs(tbl)` or `ipairs(tbl)` functions it has been with the generic for loop. Both return an iterator function that does the hard work. We are now going to write our own iterators.

We will create an iterator that works like the iterator returned by `ipairs`. It traverses the array part of a table. This function (the iterator) will be called by Lua to get the elements from a data structure (the array) until it returns `nil`. The following example illustrates when and how the iterator is called:

```lua
function iterator(tbl, key)
   print("Called iterator with tbl = "..tostring(tbl)..", key = "..tostring(key))
   if key == nil then
      return 1, tbl[1] -- return the first key/value pair if key is nil
   else
      key = key + 1 -- get the next key...
      if tbl[key] then
         -- ...and return it with its associated value if it exists
         return key, tbl[key]
      else
         return nil -- we iterated over all elements, let's break the loop
      end
   end
end

t = {"a", "b", "c"}

for i, v in iterator, t do
   print("Loop: i = "..i..", v = "..tostring(v))
end
```

This script produces the following output:

```
Called iterator with tbl = table: 0032A458, key = nil
Loop: i = 1, v = a
Called iterator with tbl = table: 0032A458, key = 1
Loop: i = 2, v = b
Called iterator with tbl = table: 0032A458, key = 2
Loop: i = 3, v = c
Called iterator with tbl = table: 0032A458, key = 3
```

So the function always receives the table to iterate over as its first argument. The second argument is the key of the last call. So key is `nil` for the first call, and the function must return the first key/value pair in this case. The iterator always returns the current key and a list of values until the last element is reached. It then returns `nil` and breaks the loop.

This iterator is not very useful, as Lua already provides such an iterator. But as an example it's designed to show how exactly that iterator is called in such a loop. The next section covers data structures, and you will see more iterators there that can be used to traverse other data structures.

Using Tables to Build Data Structures

Tables are very important and powerful in Lua. They can be used to implement all data structures, from simple arrays to complex graphs. The data structures we are going to discuss are part of many other programming languages, but Lua provides only tables. So we have to build these data structures ourselves. Virtually all scripts written in Lua use tables. You are going to use tables all the time, so it is important to understand them. You already know the basics about creating tables, so this section focuses on using them in your code.

■**Note** Remember that Lua uses one-based arrays, which means the first index is 1. Many other programming languages use zero-based arrays.

Arrays

The simplest data structure that can be created by using tables is the array. Arrays start with the index 1. The following code fragments belong together and should be placed in one file. A simple array looks like this:

```
local a = {2, 3, 5, 7, 11, 13, 17}
```

```
print(a[1]) --> 2
print(a[5]) --> 11
print(a[10]) --> nil
print(#a) --> 7
```

Arrays grow and shrink dynamically as you add or remove elements:

```
a[8] = 19
print(#a) --> 8
```

```
a[8] = nil
a[7] = nil
print(#a) --> 6
```

Every table is an array as long as its indices are consecutive integers. Using other indices uses the hash table part of the table. The length operator # only works for the array part.

Creating multidimensional arrays is also simple. You just create an array of arrays:

```
local a = {
    {2, 3, 5, 7},
    {1, 4, 9, 16}
}
print(a[1]) --> table: 0032A458
print(a[1][1]) --> 2
print(a[2][3]) --> 9
print(a[1][9]) --> nil
print(a[6][1]) --> error: attempt to index field '?' (a nil value)
```

Stacks

Stacks are another kind of quite simple data structure. This data structure works like a real-world stack; you can put something on top of the stack (this operation is called *push*), and you can remove the element that is on the top of the stack (*pop* it). The following shows a stack in Lua:

```
do
    local t = {}
    function push(v)
        t[#t + 1] = v
    end
    function pop()
        local v = t[#t]
        t[#t] = nil
        return v
    end
end

push("a")
push("b")
print(pop()) --> b
print(pop()) --> a
print(pop()) --> nil
```

Doubly Linked Lists

Doubly linked lists are a useful data structure that is easy to implement by using tables. Such a list consists of *nodes*, which each store data and a reference to the next and the previous node in the list. A singly linked list stores only one reference. The *head* of the list is a table that stores a reference to the first and last element. Nodes are also just tables, with three fields representing the previous node, the next node, and data. The following diagram shows a doubly linked list with three nodes. The field data, which is empty in this illustration, can store an arbitrary value. The arrows indicate references.

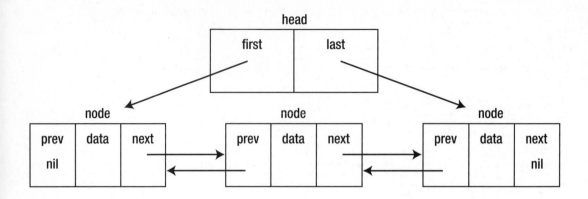

The advantage of linked lists over arrays is that lists allow us to insert or remove elements at arbitrary positions without shifting elements around. It is also easy to get from a given element to the next or previous one without knowing the index of the element. But a disadvantage compared to arrays is that there is no way to get the *n*th element of a linked list without traversing the list to count the elements. We will use such lists when we have to remove or insert elements in the middle of the list. Arrays are a better choice when we need to access a field by its index. In Chapter 9 you will see an addon that uses doubly linked lists.

Recall that tables are always passed as references, never as values. So it is easy to create doubly linked lists:

```lua
function newList()
   return {first = nil, last = nil} -- empty list head
end

function insertAfter(list, node, data)
   local new = {prev = node, next = node.next, data = data} -- creates a new node
   node.next = new -- the node after node is the new node
   if node == list.last then -- check if the old node is the last node...
      list.last = new -- ...and set the new node as last node
   else
      -- otherwise set the next nodes previous node to the new one
      new.next.prev = new
   end
   return new -- return the new node
end

function insertAtStart(list, data)
   local new = {prev = nil, next = list.first, data = data} -- create the new node
   if not list.first then -- check if the list is empty
      list.first = new -- the new node is the first and the last in this case
      list.last = new
```

```lua
    else
        -- the node before the old first node is the new first node
        list.first.prev = new
        list.first = new -- update the list's first field
    end
    return new
end

function delete(list, node)
    if node == list.first then -- check if the node is the first one...
        -- ...and set the new first node if we remove the first
        list.first = node.next
    else
        -- set the previous node's next node to the next node
        node.prev.next = node.next
    end
    if node == list.last then -- check if the node is the last one...
        -- ...the new last node is the node before the deleted node
        list.last = node.prev
    else
        node.next.prev = node.prev -- update the next node's prev field
    end
end

function nextNode(list, node)
    return (not node and list.first) or node.next
end
```

That looks like a lot of complicated code. But it is actually pretty simple. The function newList creates a table with two entries, first and last. These entries will store references to the first and last entries in our list, so they are nil if the list is empty.

The function insertAfter(*list, node, data*) takes a list created by newList, a node after which the new node will be inserted, and the data to store in the new node. The function then creates the new node. The new node's prev field is the node after which it is inserted, and the next field is the node after the old node. The function then updates the next field of the old node to point to the new node. It then checks whether the node after which we want to insert is the last node and updates the list's last field if necessary. If node is not the last node, it must have a next field pointing to another node. The function then modifies the prev field of the node after node to point to the new node. The following diagram illustrates how insertAfter works. It shows a section of a doubly linked list with the elements a and b. We want to insert the element c after the element a in this list, which means the first step is creating this element with references to a and b.

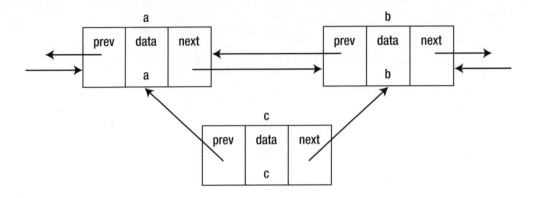

This is the first step. The next step is shown in the second diagram, where the function now modifies the next field of a and the prev field of b so that they both point to c.

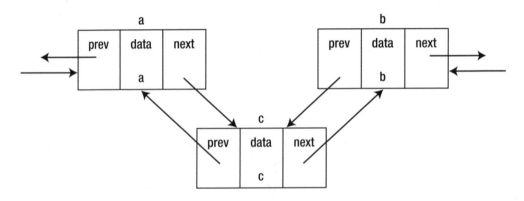

We now have a valid list with an additional element c between a and b.

The second function, insertAtStart(list, data), inserts a new node at the beginning of the list. It basically works like insertAfter, but it needs to handle the case in which the list is empty.

The function delete(*list, node*) can be used to delete a given node from the list. It needs to update the list's first and last fields if we try to delete the first or last node; otherwise it just adjusts the next field of the previous node and the prev field of the next node.

The last function, nextNode, can be used to traverse the linked list. It takes two arguments, *list* and *node*. The former is a linked list and the latter is the current element. It then returns the node after the provided node (which may be nil) or the first node from the list if *node* is nil. So this function can be used as an iterator for the generic *for*. Lua will call nextNode for all elements in the list to get the next. The current node is passed as second argument and is nil to get the first node. The for loop ends when nextNode returns nil. This happens when the last node is reached.

Other functions that are useful with doubly linked lists are insertAtEnd, insertBefore, and an iterator that starts with the last node and traverses the list backwards. It should be an easy task for you to implement them based on the provided functions.

Now, let's use that doubly linked list in a short example. You will see more uses for linked lists in the example mods discussed in the following chapters.

```lua
local l = newList()
local a = insertAtStart(l, "a")
local b = insertAtStart(l, "b")
local c = insertAtStart(l, "c")
local d = insertAfter(l, c, "d")
for node in nextNode, l do
    print(node.data)
end
print("----")
delete(l, b)
delete(l, c)
for node in nextNode, l do
    print(node.data)
end
```

The output looks like this:

```
c
d
b
a
----
d
a
```

After the first three calls to `insertAtStart`, the list looks like this: `"c" --> "b" --> "a"`. The call to `insertAfter` adds the element "d" between "c" and "b". So the output is c d b a. We then try to delete the elements b and c by calling `delete`. The output d a is the expected one, so our linked list works.

Note that we could pass an optional second argument to the iterator in the generic `for` loop to start with an arbitrary element. The following code prints only b and a.

```lua
for node in nextNode, l, d do
    print(node.data)
end
```

Cyclic lists are also possible and easy; just set the last element's `next` field to the first node and the first element's `prev` field to the last node. But don't try to use `nextNode` as an iterator on such a cyclic list, as it would never return **nil**, resulting in an infinite loop.

Graphs

Graphs are another interesting and useful data structure. A graph consists of nodes connected via arcs. Examples of addons that make use of graphs include QuestHelper and Gatherer. Another is Howling Fjord, illustrated in Figure 6-1.

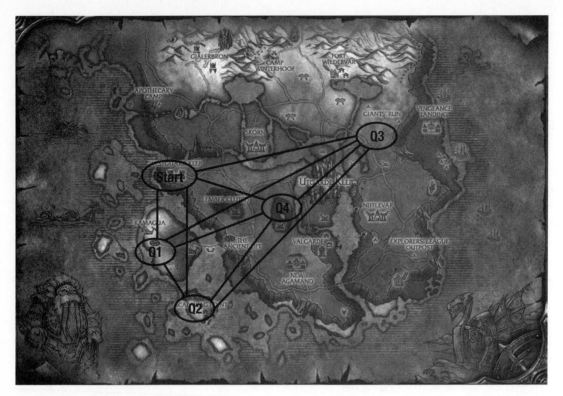

Figure 6-1. *A graph in Howling Fjord*

Imagine you are in Howling Fjord's Westguard Keep and have four open quests. A good quest addon should now calculate the optimal round trip starting and ending in Westguard Keep. This situation can be represented by using an undirected, weighted graph. *Undirected* means there are no one-way streets; *weighted* means the connections between points have a length. The points where you have to do the quests are the nodes (*vertices*), and the weight of the *edges* (connections) is the distance between two nodes.

Figure 6-1 shows the situation; we have five nodes connected via 10 edges. The following table represents this graph:

```lua
local graph = {
    Start = {Q1 = 10, Q2 = 20, Q3 = 45, Q4 = 25},
    Q1 = {Start = 10, Q2 = 10, Q3 = 50, Q4 = 30},
    Q2 = {Start = 30, Q1 = 10, Q3 = 55, Q4 = 35},
    Q3 = {Start = 45, Q1 = 50, Q2 = 55, Q4 = 20},
    Q4 = {Start = 25, Q1 = 30, Q2 = 35, Q3 = 20}
}
```

The table stores all nodes and the distances between them; such a table is also called an *adjacency matrix*. Note that the weight of each edge is stored twice, as the distance between A and B is the same as between B and A. We could optimize this representation by dropping redundant entries, but for simplicity we will work with this table.

All nodes are represented as strings, so we need another table that stores more information about these points:

```lua
local info = {
   Start = {x = 28, y = 42, type = "QuestHub"},
   Q1 = {x = 27, y = 65, type = "Quest",  objectives = "..."},
   Q2 = {x = 33, y = 76, type = "Quest",  objectives = "..."},
   Q3 = {x = 68, y = 32, type = "Quest",  objectives = "..."},
   Q4 = {x = 50, y = 53, type = "Quest",  objectives = "..."}
}
```

We use the name of the node as the key in `info` to get additional information about a node. Note that it would also be possible to use the table that stores the information directly as the key in `graph` instead of the strings. A real addon would do that, as the approach has many advantages, but using strings as indices is simpler and clearer for our graph example.

To return to our original problem, we want to find the shortest round trip that visits all nodes starting and ending at `Start`. We face what's known as the *traveling salesman problem*.

We have n nodes, so we have n - 1 possibilities for our first step, n - 2 for the second, and so on, because we can't travel to the current node and we don't want to visit an already visited node. There is no difference between the paths `Start -> Q1 -> Q2 -> Q3 -> Q4 -> Start` and `Start -> Q4 -> Q3 -> Q2 -> Q1 -> Start`, because the direction doesn't matter. So there are (n - 1)!/2 possible round trips for a graph with n nodes. A simple algorithm would just calculate the length of all available paths and return the shortest.

This might work well for our example with n = 5. But we can have up to 25 quests. Or imagine we want to write an addon like Gatherer. There are hundreds of points of interest in a zone like Howling Fjord. Our addon would need years to find the shortest path.

There is no algorithm that can find the shortest round trip in a reasonable (polynomial) time. However, there are algorithms that are faster by a magnitude than the brute force solution. But these algorithms not only require knowledge of advanced math, they are also extremely complicated and therefore far beyond the scope of this book.

But there are algorithms that can find a short path (though not necessarily the shortest) in a relatively short time. A simple algorithm that finds a round trip is the *nearest neighbor* algorithm:

```lua
function findRoundTrip(start)
   local visited = {
      [start] = true,
   }
   local path = {start}
   local currNode = start
   while true do
      local shortest = nil
      for node, distance in pairs(graph[currNode]) do
      -- search for the nearest neighbor
         if distance < (shortest and shortest.distance or math.huge)
         and not visited[node] then
            shortest = node
         end
      end
```

```
        if shortest then
            currNode = shortest
            visited[shortest] = true
            path[#path + 1] = shortest
        else -- we visited all nodes, return to the first one...
            path[#path + 1] = start
            break -- ...and break the loop
        end
    end
    for i, v in ipairs(path) do -- print the result
        print(v)
    end
end
findRoundTrip("Start")
--> Start
--> Q4
--> Q3
--> Q1
--> Q2
--> Start
```

This code uses the constant `math.huge` from the math library; no number can be bigger than this constant, as it stands for infinity.

The function is pretty simple. It looks for the nearest neighbor that has not been visited yet and appends it to the path. The solution is obviously faster than the brute force solution as it only looks for the shortest edge to a not visited node for every node instead of comparing all possible paths. It finds a short round trip for most graphs, but it is unlikely that this function finds the shortest path. In the worst case it might even return the longest path.

For our simple graph, the shortest path would be this:

```
Start -> Q1 -> Q2 -> Q4 -> Q3 -> Start
```

with a length of 120. The longest round trip is this:

```
Start -> Q2 -> Q4 -> Q1 -> Q3 -> Start
```

with the length 180. Our algorithm finds the path

```
Start -> Q4 -> Q3 -> Q1 -> Q2 -> Start
```

which has the length 125 and is the second shortest path available.

There are algorithms available that guarantee to find a path not longer than X times the shortest path. However, they are much more complicated and far beyond the scope of this chapter and book.

Metatables and Metamethods

All values in Lua can have what are called *metatables*. A metatable is a normal table, and you can store all types of data in it. Metatables can be used to modify the behavior of values. They allow you to overload (change an operator 's meaning in certain situations by providing a function that replaces the operation in those situations) the standard operators and even to call values such as tables as if they were functions. Simple data types like strings share the same metatable for all values of the same type, so you cannot modify the metatable of a specific string. But every table or userdata object can have its own metatable. (I won't discuss metatables of userdata objects here, as there is no way to create userdata objects for us.)

The basic functions used when working with metatables for tables are setmetatable(*table*, *metatable*) and getmetatable(*table*). The first one is used to attach a metatable to a table, and the second one returns the metatable of a table.

Overloading Operators

Metatables can define *metamethods*, which contain the new functionality of the operators and other table behavior. Metamethods are functions stored under special keys starting with two underscores inside the metatable. There are metamethods available to overload most operators, so we can create objects by using tables. The following example implements an object that represents a vector in 3-dimensional space (if you're not familiar with vector math yet, have a look at http://en.wikipedia.org/wiki/Euclidean_vector).

```
do
   local vectorMetatable = {}
   vectorMetatable.__tostring = function(self)
      return string.format("Vector: x = %f; y = %f; z = %f", self.x, self.y, self.z)
   end
   vectorMetatable.__add = function(v1, v2)
      return CreateVector(v1.x + v2.x, v1.y + v2.y, v1.z + v2.z)
   end
   vectorMetatable.__mul = function(v1, v2)
      if type(v1) == "number" then
         v1, v2 = v2, v1
      end
      if type(v2) == "number" then
         return CreateVector(v1.x * v2, v1.y * v2, v1.z * v2)
      else
         return v1.x * v2.x + v1.y * v2.y + v1.z * v2.z
      end
   end

   vectorMetatable.__eq = function(v1, v2)
      return v1.x == v2.x and v1.y == v2.y and v1.z == v2.z
   end
```

```lua
    function CreateVector(x, y, z)
        x = x or 0
        y = y or 0
        z = z or 0
        local obj = {x = x, y = y, z = z}
        return setmetatable(obj, vectorMetatable)
    end
end

v1 = CreateVector(1, 2, 3)
v2 = CreateVector(1, 0, 0)

print(v1) -- Vector: x = 1.000000; y = 2.000000; z = 3.000000
print(v1 + v2) -- Vector: x = 2.000000; y = 2.000000; z = 3.000000

print(v1 * 5) -- Vector: x = 5.000000; y = 10.000000; z = 15.000000
print(5 * v1) -- Vector: x = 5.000000; y = 10.000000; z = 15.000000
print(v1 * v2) -- 1

print(CreateVector(1, 2, 3) == v1) -- true
```

First, vectors can be created by the function CreateVector(x, y, z); the default value
for each coordinate is 0. The function stores the coordinates in a table, attaches the table
vectorMetatable to the table, and returns it. The function setmetatable returns its first argument, which allows you to write code like return setmetatable(obj, vectorMetatable).

Our test code then creates two vector objects v1 (1, 2, 3) and v2 (1, 0, 0) and tries to
perform a few operations on them.

Trying to convert v1 to a string (print calls tostring for all of its arguments) now invokes
the metamethod __tostring. It uses string.format from the string library to create the
returned string. The string.format function takes a string to format and a variable number
of arguments. %f is replaced by a floating point number, producing the output "Vector: x =
1.000000; y = 2.000000; z = 3.000000".

The next line then tries to add two vectors; this calls the __add metamethod, which adds
two vectors and returns a new vector as result. So arithmetic metamethods do not need to
return numbers; they can basically return any value.

The multiplication is done by calling the __mul metamethod. This function supports both
scalar multiplication and the scalar product. The scalar multiplication takes a number and a
vector, but we cannot predict whether the first or the second argument will be the number. We
can check if the first argument is a number and then swap v1 and v2. The scalar multiplication
is commutative, so swapping the arguments is no problem.

The __mul metamethod then checks whether its second argument is a number or another
vector. For a number the function does a scalar multiplication and returns a new vector. When
we call it with two vectors, it calculates the scalar product and returns a number.

The last line does an equality check. Two tables with the same values are not equal,
because the equality test compares whether two variables are actually referencing the same
table—the content of the table does not matter. But we defined the __eq metamethod, which
will be called every time we try to compare two vectors. This function checks to see that the
two vectors are the same.

Available Metamethods

Lua provides the following metamethods:

__add: Used by the + operator. This metamethod receives two arguments.

__call: This metamethod is invoked when you try to call the table. This function receives the table as first argument, followed by all arguments provided to the function.

__concat: The .. operator. This metamethod receives two arguments.

__div: The / operator. This metamethod receives two arguments.

__eq: The == operator. This metamethod receives two arguments.

__index: This metamethod is invoked when you access a field in the table that does not exist. This metamethod receives the table and the requested key. You can use the function rawget(table, key) to access a table without invoking this metamethod.

__le: The <= operator. This metamethod receives two arguments. It also handles the greater or equal operation with swapped arguments, as less or equal is an antisymmetric relation.

__lt: The < operator. This metamethod receives two arguments. It also handles the > operator with swapped arguments.

__len: The # operator. This metamethod cannot be used for metatables of tables; and because we can only use metatables attached to tables, we cannot use it at all.

__mod: The % operator. This metamethod receives two arguments.

__mul: The * operator. This metamethod receives two arguments.

__newindex: This metamethod is invoked when you try to assign a new value to a field that was not set before. You can use rawset(table, key, value) to circumvent this metamethod. This metamethod is not called when you change the value of an existing field.

__pow: The ^ operator. This metamethod receives two arguments.

__sub: The - operator. This metamethod receives two arguments.

__tostring: Called to get the string representation of an object. Receives the table and should return a string.

__unm: The unary - operator. This metamethod receives one argument.

Object Orientation

Lua supports prototype-based object orientation by using the __index metamethod. We can define a table that holds functions (*methods*) and values (*attributes*) that acts as a prototype for objects. This section provides an overview of object-oriented programming and how we can use it in Lua.

Object-oriented programming basically means that you create an abstract prototype (often called a *class*) in your code that is not used directly. This prototype in Lua is just a normal table. You can then create instances of this object by calling a function known as the *constructor*. Each instance has all the attributes and methods that were defined in the prototype. An instance will basically be a new table (with just a few or no values) that is created and returned by the constructor. But trying to access certain values in this table will forward the access to the table that acts as the prototype.

We used object orientation earlier, when we explored frames in Chapter 5. The constructor was the function CreateFrame. It returned a new table with just one entry, which contained a userdata value. Every time you accessed one of the methods of a frame, this access was silently forwarded to the prototype of this frame. Let's see how we can create such prototypes.

The Colon Operator

You have already used the colon operator, to call certain functions that required it. We will now define functions that expect to be called with this operator. The colon operator is also available when creating functions; it silently adds self as the first argument to the function:

```
local t = {}
function t:foo()
    print(self) --> table: some memory address
end
print(t) --> table: memory address
t:foo() --> table: the same memory address
```

This is just a short way to write the following:

```
local t = {}
function t.foo(self)
    print(self) --> table: some memory address
end
print(t) --> table: memory address
t:foo() --> table: the same memory address
```

A common mistake when working with this operator is to misuse it when hooking functions. It is just an abbreviation, nothing more. So you don't need to take precautions when hooking such functions. Writing code like the following is wrong:

```
local old = t:foo  --> error: function arguments expected near '<eof>'
```

Just hook it like any other function and remember that the first argument is self. Recall the example from the sidebar earlier in this chapter, where we hooked the function ChatFrame1.AddMessage, which needs to be called with the colon operator. We just added self as the first argument and passed it to the original function.

The __index Metamethod and Constructors

The colon operator can be used with the __index metamethod to implement prototype-based object orientation. In Chapter 2, the frames you worked with were actually objects. You can try to call getmetatable on a frame, and you will receive a table that holds the methods you were using repeatedly, like RegisterEvent. Now you are going to create your own objects.

First you create a table that contains all the functions (methods) and other values (attributes) you require. This table is our prototype. Then you create new tables, each with a metatable that forwards all accesses to the prototype. An access to a table is the attempt to retrieve a value from it, for example, x = foo.test is an access to the key test in the table foo. Let's look at a prototype table. This is a prototype for a monster with the attributes name, hp, dead, and damage. It implements the methods Attack(target), Say(text), and ReceiveHit(attacker). Note that there is actually no difference between methods and attributes. Methods are just attributes that hold functions.

The following code snippets belong together and should be placed in a single file.

```lua
local monsterPrototype = {}

monsterPrototype.name = "unnamed"
monsterPrototype.hp = 100
monsterPrototype.damage = 8
monsterPrototype.dead = false

function monsterPrototype:Attack(target)
   if target.dead then
      return self:Say("My target is already dead")
   end
   self:Say("Attacking "..target.name)
   target:ReceiveHit(self)
end

function monsterPrototype:Say(text)
   print("["..self.name.."]: "..text)
end

function monsterPrototype:ReceiveHit(attacker)
   self:Say("I'm being attacked by "..attacker.name)
   self.hp = self.hp - attacker.damage
   if self.hp <= 0 then
      self:Say("I died :(")
      self.dead = true
   end
end
```

Our monsters can attack other monsters, receive hits, and say something. But what we have is just the prototype for a monster. We now need to implement a constructor that creates a concrete instance (an actual mob to fight) from this abstract prototype (which acts as a template). You might be tempted to use a metatable containing objects like the following for your objects, where the __index metamethod receives two arguments: the table t and the requested key k.

```lua
local mt = {
   __index = function(t, k)
      return monsterPrototype[k]
   end
}
```

In fact, this works perfectly. The __index metamethod is invoked only if the requested key does not exist in the original table. But it has a slight performance impact, as there is a function call involved every time you invoke a method or access an unchanged attribute. So Lua provides a simpler way to implement this function—you can directly set the prototype table as an __index metamethod. So this is our constructor:

```
do
    local metatable = {
        __index = monsterPrototype
    }
    function CreateMonster()
        return setmetatable({}, metatable)
    end
end
```

The do...end block is just to limit the scope of metatable. It would also be possible to create the metatable inside CreateMonster. But that would create a new metatable for each object (monster), leading to unnecessary memory usage. It is no problem for our objects to share the same metatable.

Another possible metatable would be the table monsterPrototype after adding the entry __index, which references the table itself (such a cyclic structure is perfectly valid in Lua). You can replace the previous constructor with the following code:

```
monsterPrototype.__index = monsterPrototype
function CreateMonster()
    return setmetatable({}, monsterPrototype)
end
```

I like to keep the metatable separate from the prototype, so that is not the approach I'll use here. But you might encounter this way to define a metatable in the code of other addons.

Our constructor is now the function CreateMonster. Many other programming languages like Java using the name of the class as a constructor, so you can write monsterPrototype() instead of CreateMonster(). You can also do this in Lua, by using the __call metamethod in the metatable of the prototype, as in the following code snippet.

```
setmetatable(monsterPrototype, {__call = function(t, ...)
    -- place your constructor here or forward the call to the real constructor
    return CreateMonster(...)
end})
```

This metamethod receives the table t that was called, and all arguments passed to it. In this example, the call is just forwarded to the real constructor. But you could also place the whole code of your constructor here.

So let's create some monsters now:

```
local m1 = CreateMonster()
m1.name = "Orc"

local m2 = CreateMonster()
m2.name = "Bear"
m2.hp   = 15
```

```
m1:Attack(m2)
m1:Attack(m2)
m1:Attack(m2)
```

m1 is an orc, m2 a bear. The orc uses the default values for hp and damage, the bear has a reduced health value of 15. Calling m1:Attack(m2) is equivalent to m1.Attack(m1, m2). This call is forwarded to the function Attack(*self, target*) in the table monsterPrototype. *self* is m1, *target* is m2. So these three calls to attack produce the following output:

First call:
```
[Orc]: Attacking Bear
[Bear]: I'm being attacked by Orc
```

Second call:
```
[Orc]: Attacking Bear
[Bear]: I'm being attacked by Orc
[Bear]: I died :(
```

Third call:
```
[Orc]: My target is already dead
```

Everything is working as we expected.

Inheritance

Inheritance means that a class (or prototype) can derive methods and attributes from other, parent classes. Lua does not have support for classes; there are no keywords or functions that generate a class. But Lua's object orientation is very flexible in this way. Prototypes can also have metatables, so we can define a parent-prototype for all prototypes. When invoking a method, Lua will look it up first in the object table, then in the prototype table, and then in the parent of that prototype (also called the *superclass*).

This allows us to use a powerful concept—prototypes that inherit from other prototypes. The terms *class* and *prototype* will be used interchangeable in this section. The mechanism is very flexible as you can define an arbitrary function as the __index metamethod, so multiple inheritance is no problem in Lua.

But let's start with simple inheritance from one superclass. It is easy; we just attach a metatable containing the superclass as the __index metamethod to our prototype. So we could have an abstract class unit and another abstract class, attackingUnit, which uses unit as its superclass, inheriting all methods. Our old class monster would then inherit from attackingUnit. The following code snippets belong together and should be placed in a single file for testing:

```
local unitPrototype = {}
unitPrototype.name = "unnamed"
unitPrototype.hp = 100
unitPrototype.dead = false -- actually not required as it would start with nil...
-- ... and nil and false are the same for us in this example

function unitPrototype:Say(text)
   print(self.name..": "..text)
end
```

```lua
function unitPrototype:ReceiveHit(attacker)
    self:Say("I'm being attacked by "..attacker.name)
    self.hp = self.hp - attacker.damage
    if self.hp <= 0 then
        self:Say("I died :(")
        self.dead = true
    end
end


local attackingUnit = setmetatable({}, {__index = unitPrototype})
attackingUnit.damage = 5

function attackingUnit:Attack(target)
    if target.dead then
        self:Say("My target is already dead")
        return
    end
    self:Say("Attacking "..target.name)
    target:ReceiveHit(self)
end

local monsterPrototype = setmetatable({}, {__index = attackingUnit})
function monsterPrototype:GetType()
    return "Monster"
end
do
    local metatable = {
        __index = monsterPrototype
    }

    function CreateMonster()
        return setmetatable({}, metatable)
    end
end
```

We can use our old constructor and test code; it still works here. We just split up our class into more classes and added the method GetType(). This allows us to reuse code like the Attack and ReceiveHit functions when implementing more classes. We could now create a player or an NPC class that also inherits from attackingUnit. The following code snippet must be put in the same file as the last snippet, as it relies on having the classes we defined in that code.

```lua
local playerPrototype = setmetatable({}, {__index = attackingUnit})
playerPrototype.hp = 1000
playerPrototype.damage = 60
function playerPrototype:GetType()
    return "Player"
end
```

```
do
   local metatable = {
      __index = playerPrototype
   }
    function CreatePlayer()
      return setmetatable({}, metatable)
   end
end

local m1 = CreateMonster()
m1.name = "Orc"

local p1 = CreatePlayer()
p1.name = "Tandanu"

p1:Attack(m1)
p1:Attack(m1)
```

A player has more health than a monster and does more damage. The test code easily kills the orc, as it just got hp = 100, and a player deals 60 damage per attack. You can overwrite any attribute or method in derived classes.

Multiple Inheritance

Multiple inheritance is a bit more complicated than single inheritance. It means that one class can inherit methods from more than one parent. Let's split up our example into even more classes: we'll add the class unit, which defines basic attributes (like the name) and basic methods like ReceiveHit. The prototype attackingUnit then extends this prototype and adds a method to attack another unit. The prototype talkingUnit also inherits from unit and adds the ability to say something. We then create the prototype monster, which inherits from attackingUnit as well as from talkingUnit. This is a new example and the following code should be put in a new file:

```
local unitPrototype = {}
unitPrototype.type = "abstract unit"
unitPrototype.name = "unnamed"
unitPrototype.hp = 100
unitPrototype.canTalk = false

function unitPrototype:ReceiveHit(attacker)
   self:Say("I'm being attacked by "..attacker.name)
   self.hp = self.hp - attacker.damage
   if self.hp <= 0 then
      self:Say("I died :(")
      self.dead = true
   end
end
```

```lua
function unitPrototype:Say(text)
    if self.canTalk then
        print("["..self.name.."]: "..text)
    end
end

function unitPrototype:GetType()
    return self.type
end


local attackingUnit = setmetatable({}, {__index = unitPrototype})
attackingUnit.type = "attacking unit"
attackingUnit.damage = 5

function attackingUnit:Attack(target)
    if target.dead then
        self:Say("My target is already dead")
        return
    end
    self:Say("Attacking "..target.name)
    target:ReceiveHit(self)
end


local talkingUnit = setmetatable({}, {__index = unitPrototype})
talkingUnit.type = "talking unit"
talkingUnit.canTalk = true


local monsterPrototype = setmetatable({}, {__index = function(t, k)
    return attackingUnit[k] or talkingUnit[k]end})
monsterPrototype.type = "monster"

do
    local metatable = {
        __index = monsterPrototype
    }


    function CreateMonster()
        return setmetatable({}, metatable)
    end
end
```

```
m1 = CreateMonster()
m1.name = "Orc"
m2 = CreateMonster()
m2.name = "Bear"

m1:Attack(m2)        --> normal attack texts
print(m1:GetType()) --> monster
```

A monster is now derived from both talkingUnit and attackingUnit. So it has the method Attack and the default value canTalk = true. An interesting situation occurs when there are overlapping attributes or methods. Let's remove the line monsterPrototype.type = "monster". Calling GetType() now returns "attacking unit", as the metamethod looks in attackingUnit for the requested key and returns it if it is available; the lookup in talkingUnit is executed only if the previous table did not have the requested key. The __index metamethod in the metatable of monsterPrototype defines which overlapping attribute or method is used, as shown in the return statement in this metamethod:

```
return attackingUnit[k] or talkingUnit[k]
```

If you want to favor talkingUnit over attackingUnit for a monster, you can just swap the arguments of the or operator. Lua will then look in talkingUnit first.

You can also write helper functions to manage classes and (multiple) inheritance. A simple function that creates a class with a default constructor (a simple constructor that just applies the metatable) could look like this:

```
function CreateClass(...)
    local parents = {...} -- create a table that holds all parents of the new class
    local class = setmetatable({}, {
        __index = function(t, k)
            for i, v in ipairs(parents) do
                local attr = v[k] -- try to get the requested attribute from a parent...
                if attr ~= nil then
                    return attr -- ...and return it if it exists
                end
            end
        end
    })
    local instanceMetatable = {__index = class} -- the metatable used by instances
    class.New = function(self) -- the default constructor
        return setmetatable({}, instanceMetatable)
    end
    return class
end

local unit = CreateClass()
unit.type = "abstract unit"
function unit:GetType(text)
    return self.type
end
```

```lua
local attackingUnit = CreateClass(unit)
attackingUnit.type = "attacking unit"

local talkingUnit = CreateClass(unit)
talkingUnit.type = "talking unit"

local monster = CreateClass(attackingUnit, talkingUnit)

m1 = monster:New()
m2 = talkingUnit:New()

print(m1:GetType()) --> attacking unit
print(m2:GetType()) --> talking unit
```

The monster class inherits from attackingUnit and talkingUnit. Both attackingUnit and talkingUnit inherit from unit. The function CreateClass(...) handles the classes and provides a default constructor.

You can also use the __call field in the metatable as a constructor; this allows you to write code like local obj = Class() to create instances of your class.

Object Orientation and Data Structures

We can combine object-oriented design and the data structures we discussed earlier in this chapter. There we defined a set of functions that always took the concrete data structure to operate on as one of its arguments. The following code shows an object-oriented stack. All methods are stored in the table stack, and the constructor is stack:New(). Another minor improvement is that the constructor accepts some start values for the stack.

```lua
local stack = {}
function stack:Push(v)
    self[#self + 1] = v
end

function stack:Pop()
    return table.remove(self)
end

do
    local stackMt = {__index = stack}
    function stack:New(...)
        return setmetatable({...}, stackMt)
    end
end

local s1 = stack:New("a", "b", "c")
print(s1:Pop()) --> c
s1:Push("x")
print(s1:Pop()) --> x
```

Note that the actual stack object is still a simple array. But it now has a metatable that defines the __index metamethod which allows us to access the methods Push and Pop.

It is also possible to implement a stack by using a linked list; you can do that as an exercise if you want.

Handling Errors

You may have already encountered error messages while playing around with Lua. And you may have already noticed that there are two kinds of errors: compile-time and runtime errors. A compile-time error occurs when your script is syntactically wrong. Lua will not be able to execute anything in that file in this case. The following code does not print Hello, because it does not pass the compiler and the first line is never executed:

```
print("Hello")
hello --> '=' expected near '<eof>'
```

Runtime errors occur during execution of your script and cannot be detected by the compiler. In other words, your script is syntactically correct but logically flawed. So the following code executes the first line and prints Hello, followed by an error message:

```
print("Hello") --> Hello
print(5 > x) --> attempt to compare nil with number
```

An error will stop the execution of your script. But it will not crash the program that hosts your Lua script. In World of Warcraft, this means that if your script is syntactically wrong, WoW displays an error message when you load the mod. The affected file is not loaded at all. If the game encounters a runtime error, it stops the current execution. However, since World of Warcraft uses an event-driven model, your script is not dead after such an error. The next time an event that is registered by your addon is fired, your code will be invoked again.

Catching Errors

There are functions available to catch and handle error messages before they stop your script. One of these is pcall(*func, arg1, arg2, ...*). Its arguments are a function and the arguments to pass to it, and it returns a boolean value that indicates whether the execution of *func* was successful. The return values of *func* start with the second return value if no errors occurred. If the called function throws an error, the error message will be the second return value; the first is false as the execution was not successful. Let's look at a function that raises an error if called with incorrect arguments:

```
function myPrint(text)
    print("myPrint: "..text)
end
```

Calling myPrint(nil) will cause an error as there is no call to tostring in myPrint. We can avoid the error message by using pcall:

```
local ok, errorMsg = pcall(myPrint, nil)
print(ok)   --> false
print(errorMsg)   --> pcall.lua:2: attempt to concatenate local 'text' (a nil value)
```

However, there is a disadvantage when trying to debug such code. A normal error message in Lua also shows a nice stack traceback, allowing you to retrace the call and identify the code that caused it. You can always use the function debug.traceback() from the debug library to get the current calling stack as a string. If you are using Lua in World of Warcraft the function is debugstack() as the game does not implement the debug library. We can call debug.traceback() after catching the error in our function, but every function call that was initiated by pcall is already lost. So if our function called numerous other functions, it might be hard to reproduce the bug.

But there is a second function available that can catch errors: xpcall(*func, errorHandler*). It takes two functions. The first one, *func*, is executed and xpcall returns its return values if no error occurs. The second function is executed if the first raises an error, and it still has access to the calling stack. The following two examples also require the buggy function myPrint from the last example, so they should be in the same file as that.

```
xpcall(myPrint, function(err)
    print(err)
    print(debug.traceback())
end)
```

This produces the following output:

```
xpcall.lua:2: attempt to concatenate local 'text' (a nil value)
stack traceback:
    xpcall.lua:7: in function <xpcall.lua:5>
    xpcall.lua:2: in function <xpcall.lua:1>
    [C]: in function 'xpcall'
    xpcall.lua:5: in main chunk
    [C]: ?
```

This function also has a major disadvantage: you cannot pass arguments to the function to call. A way to circumvent this restriction is to create a closure that wraps the function call, like the following:

```
xpcall(function() myPrint("Hello!") end, function(err)
    print(err)
    print(debug.traceback())
end)
```

This is quite a lot of overhead for a simple function call and should only be used for debugging, never for a function that is called frequently.

Throwing Errors

You can also create custom error messages. Imagine you are writing a library that is used by other programmers. You define a function that expects certain arguments and might break your library if it's called with the wrong arguments. Let's go back to our very first example, the function fac(n) to calculate the factorial of a given number:

```
function fac(n)
   if n == 0 then
      return 1
   else
      return n * fac(n - 1)
   end
end
```

Calling it with nonnumeric arguments causes arithmetic errors. Calling it with negative or noninteger numbers causes a stack overflow, as the expression n == 0 is never true. So you should check the argument n and generate a custom error message that tells the programmer how to use your function. Lua provides the function assert(expression, message), which checks whether expression can be evaluated to a true value and throws an error if not. So adding the following lines to the beginning of your function is a good idea:

```
assert(type(n) == "number",➥
"Error: cannot calculate the factorial of a "..type(n).." value")
assert(n >= 0 and n % 1 == 0, "Error: n must be a positive integer")
```

Your function now generates an appropriate error message like this one:

```
assert.lua:2: Error: cannot calculate the factorial of a string value
```

However, the error seems to come from your function as it is in line 2 in this case. Users of your addon might blame you for this, even though that error message is the fault of another addon that does not use your library correctly.

But there is another function that directly throws an error message: error(*msg, level*), where *level* is the level of the calling stack: 0 is the function error itself, 1 is your function, and 2 is the function that called your function. So you can use the following code at the beginning of your function fac(n) instead of the calls to assert:

```
if type(n) ~= "number" then
   error("Error: cannot calculate the factorial of a "..type(n).." value", 2)
end
if not (n >= and n % 1 == 0) then
   error("Error: n must be a positive integer", 1)
end
```

Calling your function with the wrong argument now causes the addon that called it to be blamed. Imagine that line 14 contains the bad function call fac("hello").This function call will now result in the following error message, which shows the correct line number:

```
error.lua:14: Error: cannot calculate the factorial of a string value
```

Error messages are not limited to strings in Lua; you can use any value as an error message. This allows you to pass complex objects that describe the error. For example, it is possible to implement Java-like exceptions, which are essentially objects that precisely describe the error that occurred.

The Environment

Every function has an environment. The *environment* is a table that contains all global variables a function can access; a new function always assumes the environment of its enclosing function. Files also have an environment, since files are loaded as functions. As any programmer knows, debugging is a real and constant necessity. To make a good, workable mod, you'll need to know some basics about debugging. Here, I'll demonstrate how environments work in Lua as we build some debugging tools to use.

The Global Environment

The default environment is the global environment that is stored in the global variable _G. So this table holds all global functions and variables: _G.print = print, _G.pairs = pairs, and _G._G = _G. This means that when you access a global variable, Lua internally does a lookup in a hash table. That is why accessing local variables is always faster then using global ones.

One use of _G is that you still have access to global variables after initializing a local variable with the same name:

```
local print = function(...)
    print("<Prefix>", ...) -- this is still the global print!
end

print("Hello!")  --> <Prefix>  Hello!
_G.print("Hello!")  --> Hello!
```

First we initialize a local function print, which adds a prefix to the output. The global print is still visible in the body of that function because the scope of a local variable starts after its initialization. We can now call print in our script to get a nice prefix and we can call _G.print to get our old global print.

Another use of this table is to create or use global variables with dynamic names:

```
local x = "some string..."
_G[x] = 5print(_G["some string..."])  --> 5
```

x can be anything (except for nil); a string with an invalid identifier for a variable or any other value as _G is just a normal table. Global variables with dynamic names are very common in World of Warcraft; you already saw many them when dealing with frames. World of Warcraft provides the functions setglobal(*name*, *value*) and getglobal(*name*), which can also be used to create and access variables in the global environment.

_G is a normal table, so _G can have a metatable. This can be used to modify the default values of global variables or to track the creation of new global variables.

```
setmetatable(_G, {__index = function(t, k) return k end})
print(x)  --> x
print(some_global_variable)  --> some_global_variable
```

Not very useful, but this offers interesting opportunities. You could also define a function that throws an error message when you try to access a global variable that is not initialized. Such an __index metamethod could look like this:

```
function(t, k)
   error("Tried to access uninitialized global variable "..k, 2)
end.
```

We can also track the initialization of new variables:

```
setmetatable(_G, {__newindex = function(t, k,v)
   print("Created new global variable "..k.." = "..tostring(v))
   rawset(_G, k, v)
end})
x = 5  --> Created new global variable x = 5
test = {}  --> Created new global variable test = table: 003293C0
x = 7 --> nothing
```

This __newindex metamethod prints an info message every time it's invoked and then uses rawset to create the table entry in _G. This metamethod is only called when a new key in _G is created, so the last line, which changes the value of x to 7, does not invoke it.

It would be more powerful and useful (for debugging) to track all accesses and changes to global variables. To achieve this we would have to set the global environment to a new empty table that acts as a proxy. Using code like _G = {} does nothing as _G holds only a reference to the global environment. Let's see how we can modify that environment.

Modifying the Environment

You can use the function getfenv(*func or level*) to retrieve the environment of a given function or of the function at a given level at the call stack. The function setfenv(*func or level, environment*) can be used to set the environment of a function to a given table. Let's look at an example:

```
function foo()
   print("Hello")
end

foo() --> Hello
setfenv(foo, {print = function(...) print("<Prefix>", ...) end})
foo() --> <Prefix>  Hello
```

print is the only global variable that is visible in foo after the environment is changed. You can try to change the first four lines to these:

```
x = "Hello!"
function foo()
   print(x)
end
```

The second call to foo now prints nil because the global x is no longer visible in foo. You can change the global environment itself by using the calling stack level 0 as the first argument to setfenv. However, changing the global environment itself is a bad idea in most cases. It will break a lot of stuff, as many internal functions rely on the global environment, so you don't want to do this. It is more useful to modify the environment of the current file by providing the call stack level 1. We can now implement the previously mentioned tracking of global variables:

```lua
local _G = _G -- save a reference to the old global environment
setfenv(1, setmetatable({}, {
   __index = function(t, k)
      local v = _G[k]
      _G.print("Accessing variable "..k..": current value: "➠
.._G.tostring(v))
      return v
   end,
   __newindex = function(t, k, v)
      local oldValue = _G[k]
      print("Setting variable "..k.." to ".._G.tostring(v)..➠
"; old value: ".._G.tostring(oldValue))
      _G[k] = v
   end
}))

x = 5
x = x + 5
print(x)
```

Our new environment for the current file is now an empty table that acts as a proxy to the real global environment. All accesses are forwarded to the global environment after printing a debugging message. The table stays empty as the __newindex metamethod does not create entries in the proxy table; it creates them in the global environment. The output produced is this:

```
Setting variable x to 5; old value: nil
Accessing variable x; current value: 5
Setting variable x to 10; old value: 5
Accessing variable print; current value: function: 00324E38
Accessing variable x; current value: 10
10
```

You can use this code to test whether your addon is accessing or modifying a global variable because of bugs like a missing local, or if you tried to access a local variable outside its scope.

Namespaces

A *namespace* is basically a large container that holds many variables. In Lua, this means it is a simple table where you put all your variables. We have already used such namespaces, when we started to develop the poker mod in the last chapter. Remember, we put all our functions in the table Poker_TableBrowser; this was our namespace.

Environments can be used to create namespaces in Lua. A namespace is useful in environments where many Lua scripts are accessing the same global environment. You can simply create your own environment for your file and put all your functions into that table. You can then export certain functions or a reference to the environment into the global environment:

```
local yourMod = {}
setfenv(1, yourMod)
function foo()
    -- do something
end
```

The function foo is now in the table yourMod, and we didn't have to write `function yourMod.foo() ... end`. If you want to use the colon operator, as in `function yourMod:foo() ... end`, just add the argument `self` by hand: `function foo(self) ... end`.

However, there is a disadvantage: you can no longer access the global environment from your file, as all accesses to global variables are directed to yourMod. There are a few ways to access variables from the global environments. The simplest is to save a reference to _G in a local variable before changing the environment: `local _G = _G`. But this is not the best solution, as you have to write _G.var every time you access a global variable.

You can also store a reference to all global variables you want to use before calling `setfenv`: `local print, pairs, ipairs = print, pairs, ipairs`, and so on. This has the advantage that it also speeds up the access to these functions, as accessing a local variable is always faster than accessing a global one.

A solution that makes things easier when you need a lot of global variables is to set _G as __index metamethod in the metatable of your environment.

The Garbage Collector

You have been creating data structures like tables all the time. Did you wonder what happens to them when you don't need them anymore? There is no command to delete an object and free memory used by it.

The Old Lua 5.0 Garbage Collector

Lua 5.0, which was used in World of Warcraft until patch 2.0, provided a simple "stop-the-world" garbage collector. The collection was executed when the Lua script (in WoW, the default UI and all addons) reached a certain threshold of used memory. It then checked all tables, functions, and userdata objects if they were reachable from your code. If they were not reachable, they were deleted and the used memory freed. After freeing the memory, Lua calculated a new threshold for the next garbage collection cycle.

The name "stop-the-world" already suggests its disadvantage—performance. In World of Warcraft such a collection cycle literally stopped the world, as such a collection cycle easily collected 20 megabytes or more of garbage. Lua could not run while the collector was working, and World of Warcraft cannot run without Lua.

Many addons and the default UI created a lot of garbage by constructing and dropping numerous tables while running. This lead to addons developing the very bad reputation of having high memory usage, as everyone was afraid of these garbage collection lag spikes.

Incremental Garbage Collection

Lua 5.1 provides an incremental garbage collector that fixes the lag issue. Incremental means that the garbage collector is running all the time and the collection is done in many small steps. So there is no sudden FPS drop and no threshold that triggers the collector.

Weak References

The garbage collector checks references to determine whether an object is reachable by your script. So you basically don't need to take care of any cleanup tasks; everything is done automatically. You just drop all references to your object by setting the variables to nil, and Lua will take care of it. There are no special precautions required when dealing with cyclic data structures.

You might run into problems when you have a table that stores metadata about other tables or functions. You also have to delete the references in that table or the object will still be accessible and is therefore not considered to be garbage.

The solution is the *weak table*—that is, a table with *weak references*. These references are ignored by the garbage collector, so an object is collected when all references to it are weak. A table can have weak references for its keys and values.

You can create weak tables by using the field __mode in the metatable of the table, where __mode can be "k", "v", or "kv". The first string defines the keys as weak references, the second all values, and "kv" or "vk" makes both the keys and values weak references.

Controlling the Garbage Collector

The function collectgarbage(*option, value*) can be used to control the garbage collector. The *option* argument can be one of the following strings:

step: Performs a garbage collection step. The second argument value defines the size of the step.

collect: Performs a garbage collection cycle. This frees all unused objects.

count: Returns the amount of memory used by Lua in kilobytes.

stop: Stops the garbage collector. You don't want to do this in World of Warcraft.

restart: Restarts the garbage collector after it was stopped by stop.

setpause: Sets the pause between garbage collection steps.

setstepmul: Changes the amount of data collected per step.

Testing the Garbage Collector

We can now test the garbage collector by using collectgarbage() and weak tables. We use the following code to create a weak table for testing. This line will be the first line of all following examples:

```
local t = setmetatable({}, {__mode = "v"})
```

This creates a new table with weak values. So if we store a table or function inside this table and nowhere else, it will be collected by the garbage collector. Let's try to fill it with some new tables.

```
t[1] = {}
print(t[1])  --> table: 00329450
```

The garbage collector hasn't collected the table yet. We can't predict when it will be collected. So let's create a few more tables in a simple loop.

```
for i = 1, 100 do
   t[i] = {}
end
for i,  v in pairs(t) do
   print(v)
end
```

This code prints just a few tables, as most of the tables are already collected by the garbage collector. But we can also force it to collect tables.

```
t[1] = {}
collectgarbage("collect")
print(t[1])  --> nil
```

Calling collectgarbage("collect") forced a full garbage collection cycle. It deleted our table, so we get nil. Let's look at few other interesting situations.

```
local test = {}
t[1] = test
collectgarbage("collect")
print(t[1])  --> table: 00329470
```

The table wasn't collected this time, because it was also stored in the local variable test. The next test code checks what happens to cyclic structures.

```
local test1 = {}
local test2 = {}
test1[1] = test2
test2[1] = test2
t[1] = test1

test1 = nil -- drop the references
test2 = nil

print(t[1][1][1][1][1][1][1]) --> table: 00329470
collectgarbage("collect")
print(t[1]) --> nil
```

We create two normal tables and store the first in the second and the second in the first. We then store the reference to test1 in the weak table t. After we drop the old references test1 and test2, one of the test tables is referenced only once, in the other testing table (a strong reference!). The other table is referenced twice, in the first table (also a strong reference) and in t (a weak reference). But the garbage collector has no problem with such structures. It detects that the whole cyclic construct can be reached only through a weak reference. So it collects the construct.

More About Lua Libraries

World of Warcraft comes with an additional library that is not part of the standard Lua package (but available separately); called bitlib, it's a library for bitwise operations.

And there are functions available in the string library we haven't discussed yet; this section also looks at them.

The Bit Library

The library bitlib is not part of the Lua standard libraries but is included in World of Warcraft. I also included it in my distribution of SciTE; you can use require("bit") to load it in a Lua script. Note that loading the library is not required when you are programming for World of Warcraft, as it is loaded by default there.

If you have never heard of bitwise operations and wonder why you need to know about them for World of Warcraft addons, you will see a practical use for this library in the chapter that deals with the combat log in World of Warcraft.

When discussing a bitwise operation, we always have to look at numbers in their binary representation. For example if we have the numbers 13 and 12, we can convert them to their binary representations 1101 (13) and 1100 (12). A bitwise operation like the bitwise and now operates on each digit (which represents a single bit) of these two numbers. The bitwise and operation returns 1 if both digits passed to it are 1, 0 otherwise.

This means for our example with 1101 and 1100 that the bitwise and will be called with the arguments 1, 1 to get the first binary digit (bit) of the result, 1,1 to get the second, 0, 0 to get the third, and 1, 0 to get the last digit. The result is then 1100 = 12. The real purpose of this operation is that it allows us to check whether a specific bit is 1 or 0 by calling it with the right arguments (known as bit masks). We will see more about this when we work with the combat log.

■**Tip** An easy way to get the binary representation of a number is to use the Windows calculator. Typing "<number> in binary" in Google also works.

If you are using another IDE or your own version of Lua, you can download bitlib from its project page on LuaForge: http://luaforge.net/projects/bitlib/. The library contains the following functions:

bit.arshift(*b*, *x*): Performs an arithmetic right shift operation *x* times on *b*. Arithmetic means that it does not move the highest bit, so it can be used to divide signed integers by 2^x.

bit.band(*b1*, *b2*, ...): Performs a bitwise and operation on *b1* - *bn*.

bit.bits: The number of bits that can be manipulated by bitwise operations (32 in World of Warcraft).

bit.bnot(*b*): Performs a bitwise not operation by inverting all bits.

bit.bor(*b1*, *b2*, ...): Performs a bitwise or operation on *b1* - *bn*.

bit.bxor(*b1*, *b2*, ...): Performs a bitwise xor (exclusive or) on *b1* - *bn*.

bit.cast(*b*): Casts *b* to the integer type that is internally used by bitlib.

bit.lshift(*b*, *x*): Performs a bitwise left shift *x* times on *b*.

bit.rshift(*b*, *x*): Performs a bitwise right-shift *x* times on *b*.

The String Library: Part 2

Lua is a powerful language for string manipulation. We will have occasion to use two powerful functions, string.gmatch and string.gsub. g stands for global, meaning that these functions operate across the whole string and match multiple patterns. So whereas string.match returns the first result it finds, string.gmatch returns all results. The string.gsub function can be used for replacing complex expressions in a string. Let's look at these two functions.

string.gmatch(*str*, *pattern*)

Returns a function that can be used as an iterator for the generic for loop that iterates over all occurrences of *pattern* in *str*. This function is also available as gmatch in WoW.

The function provides all found captures in *pattern* as variables in the loop. Like its little brother string.match, it provides the whole occurrence if *pattern* does not define captures.

So if you want to get all the words in a string, you can write the following loop:

```
local text = "some long text here"
for word in text:gmatch("(%S+)") do
    print(word)
end
```

The loop prints the words some, long, text, and here, as these are all occurrences of "everything except for spaces with at least one repetition" in text.

It is also possible to use more than one capture and provide more than one variable to the generic for. Imagine that you have a very simple HTML (or BBCode for forums) parser; you could get all strings that are inside tags with their corresponding tag by using code like this:

```
local text = "fancy <b>html</b> <i>here</i>"
for tag, text in text:gmatch("<(.-)>(.-)</.->") do
    print(tag, text)
end
```

Its output is b   html and i   here. And you can also see the difference between the two modifiers - and * here! Both match one or more occurrences, but try to use * in this regular expression: it is too greedy and you get just one output, which says

b>html</b> <i   here

string.gsub(*str, pattern, repl, n*)

This function is also available as gsub in WoW. It replaces all occurrences of *pattern* in *str* with *repl*. The optional fourth argument is a number that can be used to limit the number of replacements. The function returns the new string followed by the number of replacements it made. So this function can be used to count the occurrences of a pattern, for example to count how many times the character x appears in the string *str*, we can write local n = select(2, str:gsub("x")).

The third argument, *repl*, is not required to be a string. It can also be a table or a function. This makes string.gsub a very powerful function.

The simplest way to use string.gsub is for simple replacement of patterns in strings. The string that replaces each occurrence of the pattern can contain %n, which will be replaced by the nth capture in the pattern. So if we go back to our HTML example, we can convert it to BBCode by using string.gsub:

```lua
local text = "fancy <b>html</b> <i>here</i>"
print(text:gsub("<(.-)>(.-)<(.-)>", "[%1]%2[%3]"))
```

The output we get is:

```
fancy [b]html[/b] [i]here[/i]    2
```

Note that 2 is the second return value, which indicates the number of replacements.

We can also pass a table to the gsub function, which will use captures as a key in the table and replace them with the value it finds under this key. So we can use this to format strings:

```lua
local text = "$player says: $text"
local repl = {player = "Tandanu", text = "Hello, World!"}
print(text:gsub("$(%S+)", repl)) --> Tandanu says: Hello, World! 2
```

But the most powerful thing you can do with string.gsub is to pass a function as its third argument. It will then call this function for each occurrence of the pattern. The function receives the captures of the pattern of the current occurrence as arguments. It returns the replacement for the capture.

Let's look at a real-world example from Deadly Boss Mods. The function that colors player names in raid warning messages uses gsub. Boss Mods mark player names in raid warning messages like this: >player<, so the function needs to look up the class of player and put in a fancy color code:

```lua
text = text:gsub(">%S+<", function(cap)
    cap = cap:sub(2, -2)
    local color = ClassColors[DBM:GetRaidClass(cap)] or messageColor
    return color..cap..messageColor
end)
```

I've simplified the function slightly to avoid confusion, as it contains some WoW-specific features you haven't seen yet. Let's assume that DBM:GetRaidClass(name) returns the class of the player name and that the table ClassColors contains color codes for all classes that can be used to change the color of a text. The variable messageColor is set to the default color of the current message.

Summary

This chapter covered even more about Lua. We started with a closer look at functions and how to use them for functional programming; this discussion also included recursion and closures. You also learned how to modify the behavior of tables by using metatables and metamethods to overload operators. This then allowed us to do object-oriented programming in Lua, which plays an important role in World of Warcraft programming, as all GUI-related API functions are object-oriented.

You also looked at the environment and saw how we can combine our knowledge of metatables with the environment to create powerful debugging functions. Another important part of the chapter was the description of some common data structures and how they can be implemented in Lua.

The following chapters will make heavy use of these data structures, metamethods, and object-oriented programming techniques. We will also see some functional programming in the upcoming example mods.

■ ■ ■

## CHAPTER 7

Using Advanced Lua to Extend the Texas Hold'em Poker Addon

We will now use our knowledge from the last chapter to continue working on our poker addon. Remember that we split the addon into four parts: the table browser, the game client, the server, and auxiliary functions. We have already written the simplest part, the table browser.

It's time to think about how to design the rest of the addon. This chapter will cover the auxiliary functions and some parts of the server. We will explore addon communication in the next chapter, which will allow us to finish the server and create the client. The game logic will be in the server; the client will simply display whatever the server tells it to.

Building Auxiliary Functions

We need a set of functions and objects that can be used to deal with cards and poker hands. We will put these all these functions in a new Lua file of our addon; let's call this file `PokerFunctions.lua`. Don't forget to add this file to your TOC file.

We have to create 52 tables; each one represents one card. The game client and server can then get references to these cards, and the auxiliary functions will also accept references to these cards. These functions will implement capabilities like extracting the best hand (five cards) from a set of up to seven cards or comparing hands to determine the winner. Let's start by building the tables for our cards.

■Tip None of the functions we are implementing in this section will make use of the WoW API. This means you can test them without using the game. Use `dofile("localization.en.lua")` at the beginning of your file to load the localization file when testing outside WoW.

Creating Cards

We need to think about how our card object should look before we create it. The simplest solution would be a table with just two fields: the card type (its value, 2–Ace) and the suit. We could then create another function that can generate additional information like the full name of the card from these two fields.

But we will store this additional information right in the object. This will make a few things simpler later on, as it saves us a function call like PokerLib.GetFullName(card). Our table will have the following fields: card, suit, name, value, and code. The fields card and suit contain the localized card type (such as Ace) and suit (such as Spades). The name field holds the full localized name of the card (such as Ace of Spades), value holds a numeric value so that we can compare two cards, and code is a short code that will be handy later when we have to tell another player about a card.

The following code shows a loop that generates all 52 cards. Note that we have to create these cards just once, even if we have multiple servers running. They will all use the same reference and they are not allowed to change anything in a card object.

```lua
local ranks = {"A", "K", "Q", "J", "10", "9", "8", "7", "6", "5", "4", "3", "2"}
local suits = {"H", "D", "C", "S"}
local cards = {}
local cardsByRank = {}

local value = 13
for i, r in ipairs(ranks) do
    cardsByRank[r] = {}
    for i, s in ipairs(suits) do
        cards[#cards + 1] = {
            rank = POKER_CARDS[r],
            suit = POKER_SUITS[s],
            name = POKER_CARD_NAME:format(POKER_CARDS[r], POKER_SUITS[s]),
            code = r..s,
            value = value
        }
        cardsByRank[r][s] = cards[#cards]
    end
    value = value - 1
end
```

The code first defines all 13 card types and 4 suits. It then uses two loops to iterate over all possible combinations and creates a new table cards from them. We also create the table cardsByRank here; it uses the rank of a card as a key that stores another table with the rank as key and the actual card as value. This allows us to access any card by providing a rank and suit.

The code accesses a few tables that contain localized strings of these cards and a string that is used to create the full name. So you will also need the following lines in your localization file:

```lua
POKER_CARD_NAME = "%s of %s"
POKER_CARDS = {
    ["A"] = "Ace",
    ["K"] = "King",
    ["Q"] = "Queen",
    ["J"] = "Jack",
    ["10"] = "Ten",
    ["9"] = "Nine",
    ["8"] = "Eight",
    ["7"] = "Seven",
    ["6"] = "Six",
    ["5"] = "Five",
    ["4"] = "Four",
    ["3"] = "Three",
    ["2"] = "Two",
}
POKER_SUITS = {
    H = "Hearts",
    D = "Diamonds",
    C = "Clubs",
    S = "Spades",
}
```

You can use a loop like the following to test whether the cards have been created correctly:

```lua
for i, v in ipairs(cards) do
    print(v.name)
end
```

The code prints all 52 cards. This was quite easy, but one capability is missing: we need a function that takes a card rank and suit and returns the card object.

Getting Cards

Both the server and the client must be able to request a reference to a specific card object. It would, of course, be possible for the server and client modules to build their own card objects, but having only a single instance of each card has several advantages. One is that it allows you to compare two card references to check that they are equal without using the __eq metamethod.

A function that returns all cards is also handy; the server will need this capability, as it needs the whole deck when shuffling and dealing cards. Implementing the function to get a certain card is actually quite easy, as we created the table cardsByRanks earlier:

```lua
PokerLib = {}

function PokerLib.GetCard(rank, suit)
    return cardsByRank[rank] and cardsByRank[rank][suit]
end
```

We will use the table PokerLib to store all functions that can be accessed from outside this part of our addon. The function GetCard in this table is very simple. It just uses the provided values as keys to cardsByRanks and returns the result. The and makes sure that it does not try to index a nil value if the provided rank is invalid.

The next function we need is one that returns all cards. It can also be written with just one statement by using the Lua function unpack. We used this function earlier, in our timing library in Chapter 4. Recall what it does: it takes the array part of a table and returns all the table entries as return values. That means the following function returns 52 values. Even this number of return values or arguments to a function is absolutely no problem in Lua.

```
function PokerLib.GetAllCards()
    return unpack(cards)
end
```

This was also quite easy. Let's move to a more complicated topic—extracting and rating the best hand from a set of cards. You can have up to seven cards in Texas Hold'em, but you will have to choose five from them.

A CRASH COURSE IN TEXAS HOLD'EM

Texas Hold'em is a poker variant that has gained a lot of popularity and media attention in the last few years. I will explain the basic rules so you can understand the examples in this chapter if you are not familiar with poker. You can read the excellent Wikipedia article http://en.wikipedia.org/wiki/Texas_hold'em if you want to learn more about it.

Every player gets two cards at the beginning of each round and may then bet a certain amount of game chips that go into the *pot*. Players at two rotating positions are forced to bet a certain amount (the big blind and the small blind). Every bet must at least be as high as the big blind. A betting round ends when all players bet the same amount or fold (and thus drop out of this round).

The first betting round is followed by dealing the *flop*, three community cards that are visible to all players. A second betting round takes place before the next community card; then the so-called *turn* is dealt, which is followed by the third betting round. A final fourth betting round takes place after the last (the fifth) community card, the *river*, is dealt. The game ends if only one player remains; this player gets the whole pot.

There is a final phase of the game if at least two players stay in the game until after the last betting round: the showdown. All remaining players have to show their cards, the player with the best *hand* wins all the chips from the pot. Players with equal hands split the chips from the pot. A hand consists of five cards, which can be from the community cards, and the two private cards.

The following list shows the types of hands and their hierarchy. A hand that is above another hand in this list beats it.

1. Royal Flush: Ace, King, Queen, Jack, and 10 of the same suit. This is technically just the highest possible straight flush.

2. Straight Flush: Five consecutive cards of the same suit.

3. Four of a Kind: Four cards of the same rank.

4. Full House: Three cards of the same type and two other cards of a second type.

5. Flush: Five cards of the same suit.

6. Straight: Five consecutive cards.

7. Three of a Kind: Three cards of the same type.

8. Two Pair: Two pairs.

9. Pair: Two cards of the same type.

10. High Card: None of the previous combinations. Just five random cards.

Finally, kickers are cards that don't contribute to any hands but can be used as tie-breakers when players have identical ratings. For example, in Three of a Kind, there will be two kickers left over from the five cards.

Extracting and Rating the Best Hand

There are 21 possible hands; 21 ways to select 5 cards out of 7 (7! / (5! × 2!) = 7 × 6 / 2 = 21). So a possible solution is to call the function that rates a hand for all 21 possible hands and return the best one. This would certainly work; such a solution would be called the "brute force" method, and this is rarely a nice solution. Trying all combinations works only because there are only 21 possible hands; imagine if you wanted to use it for anything else. The number of possible hands grows extremely fast, and it can become inefficient to try every possible combination for all players. We will combine the extraction and rating of a hand in one function.

This function takes up to seven cards in a table and first tries to find a straight flush in those cards. If it finds one, it returns a localized string that describes the straight flush found and a numeric value. This value is the rating of the hand; it can be compared to another hand. The hand with the higher rating will win. It then checks whether the cards contain four of a kind, and so on.

It is always easier to work with a sorted set of cards, so the first thing we need to do is sort the cards. We can just use `table.sort` with an appropriate compare function here as the cards will be passed in an array to our function. The following function compares the values of two cards, so it will sort an array of cards in descending order:

```
local function compareCards(v1, v2)
    return v1.value > v2.value
end
```

The next step is to check if the cards contain a straight flush, four of a kind, full house, and so on. The function `PokerLib.RateCards` will basically just call a lot of helper functions until one of them finds a hand. We could just write a few lines for each check instead of calling the functions, which would work but the resulting function would be quite long. A smarter way is to store the functions that try to find a hand in an array. The first entry in this array will be the function that looks for a straight flush, the last entry the function that looks for a high card. That last function should actually always find something. The following code shows the function `PokerLib.RateCards`, it assumes that the helper functions are stored in the array `findHandFunctions`, which we'll cover later in this chapter.

```
function PokerLib.RateCards(cards)
   table.sort(cards, compareCards) -- sort the cards

   for i, func in ipairs(findHandFunctions) do
      local found, text, rating = func(cards)
      if found then
         return text, rating
      end
   end
   return "error", 0
end
```

The code should never reach the last line, because we'll always find a high card. This last line just makes sure that your function still returns the expected types if your functions in findHandFunctions are broken.

We now need to add functions to this table that do the hard work. They have to calculate a rating for a hand, but how can we calculate a rating?

Calculating a Rating

This rating needs to be calculated from several variables of a hand. The function that calculates the number must also guarantee that a better hand always gets a higher rating. For example, if we have a full house with three kings and two queens, this function needs to make sure that the calculated rating is higher than the rating of a full house with three queens and two kings. So we could calculate the rating for a full house with the following formula, where *card1* is the card type of which you have three, and *card2* the pair:

(14 * card1.value) + card2.value

card1 and *card2* are the card objects, so the field value holds a numeric value that is suitable for this calculation. Let's calculate the ratings for the two example hands, starting with three kings (*card1*, value = 13) and two queens (*card2*, value = 12):

(14 * card1.value) + card2.value = (14 * 13) + 12 = 194

The other hand I mentioned earlier is very similar: it consists of three queens and two kings. So card1 is now a queen (value = 12) and card2 a king (value = 13). The expected result is a rating less than 194:

(14 * card1.value) + card2.value = (14 * 12) + 13 = 181

This system works fine when comparing two full-house hands. We now have to find a general solution that takes the hand type into account and can calculate a rating for an arbitrary hand.

A general solution for this is using a numeral system with the base 14, where a base-14 number represents the whole hand. This might sound confusing but is really the simplest way to calculate a rating. The reason for this is that there are 13 different card ranks and a single base-14 digit can store all 13 card types with a value to spare, as we'll see. We can encode the type of the hand (such as full house) in the position of the digit within the base-14 number and a value of 0 for a particular digit means that the hand represented by the number is not of the type represented by the digit. We'll expand on this throughout the section.

Base 14 means we will basically count from 0 to 9 and then from A to D. This means that D_{14} translates to 13_{10} in the decimal system. 10_{14} then translates to 14_{10}, 11_{14} to 15_{10}, and so on. In such a number like $6B7_{14}$, we will call the very right digit (7) the zeroth; the digit left of the zeroth (B) is the first, and so on. When translating a number from this system to the decimal system, we take the value of each digit, multiply it by 14 to the power of the digit's place, and add them all up. For example, when we translate $6B7_{14}$ to the decimal system we calculate $6 \times 14^2 + 11 \times 14^1 + 7 \times 14^0$ and get 1337_{10}.

There are nine hand types, and we need a digit for each of them in the base-14 number. We also need additional space to store the kickers. But the order of the kickers is not important, so we can just add them up. Two base-14 digits are sufficient to store all the kickers, which makes a total of 11 digits in the base-14 number. The hand type "high card" does not require an additional digit; we can simply take the sum of the five highest cards' values as rating. It will never be higher than the worst pair.

Let's see a few examples: the very left digit (the tenth digit) indicates that we have a straight flush. The best straight flush is a royal flush, its rating is $D0,000,000,000_{14}$ (note that the digit representing the hand is simply set to the highest card of the straight). The next digit will be set if we have four of a kind; our kicker will be stored in the very right (the zeroth) digit. For example, $01,000,000,00A_{14}$ indicates that we have four twos (the card two has the value 1 as it is the first card) and a jack. Table 7-1 shows the scoring of all card types; this score is available in the field value of a card object that we created earlier.

Table 7-1. *Card Type Scores*

Card Type	Score
Ace	D (13)
King	C (12)
Queen	B (11)
Jack	A (10)
10	9
9	8
8	7
7	6
6	5
5	4
4	3
3	2
2	1

■Note Using base 16 (hexadecimal) would also be possible and might even be easier, as you probably have more experience with base 16 than 14. But hexadecimal numbers with 11 digits reach Lua's size limit for numbers that are internally stored in double-precision floating-point.

A more interesting hand is a pair, as this means we have two cards of the same rank and three cards with different ranks. The second digit (that is, the third digit from the right side) indicates that we have a pair, and will be set to the value of the pair. But what happens with the other three cards? We have only two digits left. But we can just add the remaining three cards up to get a value that can then be added to our number. For example, suppose we have a pair of threes and an ace, a king, and a queen. We get 200_{14} for the pair and then add $D_{14} + C_{14} + B_{14} = 28_{14}$. So the total rating is 228_{14}.

We can use these last two digits to store five single cards. For example, if we just have a high card, we can store the five highest cards in these digits. The highest possible combination we can get is $D_{14} + C_{14} + B_{14} + A_{14} + 8_{14} = 3C_{14}$. This is less than 100_{14}, so we can safely use it for high cards without getting a higher rating than the worst pair.

We can now write the functions that do the actual work.

Finding and Rating the Hand

We need nine functions in the previously mentioned table findHandFunctions, one for each hand type. But I don't want to bore you by walking through all these functions. So I'll just show a few particularly interesting functions: finding a straight, a pair, and the five highest cards. You can find all the functions in the code download.

Finding Straights

Let's start with the function that finds a straight; this function takes the array cards, which contains all of a player's cards (up to 7). Note that an ace can be used here as a one, so that 5, 4, 3, 2, ace is a straight. An easy way to take this into account is to check whether the first (the highest) card is an ace and if so, insert it as a new element into the array cards. We have to remove this element before we leave the function as the function must not modify the array that is passed to it. The reason for this is that the same array will later also be passed to other functions that try to find other possible hands if it does not contain a straight.

A straight requires at least five cards, so the function just returns false if we have fewer than that. The function iterates over the array, starting with the second card. The loop always compares the current card to the last one and keeps a counter c that counts the consecutive cards. This counter starts with 1 and is increased every time the current and last cards are consecutive, unchanged if it encounters two equal cards, and reset to 1 otherwise. The array contains a straight if this counter reaches 5. Another local variable, called high, stores the highest card in the sequence. Let's look at the code of this function:

```
local function findStraight(cards)
    if #cards < 5 then
        return false
    end
    if cards[1].value == 13 then
        cards[#cards + 1] = cards[1]
    end
    local c = 1
    local high = cards[1]
```

```
for i = 2, #cards do
   local prev = cards[i - 1]
   local cur = cards[i]
   if (prev.value - cur.value) == 1 or (prev.value - cur.value) == -12 then
      c = c + 1
      if c == 5 then break end
   elseif prev.value == cur.value then
      -- do nothing
   else
      c = 1
      high = cur
   end
end
if cards[1].value == 13 then
   cards[#cards] = nil
end
if c == 5 then
   return true, POKER_STRAIGHT:format(high.rank), 14^6 * high.value
else
   return false
end
end
```

Two cards are considered consecutive if the difference of their values is 1 or –12. (A value of –12 means that an ace is used as a one.) The code leaves the loop if it finds five cards.

It then returns true, a localized text and the rating if the counter is five, otherwise false. Remember how we want to calculate the rating of a hand. The sixth digit is used for a straight, so we need to calculate 14 (our base) to the power of 6 and multiply it with the value of the highest card.

Note that we also need the following line in the localization file as our function also returns a localized string:

```
POKER_STRAIGHT = "%s-high Straight"
```

We now have to add the function to the table findHandFunctions. The local variable holding the table needs to be placed above the function PokerLib.RateCards.

```
local findHandFunctions = {
   findStraight
}
```

We can now call the function RateCards with test values. We can get references to cards by using the function GetCard. Remember that we need to pass the cards in a table:

```
print(PokerLib.RateCards{
   PokerLib.GetCard("2", "H"),
   PokerLib.GetCard("3", "H"),
   PokerLib.GetCard("5", "H"),
   PokerLib.GetCard("5", "H"),
   PokerLib.GetCard("4", "H"),
```

```
    PokerLib.GetCard("3", "H"),
    PokerLib.GetCard("A", "H")
})
```

We don't need parentheses when we pass only a single table to a function, so we can save a few brackets here. This code will produce the following output:

```
Five-high Straight    30118144
```

Play around with the values to satisfy yourself that the function is working properly.

Finding Pairs

Finding pairs is basically quite easy. Remember that we have a few preconditions when this function is called. The cards have been sorted and do not contain two pair, three of a kind, or a full house, as the functions to find these hand types have already been called and returned `false`. This means that if the cards contain a pair, both cards of this pair are consecutive in the array. We just need a simple loop that goes over the array and compares the value (card type) of the current card to the next card.

If we find a pair we have to find the three highest cards (our kickers, not part of the pair) and add their values. This sum is then added to the rating, which is calculated as $14^2 \times$ pair value. But how can we calculate this sum? Remember that we must not modify the table that is passed to this function, as another function might also use this table, so we may not remove the pair from it without putting them back later. We could take this approach. We could also write a loop that traverses the table and adds the values of the three highest elements (except for the pair itself) to the rating. But the purpose of this example is not only to write a poker game; it is also to teach the Lua language and its programming techniques. Lua is a great functional programming language, and we haven't seen much functional programming yet.

Let's do some functional programming with a few recursive functions here. We will work with varargs to extract the kickers from the cards. The following code shows the function `findPair`, which checks whether a set of cards contains a pair:

```
local function findPair(cards)
    local found = nil
    local pos = nil
    for i = 1, #cards - 1 do
        if cards[i].value == cards[i + 1].value then
            found = cards[i]
            pos = i
            break
        end
    end
    if found then
        local kickers = addHighest(3, removeArg(pos, removeArg(pos, unpack(cards))))
        return true, POKER_PAIR:format(found.rank), 14^2 * found.value + kickers
    else
        return false
    end
end
```

Let's go through this function line by line. It first initializes two local variables, found and pos, with nil. The next step is traversing the array from the first to the penultimate entry. The loop compares the current entry to the next entry. If it finds two cards with the same value it saves the found card and its position in found and position.

If it doesn't find a pair, it just returns false. Otherwise it calls unpack on the cards and passes these values to the function removeArg(pos, ...), which returns all arguments passed to it except the argument at *pos*. Such a function does not exist by default; we will have to write it. The function is called twice to remove both cards of the pair from the result of unpacking. The remaining cards are now passed to the function addHighest(n, ...), which calculates and returns the sum of the *n* highest cards passed to it.

The findPair function then returns true, followed by a localized description of the pair and the rating. You need the following line in your localization file for this:

```
POKER_PAIR = "Pair: %s"
```

We now need to write removeArg and addHighest. Let's start with removeArg, as it is quite easy to implement using recursion. We will implement both functions so that they can act as general-purpose functions for a list of unsorted cards. We will ignore the fact that the arguments will be always sorted when they are called from PokerLib.RateCards.

Writing removeArg(*n*, ...)

The first thing the function does is check whether the position is in the bounds of the vararg. If that is not the case, it just returns all values. Otherwise, it checks for the position 1; if this is the case the function just returns all values from the varargs except for the first one, by calling select.

The interesting part of this function is the else block, which contains the recursive call. It returns the first value from the vararg followed by a call to itself, with the position reduced by one and the remaining values from the vararg. Here is the code of this function:

```
local function removeArg(n, ...)
   if n > select("#", ...) then
      return ...
   elseif n == 1 then
      return select(2, ...)
   else
      return select(1, ...), removeArg(n - 1, select(2, ...))
   end
end
```

So the function essentially goes over the vararg until it reaches the position to remove. It then skips this argument and returns the rest.

Note that select can only cut off arguments at the start, not at the end. And even if we had a function that could do this, we could not write code like the following:

```
return cutEnd(n + 1, ...), select(n - 1, ...)
```

Well, we could write such code but it wouldn't work as expected. The reason is that a function that returns multiple results will only use all of these results if it is the last value in a list of values. Otherwise, only the first return value is used.

Our next task is to write the function addHighest(n, ...), which calculates the sum of the n highest cards in the vararg.

Writing addHighest(n, ...)

We actually need one more argument than n and the cards, as we need to store the already calculated sum somewhere. An argument is always a good place to store a value over recursive calls; you just have to pass the value in each recursive call. But we don't want to pass this additional argument to the function. Because it would always be 0 in the initial call, we can just write a wrapper function that adds this argument in a tail call.

Another task that can be done by this wrapper is checking whether n is greater than the number of cards passed to the function. We will set n to the number of cards in this case to avoid issues with nil values.

We will call the function that does the real work, _addHighest, and limit its scope to the wrapper function by using a do-end block. Let's take a look at this function.

```lua
local addHighest
do
    local function _addHighest(n, sum, ...)
        if n == 0 then
            return sum
        else
            local max, maxPos = getMax(...)
            return _addHighest(n - 1, sum + max, removeArg(maxPos, ...))
        end
    end

    function addHighest(n, ...)
        return _addHighest(math.min(n, select("#", ...)), 0, ...)
    end
end
```

First _addHighest checks whether n is 0 and returns sum in this case. This will happen when the function has finished adding up all cards to sum. Otherwise, it calls a function getMax(...) that returns the highest card from the vararg and its position. It then does a recursive tail call to itself with n reduced by one, max added to sum, and without the highest element in the vararg by calling removeArg with maxPos.

We now need to write the function getMax(...).

Writing getMax(...)

This function just iterates over all cards passed to it to determine the highest one and then returns the value of this card and the position. It needs to be visible in _addHighest, so it must be placed above it.

```
local function getMax(...)
    local max = select(1, ...).value
    local maxPos = 1
    for i = 2, select("#", ...) do
        if select(i, ...).value > max then
            max = select(i, ...).value
            maxPos = i
        end
    end
    return max, maxPos
end
```

The function initializes two variables, max and maxPos, with the value of the first card and its position. The loop then starts with the second argument and traverses all arguments to determine the highest card and saves its value and position in max and maxPos. These values are then returned.

Insert this function above, addHighest, which needs to see getMax. Another solution is to create all local variables at the beginning of the file and remove the keyword local from the functions.

Testing findPair(cards)

We can now add findPair to the table findHandFunctions after findStraight.

```
local findHandFunctions = {
    findStraight,
    findPair
}
```

We can test the function with the same code that we used to test findStraight. But keep in mind that you must not use hands that contain a two pair or a full house, as we haven't implemented the function to find these hand types yet. They would be filtered by functions we haven't created yet, so the results of such hands might be wrong.

```
print(PokerLib.RateCards{
    PokerLib.GetCard("3", "H"),
    PokerLib.GetCard("2", "C"),
    PokerLib.GetCard("Q", "C"),
    PokerLib.GetCard("A", "C"),
    PokerLib.GetCard("9", "H"),
    PokerLib.GetCard("K", "H"),
    PokerLib.GetCard("2", "H")
})
```

This will print Pair: Two and 232. Let's check whether 232 is correct. The best hand in these seven cards is a pair of twos and the ace, king, and queen. So the rating should be $14^2 \times 1 + 13 + 12 + 11 = 232$. It seems to work properly. You can test it with other cards as well. It is a good idea to add print(kickers) to findPairs(), so you can quickly confirm that addHighest calculates the correct value.

Finding High Cards

We have already written the necessary helper function addHighest, so finding the five highest cards is really easy. Note that the array cards is sorted by rank, so cards[1] is always the highest card. We could also just add cards[1] to cards[5] to get the result, but simply calling addHighest, as in the following code, is shorter and easier:

```
local function findHighCard(cards)
    return true, POKER_HIGH_CARD:format(cards[1].rank), addHighest(5, unpack(cards))
end
```

Add the function to the end of the array findHandFunctions if you want to test it. Note that you also need the following line in your localization file for testing:

```
POKER_HIGH_CARD = "High Card: %s"
```

You can find the remaining functions in the code download; again, I won't go through them here. Our set of auxiliary functions is now finished. We can move to the next part of our addon—the server.

Building the Server

We will now begin building the poker server. We can't build the whole server, as we haven't discussed addon communication yet. But we will create the key parts of the server here; and then communication, in Chapter 8, will be just another part of the server.

Let's start by thinking about what such a poker server does. It needs to handle the whole game logic and it will utilize the poker library we just implemented. We will here implement the most interesting and important parts of the game logic like managing the different states a poker game can be in.

We will later start the whole server by clicking a button in the GUI which calls a function that tells our server to start with certain parameters. What happens if you click that button again? Can we run multiple servers at the same time? Why not? We will use object-oriented programming (OOP) here to allow us to host many servers at the same time without any problems or difficult code.

Creating a Player Object

The following code is part of the file Server.lua (don't forget to add this to your TOC) and shows a skeleton player object. It just consists of an empty prototype with a constructor that initializes the player object with three basic values: a name, a position, and the amount of chips the player starts with.

```
local createPlayer

local player = {}
local playerMt = {__index = player}-- metatable for the player object
```

```lua
function createPlayer(name, position, chips)
   return setmetatable({
       name = name,
       position = position,
       chips = chips
   }, playerMt) -- add the metatable to the new object
end
```

We will later add methods like sending a message to the player object. But this simple object is sufficient for now.

Creating a Server Object

The server object is more complicated than the player object we just worked with, as it needs a lot of attributes. The obvious attributes are those we used in the "host a table" dialog: the server's name, maximum allowed number of players, blinds, and permissions. Besides the name, the server will also need a unique ID as we need to be able to identify it. The name is not necessarily unique if we are hosting more than one server.

We also need an array (table) that keeps track of all players currently connected to the server. It might also be useful to include another table to hold all players on the server by using the position as the table index.

The next attribute we clearly require is a data structure that holds all cards. An obvious choice of data structure to represent a deck of cards is a stack. All cards will be pushed on the stack in a random order when a round starts, and drawing a card equals a pop operation. After the round, the server "collects" all cards and fills the stack in a random order. But how do we get the cards back? We could track all cards that are removed from the stack during the game, but there is a better solution. Our pop operation won't remove a card; instead it will increment a counter. This counter is what is called a *stack pointer*. It starts at 1 and is used as an index into the array that stores the objects on the stack. The stack pointer moves down the stack following pops and up the stack following pushes, which makes it look like the stack is empty when the pointer reaches its end. This implementation of a stack is especially useful here, as we have the same 52 objects on the stack all the time. We actually won't do a single push operation; we will just use `table.sort` on the array to get a new random order. The stack pointer is reset to 1 after the array has been re-sorted.

Another attribute our server needs is its current state. What is a state, and why does our server need one? You'll find out in the coming sections, but for now, a smart way to design a server for a game like poker is as what is called a *finite-state machine*. Let's first look at the server prototype and its constructor. We will start with an empty prototype without any methods and add them later.

```lua
local servers = {}

local server = {}
local serverMt = {__index = server}
```

```lua
function Poker_CreateServer(name, maxPlayers, smallBlind, bigBlind,➥
allowEveryone, allowGuild, allowGroup, allowFriends)
    local obj = {
        name = name, -- server name
        maxPlayers = maxPlayers,
        smallBlind = smallBlind,
        bigBlind = bigBlind,
        allowEveryone = allowEveryone,
        allowGuild = allowGuild,
        allowGroup = allowGroup,
        allowFriends = allowFriends,
        players = {}, -- list of connected players
        playersByPosition = {}, -- key: player position (1-10), value: player
        cards = {PokerLib.GetAllCards()}, -- all cards
        stackPointer = 1, -- increased by 1 when a card is drawn
        communityCards = {}, -- community cards
        id = #servers + 1, -- server id (for multiple servers)
        state = "waitingForPlayers" -- current server state
    }
    servers[#servers + 1] = obj
    return setmetatable(obj, serverMt)
end
```

The table servers will hold all servers that are currently running. The constructor takes care of adding new servers to this table.

Finite-State Machines

A finite-state machine (FSM) is a model that describes a machine or system. It consists of a finite number of *states* the system can assume. There are so-called *transitions* between those states. A transition occurs when certain transition conditions in a current state are met. For example, our server starts in the state waitingForPlayers; a good transition condition would be this: (number of players with chip value > 0) >= 2. The transition will then change the state of the server to another state, like bettingRoundStarted. Note that a state might be quite complex and consist of multiple variables that contain additional information about the current state. In this example, bettingRoundStarted will also get the additional information that it is the first one. An external input like a network message from a player can satisfy a transition condition and thus trigger a transition.

The following *bubble diagram* shows all states of a finite state machine as bubbles. The arrows between these bubbles are the transitions; the text on the arrow is the transition condition. This diagram shows a rough sketch of our poker server. A full diagram that takes everything into account would be quite large and complicated.

We basically have four states: we will start in the state waitingForPlayers. The next state is bettingRoundStarted, which is always left immediately for waitingForBet or showdown. Both of these states return to bettingRoundStarted. This diagram does not cover the contingency that we have to return to waitingForPlayers if a player leaves, and it also does not go into detail about betting rounds. It just defines the transition condition "betting round over," which leaves waitingForBet. This state is more complicated than it seems to be in this diagram.

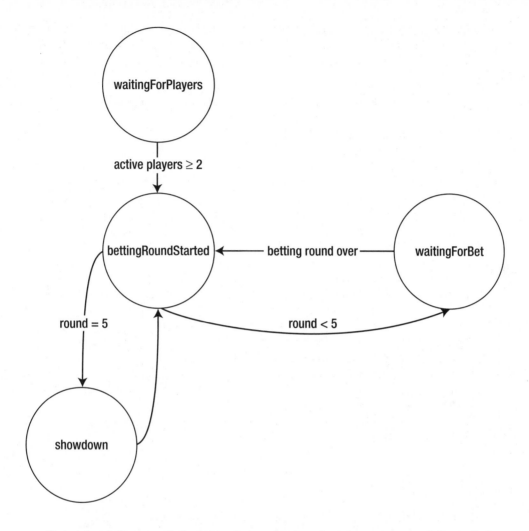

States also define so-called *entry actions* and *exit actions*. An entry action is basically Lua code that is executed when the system enters the given state. The exit action is executed when the system leaves the state. For example, a useful entry action for "bettingRoundStarted" would be shuffling and dealing cards if it is the first round. The exit action would be empty. It is also possible to define actions that occur on certain transitions, so-called *transition actions*. Another type of action is the *input action*, which occurs when the state machine receives an input in a certain state.

We will use methods with the prefix On like OnReceiveJoinRequest to indicate that these methods are called on external inputs. Let's look at this method, which adds a new player to the table.

Joining a Game

The very basic functionality a server needs is allowing players to join. This join request is an input, so the name of this method is OnPlayerJoin. The method receives the name of the player who wants to join, and it is called by the communication module of the server. The method SendMessage will also forward the call to the communication module. It's up to the communication module to check whether the player is actually allowed to join your table, so we do not check that here. The following code shows this method:

```lua
function server:OnPlayerJoin(name)
    -- the network code checks if the player is eligible and if we have a free slot
    local player
    for i = 1, self.maxPlayers do -- find free slot
        if not self.playersByPosition[i] then
            player = createPlayer(name, i, self.bigBlind * 30)
            player.inactive = true -- the new player will be active in the next round
            self.playersByPosition[i] = player
            table.insert(self.players, player)
            break
        end
    end
    -- tell everyone about the new player
    self:BroadcastMessage("PlayerJoined", name, player.position, player.chips)
    -- tell the player that we accepted him
    player:SendMessage("JoinAccepted", player.position, player.chips)
    player:SendState() -- send the current state of the game to the player
    -- check if we are currently wating for players
    if self.state == "waitingForPlayers" then
        -- the transition condition from this state to the state "bettingRoundStarted"
        -- might have become true, so check this
        local playersWithChips = 0
        for i, v in ipairs(self.players) do -- count players with chips
            if v.chips > 0 then
                playersWithChips = playersWithChips + 1
            end
        end
        if playersWithChips >= 2 then -- check transition condition
            - change state to "bettingRoundStarted" with round = 1 (deal cards)
            self:StartBettingRound(1)
        end
    end
end
```

It basically finds the first free seat on the table and creates a new player object with this position, name, and 30 times the big blind as chips. We use the attribute inactive to indicate that this player is not yet participating. The player is then inserted in the table players and playersByPosition. The next task of the method is to tell all players on the table that this player has just joined the table, so each client can update its game screen. The method also sends the new player a message that his join request has been accepted, showing his position and initial chips. The method SendState then sends the new player the current state of the table, so he or she can watch the ongoing round.

The if block at the end checks if we are currently in the state "waitingForPlayers" as its transition condition might have changed. So we have to count the number of players on the table with at least 1 chip. If we find two players, we have to change the state to "StartBettingRound". This is the next function we are going to implement.

■Tip We are often referring to methods that do not exist yet, so testing the code is somewhat difficult. You can implement these methods and fill them with dummy code like printing all arguments they receive to test the addon.

Starting Betting Rounds

Starting a betting round is a more complicated state than we've looked at so far. It does not just consist of a single string. We also need to store the betting round that can assume four states: pre-flop, flop, turn, and river. We will use the numbers 1, 2, 3, and 4 to identify these states as this allows us to transit to the next state (read: next betting round) by adding 1. We also need to store some values about the minimum allowed raise and the amount of chip value needed to call.

The following code shows the method StartBettingRound, which sets the state and executes an entry action. Note that this state has a transition condition that is always true, so it immediately changes the state to waitingForBet.

```lua
function server:StartBettingRound(counter)
   -- set new state
   self.state = "bettingRoundStarted"
   self.bettingRound = counter
   self.minRaise = self.bigBlind
   self.call = self.bigBlind
   -- entry action depends on "sub-state" bettingRound
   -- 1 = first betting round; pre-flop
   -- 2 = flop
   -- 3 = turn
   -- 4 = river
   -- 5 = showdown; actually not a betting round
   if counter == 1 then
      table.wipe(self.communityCards) -- remove community cards
      self:ShuffleCards() -- shuffle cards...
      -- ...before dealing them
      for i, v in ipairs(self.players) do
         -- set inactive players to active if they have chips (new players)
         if v.inactive and v.chips > 0 then
            v.inactive = false
         end
```

```lua
            -- check if the player is active
            if not v.inactive then
                -- draw 2 cards and send them to the player
                v:SendCards(self:DrawCard(), self:DrawCard()) --
            end
        end
        -- move the dealer button after the previous loop
        -- as this loop removes the inactive state from new players
        self:MoveDealerButton()
        -- small/big blinds
        self.playersByPosition[self.smallBlindPos]:Bet(self.smallBlind)
        self.playersByPosition[self.bigBlindPos]:Bet(self.bigBlind)
    elseif counter == 2 then
        -- draw the flop
        self:AddCommunityCard(self:DrawCard())
        self:AddCommunityCard(self:DrawCard())
        self:AddCommunityCard(self:DrawCard())
    elseif counter == 3 then
        -- turn
        self:AddCommunityCard(self:DrawCard())
    elseif counter == 4 then
        -- river
        self:AddCommunityCard(self:DrawCard())
    elseif counter == 5 then
        -- change state to showdown, so we return here
        return self:Showdown()
    end
    -- we will leave this state immediately
    self.currentPlayer = self.bigBlindPos
    self:WaitForBet(self:GetNextPlayer())
end
```

The entry action depends on the betting round. If it is the first one, we have to move the dealer button to the next position, shuffle and deal cards, and bet the blinds. The entry action for the second betting round draws the flop, the third draws the river, and the fourth the turn. The fifth round is actually not a betting round, so we change the state to showdown here.

We transit to the state waitingForBet after executing this entry action, as we have a transition condition that is always true. This state also contains additional information; namely, the player we are waiting for. We use the method GetNextPlayer for this; it will return the next player object. The attribute currentPlayer stores the position of the current player, which here is the big blind position.

The method makes use of a lot of methods we haven't implemented yet. Among those, let's start with shuffling and drawing cards.

Shuffling and Drawing Cards

I mentioned earlier that we will use `table.sort` to sort the table that holds the cards. We need a criterion the cards will be sorted by. It has to be random, as we need them in a random order. The simplest way to do this is to assign a new field that holds a random value in each table that represents a card. The cards will then be sorted by this field, so let's call it just `random`. The following code shows the method `ShuffleCard` with its helper function `compare`:

```lua
do
    -- compare function
    local function compare(v1, v2)
        return v1.random > v2.random
    end

    function server:ShuffleCards()
        self.stackPointer = 1 -- reset the stack pointer
        for i, v in ipairs(self.cards) do
            v.random = math.random() -- assign random values to all cards
        end
        table.sort(self.cards, compare) -- sort the array
    end
end
```

The attribute `stackPointer` of the server object holds the stack pointer for our stack; we reset it here as we want to shuffle all cards. The code then assigns a random value between 0 and 1 to each card and uses `table.sort` to sort them by this random value.

PSEUDO RANDOM NUMBER GENERATORS

An important thing to know about `math.random` is that usually in Lua, you must use `math.randomseed` beforehand. However, World of Warcraft does this automatically and `math.randomseed` is not available in the game. The following is still important if you are using Lua outside the game.

The reason `math.randomseed` is important is that your computer cannot generate random numbers without special hardware. Random functions like `math.random` will always generate so-called *pseudo random numbers*, which seem to be random but are just calculated from another number, the so-called *seed*. If you use the same seed you will get the same sequence of numbers from `math.random`. If you provide no seed at all, the function uses a default seed that also gives you the same numbers every time you run your script. You can test this by creating a Lua file and filling it with the following code:

```lua
for i = 1, 10 do
    print(math.random(1, 100))
end
```

Every time you execute this file with Lua, you'll get the same sequence of numbers between 1 and 100. This time, try adding `math.randomseed(os.time())` in the first line to seed the PRNG (pseudo random number generator) with the current time. You get a different sequence of numbers every time the script is executed.

We now need to draw a card; this means we have to pop it off the stack. To do that, we get the current object the stack pointer is pointing to, increment the stack pointer, and return the object we retrieved:

```
function server:DrawCard()
    local card = self.cards[self.stackPointer] -- get the card
    self.stackPointer = self.stackPointer + 1 -- increment stack pointer
    return card -- return the card
end
```

We can now shuffle and draw cards, so the first part of our function that deals the cards works. Let's look where the cards we draw go. We are passing them to the methods SendCards and AddCommunityCard.

Player Cards and Community Cards

Let's start by building the method that sends cards to a player.

```
function player:SendCards(card1, card2)
    self.card1 = card1
    self.card2 = card2
    self:SendMessage("YourCards", card1.code, card2.code)
end
```

We just store the two cards in two fields of the player object. We then tell the player the codes of the cards he or she received. Working with community cards is even simpler:

```
function server:AddCommunityCard(card)
    self.communityCards[#self.communityCards + 1] = card
    self:Broadcast("CommunityCard", card.code)
end
```

The code just adds the card to the table communityCards, which holds all community cards and broadcasts a message that tells everyone on the table about the new card.

The next task is moving the dealer button to the next player. This might be confusing, as the dealer button is usually moved before you deal the cards. But moving the button first would require an additional loop, as we need to enable inactive players who just joined the table. These players must be enabled because MoveDealerButton needs to determine the next active player.

Moving the Dealer Button

We can't just add on the current position, as the next seat might be empty or the player may have run out of chips. So we need a method that returns the next position with a player after a given position. We also need to set an initial value for the dealer position if we haven't placed the dealer button yet (which is the case if it is the first round on the table). The following code shows the method MoveDealerButton, which makes use of the method FindNextPosition:

```
function server:MoveDealerButton()
   if not self.dealerPos then -- first round on this table
      -- initial button position
      self.dealerPos = self:FindNextPosition(1)
   else
      -- move the button
      self.dealerPos = self:FindNextPosition(self.dealerPos)
   end
   -- set small blind position
   self.smallBlindPos = self:FindNextPosition(self.dealerPos)
   -- set big blind position
   self.bigBlindPos = self:FindNextPosition(self.smallBlindPos)
   -- tell all clients to move the button
   self:BroadcastMessage("ButtonMoved", self.dealerPos, self.smallBlindPos,➥
self.bigBlindPos)
end
```

The last line in the function simply calls the method BroadcastMessage, which tells all currently connected clients to move the dealer button and the new small/big blind positions. The clients could also calculate the blind positions from the big blind positions, but it is easier to do this calculation just once in the server. Remember, our client will know nothing about the game logic; it will simply display whatever the server says.

We now need the method FindNextPosition, which consists only of a single loop:

```
function server:FindNextPosition(pos)
   for i = 0, self.maxPlayers - 1 do
      local p = (pos + i) % self.maxPlayers + 1
      if self.playersByPosition[p] and not self.playersByPosition[p].inactive then
         return p
      end
   end
end
```

We use the modulo operator % here. This operator returns the remainder of the division of two numbers and thus allows us to use only one loop in the function, as the variable p restarts at 1 when it reaches the last position.

The next state we look at is "showdown". The state is entered from "bettingRoundStarted" if it is the fifth round.

The Showdown

The method server:Showdown() needs to calculate the ratings of all players who are still in the game. It then determines and broadcasts the winner. Afterward, it transits into the state "bettingRoundStarted" with round = 1, starting a new round.

```
do
    local function sortPlayers(v1, v2)
        return v1.rating > v2.rating
    end

    function server:Showdown()
        self.state = "showdown"
        local winners = {} -- array of all players who haven't folded
        -- fill the array
        for i, v in ipairs(self.players) do
            -- not inactive and didn't fold
            if not v.inactive and not v.folded then
                winners[#winners + 1] = player
                -- rate the player's cards
                player.rating = PokerLib.RateCards{player.card1, player.card2,➥
unpack(self.communityCards)}
                -- the player has to show his or her cards
                self:Broadcast("Showdown", player.position, player.card1, player.card2)
            end
        end
        -- sort the table descending
        table.sort(winners, sortPlayers)
        if winners[1].rating == winners[2].rating then -- split pot
            self:SplitPot(winners)
        else
            -- todo: side pots etc
            self:Broadcast("TheWinner", winners[1].position, self.pot)
        end
        self:StartBettingRound(1)
    end
end
```

The function does not support side pots yet, as we haven't even thought about betting yet. It will be much easier to code that when we know where the bets and all other conditions we need to take into account for side pots are stored.

Let's take a closer look at betting by implementing the method WaitForBet, which transitions the server into the state "waitingForBet".

Waiting for Bets

This state not only consists of a single string, it also has to store the player we are currently waiting for. The first task of this function is to check whether we are at the first player. If this is the case, the function checks whether all players bet the same amount and if so, changes the state to "bettingRoundStarted". Otherwise we stay in the state "waitingForBet" until the player we are waiting for sends us a message or a timeout of 45 seconds expires.

```lua
function server:WaitForBet(player)
   -- set new state
   self.state = "waitingForBet"
   self.waitingFor = player
   -- check if we are at the first player
   if player.position == self:FindNextPosition(self.bigBlindPos) then
      -- if all active players bet the same amount we move to the next betting round
      for i, v in ipairs(self.players) do
         -- player is active and didn't check yet
         if not v.inactive and v.bet ~= self.call then
            -- change state to "bettingRoundStarted" with bettingRound + 1
            -- this means we have to return here!
            return self:StartBettingRound(self.bettingRound + 1)
         end
      end
   end
   player:SendMessage("YourTurn", self.check, self.minRaise) -- your turn, player!
   -- set timeout: 45, self:BetTimeout(player)
   self:Schedule(45, self.BetTimeout, self, player)
end
```

This was actually the last state from the simplified bubble diagram shown earlier. We now have nearly all our states and transitions defined. The state "showdown" is not completely implemented yet, but it is not complicated at all. Get all cards from all players, calculate the rating of the hands, get the player with the best hand, and tell everyone on the table who won.

This is the skeleton of a fully functional poker game logic. There are two tasks remaining: adding the communication-related methods and thinking of a smart protocol to tell the client what to display. We will do this in Chapter 8. The second task is to implement the missing parts of the game logic. If that sounds like a lot of work, you are right. But it is not difficult, as we have already completed the most important part of the logic. We just need to add a lot of methods. But this is rather boring and repetitive work, and you probably wouldn't learn much from seeing all the code here. You can find the complete code of the server in the code download.

We call the method Schedule in the code here that will forward the call to our timing library. But there is a small problem with this timing library: it is not object-oriented. This means if one of our server objects tries to unschedule all calls to self.BetTimeout, it will also unschedule all calls of the other running servers. This could be solved by also providing the first argument as a unique identifier for the server. But it would be much clearer if the timing library would be object-oriented. We could then just create an instance of it and safely use schedule and unschedule methods on this instance without worrying to interfere with other addons or objects using other instances of the library. Let's fix this, as it is more interesting than implementing poker game logic.

Simple Timing Library 2.0

This part of the chapter deals with our old library SimpleTimingLib; we will add object-orientation to it. You don't have to delete the old version of SimpleTimingLib, as we can re-use most parts of it.

Our first design decision for this second version of the timing library is whether to use a separate task storage for each instance or just one for all instances. The advantage of using separate storage for each instance is that tasks of different instances are clearly separated. But each instance would need its own OnUpdate handler. The prototype would have numerous methods to handle this.

Object-Oriented Timing Library

We are going to use just one task storage, so our OnUpdate handler stays simple and the whole timing library prototype is quite small. We just need to store the instance a task belongs to somewhere in the table that represents a task. The prototype is then simply a wrapper for the real functions. The following code shows the prototype, which simply consists of two wrapper methods and a constructor. Add it to the end of the file SimpleTimingLib.lua of the addon SimpleTimingLib.

```
SimpleTimingLib = {}
function SimpleTimingLib:Schedule(time, func, ...)
    return schedule(time, func, self, ...)
end

function SimpleTimingLib:Unschedule(func, ...)
    return unschedule(func, self, ...)
end

do
    local metatable = {__index = SimpleTimingLib}
    function SimpleTimingLib:New() -- constructor
        return setmetatable({}, metatable)
    end
end
```

The method Schedule just forwards the call to the real schedule function, schedule, with self as an additional argument. Unschedule forwards to unschedule and also adds self. These two functions are basically our old functions SimpleTimingLib_Schedule and SimpleTimingLib_Unschedule; let's copy and paste them and add support for the additional argument that identifies the calling instances. The following code shows the schedule function, which needs to be placed right above the three methods we just added, which require it:

```
local function schedule(time, func, obj, ...)
    local t = {...}
    t.func = func
    t.time = GetTime() + time
    t.obj = obj -- new
    tasks[#tasks + 1] = t
end
```

Note that we are keeping our old array tasks, which stores all tasks. This new function just adds the additional field obj to the table that stores the task. The new unschedule function has to read obj. The following function also needs to be placed above the three new methods:

```lua
local function unschedule(func, obj, ...)
   for i = #tasks, 1, -1 do
      local val = tasks[i]
      if value.obj == obj and (not func or val.func == func) then
         local matches = true
         for i = 1, select("#", ...) do
            if select(i, ...) ~= val[i] then
               matches = false
               break
            end
         end
         if matches then
            table.remove(tasks, i)
         end
      end
   end
end
```

The only change here, beside the function's head, is the if statement in the loop. It now checks whether the task was created by our object. It is now also possible to pass nil as the function to unschedule. This will cancel all tasks that were scheduled by the current instance.

Note that we don't have to rewrite the OnUpdate handler; we can just use the old one. This handler does not need to know which instance scheduled the task; it just executes the given function.

Let's use this library now by implementing the methods Schedule and Unschedule of the poker server. This is actually quite simple as they receive the same arguments as the Schedule/Unschedule methods of the timing library, so we can just forward the call. Add the following two method declarations to the server module of the poker addon:

```lua
function server:Schedule(...)
   return self.timingLib:Schedule(...)
end

function server:Unschedule(...)
   return self.timingLib:Unschedule(...)
end
```

This instance of the timing library needs to be created in the constructor; do that by assigning the return value of SimpleTimingLib:New() to the attribute timingLib of the new object.

But what happens to mods that are already using the old version of the timing library, like the DKP addon we wrote in Chapter 4?

Supporting the Old Timing Library

We could just keep the old functions. They would create entries without the field obj, and the unschedule function would be able to unschedule functions from all instances. But we have a lot of duplicate code here at the moment. We can update the old functions to forward to the local schedule and unschedule functions, with obj = nil.

```
function SimpleTimingLib_Schedule(time, func, ...)
    return schedule(time, func, nil, ...)
end

function SimpleTimingLib_Unschedule(func, ...)
    return unschedule(func, nil, ...)
end
```

The function SimpleTimingLib_Unschedule can no longer unschedule tasks from all instances, but we actually never wanted this functionality. You can change the if statement in the unschedule function if you want this functionality.

Using Another Data Structure?

We are using an array to store all tasks. Based on what we know about data structures, a question that comes up is this: is it really very smart to use an array here? We have to traverse the whole array every time OnUpdate is called. We also had problems with tasks that unscheduled other tasks in an array.

We could use a linked list instead of an array here, which would allow us to do a few smart optimizations. But a linked list might lead to problems when more than one consecutive task in this list is due in the same OnUpdate task. We could certainly work around this or use a double linked list. But a really smart data structure for such a scheduler is what is called a *priority queue*. You will see more about data structures, performance, and other implementations of this library in Chapter 13.

Our server is now pretty much finished (except for the game logic, which is not worth discussing here). We can now add functionality to the button in the GUI (the table browser) that creates a new table. This can be done with a single function call. But a nice feature would be the ability to save and restore the settings from the last session. This is more interesting, as it leads us back to a question I promised to answer earlier in this book: how can we save multiple values in a persistent table without running into problems?

Saved Variables and Metatables

When we discussed saved variables in Chapter 3, I mentioned that there is a smart method to solve the problem with saved tables. The original problem is that we want to save a table that contains a lot of options.

The Problem: Saving Tables

Let's look at an example table that is created in an addon.

```
TestTable = {
    testEntry = 1,
}
```

The variable TestTable is added as SavedVariables in the TOC file of the addon. We now load the addon for the first time, but there is no saved variable yet. Nothing happens. We set the field testEntry of the table to 2. Reloading the addon now initializes TestTable with the new table, but the saved variables are loaded after the addon. These saved variables overwrite the variable TestTable with a new table and TestTable.testEntry is 2.

The problem is that if we now add a new field (for example otherTestEntry = 5) to TestTable in the Lua file, it will never be saved. The game will always drop the table that is created in the Lua file when the old table from the saved variables is loaded; this old table does not have the entry otherTestEntry yet, as it didn't exist when the table was saved. The addon might now rely on getting a numeric value from this entry, but it gets nil. This will then lead to error messages when the addon tries to perform arithmetic operations on the value.

Note that this issue only happens if a user updates from a version that did not have the entry otherTestEntry to a new version with this entry. New users of the addon are unaffected.

Let's use the table browser part of the poker addon as an example. Let's add a saved variable that remembers the settings of the Create Server dialog. Add the following code to the first lines of TableBrowser.lua:

```
local defaultSavedVars = {
    Name = "My Table",
    Players = 6,
    SmallBlind = 10,
    BigBlind = 20,
    AllowEveryone = false,
    AllowGuild = true,
    AllowGroup = true,
    AllowFriends = true
}
Poker_TableBrowserSavedVars = {}
```

This sets up a few suitable default values that will be stored in the local variable defaultSavedVars. The global variable Poker_TableBrowserSavedVars holds an empty table and will be saved. This means you need to add the following line to your TOC file:

```
## SavedVariables: Poker_TableBrowserSavedVars
```

Don't forget that you must restart your game after a change to the TOC file.

The Solution: Metatables

We now need a metatable that is attached to the saved table. This table is available after the saved variables are loaded, which is indicated by the event ADDON_LOADED. The first argument of this event is the name of the addon that was loaded. We need an event handler for the file TableBrowser.lua, as we don't have one at the moment. You can add the event handler anywhere in the file; it doesn't matter as it neither refers to nor creates local variables.

```lua
do
    local frame = CreateFrame("Frame")
    frame:RegisterEvent("ADDON_LOADED")
    frame:SetScript("OnEvent", function(self, event, ...)
        return Poker_TableBrowser[event](...)
    end)
end
```

The event ADDON_LOADED will now call the function Poker_TableBrowser.ADDON_LOADED, so we need to add the metatable there. But what will be in that metatable? It needs to forward accesses to the table that contains the default options. So an option will be saved as soon as you change it. If you try to read a variable, Lua will first look in the saved table. If there is no option set, it will instead return the value from the table containing the default values. Note that we need to add this metatable recursively for all subtables that might be in the metatable. The following code shows a function that adds suitable metatables to all tables in a given table:

```lua
do
    local function addOptionMt(options, defaults)
        setmetatable(options, {__index = defaults})
        for i, v in pairs(options) do
            if type(v) == "table" and not getmetatable(v) then
                addOptionMt(v, defaults[i])
            end
        end
    end

    function Poker_TableBrowser.ADDON_LOADED(addon)
        if addon == "Texas_Hold'em" then
            addOptionMt(Poker_TableBrowserSavedVars, defaultSavedVars)
        end
    end
end
```

Note that we do not have any subtables in this example, but this function is a general solution for the problem of storing tables in saved variables. You can use it in all of your other addons.

We now need to save the options from the Create Game dialog; we can update the function CreateGame for this. But we have a small problem there as we cannot store nil in our new saved table. nil means that the field is empty, so Lua will instead return the default value from the table defaultSavedVars. But why would we get a nil value here? The method GetChecked of CheckButtons returns 1 if it is checked and nil otherwise. Many API functions where you might expect a boolean actually return 1 or nil. This is a residue from Lua 4.0, which did not have the type boolean. So we need a helper function that converts (*casts*) its argument to true or false. Let's call this function toboolean.

```
function Poker_TableBrowser.CreateGame(...)
   Poker_TableBrowserSavedVars.Name = select(1, ...)
   Poker_TableBrowserSavedVars.Players = select(2, ...)
   Poker_TableBrowserSavedVars.SmallBlind = select(3, ...)
   Poker_TableBrowserSavedVars.BigBlind = select(4, ...)
   Poker_TableBrowserSavedVars.AllowEveryone = toboolean(select(5, ...))
   Poker_TableBrowserSavedVars.AllowGuild = toboolean(select(6, ...))
   Poker_TableBrowserSavedVars.AllowGroup = toboolean(select(7, ...))
   Poker_TableBrowserSavedVars.AllowFriends = toboolean(select(8, ...))
   print("Creating game...")
   Poker_CreateServer(...)
end
```

The function toboolean is also quite simple; remember that not always returns true or false. So using not twice does the job:

```
local function toboolean(val)
   return not not val
end
```

Note that this function (or the initialization of the local variable toboolean) must be above the function CreateGame.

This stores the settings, but we also need to restore them when opening the frame. We can use the OnShow method here. Note that using _G is equivalent to getglobal: I'm using _G most of the time as it is shorter. The following code can be put in the OnShow element of the Scripts element of the frame Poker_CreateTable in the XML file:

```
local name = self:GetName()
_G[name.."TableName"]:SetText(Poker_TableBrowserSavedVars.Name)
_G[name.."Players"]:SetValue(Poker_TableBrowserSavedVars.Players)
_G[name.."SmallBlind"]:SetValue(Poker_TableBrowserSavedVars.SmallBlind)
_G[name.."BigBlind"]:SetValue(Poker_TableBrowserSavedVars.BigBlind)
_G[name.."AllowEveryone"]:SetChecked(Poker_TableBrowserSavedVars.AllowEveryone)
_G[name.."AllowGuild"]:SetChecked(Poker_TableBrowserSavedVars.AllowGuild)
_G[name.."AllowGroup"]:SetChecked(Poker_TableBrowserSavedVars.AllowGroup)
_G[name.."AllowFriends"]:SetChecked(Poker_TableBrowserSavedVars.AllowFriends)
```

You can now test this in-game. You can also try to add new fields to the default values to satisfy yourself that it is working properly.

Summary

This chapter featured a few examples showing how we can use our advanced knowledge of Lua in World of Warcraft addons. The focus here was on object-oriented programming, as this approach is important in addons. The whole frame/widget API is object-oriented, so you are going to use OOP all the time.

The main example of this chapter was the Texas Hold'em Poker addon. But we didn't see a lot of code that was actually running in the game. This will change in the next chapter, which covers addon communication; we will build the communication module and client of the poker addon there. You will have a fully featured poker addon after the next chapter!

■ ■ ■

## CHAPTER 8

Building a Poker Game Client with Addon Communication

Our poker addon is almost finished. The last part that remains is the client that connects to a server and displays the actual game. Remember that the whole game logic is already in the server; the client only needs to display the data it receives from the server. But how can we send data from one player who runs a given server to another player who wants to play on that server? World of Warcraft provides what it calls *addon messages*, which are basically just invisible chat messages. You can send such a message to other players through the raid, party, battleground, guild, and whisper channels. WoW fires the event CHAT_MSG_ADDON every time it receives such an addon message.

In writing the client, you will learn how addon messages can be used to provide your addons with basic networking capabilities. There are a few very important things one has to keep in mind when using addon messages; security is especially important when receiving commands from other players. These other players could try to send you forged or malformed addon messages that lead to crashes, or the remote player might even be able to take control of the addon. You will learn how this can be prevented and what needs to be checked when receiving such an addon message.

Chapter 7 was more focused on Lua and not on World of Warcraft, but this chapter will again focus on using Lua in World of Warcraft. You are now probably afraid that we are going to see a lot of XML, as I just told you that we're going to build a poker client. But I've provided a basic client in the code download that comes with a simple GUI and functions like SetPlayerCards(*card1*, *card2*) or AddCommunityCard(*card*). We will implement only a few particularly interesting functions, like those for communication.

The reason I provide this template instead of discussing the whole game client here is that most parts of the poker client are really boring; it is basically a frame with a few textures for a table, cards, and player portraits in it. We've already discussed how to create such frames in Chapter 5, so you would learn nothing new here.

Addon Communication Basics

An addon message works like a chat message, with the only difference that the default UI does not display it. However, it's easy to write a function that displays addon messages like regular chat messages. This is incredibly useful for debugging, so we will see how to do this in just a bit.

Sending Messages

Sending addon messages is very similar to sending chat messages. The function `SendAddonMessage(prefix, msg, channel, target)` sends such an addon message. The `prefix` argument is used as a prefix to identify the addon that sent a message, as there are probably a lot of different addons communicating on the same channel, and the messages must be distinguishable.

■Tip A good name for a prefix is a unique abbreviation of your addon's name. For example, Deadly Boss Mods uses DBMv4 as a prefix; this is certainly unique and does not conflict with any other addon, not even with older versions of DBM, which used a different communication protocol.

The `msg` argument is the actual message you want to send; the maximum length of the message and the prefix together is 254 characters. The game uses a tab (\t) as a delimiter between the prefix and the message internally. You must therefore not use \t in the prefix, but you can use all characters in the message. The `channel` argument defines the channel the message will be sent to; all available channels can be found in Table 8-1. The fourth argument, `target`, can only be used together with the channel WHISPER and defines the player the message is sent to.

Table 8-1. *Available Addon Message Channels*

Channel	Description
GUILD	Sends a message to all guild members.
PARTY	Sends a message to members of your party.
RAID	Sends a message to your raid.
BATTLEGROUND	Sends a message to all players of the same faction in your battleground.
WHISPER	Sends a message to a player specified with the fourth argument, *target*.

Note that many chat message channels are not available. Most of these channels, like SAY, would not make sense for addon messages. But CHANNEL is also not available, even though it could be very helpful when you want to communicate with multiple players that are in neither your group nor your guild. Our poker addon could use such a channel for a server-wide broadcast of currently opened games, but we will have to stick to raid and guild communication here.

Receiving Messages

Receiving an addon message is also very similar to receiving chat messages. The event CHAT_MSG_ADDON is fired every time you receive an addon message. Table 8-2 shows the event arguments that are passed to the event handler after *self* and *event*.

Table 8-2. *CHAT_MSG_ADDON Event Arguments*

Channel	Description
prefix	The prefix used.
msg	The message that was sent.
channel	One of the channel types from Table 8-1.
sender	The player who sent the message.

This is basically everything you need to know in order to use addon messages. So let's try it.

Playing Around with Addon Messages

We can test a few addon messages by writing a simple script that displays all received addon messages with the prefix Test. The following code shows an example event handler that can be used to print messages to the chat frame. This can also come in handy when you have to debug an addon.

```
local f = CreateFrame("Frame")
f:RegisterEvent("CHAT_MSG_ADDON")
f:SetScript("OnEvent", function(self, event, prefix, msg, channel, sender)
    if prefix == "Test" then
        print(string.format("[%s] [%s]: %s %s", channel, sender, prefix, msg))
    end
end)
```

You can remove the check for the prefix to see all addon messages you receive, but this can produce a lot of spam as many addons constantly send messages to the raid and guild channel. You can now execute the following function calls to send test messages:

```
SendAddonMessage("Test", "Whisper test", "WHISPER", UnitName("player"))
SendAddonMessage("Test", "Party test", "PARTY") -- requires a party
SendAddonMessage("Test", "Raid test", "RAID") -- requires a raid
SendAddonMessage("Test", "Guild test", "GUILD") -- requires a guild
```

The produced output will be

```
[WHISPER] [Tandanu]: Test Whisper test
[PARTY] [Tandanu]: Test Party test
[RAID] [Tandanu]: Test Raid test
[GUILD] [Tandanu]: Test Guild test
```

You will, of course, see the name of your character instead of Tandanu (the name of my Priest). You can also test this with guild mates to see for yourself that it really works and sends invisible addon messages around.

This simple example can be used to chat through these messages; one advantage of such a chat addon could be that you can easily implement messages that are longer than 255 characters by splitting long messages into several addon messages.

But many addons, like our poker addon, want to do more than simply display the messages. For example, addons like Gatherer can use these messages to synchronize information about mining or herb spots. Players can inform their whole guild or raid that they've just harvested a given herb spot, and your gatherer client will mark the spot as empty so you can efficiently farm an area with many people in your guild. Another example would be an addon for questing that shares detailed information about your open quests and progress with your group.

But there is one important topic to keep in mind when working with addon messages—security.

Security and Addon Messages

Security is always important when you receive messages sent by other players. The first thing you have to do is to check whether the player who sent the message is actually allowed to execute the given message.

Many actions in raid mods should be restricted to raid leaders and assistants. For example, Deadly Boss Mods allows raid leaders and assistants to create custom timers and send them to the raid or party. We will use the custom timer implementation as an example of security in this section before we start working on the poker client in the next section.

The following checks need to be performed before any action (other than ignoring the message) can be taken:

- Where was the message sent to? You probably don't want to accept certain commands from whisper or battleground messages. The reason for this is that you probably trust a member of your guild or raid to send you correct information, but you don't want a random player from a battleground (or even a whisper message, which could come from anywhere) to be able to send you certain commands.

- Who sent the message? Has the sender sufficient rights (raid leader or assistant) to send the message?

- Is the message well formed? Imagine you are expecting a message that contains a number, but it contains a string. You now try to extract a number and perform an arithmetic operation on it and what you get is an error message. You don't want other players to be able to trigger error messages remotely.

- Do the contents of the message make sense? You should perform checks on any received values to prevent problems caused by extremely long strings or huge numbers. For example, consider the previously mentioned custom timer broadcast; you probably don't want to receive timers that last several hours.

Let's take a look at the timer broadcast system of DBM and how it performs these checks. The event handler for CHAT_MSG_ADDON first checks the channel and prefix and dispatches a call to an appropriate function for the specific prefix, as DBM handles various types of prefixes. The dispatcher is very similar to those we saw in combination with events, and you should consider using event handlers with such a dispatcher when you have to handle a lot of prefixes in your addon. Our poker addon won't need it, as it just needs a few prefixes.

The event handler never accepts any messages from the GUILD channel, as the addon does not expect messages to be sent there. So a message that somehow gets to the GUILD channel is potentially malicious. The function also makes sure that any incoming whisper message is sent from a player in the current party or raid by calling the auxiliary method DBM:GetRaidUnitId(*playerName*), which returns the unit ID none if the player is not in your raid or party. Note that none is a unit ID that is valid but never refers to an existing unit; returning nil could cause problems, as the result of this function is often passed to API functions that expect a valid unit ID. Messages from players outside the raid are never accepted.

The next security check here is to distinguish between broadcast messages that are received in the PARTY, RAID, or BATTLEGROUND channel and unicast WHISPER messages from raid members. All addon message handlers that expect broadcast messages are stored in the table syncHandlers, while all unicast messages are stored in whisperSyncHandlers. For example, a custom timer is never accepted if it was received via whisper, because the handler function responsible for this is stored in syncHandlers and not in whisperSyncHandlers.

Here's the complete event handler:

```
function DBM:CHAT_MSG_ADDON(prefix, msg, channel, sender)
    if channel ~= "WHISPER" and channel ~= "GUILD" then
        -- channel is a "group channel": RAID, PARTY or BATTLEGROUND
        local handler = syncHandlers[prefix]
        if handler then
            return handler(msg, channel, sender)
        end
    elseif channel == "WHISPER" and self:GetRaidUnitId(sender) ~= "none" then
        local handler = whisperSyncHandlers[prefix]
        if handler then
            return handler(msg, channel, sender)
        end
    end
end
```

This event handler performs the first important check: where did the message come from? Let's look at the function that is responsible for the custom timer. The prefix that is used is DBMv4-Pizza (the custom timer was originally known as "Pizza Timer" in earlier versions of Deadly Boss Mods). The first thing the function needs to check is whether the sender has sufficient rights to send you a custom timer. The method DBM:GetRaidRank(*name*) is used to determine the rank of a player; 0 means no special role, 1 raid assistant, and 2 raid leader. The function also rejects the timer if you are currently in a battleground, as you usually don't trust a random raid leader in a battleground as much as you trust your guild's raid leader. This prevents you from being spammed with custom timers in battlegrounds. DBM rejects most sync messages in battlegrounds that are normally accepted. You would also ignore a custom timer if you are the sender of the message, as the timer will already be started locally when broadcasting it.

The third check is whether the message is well formed. Its expected format is the time in seconds followed by a tab as delimiter and the name of the timer. The sync handler tries to extract these two arguments from the message and propagates the call to another method, which handles the actual creation of the custom timer if the message was well-formed:

```
syncHandlers["DBMv4-Pizza"] = function(msg, channel, sender)
    if select(2, IsInInstance()) == "pvp" then return end
    if DBM:GetRaidRank(sender) == 0 then return end
    if sender == UnitName("player") then return end
    local time, text = strsplit("\t", msg)
    time = tonumber(time or 0)
    text = tostring(text)
    if time and text then
        DBM:CreatePizzaTimer(time, text, nil, sender)
    end
end
```

The method DBM:CreatePizzaTimer(*time, text, broadcast, sender*) does a few checks on the arguments provided and then displays the timer. For example, timer names with more than 16 characters are not allowed, and the maximum time for a timer is 2 hours.

You always have to perform these checks. Bad things can happen if you don't. For example, I once read the code of a raid management addon that was used during raids a few years ago; This particular addon was very popular, and the whole raid (40 players) used it. I figured out that the check for well-formed messages was missing for the message that informs other players about the current main tank settings. So I tried to send an invalid main tank broadcast to the raid; it basically said that we currently have three main tanks, but I didn't provide the names of the tanks.

This addon accepted the invalid message and tried to modify the main tank display, and this task failed. The raid frames that were provided by the addon stopped working for the whole raid; it was no longer possible to click on them, and the addon produced error messages all the time. I did this during a fight in Naxxramas, so our raid wiped and everyone was upset about that addon, as it killed them (well actually I killed them, but my guild mates didn't know that). All players tried to reload their user interfaces or logged out and back in. But that didn't help, as one of the first things this addon did when joining a raid was to ask for the current status, like the main tank settings. It simply broadcast the malicious message again and again; the only way to solve the problem was to disband and reform the whole raid group.

You don't want this to happen with your addon, so make sure you always check addon messages you receive in your addon. Also, the code that receives and interprets the messages must be very robust; it must not throw error messages just because a value is missing or of the wrong type.

That was the theory. Now let's use addon messages to finish the poker addon.

Building the Poker Client

You can find a basic version of the whole poker addon in the code download, as mentioned in the chapter introduction. It contains the full server implementation with the whole game logic and a client with methods like adding players and community cards. Again, the reason we are not implementing the whole client here is that it is a lot of code and most of it is really boring. Creating a GUI with XML is not so exciting that we need another chapter that deals with it. The pre-implemented methods basically deal with calling the methods Show, Hide, and SetTexture on texture objects. You can read the code of the provided methods if you are curious how it works.

The Different Message Types We Need

There are a few different message types we need in our poker addon, and we are going to use different prefixes for them. It is always good to think about what message types you need before you start programming. The following list shows the prefixes we will use:

> Poker-GA: The notation GA stands for "Game Announce"; this message broadcasts all games you are currently hosting to your party, raid, and guild.

> Poker-S2C: The notation S2C stands for "Server to Client" and will be used for messages sent from the server to the client.

> Poker-C2S: The notation C2S stands for "Client to Server" and will be used for messages that are sent from the client to the server.

The server-to-client and client-to-server messages are using separate prefixes because it prevents possible issues when you are playing on your own server. Imagine that your server receives client-to-server messages from other players that might be misinterpreted as server-to-client messages directed to your game client and not to your server.

Another thing we need to keep in mind is that we could potentially be running multiple servers at the same time. This means we need to be able to distinguish two messages that are directed to two different running server instances. One way would be to include the server ID in the prefix, but the prefix is usually static. The reason for this is that you are probably receiving many addon messages from other addons, and performing string operations on every single addon message you receive can be too expensive. We are going to include the server ID (a number that increases by 1 for every server you create) in the body of the client-to-server messages for this reason.

Sending Game Announcements

The first things we need to create are the game announcement, which is actually part of the server (sending the announcements), and the table browser (receiving and displaying the games).

We will broadcast currently running server instances to the party, raid, and guild chat. The simplest way to do this is to broadcast the tables every few seconds to these channels. Another possible way would be to implement a "request game list" command that is sent by the player who is interested in the game list. All servers that see the message would then whisper all their games to the requesting player and also inform the player about any changes in these games. This seems to be a better solution than simply broadcasting the game all the time, but it has the disadvantage that it is more complicated to implement. You have to keep track of players who want to be informed about changes, and you have to send updates every time something changes. We would also need an additional broadcast message when opening the game to inform all clients.

We will stick to the simple solution and broadcast all opened tables to all channels if the players in these channels are allowed to join the game. It would obviously not make sense to send information about games that cannot be joined by raid members to the RAID channel. One might argue that it is a waste of bandwidth or CPU cycles, but we will be broadcasting the games only every three seconds to a maximum of two channels (GUILD and RAID or PARTY). Also, the message is relatively short, with a maximum of 51 characters (8 for the prefix, up to 4 for the current and maximum players, up to 8 for the small/big blinds, 26 for the game name, and 5 tabs as delimiters). Even if you had opened five games at the same time (which is extremely unlikely), and all of them were broadcast to two channels, you would only generate 136 bytes-per-second traffic, which is acceptable as you probably don't need the game for anything else while playing poker. You should not have to worry about sending too much addon message content as long as you are not sending multiple long messages per second, which is not the case here. Everything else is just fine.

Another thing we need to keep in mind is that you always want to be able to see your own table in the table browser. You might think that was already the case, as you are a member of your own group and guild and therefore receive your own broadcast commands. However, imagine that you do not have a guild and no group, and you want to host a table that can only be joined by your friends by entering your name. Even though your friends obviously have to enter your name to join the game, as there is no suitable broadcast channel, you would still expect the addon to show your own game in this case. So we are going to fake a CHAT_MSG_ADDON event for ourselves if we don't send any sync message at all.

Let's take a look at this functionality, which is already in the template from the code download; you can find it at the end of Server.lua:

```lua
local frame = CreateFrame("Frame")
local elapsed = 0

frame:SetScript("OnUpdate", function(self, e)
    elapsed = elapsed + e
    if elapsed >= 3 then
        elapsed = 0
        for i, v in ipairs(servers) do
            if #v.players < v.maxPlayers then
                local msg = string.format("%d\t%d\t%d\t%d\t%d\t%s", ➥
#v.players, v.maxPlayers, v.smallBlind, v.bigBlind, v.name)
                local sentMsg
                if IsInGuild() and (v.allowGuild or v.allowEveryone) then
                    SendAddonMessage("Poker-GA", msg, "GUILD")
                    sentMsg = true
                end
                if v.allowGroup or v.allowEveryone then
                    if GetNumRaidMembers() > 0 then
                        SendAddonMessage("Poker-GA", msg, "RAID")
                        sentMsg = true
                    elseif GetNumPartyMembers() > 0 then
                        SendAddonMessage("Poker-GA", msg, "PARTY")
                        sentMsg = true
                    end
                end
            end
```

```
            if not sentMsg then
                Poker_TableBrowser("Poker-GA", msg, "GUILD", UnitName("player"))
            end
        end
    end
end
end)
```

This broadcasts the information; the next thing we need to do is to receive it in the table browser module.

Receiving Game Announcements

Besides the new event handler, two other changes need to be made in the table browser: First, we are currently creating dummy entries with the purpose of testing the GUI, and they need to be removed. We also need to register the event CHAT_MSG_ADDON. These two changes and the following event handler are already included in the package from the code download; you can find the event handler at the end of the file TableBrowser.lua.

The following function is the event handler that does all necessary checks: First it checks whether the message came from the right channel; we do not want to accept anything that came from the whisper channel. We don't need to check whether the player is permitted to send this, as everyone may host poker games. The function then tries to extract the data from the message, and it makes sure that possible nil values do not cause an error when trying to convert them into a number. The function returns if the message is malformed. It also returns if one of the security checks fails; we do not want to receive tables that have obviously wrong values for the number of allowed players or too long names.

A table representing the poker game is created (or updated if the game is already in our list) if none of these checks fails. Here's the complete function:

```
function Poker_TableBrowser.CHAT_MSG_ADDON(prefix, msg, channel, sender)
    if prefix == "Poker-GA" and➥
(channel == "GUILD" or channel == "RAID" or channel == "PARTY") then
        local players, maxplayers, smallBlind, bigBlind, tableName =➥
string.split("\t", msg)
        players = math.floor(tonumber(players or ""))
        maxplayers = math.floor(tonumber(maxplayers or ""))
        smallBlind = math.floor(tonumber(smallBlind or ""))
        bigBlind = math.floor(tonumber(bigBlind or ""))
        if not (players and maxplayers and smallBlind and bigBlind and tableName) then
            return -- message is malformed; reject it
        end
        -- check arguments for valid values
        if players > 10 or players < 0 or maxplayers > 10 or maxplayers < 0
        or smallBlind > 1000 or smallBlind < 0 or bigBlind > 1000 or bigBlind < 0
        or smallBlind > math.floor(bigBlind / 2) or #tableName > 26 then
            return
        end
```

```
            local key = #Poker_TableBrowser.Tables + 1
            -- check if we already have the server in our list
            for i, v in ipairs(Poker_TableBrowser.Tables) do
                if v[1] == tableName and v[2] == sender then
                    -- found it, return
                    key = i
                    break
                end
            end
            -- key is now either the first free slot in the array
            -- Poker_TableBrowser.Tables that holds all open servers
            -- or it is the old entry that will be updated
            Poker_TableBrowser.Tables[key] = Poker_TableBrowser.Tables[key] or {}
            local entry = Poker_TableBrowser.Tables[key]
            entry[1] = tableName
            entry[2] = sender
            entry[3] = players
            entry[4] = maxplayers
            entry[5] = smallBlind
            entry[6] = bigBlind
            entry.lastUpdate = GetTime()
            Poker_TableBrowser.Update() -- update the GUI
        end
end
```

The field lastUpdate in the poker table is new; it is the time the table was last updated. This allows us to remove tables that are no longer announced by the server because they are full or have been closed. The following OnUpdate script, which is also already in the file, regularly scans the array for outdated entries and removes them:

```
local elapsed = 0
frame:SetScript("OnUpdate", function(self, e)
    elapsed = elapsed + e
    if elapsed >= 5 then
        elapsed = 0
        local time = GetTime()
        -- remove outdated entries
        for i = #Poker_TableBrowser.Tables, 1, -1 do
            if time - Poker_TableBrowser.Tables[i].lastUpdate > 5 then
                table.remove(Poker_TableBrowser.Tables, i)
            end
        end
        Poker_TableBrowser.Update() -- update the GUI
    end
end)
```

You can verify that it is working by opening the table browser with the slash command /poker and creating one or more games that will show up in the table list.

We can now move on to the topic you are probably waiting for: creating the communication module of the poker client. This will be relatively short and easy, as there is not really much to do and the whole game logic is already in the server.

But we will also see a few parts of the server again, as communication always requires two parts: something that sends a message and something else that receives it. The first thing we need to be able to do is join a game.

Joining Games

The table browser calls the method `PokerClient:JoinTable()`, which we are going to implement in the file `Client.lua` now. You can already find an empty function body for this function there. I'm using the colon notation here, even though the client is not object-oriented and you cannot have multiple clients open at the same time. The reason for this is that the methods of the poker client will often call its other methods, and it is just shorter to write `self:SomeMethod()` instead of `PokerClient:SomeMethod()`. You will often see addons that are not object-oriented but use methods with the colon notation for this reason.

Sending Join Requests

This function will send our first client-to-server message, so you might expect it to be a one-line function that just calls `SendAddonMessage`. But we will wrap the call to `SendAddonMessage` in another function, as this frees us from providing the host of the current table every time we want to send a message. This method will simply be called `PokerClient:SendMessage(msg)`; you can already find an empty body of it at the beginning of the file.

We also need to store the server ID somewhere, as the host might host multiple servers; this server ID will be sent to us once our join request has been accepted. The local variable `curHost`, which is defined at the beginning of the file, stores the host, and `curServerID` stores the ID of the server. The ID will be added to all server-to-client messages we are going to send with the `SendMessage` function. Note that we don't have the ID yet, as we are not connected yet, so we will simply use 0 as the ID here. This tells the server that we don't know the ID yet and that this message is a join attempt.

A good function to send messages would therefore look like the following. It accepts a variable number of arguments that will all be converted to strings and separated with tabs. The communication module of the server can then use `string.split` to get the used strings back.

```
function PokerClient:SendMessage(...)
   if not curHost then
      return
   end
   SendAddonMessage("Poker-C2S", string.join("\t",➡
curServerID or 0, tostringall(...)), "WHISPER", curHost)
end
```

The method `JoinTable` is now really simple; it merely sets the `curHost` variable and calls `SendMessage`:

```
function PokerClient:JoinTable(host, name)
   curHost = host
   self:SendMessage("JoinRequest", name)
end
```

Our server will respond to this message with three possible response codes: AccessDenied if you do not have sufficient rights to join the table, ServerFull if all slots are occupied, or Welcome to inform you that your join request was successful. This also needs additional arguments: the server ID that should later be used in addon messages to identify the server, your slot on the table, and your initial amount of chip value.

Receiving Responses

We now need to be able to receive server-to-client messages. I already prepared an event dispatcher for the client and an empty method for the event CHAT_MSG_ADDON. We can use a very minimal event handler that does a few basic checks and decodes the message with string. split before forwarding the call to a method, named OnMessage, that receives all results from string.split as arguments. These basic checks are whether the message was sent by the host of the table we are currently playing on, whether the prefix indicates that it is a server to client message in our addon, and whether it was a whisper message, as we only expect whispers. Here's the code:

```
function PokerClient:CHAT_MSG_ADDON(prefix, msg, channel, sender)
    if sender ~= curHost or prefix ~= "Poker-S2C" or channel ~= "WHISPER" then
        return
    end
    return self:OnMessage(string.split("\t", msg))
end
```

The function OnMessage can also be very simple. It continues decoding the message by extracting the first argument, which is used to identify the message type, and dispatches another call to a method based on the first argument:

```
function PokerClient:OnMessage(id, ...)
    if self["On"..id] then -- avoid error messages on invalid addon messages
        return self["On"..id](self, ...)
    end
end
```

We can now simply create methods named after the response codes to handle them. The two simplest response codes we need to handle here are AccessDenied and ServerFull; they just display a message and set curHost back to nil:

```
function PokerClient:OnAccessDenied()
    self:AddMsg("Access denied!")
    curHost = nil
end
```

```
function PokerClient:OnServerFull()
    self:AddMsg("The server is currently full.")
    curHost = nil
end
```

Being accepted is more interesting, as you receive additional arguments. Note that these additional arguments will always be strings, so we have to convert them to numbers here.

These numbers will then be used to display our portrait in the given slot by calling the predefined method SetSlot and updating the chip display for our slot by calling SetChips:

```
function PokerClient:OnWelcome(serverId, slot, chips)
    serverId = tonumber(serverId)
    slot = tonumber(slot)
    chips = tonumber(chips)
    curServerID = serverId
    playing = true
    self:SetSlot(slot)
    self:SetChips(slot, chips)
end
```

You might think there is something missing, as I'm not checking whether the three arguments were provided and valid. This could cause an error message if you are trying to join a game of a malicious host. However, I'm not doing all the checks here, because you have to trust the host anyway. You have a bigger problem than an error message if you don't trust the host of your game. The host can cheat because he knows how the cards are sorted and can even modify them.

Adding all the checks that would normally be necessary would blow up the code and is not really necessary here, as the host is not a random person from your group or guild but a trustworthy person. An error message means that probably something went wrong in the game client or server and not that the host is trying to annoy you.

We are now sitting at the table, but we still don't know what's going on there.

Receiving Status Updates

You might have expected to receive more information in the Welcome message. For example, we don't know who else is on the table with us. The server will send us NewPlayer commands (which are also used if a new player joins the table) to inform us about the other players:

```
function PokerClient:OnNewPlayer(slot, name, chips, status)
    slot = tonumber(slot)
    chips = tonumber(chips)
    status = tonumber(status)
    self:AddPlayer(slot, name)
    self:SetChips(slot, chips)
    self:SetStatus(slot, status)
end
```

This returns all the necessary information about the player. The status is a number that represents the status of the player: 1 means waiting, 2 means active (it's that player's turn), 3 means folded, and 4 means sitting out.

Next we need to know about the community cards, so we can follow the game:

```
function PokerClient:OnNewCommunityCard(cardCode)
    self:AddCommunityCard(cardCode)
end
```

The function AddCommunityCard is also not really interesting; it gets the card from the card code by using the poker library and inserts that card into a table. It then calls SetTexture on a texture to show the card and returns.

Another piece of information we still need is the size of the pot. However, I think you now have the concept of all these addon messages, and you can imagine what all of the following functions will look like. They just need to display things, which is really easy and not worth discussing it here. We've covered the important parts of the communication modules, and you learned how addon communication works. I don't want to bore you with method definitions that just forward calls to other methods that then show and hide textures.

Summary

This chapter covered everything you need to know about addon messages: how to send them with the function SendAddonMessage(prefix, msg, channel, target), and how to listen to them with the event CHAT_MSG_ADDON. The next important topic was security when working with addon messages. I showed you a few examples of how to use addon messages in a smart way and how not to use them. You must never forget to check all code that is related to addon messages twice. You don't want to have bugs in this code.

In the second part of the chapter, we then tried out a practical use for addon messages, when we continued working on the poker mod. We did not discuss all of the sync methods there, as they are very similar. After you've seen a few of the communication methods, they all look alike and don't do exciting stuff. You can, as always, find the finished version of the poker addon in the code download package for this chapter. Have fun with this addon, and don't use it while raiding, or you will probably wipe out the raid (I'm speaking from experience here).

■ ■ ■

## CHAPTER 9

Using the Combat Log to Build a Cooldown Monitor

We have already used many events. But there are two particularly interesting events we haven't discussed yet: `COMBAT_LOG_EVENT` and `COMBAT_LOG_EVENT_UNFILTERED`. Both events are related to the combat log and can receive numerous arguments (up to 20). We will see the meaning of these arguments in this chapter. The combat log events are fired for all combat-related occurrences; for example, when anyone in your vicinity attacks a mob or anyone gets hit. The event arguments tell you exactly what happened.

The example mod we will write in this chapter will be called Cooldown Monitor, an addon that displays important cooldowns, like Heroism/Bloodlust or Rebirth, from members of your raid group. This means we have to find the type of combat log event that is fired when someone in your raid casts such a spell.

Working with Combat Log Events

I mentioned that there are two combat log events: `COMBAT_LOG_EVENT` and `COMBAT_LOG_EVENT_UNFILTERED`. Both receive the same arguments; the only difference is that the unfiltered event is fired for all combat log events. `COMBAT_LOG_EVENT` uses a filter that filters certain events. This filter is your combat log setting, and every `COMBAT_LOG_EVENT` is displayed in your combat log chat frame. Changing the setting of your combat log chat frame changes this filter. This means that you will be working with the unfiltered version of this event most of the time. In almost all of your addons, you don't want a user-defined filter for your events. The filtered version is useful only if you want to replace the default combat log chat frame with your addon.

Combat Log Arguments

The first eight arguments of a combat log event are always the same for all types of combat log events. Table 9-1 lists them.

Table 9-1. *The First Eight Combat Log Arguments*

Argument	Description
timestamp	A time stamp that contains the exact time when the event occurred. This can be used as the second argument to date(*fmt, time*).
event	The subevent.
sourceGUID	The GUID (globally unique identifier) of the entity that generated the event. We will see how we can get information from a GUID later.
sourceName	The name of the entity that generated the event. For example, if you cast a spell, this is your name.
sourceFlags	Flags that contain additional information about the entity that generated this event. This is a bit field which was already mentioned in Chapter 6; we will see how we can extract information from this bit field later.
destGUID	The GUID of the target.
destName	The target's name.
destFlags	The target's flags.

The most interesting argument is the second one, event. Don't confuse this with the real event COMBAT_LOG_EVENT. The event argument acts as a subevent that identifies the combat log action; for example, if you begin casting a spell, event will be SPELL_CAST_START. If you finish casting a spell, it is SPELL_CAST_SUCCESS. If the spell hits your target, event is SPELL_DAMAGE. You can find all subevents of combat log events in Appendix B.

This subevent also determines all additional arguments the event handler receives. If the subevent starts with SPELL or RANGE, like the previous example events, the arguments from Table 9-2 will be the next three arguments.

Table 9-2. *Additional Arguments of SPELL and RANGE Events*

Argument	Description
spellId	The ID of the spell. This is the same ID that is also used by many WoW database sites, like Wowhead. You can build a URL with the following pattern to retrieve additional information about a spell ID from such a site: http://www.wowhead.com/?spell=<spellId>
spellName	The name of the spell.
spellSchool	The school of the spell. This is a bit field and will be discussed in detail later in this chapter.

If the event starts with ENVIRONMENTAL (for example ENVIRONMENTAL_DAMAGE), the next argument is environmentalType, a string that identifies the environment type (for example "LAVA").

The arguments shown in Table 9-3 depend on the suffix of the combat log event. There are suffixes that do not add additional arguments, like SPELL_CAST_START and SPELL_CAST_SUCCESS in the example earlier. These two events receive the eight standard arguments and the additional three spell arguments. These arguments provide all the information you need: who cast which spell on whom. But the event SPELL_DAMAGE obviously requires even more arguments, as you also need to know how much damage the spell did or if it was a critical hit, and so on. Table 9-3 shows the additional arguments of all events that end with DAMAGE like SPELL_DAMAGE or SWING_DAMAGE (a normal white melee hit).

Table 9-3. *Additional Arguments of Events with the Suffix DAMAGE*

Argument	Description
amount	The amount of damage the attack did.
overkill	The overkill damage if the target died from the attack.
school	The school of the damage; this is a bit field, just like the spell's school. We will see how we can get information from this later.
resisted	The amount of damage that was resisted.
blocked	The amount of blocked damage.
absorbed	The amount of absorbed damage.
critical	1 if the hit was critical, nil otherwise.
glancing	1 if it was a glancing strike, nil otherwise.
crushing	1 if it was a crushing blow, nil otherwise.

There are more suffixes with even more arguments. Appendix B contains a table that lists all arguments for all combat log events.

Let's see a practical use for these events now.

Building an Event Handler

Dealing with a subevent is essentially no different than with a normal event, so you can just use your normal event handler. But it might be sometimes useful to treat the subevents like real events. The following code shows an event handler that does this:

```
MyMod = {}

local function onEvent(self, event, ...)
   if event == "COMBAT_LOG_EVENT_UNFILTERED" then
      return onEvent(self, select(2, ...), ...)
   elseif MyMod[event] then
      return MyMod[event](...)
   end
end

local frame = CreateFrame("Frame")
frame:RegisterEvent("COMBAT_LOG_EVENT_UNFILTERED")
frame:SetScript("OnEvent", onEvent)
```

The trick of this event handler that it just calls itself if the event is a combat log event. It replaces the combat log event with its subevent in this tail call. For example, we can now use the following function to print all SPELL_CAST_START subevents to the chat frame:

```
function MyMod.SPELL_CAST_START(...)
   print(string.join(",", tostringall(...)))
end
```

tostringall is an auxiliary function that is created by the default UI; it works just like tostring, but with many arguments. The string.join function is then used to concatenate all arguments, separated by commas. This will print all arguments of this subevent to your chat frame every time someone near you begins casting a spell. So using this in a city or even during a raid will spam a chat frame with a lot of events. The following example output is produced when I cast a Flash Heal:

```
1236219351.848,SPELL_CAST_START,0x00000000001517FB,Tandanu,1297,➥
0x0000000000000000,nil,-2147483648,48071,Flash Heal,2
```

The format of this output might look familiar if you have ever read a combat log in its raw form. You can create combat logs by typing /combatlog; this dumps all COMBAT_LOG_EVENT_ UNFILTERED events to the file World of Warcraft\Logs\WoWCombatLog.txt. Each line in this file holds an event with all its arguments separated by commas.

The first argument is the current time, and the second the subevent. The third argument is more interesting; it is my GUID. Note that this is a string, as a Lua number cannot represent such a large number. A GUID is always unique on the server, which means that there is no other player or NPC with the same GUID as mine. Note that even two mobs of the same type at the same spawn location will always have different GUIDs. This means you can use this ID to track an NPC or player in a combat log mod. Statistics addons like DamageMeters can use this ID to tell apart two mobs with the same name.

The fourth argument is my name. The fifth argument stores additional information about the caster (me); you will see how we can extract information from this bit field in the next section. The next three arguments, called destGUID, destName, and destFlags, refer to the target of the action. The event SPELL_CAST_START does not provide target information, so you cannot predict on whom a spell is cast. This information will be available when the spell hits the target. This means the GUID is just 0, the name is nil, and the flags seem to contain a pointless number.

The next three arguments are spellId, spellName, and spellSchool. The ID of the highest Flash Heal rank is 48071, which you can check by looking up the spell on Wowhead (http:// www.wowhead.com/?spell=48071). The name is obviously Flash Heal, and the school is 2, which indicates that the spell is a holy spell; we will see other possible values for spellSchool later in this chapter.

Working with GUIDs and Units

Every unit in the game has a unique GUID that identifies the object. The term *unit* refers to objects like mobs, players, NPCs, or vehicles. Every single NPC or player on the server has a unique GUID.

The GUID of a player or pet will change only when you rename your character or transfer it to another server. The GUID of an NPC is used until it dies; all respawned NPCs will have a new and different GUID.

A GUID is always represented as a string in hexadecimal notation. You cannot convert it to a Lua number, as this number is much too big. This number contains valuable information about its owner. For example, here is the GUID of a mob:

0xF1300070BB00004A

The purpose of the first two digits, F and 1, is unknown. (Note that 0 and x do not count as digits; 0x simply indicates a hexadecimal number.) The third digit (3) indicates the type of the unit; 3 stands for NPC. Other possible values are 4 for pet, 5 for vehicle, and 0 for player. All other digits depend on the type of the unit.

NPC and Vehicle GUIDs

The purpose of the next three digits is unknown here, but they are always 0. The next four digits (70BB in our example) contain the most valuable information we can extract from a GUID. This portion is the NPC ID of the NPC or vehicle. We can use the following function to extract the NPC ID from a GUID:

```
local function GetNPCId(guid)
    return tonumber(guid:sub(9, 12), 16)
end
```

```
print(GetNPCId("0xF1300070BB00004A")) --> 28859
```

We use the second argument of tonumber(*str, base*) here, which can be used to tell tonumber the base of the numeral system the given string is in. Note that this is not required for hexadecimal numbers if they are prefixed with 0x.

We call the function with our example GUID, and the result we get is 28859. This creature ID is, just like spell IDs, also used by almost all WoW database sites. We can use Wowhead to get the name and additional information about the NPC by opening the URL http://www.wowhead.com/?npc=28859. The page tells us that the GUID from the example was taken from Malygos.

We could also just look up the name, which is also passed as an argument, so this seems to be somewhat pointless. The real purpose of having these NPCs is that they do not depend on your localization. If you write a mod that looks for a certain NPC ID, it will work with all client languages. The name of the mob will certainly be different in a localized World of Warcraft client. The same applies for spell IDs.

■Tip Use the ID to identify a creature or spell and use sourceName, destName, and spellName to get its localized name for output.

The remaining six digits are a spawn-counter that is increased by one for every new mob of same type, to guarantee that the GUID is unique. This counter is reset when the server is restarted, so NPC (non-player character) and vehicle GUIDs are unique only for the current week.

Player and Pet GUIDs

The whole GUID of a player is just a counter that is increased every time someone creates a new character. This means you can compare the creation date of two characters by comparing their GUID. Note that a server transfer or name change will also give you a new GUID.

Pets are very similar to players. They also have a counter that is increased every time someone tames a new pet. This counter is stored in seven digits, starting with the fourth digit. The last six digits are a spawn counter for this specific pet, which is increased every time you summon your pet.

GUID Examples

An addon that works with GUIDs all the time is Deadly Boss Mods, which relies on having values that do not depend on the client language. The following code fragment shows a slightly simplified version of DBM's UNIT_DIED handler. The purpose of this handler is to detect the death of the boss you are currently fighting against. The handler is invoked every time a player or NPC dies; destGUID is the GUID of the dead unit. The method checks whether it was an NPC or a vehicle and then extracts its NPC ID, which is then passed to the method OnMobKill:

```
function DBM:UNIT_DIED(_,_,_,_,_,destGUID)
    if destGUID:sub(5, 5) == "3" or destGUID:sub(5, 5) == "5" then
        self:OnMobKill(tonumber(destGUID:sub(9, 12), 16))
    end
end
```

OnMobKill does the hard work. It uses a loop to iterate over all boss mods (small modules of DBM that handle boss fights) that are currently in combat; these mods are stored in the table in the local variable inCombat. Such a boss mod object then contains the field combatInfo, a table that holds all information about how to detect the pull and kill off the boss. The field mob in this table holds the NPC ID of the boss, which is also used for the pull detection. The following code snippet shows a slightly simplified version of the OnMobKill handler. The complete method has a lot of additional code for bosses with multiple mobs that need to be killed.

```
function DBM:OnMobKill(cId, synced)
    for i = #inCombat, 1, -1 do
        local v = inCombat[i]
        if cId == v.combatInfo.mob then
            if not synced then
                sendSync("DBMv4-Kill", cId)
            end
            v:EndCombat()
        end
    end
end
```

The function also syncs this event to the raid group to tell players who are out of range that the fight has ended. This sync will then again call OnMobKill with the second argument synced = true to prevent a sync loop.

The code then calls the method EndCombat of all boss mods that used the given NPC ID. This method prints out the victory chat message, ends all timers, and saves a few statistics.

Another important use of GUIDs is a very obvious one: using them as identifiers. They are, after all, globally unique identifiers. An example of this use is the Malygos boss mod. All players are using a vehicle (a dragon) during the third phase of this fight, and spells like Power Surge are then cast on these vehicles and not on the players. However, a boss mod still needs to be able to determine the target of Malygos' spells. But the only information it gets is the name and GUID of the affected vehicle. It's not possible to use the name to get the owner of the dragon, as all dragons have the same name. So we need to use the GUID for that.

The idea is to use the GUID as the key in a table and store the name of the vehicle's owner as the value there. The following code shows the function `buildGuidTable`, which is called a few seconds after Phase 3 starts. It uses the function `GetNumRaidMembers()`, which returns the number of players in your raid. It then builds a string from this number that identifies raid members and their pets. We will see more about unit IDs in the next section. `UnitGUID` is used to get the GUID of a unit and `UnitName` to get the name.

```
local guids = {}

local function buildGuidTable()
   for i = 1, GetNumRaidMembers() do
      guids[UnitGUID("raid"..i.."pet") or ""] = UnitName("raid"..i)
   end
end
```

This function builds the table `guids`, which allows us to use the GUID of a dragon to get its owner. The following example shows a code fragment that is responsible for displaying a huge warning text if Malygos casts a Power Surge on you. `specWarnSurge` is an object that represents a warning; its method `Show` displays this warning:

```
local target = guids[destGUID]
if target == UnitName("player") then
   specWarnSurge:Show()
end
```

The loop that built the table `guids` from this example made extensive use of unit IDs. Let's see how they work.

Unit IDs

A unit ID is a short string that identifies a unit like a player or an NPC. We just saw a few quite complicated unit IDs like `raid1target`. But we already saw a simpler unit ID earlier in this book: `player`. `player` always refers to you and it can be, like all unit IDs, passed to API functions like `UnitName`. There are many such functions to get the various attributes of a unit, like its current mana (`UnitMana`), health (`UnitHealth`), or GUID (`UnitGUID`). Appendix B contains a reference for all unit-related functions.

Unit IDs always consist of a prefix that can be followed by multiple suffixes. Table 9-4 lists all possible prefixes for unit IDs.

Table 9-4. *Unit ID Prefixes*

Prefix	Description
focus	Your focus target.
player	You.
pet	Your pet.
party*n*	The *n*th party member. Note that you are not your own party member, meaning that you cannot refer to yourself by using a such a unit ID. 0 < *n* < 5.
raid*n*	The *n*th raid member. This can, unlike party*n*, be you.
target	Your current target.
mouseover	The unit your mouse is currently over.
none	Refers to no unit.
npc	The NPC you are currently interacting with. Interacting means that you have a window opened like the flight map or quest dialog of the NPC.

This prefix can then be followed by suffixes. There are just two suffixes available: target and pet. The former always refers to the target of the unit identified by the prefix, the latter to its pet. An example of a unit ID would be raid1targetpettarget, which refers to the target of the pet of the target of the first raid member. The first raid member is the player who opened the raid group, the second one is the player who was the first to join, and so on. The following loop iterates over all raid members and prints their name and current target. It is very similar to the loop from the previous example that built the lookup table for the Malygos mod.

```
for i = 1, GetNumRaidMembers() do
    print(UnitName("raid"..i), UnitName("raid"..i.."target"))
end
```

Note that there will never be a hole in the raid unit IDs, and no player will ever get a unit ID greater than GetNumRaidMembers(), as the raid IDs shift down when a player leaves the raid group.

Other important arguments of combat log events are the unit flags and spell school. We have already seen the spell school 2, which told us that the spell was a holy spell. But what is the meaning of this number?

Unit Flags and Spell Schools

Unit flags and spell schools are bit fields; I mentioned them in Chapter 6 when we discussed the bit library. Let's take a closer look at bit fields now. A bit field is basically just a number that holds a series of boolean values. We have to look at the binary representation of a number to understand how it can hold booleans.

Bit Fields

Consider the number 20. Its binary representation is 10100. Each binary digit can either be 1 or 0, where 1 corresponds to true and 0 to false. This means we can store up to n boolean values in a binary number with n digits. These booleans are also called *flags*. The value 20 from the example stores five boolean values. We will refer to the very right bit as the zeroth bit, the bit left to this as the first bit, and so on. This means that in our example number 20, the zeroth boolean value that is stored in it is `false`. The first is also `false`, the second is `true`, the third is `false`, and the fourth is `true`.

As you can see, a relatively small number can store a lot of boolean values. So the use for bit fields is to save space. We will see bit fields that store up to 25 boolean values in just one number when we look at unit flags later in this section. Imagine that all those 25 booleans were passed as additional arguments to combat log events. It would certainly be possible, but working with the code would be really painful.

Reading Bits

We will now use the bit library to extract this information. Use the following code to load this library if you want to test the following examples in a normal Lua interpreter:

```
require("bit")
```

This is not necessary in World of Warcraft as the library is already loaded there. The function `require` is not even available in the game.

The bitwise operation that is needed to read a specific bit is the binary operator AND, which is available in the function `bit.band`. Table 9-5 lists the *truth table* of this operation, which shows the results of all possible combinations of operands. You can read the table by looking up the first operand in the left column and the second operand in the top row; the result is then in this row and column.

Table 9-5. *Truth Table of the Binary AND*

AND	1	0
1	1	0
0	0	0

Recall how these bitwise operations work. They use the binary AND operation on each bit of two numbers, starting with the very right bit. The corresponding bit in the resulting number is then set according to the table. This means that it is 1 only if the bits of both operands are also 1; otherwise it is 0.

For example, if we want to check that the fourth bit (remember to start counting with 0 at the least significant bit, the bit at the very right) is set in our earlier example, we can use the binary number 10000 (16 in decimal) as the second operand to the binary AND. This second operand is also called a *bit mask* and in the result of the operator will clear all the bits that are set in the number we are testing, except for the ones it has set. In the following code the 20 is our bit field and 16 is our bit mask:

```
print(bit.band(20, 16))
```

This prints 16, as 10100 band 10000 equals 10000. The function returns 0 if the fourth bit is not set, as, for example, in the number 15 (binary 01111). You can use the following expression to check whether the nth bit is set in a given bit field bf:

```
local isBitSet = bit.band(bf, 2^n) ~= 0
```

Replace n with the bit to check. Don't forget that 0 is the least significant bit. The expression evaluates to true if the bit is set; to false otherwise.

Note that the expression 2^n always evaluates to a number with the binary representation 100...00. Another possible way to create a bit mask is using the function bit.lshift(bitfield, n). This is the left shift operation; it shifts all bits in a field n places to the left. The new digits to the right will be filled with zeros. The following code also checks whether the nth bit is set:

```
local isBitSet = bit.band(20, bit.lshift(1, n)) ~= 0
```

Tip People who are familiar with working with hexadecimal numbers and bit fields often directly use hexadecimal values to create bit fields. A digit in a hexadecimal number always represents four bits, which makes it really easy to convert from binary to hex representation and back. Important hex digits in bit fields are 0, 2, 4, and 8. Their binary representation is 0000, 0010, 0100, and 1000 respectively.

It is also possible to use bit masks with more than one set bit. Such a bit mask returns 0 if none of the bits are set. This means they can be used to check whether at least one bit of a set of bits is set.

Setting Bits

You also need to be able to store information in a bit field. The operation we need for this is the bitwise OR. Table 9-6 shows the truth table of the binary OR. It returns 1 if one of the operands is 1; 0 if both are 0.

Table 9-6. *Truth Table of the Binary OR*

OR	1	0
1	1	1
0	1	0

The bit mask that is used to set a bit is the same bit mask that is used to read that bit. This means we can use the following code to set the third bit in our example bit field to 20 (10100):

```
local field = 20 -- 10100
local mask = 2^3 -- 01000

print(bit.band(field, mask) ~= 0) --> false, bit 3 not set
field = bit.bor(field, mask) -- set bit 3
print(bit.band(field, mask) ~= 0) --> true, bit 3 is now set
print(field) --> 28 (binary: 11100)
```

The bitwise OR operation successfully set the third bit in this example. Note that in a real addon you might want to store the bit masks in variables. So you can just use a variable with a meaningful name as a bit mask in read and set operations. You will see how real addons deal with bit fields later in this chapter.

We can now set bits to 1 in a bit field. But how can we set a bit to 0?

Resetting Bits

We also need the bitwise AND to reset a bit. But the bit mask that is required here needs a 0 at the location of the bit we want to reset, and all other bits need to be 1, as we don't want to modify any other bit. We need another operation to create such a bit mask from the original bit mask: the bitwise NOT.

The binary NOT is a unary operation, meaning it takes only one operand. It returns 1 if this operand is 0 and 0 if it is 1; that is, it inverts the bit. The bitwise NOT then inverts all bits in a bit field. So we can use the function `bit.bnot(bitfield)` on the original bit mask; this function is also used to read or set bits to get a bit mask that can be used to reset a bit.

The following code shows how we can use these operations to reset the fourth bit in our example bit field to 20 (10100):

```
local field = 20 -- 10100
local mask = 2^4 -- 10000

print(bit.band(field, mask) ~= 0) --> true, bit 4 is set
field = bit.band(field, bit.bnot(mask)) -- reset bit 4
print(bit.band(field, mask) ~= 0) --> false, the bit is no longer set
print(field) --> 4 (binary 00100)
```

The code works as expected. So we can now read bits, set bits, and reset bits in bit fields. Another operation that can come in handy is toggling a specific bit.

Toggling Bits

The operation we need here is the bitwise XOR. This operation is the exclusive OR, meaning that it returns 1 if one of the operands is 1, but 0 if both operands are 1 or both are 0. Table 9-7 shows the truth table of the binary XOR.

Table 9-7. *Truth Table of the Binary XOR*

XOR	1	0
1	0	1
0	1	0

We can use this operation to toggle a bit in a bit field with a bit mask. All fields that are 0 in that bit mask remain unchanged, and all fields that are 1 will be toggled. The following code toggles the fourth bit in our example bit field, 20:

```
local field = 20 -- 10100
local mask = 2^4 -- 10000

print(bit.band(field, mask) ~= 0) --> true, bit 4 is set
field = bit.bxor(field, mask) -- toggle bit 4
print(bit.band(field, mask) ~= 0) --> false, the bit is no longer set
field = bit.bxor(field, mask) -- toggle bit 4
print(bit.band(field, mask) ~= 0) --> true, bit 4 is set again
```

We can now perform all necessary operations on bit fields to extract information from them or to store information in them. But how many bits can a bit field contain?

Limits of Bit Fields

The size of a bit field is limited to 32 bits in Lua with bitlib. All larger numbers will be interpreted as –2147483648 (binary: a one followed by 31 zeros, hex: 0x80000000). This was also the value for destFlags we got in the previous example, where our combat log event didn't have a target.

Bit Fields vs. Booleans

You should use bit fields only if it really makes sense. For example, if you just have a few booleans, it is in most cases better to just use variables. You should consider using a bit field as soon as you have a lot of booleans (four or more) that belong together and are used frequently in your code.

But keep in mind that your most important goal should always be to write readable code. Code that uses bit fields is often harder to understand than code that uses normal variables. You should at least use meaningful variable names for your bit masks and not just magic numbers in your code. As you'll see in the next section, Blizzard provides variables with meaningful names for all important bit masks you need when working with the combat log.

Spell Schools

One of the bit fields you saw in combat log events is the school of a spell. The same bit field is also used for the school of a damage, which is not necessarily of the same school as the spell. For example, these two values differ for wand attacks of casters. The spell here is always the physical spell "Shoot," but the damage school depends on the wand the caster is using.

In the earlier example that showed a Flash Heal SPELL_CAST_START event, the spell school was 2 (binary 10). So this bit in this field stands for holy spells. There are bit masks available in global variables that can be used to work with spell schools. Table 9-8 lists all these bit masks with their value. The names of the variables are self-explanatory.

Table 9-8. *Bit Masks for Spell and Damage Schools*

Variable	Bit Mask
SCHOOL_MASK_NONE	00000000
SCHOOL_MASK_PHYSICAL	00000001
SCHOOL_MASK_HOLY	00000010
SCHOOL_MASK_FIRE	00000100
SCHOOL_MASK_NATURE	00001000
SCHOOL_MASK_FROST	00010000
SCHOOL_MASK_SHADOW	00100000
SCHOOL_MASK_ARCANE	01000000

Note that spell schools are not mutually exclusive; there are spells that belong to more than one school. An example of such a spell is Frostfire Bolt, which is both a frost and a fire spell and therefore has the spell and damage schools frost and fire. The bit field that appears in a combat log event when someone casts a Frostfire Bolt is 0000010100 (20 in decimal).

We can now use these bit masks and our knowledge of bitwise operations to create a small example mod. This mod displays a message in your chat frame every time your target begins casting a holy spell.

```
MyMod = {}

local function onEvent(self, event, ...)
    if event == "COMBAT_LOG_EVENT_UNFILTERED" then
        return onEvent(self, select(2, ...), ...)
    elseif MyMod[event] then
        return MyMod[event](...)
    end
end

local frame = CreateFrame("Frame")
frame:RegisterEvent("COMBAT_LOG_EVENT_UNFILTERED")
frame:SetScript("OnEvent", onEvent)

function MyMod.SPELL_CAST_START(_, _, srcGUID, srcName, _, _, _, _, _,➥
spellName, spellSchool)
    if srcGUID == UnitGUID("target") then
        if bit.band(spellSchool, SCHOOL_MASK_HOLY) ~= 0 then
            print(srcName.." begins to cast "..spellName.."!")
        end
    end
end
```

It uses the function UnitGUID(unitId) to get the GUID of your current target and compares it to the srcGUID of the SPELL_CAST_START event. The unit ID target always refers to your current target; another possible unit ID here is focus, which always refers to your focus target. Appendix B lists all unit IDs and all unit-related API functions.

You can check for multiple spell schools at the same time by using bit.bor on the bit masks of the schools. For example, if you want to display all holy and shadow spells, change the expression in the inner if statement to the following:

```
bit.band(spellSchool, bit.bor(SCHOOL_MASK_HOLY, SCHOOL_MASK_SHADOW)) ~= 0
```

I also mentioned another bit field argument earlier—the unit flags. Let's take a look at this bit field.

Unit Flags

This bit field contains information about the unit's affiliation, reaction, ownership, type, and raid role. There are also global variables available that contain bit masks that read all flags from a given bit field. Table 9-9 lists these variables and each one's value in hexadecimal representation. Note that these bit fields make use of almost all 32 bits, which makes the binary representation somewhat unclear and long. The meaning of a bit mask is explained by the name of the variable.

Table 9-9. *Bit Masks for Unit Flags*

Variable	Bit Mask
COMBATLOG_OBJECT_AFFILIATION_MINE	0x00000001
COMBATLOG_OBJECT_AFFILIATION_PARTY	0x00000002
COMBATLOG_OBJECT_AFFILIATION_RAID	0x00000004
COMBATLOG_OBJECT_AFFILIATION_OUTSIDER	0x00000008
COMBATLOG_OBJECT_REACTION_FRIENDLY	0x00000010
COMBATLOG_OBJECT_REACTION_NEUTRAL	0x00000020
COMBATLOG_OBJECT_REACTION_HOSTILE	0x00000040
COMBATLOG_OBJECT_CONTROL_PLAYER	0x00000100
COMBATLOG_OBJECT_CONTROL_NPC	0x00000200
COMBATLOG_OBJECT_TYPE_PLAYER	0x00000400
COMBATLOG_OBJECT_TYPE_NPC	0x00000800
COMBATLOG_OBJECT_TYPE_PET	0x00001000
COMBATLOG_OBJECT_TYPE_GUARDIAN	0x00002000
COMBATLOG_OBJECT_TYPE_OBJECT	0x00004000
COMBATLOG_OBJECT_TARGET	0x00010000
COMBATLOG_OBJECT_FOCUS	0x00020000
COMBATLOG_OBJECT_MAINTANK	0x00040000
COMBATLOG_OBJECT_MAINASSIST	0x00080000
COMBATLOG_OBJECT_RAIDTARGET1	0x00100000

Variable	Bit Mask
COMBATLOG_OBJECT_RAIDTARGET2	0x00200000
COMBATLOG_OBJECT_RAIDTARGET3	0x00400000
COMBATLOG_OBJECT_RAIDTARGET4	0x00800000
COMBATLOG_OBJECT_RAIDTARGET5	0x01000000
COMBATLOG_OBJECT_RAIDTARGET6	0x02000000
COMBATLOG_OBJECT_RAIDTARGET7	0x04000000
COMBATLOG_OBJECT_RAIDTARGET8	0x08000000
COMBATLOG_OBJECT_NONE	0x80000000

These bit masks can be divided into five categories: affiliation, reaction, control (the ownership), type, and raid role. The flags in the first four categories are mutually exclusive; there will never be two bits of the same category set in a unit flag.

■**Caution** Players in your raid group who are in the same raid subgroup as you do not have their `raid` affiliation bit set. They only have the `party` bit set. Also, your own unit flags will always have the `mine` bit set in this category and never the `party` or `raid` flag.

We can now update the function MyMod.SPELL_CAST_START from the previous example by using these bit masks. We can change the function to warn us about all holy casts from hostile players. The masks COMBATLOG_OBJECT_REACTION_HOSTILE and COMBATLOG_OBJECT_TYPE_PLAYER can be used for this:

```
function MyMod.SPELL_CAST_START(_, _, srcGUID, srcName, srcFlags, _, _, _, _,➥
spellName, spellSchool)
    if bit.band(spellSchool, SCHOOL_MASK_HOLY) ~= 0
    and bit.band(srcFlags, COMBATLOG_OBJECT_REACTION_HOSTILE) ~= 0
    and bit.band(srcFlags, COMBATLOG_OBJECT_TYPE_PLAYER) ~= 0 then
        print(srcName.." begins to cast "..spellName.."!")
    end
end
```

The bit masks related to raid role can be used to check if the object is your main tank, main assist, or a marked target; they also open up interesting opportunities. It is very easy to write a function that only processes events related to marked targets or to your main tank. Let's change that function a second time so that it warns you about every holy spell cast by marked units. This means we need to check if one of the raid target bits is set. We can either use eight bit.band calls (one for every bit) or use a bit mask that has all raid target bits set. Building such a bit mask is obviously the better solution, and we actually don't even have to build it. The file Interface\FrameXML\Constants.lua already defines the variable COMBATLOG_OBJECT_RAIDTARGET_MASK, which can be used:

```
COMBATLOG_OBJECT_RAIDTARGET_MASK = bit.bor(
    COMBATLOG_OBJECT_RAIDTARGET1,
    COMBATLOG_OBJECT_RAIDTARGET2,
    -- ...3, 4, 5, 6, 7...
    COMBATLOG_OBJECT_RAIDTARGET8
)
```

We can just use this bit mask in our `if` statement to check whether the caster is marked with a raid target:

```
function MyMod.SPELL_CAST_START(_, _, srcGUID, srcName, srcFlags, _, _, _, _,➡
spellName, spellSchool)
    if bit.band(spellSchool, SCHOOL_MASK_HOLY) ~= 0
    and bit.band(srcFlags, COMBATLOG_OBJECT_RAIDTARGET_MASK) ~= 0 then
        print(srcName.." begins to cast "..spellName.."!")
    end
end
```

There are many addon types that can benefit from using these flags wisely. For example, PvP (Player vs. Player) addons can make use of unit flags to identify hostile and friendly players, and raid mods can use them to identify main tanks or marked mobs.

I told you that we were going to write an example mod, but everything you have seen so far in this chapter has been a highly theoretical description of the arguments of combat log events. Let's get some practice and build a real addon.

Building a Cooldown Monitor

We will build an addon that displays cooldowns of your raid member's spells like Heroism/Bloodlust or Rebirth. Let's call this addon just CooldownMonitor. Create a folder for it and a `.toc` file with the following entries:

```
## Interface: 30100
## Title: Cooldown Monitor
CooldownMonitor.xml
CooldownMonitor.lua
CooldownBars.lua
```

You should also create the XML and both Lua files right now, so you don't have to restart your game when we make use of these files later. Let's start by building the main Lua file `CooldownMonitor.lua`.

Detecting Spells

The addon needs to detect certain spells and respond to them. The simplest solution would be a long `if-then-elseif-end` block in the event handler that checks whether the event is one of our spells. A better solution is to use a table that stores the information about all spells we want to use. All we need to store are the event of the spell, its spell ID, and its cooldown. The following table stores this information for a few interesting spells with their events.

```lua
local spells = {
    SPELL_CAST_SUCCESS = {
        [29166] = 360,   -- Druid: Innervate (6 min cooldown)
        [32182] = 600,   -- Shaman: Heroism (Alliance)
        [2825] = 600,    -- Shaman: Bloodlust (Horde)
        [22700] = 600,   -- Field Repair Bot 74A (10 min duration)
        [44389] = 600,   -- Field Repair Bot 110G (10 min duration)
    },
    SPELL_RESURRECT = {
        [20748] = 1200,  -- Druid: Rebirth (20 min cooldown)
    },
    SPELL_CREATE = { -- SPELL_CREATE is used for portals, and they vanish after 1 min
        [53142] = 60,    -- Portal: Dalaran (Alliance/Horde)
        [33691] = 60,    -- Portal: Shattrath (Alliance)
        [35717] = 60,    -- Portal: Shattrath (Horde)
        [11416] = 60,    -- Portal: Ironforge
        [10059] = 60,    -- Portal: Stormwind
        [49360] = 60,    -- Portal: Theramore
        [11419] = 60,    -- Portal: Darnassus
        [32266] = 60,    -- Portal: Exodar
        [11417] = 60,    -- Portal: Orgrimmar
        [11418] = 60,    -- Portal: Undercity
        [11420] = 60,    -- Portal: Thunder Bluff
        [32667] = 60,    -- Portal: Silvermoon
        [49361] = 60,    -- Portal: Stonard
    },
}
```

You can easily add new spells to it; just look up the spell ID on Wowhead or in your combat log and add it to the correct event. The correct event for a spell can be determined by using the combat log file that is created when you run the slash command /combatlog. It might be a good idea to add a simple spell for testing purposes. I added the following table as a subtable to spells for testing; 48071 is the spell ID of Flash Heal (Rank 11):

```lua
SPELL_HEAL = {
    [48071] = 60 -- Flash Heal (Test)
},
```

The event handler now needs to read that table. The following code makes use of select on the vararg to retrieve the interesting arguments. You could also add all ten arguments we need to the header of the function, but that approach would not be very clear. We need only the subevent, the caster's name, the caster's flags, the ID of the spell, and the name of the spell. We can then use the event and spell ID to check if our table contains the spell/event combination.

The caster's flags are used to check if the player is in our raid or party; this is the case if the affiliation: outsider flag is not set. It would also be possible to check if one of the mine, party, or raid flags is set. But these four flags are always mutually exclusive. Every unit will have always exactly one of them set. This means that if the outsider flag is not set, one of the others must be set.

We will also use a table called CooldownMonitor, placing all functions that need to be accessed from the outside in this table. Another thing we need to do here is creating the local variable onSpellCast, which is accessed by our event handler; we will later store a function in it:

```
CooldownMonitor = {}
local onSpellCast

local function onEvent(self, event, ...)
    if event == "COMBAT_LOG_EVENT_UNFILTERED" then
        local event = select(2, ...) -- get the subevent
        local sourceName, sourceFlags = select(4, ...) -- caster's name and flags
        local spellId, spellName = select(9, ...) -- spell ID and name
        -- check if we need the event and spell ID
        -- and check if the outsider bit is not set, meaning the unit is in our group
        if spells[event] and spells[event][spellId]
        and bit.band(sourceFlags, COMBATLOG_OBJECT_AFFILIATION_OUTSIDER) == 0 then
            local cooldown = spells[event][spellId]
            onSpellCast(cooldown, sourceName, spellId, spellName)
        end
    end
end

local frame = CreateFrame("Frame")
frame:RegisterEvent("COMBAT_LOG_EVENT_UNFILTERED")
frame:SetScript("OnEvent", onEvent)
```

This calls the function onSpellCast every time someone casts one of the spells we defined earlier. onSpellCast then calls startTimer (we will write this function later) to show a cast bar for the cooldown of the spell with the player's name and the spell. Another capability we can put in the function onSpellCast is generating and displaying a short notification in the chat. Such a message could look like this:

```
[player] just cast [spell] (Cooldown: x Minutes)
```

where [player] and [spell] should be clickable links. We worked with chat links when we built the DKP mod. But we haven't created any links yet. It would also be nice to have some colors in such a message to highlight the link. We need escape sequences in order to create links and colored text in the chat frame.

Using Escape Sequences in Chat Frames

Escape sequences (sequences with a special meaning like color codes) can be used in all chat frames and font strings in the game. The escape character is the pipe symbol |. We can test this with a simple example, which should print some red text (more on colors in the next section):

```
print("|cFFFF0000red text!")
```

This will work only if you write it in a Lua file of an addon. Trying to execute it via /script or an in-game editor like TinyPad will just print the raw code without a color. The reason for this is that the game automatically replaces | in user inputs with ||. Two pipe symbols || are used to represent a normal pipe symbol without a special meaning, just like the backslash in Lua strings.

But there is a Lua escape code that allows us to inject a normal pipe into a Lua string that is entered in the game: \124. Try typing the following in the game:

```
print("\124cFFFF0000red text!")
```

This shows a red message saying red text! in your chat frame. But why is it red and what's the meaning of these apparently hexadecimal numbers?

Colored Texts

The format of a color code is |cAARRGGBB. It consists of four values: alpha (A), red (R), green (G), and blue (B). All of these values are written with two hexadecimal digits, meaning that the lowest possible value is 00 and the highest FF (255 in decimal). The alpha value is actually ignored by the game; you can use any valid hexadecimal value here. But you should use FF (full visibility) here in case a patch adds support for this. The color is then built from the three values for red, green, and blue. (The Wikipedia article http://en.wikipedia.org/wiki/RGB_color_model has an excellent explanation of the RGB color model if you are not familiar with it.)

For example, |cFF00FF00 produces green text, |cFF0000FF blue text, and |cFF111111 gray text. |cFF000000 is black and |cFFFFFFFF is white. The color codes are not case-sensitive, so you can also use lowercase letters.

Once defined, the color is used until the next color definition or until the game encounters the color reset code |r. The text after the color reset will be in the default color of that text element. The default color of a line added by calling print is always white. But it is also possible to add a line to your chat frame with another default color by using the method AddMessage of a chat frame object.

You saw the chat frame objects earlier when we wrote the addon ChatlinkTooltips; they are stored in the global variables ChatFrame1 to ChatFrameN. But which chat frame is the default? It's is very likely that it is ChatFrame1 but you can't be sure. So the UI defines another global variable that always holds the default chat frame: DEFAULT_CHAT_FRAME. This means we need to call the method AddMessage of this frame with the following arguments in order to print a message with our default color:

```
DEFAULT_CHAT_FRAME:AddMessage(message, r, g, b)
```

The arguments r, g, and b hold the red, green, and blue color values. Note that the maximum value here is 1 and the minimum value 0. So $r = 1$, $g = 1$, and $b = 1$ produces a white default color.

If you want to color the whole chat message, it is always better to apply a default color with AddMessage than to use a |c escape-sequence. This default color will also be used by hooks that add a time stamp to the chat frame, like the mini-mod we wrote in Chapter 6. Using print would always result in a white time stamp.

■**Note** It is not possible to embed color codes in chat messages. Using a color code in a string that is passed to SendChatMessage generates an error message.

Many addons use a wrapper function for the AddMessage method that adds the addon's name as prefix and sets a color. Let's write such a function for our cooldown monitor. It's sufficient to keep this function in a local variable for a small addon like ours. A larger addon should store its print handler in a table (which acts as namespace for the addon), as the function would be accessible there to many files. We'll simply create a local variable called print in the scope of the file CooldownMonitor.lua, so we can just use print as we did it in our previous addons. This function should be placed at the beginning of the file to ensure that the local variable is visible in all other functions in the file.

```
local chatPrefix = "|cffff7d0a<|r|cffffd200CooldownMonitor|r|cffff7d0a>|r "
local function print(...)
    DEFAULT_CHAT_FRAME:AddMessage(chatPrefix..string.join(" ", tostringall(...)),➡
    0.41, 0.8, 0.94)
end
```

The function makes use of tostringall and string.join, so it behaves just like the original print handler. But it adds a nicely colored prefix to our message.

Hyperlinks

A link is created by using an escape sequence with the following format:

|H*link*|h*text*|h

|H marks the beginning of a link, and the following *link* is the data of the link. The end of the data string is marked by |h and followed by the displayed and clickable *text*, which is also followed by |h. We saw some link types earlier, when we created the DKP addon; a link is basically just a string that is passed to the event handlers that deal with hyperlink events like OnHyperlinkClicked. Let's look at a complete item link with the text. We have already seen the link for an item, which consists of a long string of numbers that describe the item. The code behind a small link to a Runed Titanium Rod, for example, looks like this:

|cff0070dd|Hitem:44452:0:0:0:0:0:0:0:1352691344:80|h[Runed Titanium Rod]|h|r

We can clearly see the color of the link at the beginning, the link ID, and the displayed text at the end, followed by the end codes for the link (|h) and color (|r).

■**Note** It is not possible to link an item that is unknown to the server. Such items might be drops from bosses that are not yet killed in your battlegroup. The server will also check the name and color of links in chat messages. The link will be removed from the chat message if the name or color is incorrect.

The substring until the first colon in the link is used to indicate the type of the link. The type of this example is an item link, but we need a player and a spell link. A player link looks like this:

```
|Hplayer:name|htext|h
```

and a spell link like this:

```
|Hspell:spellId|htext|h
```

We can now start creating the function onSpellCast. Add this function to the end of the file CooldownMonitor.lua:

```
local castInfo = "|Hplayer:%1$s|h[%1$s]|h cast |cFF71D5FF|Hspell:%d|h[%s]|h|r➥
(Cooldown: %d minutes)"
function onSpellCast(timer, player, spellId, spellName)

    print(castInfo:format(player, spellId, spellName, timer / 60))
    CooldownMonitor.StartTimer(timer, player, spellName,➥
texture)
end
```

The format string that is used here might look more difficult than it is. First is the player link, which needs the name of the player twice: as link and as displayed text. We can select one of the arguments that is passed to string.format by starting the replacement directive with %n$s, where n is the number of the desired argument (s can also be any other format directive). This allows us to use the first argument twice here. The second link is a spell link, whose default color is taken from the default UI.

Another nice feature would be to include a small icon of the spell in the message. We can also create that with these escape codes.

Textures

An escape sequence that represents a texture looks like this:

```
|Tfile:height:width:xoffset:yoffset|t
```

All arguments except for the file and height are optional. The default width is the same value as the height, and the default offsets are 0. The height of the font is used if *height* is set to 0. You should always set *height* to 0, as wrong values can distort the font. If *height* is 0 and *width* is set, it will be interpreted as a value relative to the height of the font.

For example, the code |Tfoo.tga:0|t displays the texture from the file foo.tga scaled to a square width the same height as the text, |Tfoo.tga:0:2|t displays the same texture with the height set to the font height and the width set to two times the font height, and |Tfoo.tga:10:20|t displays foo.tga with the size 10 × 20.

Note It is not possible to embed a texture into a chat message for security reasons.

We now have the ID of the spell, but we need its texture. There is an API function available that returns almost all information we will ever need about a spell. The name of this function is GetSpellInfo, and its argument can either be a spell ID, a spell's name, or a spell link.

```
name, rank, iconTexture, cost, isFunnel,
powerType, castTime, minRange, maxRange
= GetSpellInfo(spell)
```

We just need the third return value, which holds the file name of the texture that is associated with this spell. Replace the old version of the function onSpellCast with this new and improved one, which also displays an icon in your chat:

```
local castInfo = "|Hplayer:%1$s|h[%1$s]|h cast |T%s:0|t|cFF71D5FF➡
|Hspell:%d|h[%s]|h|r (Cooldown: %d minutes)"
function onSpellCast(timer, player, spellId, spellName)
    local texture = select(3, GetSpellInfo(spellId))
    print(castInfo:format(player, texture, spellId, spellName, timer / 60))
    CooldownMonitor.StartTimer(timer, player, spellName, texture)
end
```

The code added a |T escape-sequence right in front of the spell link and added the texture as additional argument to string.format. This adds a small icon to the info message. The path of the texture is now also passed to startTimer because a texture is also useful in the timer.

One minor issue remains: what happens if we have a spell that has a cooldown of only one minute? The text would still say "Cooldown: 1 minutes". The game provides us a simple way of dealing with situations like this.

Grammatical Escape Sequences

There are three escape sequences available that deal with grammatical issues that might occur when formatting text. The first has the following format:

digit |1*singular*;*plural1*;*plural2*;

This will display *singular* if the preceding digit is 1; *plural1* otherwise. *plural2* is optional and it will be used instead of *plural1* if it is provided and the digit is 2. This second form of the plural is useful for languages like Russian.

This escape sequence takes into account only the digit immediately to its left. So 11 |1*singular*;*plural*; will result in 11 *singular*. This escape sequence is rarely needed; the following one is more useful, as it takes the whole number into account:

number |4*singular*:*plural1*:*plural2*;

This works just like |1 but uses the whole number to determine whether to use *singular* or *plural1/2*. The plural2 text is again optional. So this is the one we need in our format string castInfo. Let's change that string to the following string:

```
local castInfo = "|Hplayer:%1$s|h[%1$s]|h cast |T%s:0|t|cFF71D5FF➡
|Hspell:%d|h[%s]|h|r (Cooldown: %d |4minute:minutes;)"
```

■**Caution** |1 uses semicolons to separate the different forms, while |4 requires colons as separators but a semicolon at the end.

The third escape sequence is |2. The format is simply |2*sometext*. It will be shown as d'*sometext* if *sometext* starts with a vowel, otherwise it shows up as de *sometext*.

■**Note**   These grammatical escape sequences cannot be used in chat messages.

We can now print pretty messages to the chat frame, and the function onSpellCast is finished. Our next task is building the function CooldownMonitor.StartTimer, which creates a visual timer and displays it on your screen. We will create this function together with all its helper functions in a separate file (you might have guessed the name: CooldownBars.lua) so that we can easily replace it with a library in the next chapter. A good frame type for such a cooldown timer is the status bar. It represents a progress bar and is used by all cast bars, health bars, and mana bars you see on the screen. Status bars are very similar to sliders, as they have a minimum value, a maximum value, and a value that is currently set. Timers that are displayed by using a status bar are often called "status bar timers" because of the name of the frame type.

Building Status Bar Timers

Let's start by building an XML template for such a timer. The first question when creating a template is always, is there already a template defined by Blizzard? The answer is yes, the file Interface\FrameXML\CastingbarFrame.xml defines the template CastingBarFrameTemplate, which is suitable for our purposes.

Building a Template

We need to change a few things in this template before we can use it. The default cast bar does not display a timer, so we will have to add that, preferably as a small font string in the right part of the frame. Another issue is that the text of this cast bar is centered in the frame. We want to anchor it to the left as we need additional space in the right half of the frame for our cooldown timer. The third issue is that the template defines a few script handlers that are specific to cast bars. We will have to overwrite them.

We will derive our template from this existing template as it is still easier than rewriting the whole template. The following code shows our new template. Please open the template CastingBarFrameTemplate in the file Interface\FrameXML\CastingbarFrame.xml while looking at the following code. This makes it easier to understand what the complete template will look like.

The following code shows the file CooldownMonitor.xml:

```
<Ui xmlns="http://www.blizzard.com/wow/ui/" ➥
xmlns:xsi="http://www.w3.org/2001/XMLSchema-instance" ➥
xsi:schemaLocation="http://www.blizzard.com/wow/ui/
..\FrameXML\UI.xsd">
    <StatusBar name="CooldownBarTemplate" virtual="true" minValue="0"➥
maxValue="1" inherits="CastingBarFrameTemplate">
        <Size>
            <AbsDimension x="195" y="13"/>
        </Size>
        <Layers>
            <Layer level="ARTWORK">
                <!-- add a fontstring that shows the timer -->
                <FontString name="$parentTimer" justifyH="RIGHT"➥
inherits="GameFontHighlight">
                    <Anchors>
                        <Anchor point="RIGHT">
                            <Offset>
                                <AbsDimension x="-6" y="3"/>
                            </Offset>
                        </Anchor>
                    </Anchors>
                </FontString>
            </Layer>
        </Layers>
        <Scripts>
            <OnShow/>  <!-- we do not want the old OnShow handler -->
            <OnEvent/> <!-- the old OnEvent handler is also not required -->
            <OnLoad> <!-- modify the text and icon -->
              _G[self:GetName().."Text"]:ClearAllPoints()
              _G[self:GetName().."Text"]:SetPoint("LEFT", 6, 3)
              _G[self:GetName().."Text"]:SetWidth(155)
              _G[self:GetName().."Text"]:SetJustifyH("LEFT")
              _G[self:GetName().."Icon"]:ClearAllPoints()
              _G[self:GetName().."Icon"]:SetPoint("RIGHT", self, "LEFT", -5, 2)
              _G[self:GetName().."Icon"]:SetWidth(20)
              _G[self:GetName().."Icon"]:SetHeight(20)
            </OnLoad>
            <OnUpdate> <!-- the function's head is function(self, elapsed) -->
                self.obj:Update(elapsed)
            </OnUpdate>
        </Scripts>
    </StatusBar>
</Ui>
```

Our template CooldownBarTemplate now has the following children:

- Text: A font string that is anchored in the center of the frame. This is defined by the original template, and the only way for us to modify it is to use the OnLoad handler.

- Timer: The remaining time; this font string is added by our template.

- Border: The border around the frame, defined by the original template.

- Icon: A 16 × 16 texture to the left of the timer. It will show the spell's icon later. This is also defined by the original template. The size of this icon is changed to 20 × 20 in the OnLoad handler, and its position is slightly adjusted.

- Spark: A glow effect texture that needs to be moved to the current position of the status bar. This is also created by the original template.

- Flash: A texture that can be used to add a flash effect to the bar. This child is created by the original template.

We won't use this template in our XML file as we won't create our frames with XML. There is no way to predict how many timers will be needed by the addon; there might be ten simultaneous cooldowns or only one. We will use CreateFrame to create timers from this template dynamically. We can test whether the template works properly by executing the following code. Note that it will generate an error message, because we haven't implemented the OnUpdate method yet. Ignore this error or disable the OnUpdate method by marking it as a comment.

```
local f = CreateFrame("StatusBar", "TestTimer", UIParent, "CooldownBarTemplate")
_G[f:GetName().."Text"]:SetText("Test Timer!")
_G[f:GetName().."Timer"]:SetText("1:00")
_G[f:GetName().."Flash"]:Hide()
f:SetPoint("CENTER")
```

The first line creates a new frame of the type StatusBar that inherits from our template. Its name is TestTimer and its parent is UIParent. The second line accesses the child Text of the frame and calls SetText on this font string to set a test text. The third line does the same with the timer, and the fourth line hides the texture Flash that is displayed by default. The last line sets a point so that our frame is visible in the center of the screen. You can try to play around with the various children like the icon. Another interesting test is trying to set a long string as text to check if it is truncated properly.

But the timer doesn't work yet. It doesn't count down, and the spark is in the middle instead of the end. We will need the OnUpdate method for this. It will update the position of the status bar by calling its method SetValue, setting the position of the spark to match the bar and the text of the timer. It will also hide it when the time is 0.

This functionality is stored in the method Update of the object that is stored under the key self in the status bar. It would also be possible to use the status bar frame as the object, but it already has its own metatable. We would have to forward calls to this original metatable, so it is just easier to store an object in the table that represents a frame.

Handling the Timers

A good data structure that represents a set of status bar timers is a doubly linked list. It allows us to get the previous and next timers just by accessing fields in a table. This allows us to remove a timer in the middle of our set of frames. Each entry in this doubly linked list is a timer object.

All of the following Lua functions should be placed in the file CooldownBars.lua. We first need to create a few local variables that will be used later:

```
-- the first and last timer objects in the double-linked list
local firstTimer, lastTimer

-- prototype for the timer object
local timer = {}
```

We now need to build the actual timer object. Our constructor is the function startTimer. It creates a status bar object and displays it. The actual object is also stored in this frame. This object holds a reference to the frame, so we can easily get the frame that belongs to this object. This object is added to the doubly linked list that represents a set of timers.

But what happens if the timers expire and the frame is hidden? There is no way to delete an existing frame (the garbage collector cannot delete frames), so it is a good idea to reuse it. We need to store all currently unused frames somewhere, and the constructor will just recycle an old frame if there is one. A good data structure to store the unused frames is a stack. We push the objects of expired timers on the stack. The pop operation here is slightly different from the stacks we saw in previous examples; it will never return nil, as it just creates a new frame and returns it if the stack is empty. We will call the function popOrCreateFrame to indicate this behavior.

Each frame needs to have a name, as we need this name to get the frames' children. We just use a counter here that counts up every time the pop operation has to create a new frame.

The following code fragment shows such a stack. It is implemented here as a linked list, which means we just store the object that is currently on the top of the stack in a variable (in this case, frameStack). This object then has the field next, which points to the next object on the stack.

```
local popOrCreateFrame, pushFrame
do
    local id = 1
    local frameStack -- the object on the top of the stack

    -- pops a frame from the stack or creates a new frame
    function popOrCreateFrame()
        local frame
        if frameStack then -- old frame exists
            frame = frameStack -- re-use it...
            -- ...and remove it from the stack by changing the object on the top
            frameStack = frameStack.next
            frame:Show() -- make sure that it's shown as it might be hidden
```

```
        else -- stack is empty...
            -- ...so we have to create a new frame
            frame = CreateFrame("StatusBar", "CooldownMonitor_Bar"..id,➥
CooldownMonitor_Anchor, "CooldownBarTemplate")
            id = id + 1 -- increase the ID
        end
        return frame
    end

    -- pushes a frame on the stack
    function pushFrame(frame)
        -- delete the reference to the object to allow
        -- the garbage collector to collect it
        frame.obj = nil
        -- the next object on the stack is the one that is currently on the top
        frame.next = frameStack
        -- the new object on the top is the new one
        frameStack = frame
    end
end
```

We are referencing a currently undefined frame in the pop function. The name of this frame is CooldownMonitor_Anchor. It will be the anchor of the first bar and the parent of all bars. The second bar will then be anchored to the first one, and so on. The position of this anchor is saved by using the frame's method SetUserPlaced. Place the following frame in the <Ui> tag of the file CooldownMonitor.xml. It does not matter whether you put this code before the template or after. Just do not put it in the template, as it is a completely new frame that has nothing to do with our status bar template.

```
<Frame name="CooldownMonitor_Anchor" movable="true" parent="UIParent">
    <Anchors>
        <Anchor point="CENTER">
            <Offset>
                <AbsDimension x="300" y="0"/>
            </Offset>
        </Anchor>
    </Anchors>
    <Size> <!-- required in order to make the frame visible -->
        <AbsDimension x="1" y="1"/> <!-- 0x0 would not work here! -->
    </Size>
    <Scripts>
        <OnLoad>
            self:SetUserPlaced(1)
        </OnLoad>
    </Scripts>
</Frame>
```

■**Caution** Frames without a valid size are not only invisible, they are also unusable by other frames as anchors. 0 × 0 is not a valid size. Multiple anchors that span the frame can also be used.

It would be shorter if we could just create the frame in Lua and store it in a local variable. But the method SetUserPlaced requires our frame to have a name, as the name is used to identify the frame. Thus we need a global variable, anyway. We also need to take care of the default position when creating the frame with Lua. We must not overwrite the saved position after the frame is created by calling SetPoint. This means we have to check whether there is already a saved position before we set the default position. Because of these issues, it is easier to use XML here to create the frame.

We now have the frame template and the anchor. Our next task is building the constructor of the frame object.

The Status Bar Timer Constructor

This constructor creates a timer object with a corresponding frame and adds this object to the doubly linked list. It also sets the text that is displayed on the timer, the texture of the spell icon, and the color of the timer. We will use the class color of the player that cast the spell for the timer. We need a helper function that takes the name of a player and returns the class of this player. This function needs to iterate over the whole party or raid to find the player.

The following code should be placed at the end of the file CooldownMonitor.lua:

```lua
-- gets a class of a player in your party or raid
function CooldownMonitor.GetClassByName(name)
    -- check if we are looking for ourselves
    if UnitName("player") == name then
        -- the first return value of UnitClass is localized, the second one is not
        return select(2, UnitClass("player"))
    end
    -- iterate over the party (if we are in a party)
    for i = 1, GetNumPartyMembers() do
        if UnitName("party"..i) == name then
            return select(2, UnitClass("party"..i))
        end
    end
    -- still no match, iterate over the whole raid (if we are in a raid)
    for i = 1, GetNumRaidMembers() do
        -- no need to work with the GUID here as the player's name is unique
        if UnitName("raid"..i) == name then
            return select(2, UnitClass("raid"..i))
        end
    end
    -- that player isn't part of our party/raid
    return "unknown"
end
```

We can now create the function CooldownMonitor.StartTimer, which resembles the constructor of the status bar timer object. It does all the hard work and creates a new status bar timer and starts it. Place it at the end of CooldownBars.lua.

```lua
local mt = { __index = timer} -- metatable
-- the constructor
function CooldownMonitor.StartTimer(timer, player, spell, texture)
   local frame = popOrCreateFrame() -- create or recycle a frame
   local class = CooldownMonitor.GetClassByName(player)
   -- set the color the status bar by using color informations from the table
   -- RAID_CLASS_COLORS that contains the default colors of all classes
   if RAID_CLASS_COLORS[class] then
      local color = RAID_CLASS_COLORS[class]
      frame:SetStatusBarColor(color.r, color.g, color.b)
   else -- this should actually never happen
      frame:SetStatusBarColor(1, 0.7, 0) -- default color from the template
   end
   -- set the text
   _G[frame:GetName().."Text"]:SetFormattedText("%s: %s", player, spell)
   -- and the icon
   local ok = _G[frame:GetName().."Icon"]:SetTexture(texture)
   if ok then
      _G[frame:GetName().."Icon"]:Show()
   else -- hide the texture if it couldn't be loaded for some reason
      _G[frame:GetName().."Icon"]:Hide()
   end
   -- add a short flash effect by fading out the flash texture
   UIFrameFadeOut(_G[frame:GetName().."Flash"], 0.5, 1, 0)

   local obj = setmetatable({ -- this is the actual object
      frame = frame, -- the frame is stored in the object...
      totalTime = timer,
      timer = timer -- this is the remaining time, it will be decremented later
   }, mt)
   frame.obj = obj -- ...and the object in the frame
   -- add the object to the end of the list
   if firstTimer == nil then -- our list is empty
      firstTimer = obj
      lastTimer = obj
   else -- our list is not empty, so append it after the last entry
      -- the element in front of our object is the old last element
      obj.prev = lastTimer
      -- the element after the old last element is our object
      lastTimer.next = obj
      -- the new last element is our object
      lastTimer = obj
   end
```

```
    obj:SetPosition()
    obj:Update(0)
    return obj -- return the object
end
```

The function gets a frame from popOrCreateFrame and initializes it by setting its text, icon, and color. It then uses the UI function UIFrameFadeOut on the texture flash, which results in a flash effect. The constructor then creates the actual object and adds it to the doubly linked list.

It then calls the object's SetPosition method, which will set the frame's position; we will implement this method next. It also calls the method Update with the argument 0; this will set the initial value of the status bar and the text of the font string Timer.

Positioning

Let's create the method SetPosition (place it at the end of your file). The method just needs to set the point depending on the position of the frame in the linked list. It needs to anchor to our previously created anchor if it is the first element in the list; otherwise it uses the previous frame as anchor.

```
function timer:SetPosition()
    self.frame:ClearAllPoints()
    if self == firstTimer then -- it's the first timer
        self.frame:SetPoint("CENTER", CooldownMonitor_Anchor, "CENTER")
    else -- it's not the first timer, anchor it to the previous one
        self.frame:SetPoint("TOP", self.prev.frame, "BOTTOM", 0, -11)
    end
end
```

This method shows why it was smart to choose a doubly linked list here. We can just write self.prev to get the previous timer object and self.prev.frame to get its frame.

Our next method is the Update method, which updates the frame.

Updating Timers

The Update method decrements the attribute timer of our object by the time that elapsed since the last call to it. The method cancels the timer if the remaining time is less than or equal to 0. If this is not the case, it updates the value of the status bar, the text of the timer, and the position of the spark. We need a small helper function here that formats the timer into a human-readable format that is then displayed. This function should be placed at the end of the file.

```
local function stringFromTimer(t)
    if t < 60 then -- less than 60 seconds --> don't show minutes
        return string.format("%.1f", t)
    else -- 60 seconds or more remaining --> display minutes
        return string.format("%d:%0.2d", t / 60, t % 60)
    end
end
```

```
function timer:Update(elapsed)
    self.timer = self.timer - elapsed
    if self.timer <= 0 then -- time's up
        self:Cancel() -- cancel the timer
    else
        -- currentBarPos holds a value between 0 and 1
        local currentBarPos = self.timer / self.totalTime
        -- the min value of a status bar timer is 0 and the max value 1
        self.frame:SetValue(currentBarPos)
        -- update the text
        _G[self.frame:GetName().."Timer"]:SetText(stringFromTimer(self.timer))
        -- set the position of the spark
        _G[self.frame:GetName().."Spark"]:SetPoint("CENTER", self.frame, "LEFT",➥
self.frame:GetWidth() * currentBarPos, 2)
    end
end
```

Note The OnUpdate script handler is invoked only if the frame is shown. So we can assume here that the timer is running.

Our next task is creating the method Cancel to cancel the timer. This Cancel method has to take care of removing the object from the doubly linked list and recycling the frame.

Canceling Timers

The Cancel method basically just removes a timer from the list, hides the frame, and pushes the frame onto our stack, which stores currently unused frames. This function should be placed at the end of our Lua file:

```
function timer:Cancel()
    -- remove it from the list
    if self == firstTimer then
        firstTimer = self.next
    else
        node.prev.next = node.next
    end
    if self == lastTimer then
        lastTimer = self.prev
    else
        self.next.prev = self.prev
    end
    -- update the position of the next timer if there is a next timer
```

```
     if self.next then
        self.next:SetPosition()
     end
     self.frame:Hide() -- hide the frame...
     pushFrame(self.frame) -- ...and recycle it
  end
```

The addon now works as we expected it to. But one issue remains: we currently cannot move the bars to a different position.

Moving the Timers

We need a slash command handler displaying a dummy timer that can be moved. The slash commands move or unlock will initiate the movement process. Our slash command handler will unlock the frames for 45 seconds and display a timer that shows the remaining time. We also need our timing library SimpleTimingLib to lock the frames after 45 seconds, so make sure that it is still installed and add it as a dependency. We will use the anchor's unlocked attribute to indicate that it is unlocked.

The following code shows the slash commands; it should be placed at the end of the Lua file:

```
local timingLib = SimpleTimingLib:New()
local function lock()
   CooldownMonitor_Anchor.unlocked = false
end

SLASH_COOLDOWNMONITOR1 = "/cooldownmonitor"
SLASH_COOLDOWNMONITOR2 = "/cm"
SlashCmdList["COOLDOWNMONITOR"] = function(msg)
   local cmd = msg:trim():lower()
   if cmd == "unlock" or cmd == "move" then
      startTimer(45, "Status", "unlocked")
      CooldownMonitor_Anchor.unlocked = true
      timingLib:Schedule(45, lock)
   end
end
```

Note that our addon now depends on SimpleTimingLib, so you should add it as a dependency to the TOC file. We will see how we can get rid of this dependency and embed the library into our addon in the next chapter, which explains libraries in detail.

But the timers do not become movable just because we have set an attribute here. We need a few more script handlers in our template. We need to use the method RegisterForDrag on our status bars to receive the drag mouse events. We can include it by adding the following line to the OnLoad script handler of the status bar template CooldownBarTemplate in the XML file:

```
self:RegisterForDrag("LeftButton")
```

We then need to add an OnDragStart script handler to the <Scripts> element of the status bar template CooldownBarTemplate. Note that we are moving the parent (the anchor) and not the status bar:

```
<OnDragStart>
    if self:GetParent().unlocked then
        self:GetParent():StartMoving()
        self:GetParent().moving = self
    end
</OnDragStart>
```

The handler checks whether the attribute unlocked of anchor (the parent) is set and attaches the parent to the mouse if this is the case. We also save the frame that initiated the moving process in the anchor.

We need to tell this anchor to stop moving if we stop dragging or if the frame is hidden while we move it around. Hiding the frame does not trigger the OnDragStop script, so our frame would keep moving if the timer we clicked expires while we move it.

The OnHide handler stops the anchor only if the user clicks on the frame that initiated the movement. This prevents the positioning from stopping if another timer expires while we move it.

```
<OnDragStop>
    self:GetParent():StopMovingOrSizing()
</OnDragStop>
<OnHide>
    if self:GetParent().moving == self then
        self:GetParent():StopMovingOrSizing()
    end
</OnHide>
```

We now have a fully functional cooldown monitor. But it has a problem. We didn't take into account one important thing, and our addon is currently not working properly under certain circumstances. Did you notice that bug?

Fixing the Last Bug

We currently rely on the frame's OnUpdate script handler when counting down a timer. But who can guarantee that our status bar timers are shown all the time? They will pause if they are hidden for any reason; for example, they might be hidden because the user has pressed Alt-Z to hide UIParent. Or the user might open the world map while a timer is running. You can test this bug by typing /cm move and opening the world map. The timer will freeze for the duration the world map is opened. But SimpleTimingLib won't. So you will still see the "Status: unlocked" timer after you close the world map, but the 45 seconds might be over and the frames locked again.

Helpful here is the method IsVisible of frame objects. It returns nil if the frame is not shown or if its parent is not shown. This means we can detect whether the World Map is open or the UI hidden if our anchor is shown but not visible. We create a frame that is not a child of UIParent and use its OnUpdate method to check if we are missing OnUpdate events. Place this at the end of your file CooldownBars.lua:

```
local updater=CreateFrame("Frame")
updater:SetScript("OnUpdate", function(self, elpased)
    if CooldownMonitor_Anchor:IsShown() and
    not CooldownMonitor_Anchor:IsVisible() then
        local timer = firstTimer
        while timer do
            timer:Update(elapsed)
            timer = timer.next
        end
    end
end)
```

Note that we implemented only a few functions of our doubly linked list. We did not implement an iterator, and it's not worth the effort for just one loop. So we're just using a while loop here. The loop calls the Update method from all frames.

This last bug is now fixed and we have a working cooldown monitor that you can use to track your raid group's cooldowns.

Summary

The chapter covered working with the combat log. You can now create mods that respond to combat events. We also discussed bit fields and how they are used in combat log events in World of Warcraft. Many popular mods, like Damage Meters or Scrolling Combat Text, deal only with combat log events. You can now write your own combat log addon by using these events; there are a lot of exciting opportunities.

The example mod we wrote during this chapter is a fully featured cooldown monitor with a quite decent display for cooldowns. The next chapter is about libraries and how to use them. As a demonstration, we will replace our implementation of status bar timers with a library. These libraries will give our addon a brand new look (with a lot of eye candy) and add a few other exciting features, like a configuration menu.

CHAPTER 10

■ ■ ■

Using Libraries

A library is an addon that provides a set of functions that can be used by other addons. The addon `SimpleTimingLib` we wrote in Chapter 4 is a library. But there are a few issues involved when working with libraries. Let's assume you wrote an addon that depends on that library and you want to publish it. You can either include the library in your zip file or tell the users to install the library themselves.

The first solution, including the library, exposes its weakness when a user who already has this library tries to install your package. He will overwrite the version of the library he already had with your version of the library. But what happens if he had a newer version of the library? And what happens if he had an older version, but another addon that uses the library is incompatible with the newer version? This solution almost certainly breaks the user's interface as soon as there are different versions of your library around. And the user currently cannot even distinguish an older version of a library from the newer one, as it doesn't have a version number.

The other solution, telling the user to download a specific version of the required library from somewhere else, would work perfectly if your addon is designed to be a plugin for another, larger framework or library. Let's assume you have written a boss mod for a new instance, and you've used Deadly Boss Mods for this. You will then publish this boss mod somewhere (such as on `curse.com`) with a note like "This is a plugin for Deadly Boss Mods; you need to have DBM from `http://www.deadlybossmods.com` installed in order to use this boss mod." Your users will certainly understand that a boss mod can be based on a boss mod creation framework and therefore requires DBM.

But there are a lot of mods that make use of ten or more libraries out there. You will see such mods in this chapter. It is quite an effort for the user to download by hand all the libraries your mod requires. And a lot of people out there will fail at this task and send you an email saying "your mod doesn't work; I'm always getting an error about a missing dependency!"

We will see in this chapter how this problem can be solved in World of Warcraft by using *embedded libraries*, which are embedded in your addon's main folder and not as separate addons.

Embedded Libraries

An embedded library is a library that is embedded in your addon, meaning it will be in the same folder as your addon. Such a library usually consists of a single Lua file that is simply added to your TOC file. You can then just pack your addon folder into a zip file and publish it together with all libraries it makes use of.

What happens if I have two addons that embed the same library? Will I have this library twice? The answer to that question is both yes and no. You will have the library twice on your hard disk, but each version will be loaded only once. But our libraries currently do not even have version numbers, so two different versions of SimpleTimingLib would not be distinguishable; and the library needs to be able to determine whether it is already loaded or not. What would be a good version number for a library?

Versioning Libraries

A version number for a library usually consists of two parts: its major version, which is basically the name followed by a normal version number, for example LibFoo-1.1. A change to this version number indicates a major change to the library. The second part of this version number is its minor version, which is increased with every minor change to the library; this minor version is just represented as a number and could be, for example, 9. Later you will see how we can set these version numbers of a library.

Let's assume we have an embedded library that is called LibFoo. We have the following addons with the following versions of LibFoo installed:

- Addon1: LibFoo-1.0 (minor: 1)

- Addon2: LibFoo-1.0 (minor: 3)

- Addon3: LibFoo-1.0 (minor: 2)

- Addon4: LibFoo-1.1 (minor: 9)

Addons are always loaded in alphabetical order if they are not load-on-demand. This means that the first addon that will be loaded is Addon1. This addon then loads version 1.0 of LibFoo. The next addon that is loaded is Addon2, which also embeds version 1.0 of LibFoo. The situation now becomes interesting, as there is already an older version of the same library loaded, as indicated by the minor version numbers.

LibFoo-1.0 of Addon2 now detects that there is already an older version of it; you will soon see how we can implement this functionality. It now has to replace this older version of the library with the new one. This new version must be compatible with the old library, as other addons might rely on this old version.

The next addon is Addon3, which tries to load yet another minor version of LibFoo-1.0: the minor version 2, which is older than the currently loaded version 3. This version of LibFoo-1.0 now detects that there is already a newer version (3) of itself, and it just does nothing. To instruct the program to do nothing you could use a large if-block around all code in your file, but there is a better solution: using return outside a function. Recall that a Lua file is internally handled as a huge function that is executed once when the addon is loaded. Calling return outside of a function in the file is like calling return in the function that represents the file. This means that this return call cancels loading the file. The following code shows what such a return statement could look like:

```
if dontLoadMe then
    return
end
```

This stops loading the file if dontLoadMe is true. We will see examples for a library and how we can handle this detection later in this chapter.

The last addon that is loaded is Addon4. It loads a new major version of this library. This version contains a lot of changes and is not compatible with older versions of the library; it has the major version LibFoo-1.1 for this reason. It does not replace the old 1.0 version of the library if it is loaded; it is treated as a completely different library because of possible compatibility issues. You will have two versions of this library loaded in your memory from this point on.

All addons that depend on LibFoo-1.0 will use LibFoo-1.0 with the minor version 3, and all addons that require LibFoo-1.1 will then use LibFoo-1.1 with the minor version 9. This works for all addons and all libraries that are backward-compatible within one major version.

Problems with Embedded Libraries

But what happens if a library is not 100% backward-compatible within a major version? Or what happens if an addon only works with a library because of a bug in that library? A newer version of the library now fixes that bug, and the old addon breaks. This should not happen, and it can actually be quite hard to maintain complete backward compatibility in a new version. The simple solution to this issue is that the major version is increased with every major change that might cause such issues. The minor version is only increased for minor changes that do not affect the functionality of the library.

Another disadvantage is that embedded libraries might slow down the loading process of your addons, especially if you have a lot of different versions of a library installed. It might be replaced multiple times while loading the UI.

The whole problem with libraries and different versions of them that are shared by multiple addons or programs is not entirely solved. This is not only true for World of Warcraft; every system that makes use of libraries that are shared between many programs has the same problems. For example, in Windows this problem is known as "DLL Hell." You know what I'm talking about if you've ever had a missing DLL (dynamic link library) file under Windows.

Embedded libraries are quite a good solution for this problem, but they are far from being perfect.

Let's look at how these embedded libraries can be implemented. There is basically one main library that acts as a helper library for libraries: LibStub.

Using LibStub

LibStub is an embedded library that manages other embedded libraries. You can always download the latest version of it on its project page on wowace.com: http://www.wowace.com/projects/libstub/.

It provides three functions that are accessible by addons and libraries: LibStub:NewLibrary(*major, minor*), LibStub:GetLibrary(*major, silent*), and LibStub:IterateLibraries(). The last is just a helper function that can be used in the generic for loop to iterate over all libraries that are currently loaded.

The method NewLibrary creates a new library and registers it. The first argument to this function is a string that acts as unique identifier for the library. This identifier is referred to as the major version of this library. In our previous example with LibFoo, this could be LibFoo-1.0 for LibFoo-1.0 and LibFoo-1.1 for LibFoo-1.1. The second argument to this function is a number that represents the minor version of the library. This number should be increased with every single change to that library to ensure that a newer version always replaces older versions.

LibStub then checks whether a library with the same major version already exists. It returns a new empty table if that is not the case. This empty table will then be used by the library as a namespace, meaning that all functions and variables of the library will be put in this table. If there is already such a library loaded with a newer minor version, it returns nil. The library's loading process should then be canceled, as this means that it is outdated and a newer version is already loaded.

The third case is that there is already a library with the same major version loaded but the old minor version is lower than the minor version of the new library. LibStub then returns this old library (which is just a table) followed by the minor version of the old library. The new library can now overwrite all functions and other values in the table that was used by the old version of the library. This process completely replaces the old version of the library with your new version.

The last method is LibStub:GetLibrary(*major, silent*); it returns the requested library followed by its minor version and throws an error message if that library doesn't exist. The second optional argument can be set to true to suppress that error message.

LibStub is quite simple and short, so we can take a look at its source code here. Note that it is also an embedded library, which means it also has to take care of replacing old versions of itself and must be able to cancel the load process. Recall that _G is the table that holds all global variables; this means that LibStub will be stored in the global variable LibStub in the following code:

```
-- LibStub is a simple versioning stub meant for use in Libraries.
-- http://www.wowace.com/wiki/LibStub for more info
-- LibStub is hereby placed in the Public Domain
-- Credits: Kaelten, Cladhaire, ckknight, Mikk, Ammo, Nevcairiel, joshborke
local LIBSTUB_MAJOR, LIBSTUB_MINOR = "LibStub", 2
local LibStub = _G[LIBSTUB_MAJOR]

if not LibStub or LibStub.minor < LIBSTUB_MINOR then
    LibStub = LibStub or {libs = {}, minors = {} }
    _G[LIBSTUB_MAJOR] = LibStub
    LibStub.minor = LIBSTUB_MINOR

    function LibStub:NewLibrary(major, minor)
        assert(type(major) == "string", "Bad argument #2 to `NewLibrary' (string➥
expected)")
        minor = assert(tonumber(strmatch(minor, "%d+")), "Minor version must➥
either be a number or contain a number.")
```

```
    local oldminor = self.minors[major]
    if oldminor and oldminor >= minor then return nil end
    self.minors[major], self.libs[major] = minor, self.libs[major] or {}
    return self.libs[major], oldminor
end

function LibStub:GetLibrary(major, silent)
    if not self.libs[major] and not silent then
        error((("Cannot find a library instance of %q."):format(tostring(major)), 2)
    end
    return self.libs[major], self.minors[major]
end

function LibStub:IterateLibraries() return pairs(self.libs) end
setmetatable(LibStub, { __call = LibStub.GetLibrary })
end
```

The major version of `LibStub` here is just `LibStub`, and it is used as a global variable to store the library. The minor version here is 2. It checks whether there is already an older version of `LibStub` loaded and does nothing (by using a large if-block) if this old version exists and the minor version of the old instance of `LibStub` is greater than or equal to the minor version from this instance.

Otherwise, it initializes `LibStub` with a table that holds all libraries and one that holds the minor versions of all libraries. It will just use the table (namespace) that was used by an older version of `LibStub` if it is overwriting an old version. The library then defines its three methods.

The metatable assignment in the last line just allows you to use `LibStub("`*`libname`*`")` instead of `LibStub:GetLibrary("`*`libname`*`")`.

We can now use `LibStub` to create an embedded library.

Creating Our Own Embedded Library

Let's update our `SimpleTimingLib` to use `LibStub`. We need to set up a new addon that acts as a test for our library to check whether it works. We need this test addon because an embedded library cannot be used without the addon it's embedded in. The folder `SimpleTimingLib`, which currently contains the library, will no longer be required after we finish this embedded version. We can then later embed a working version of this library in our other addons that currently make use of `SimpleTimingLib`. Let's call our test addon SimpleTimingLibTest.

Building a Skeleton Addon for our Library

Create a folder called `SimpleTimingLibTest` for the library and place the following TOC file in it:

```
## Interface: 30100
## Title: Test Addon for SimpleTimingLib-1.0
## OptionalDeps: SimpleTimingLib-1.0
libs\LibStub\LibStub.lua
libs\SimpleTimingLib-1.0\SimpleTimingLib-1.0.lua
SimpleTimingLibTest.lua
```

We are using the field `OptionalDeps` here. This ensures that our addon is loaded after the addon `SimpleTimingLib-1.0` if such an addon exists, allowing us to create stand-alone versions of our library later. Such a stand-alone version has the advantage that it is loaded just once during the loading process. The disadvantage is that the user has to take care of updating the stand-alone version of the library. The solution to this is using an updater for your addons, but there is currently no updater available that can extract the embedded libraries from an addon. The old WowAce updater had this feature, but its successor, the Curse Client, does not provide this functionality yet. It is planned for a future version and might already be available by the time you read this.

The next three lines deal with loading the required files. It is common to use the subfolder `libs` to place all libraries there. Note that the order in which the files are listed here is important: the first thing that must be loaded is `LibStub`, as it is required by both our library and our test file. The next file that needs to be loaded is our library, as it is required by our test file and depends on `LibStub`. The last file is our simple script that tests whether the library works properly; it requires `SimpleTimingLib-1.0` and `LibStub`.

Many addons embed a lot of libraries, so this list in your TOC file can quickly become quite long and unclear. But using XML, there is a simple way to separate the libraries from the files that belong to your addon. Recall that XML files can embed Lua code by using the element `<Script>`. This means you can create an XML file with the sole purpose of loading other Lua files. The following code shows an XML file that can be used instead of the two library-related entries in the previous TOC file:

```
<Ui xmlns="http://www.blizzard.com/wow/ui/"➥
xmlns:xsi="http://www.w3.org/2001/XMLSchema-instance"➥
xsi:schemaLocation="http://www.blizzard.com/wow/ui/..\FrameXML\UI.xsd">
    <Script file="libs\LibStub\LibStub.lua"/>
    <Script file="libs\SimpleTimingLib-1.0\SimpleTimingLib-1.0.lua"/>
</Ui>
```

Such an XML file is often called `embeds.xml`. It is then added to the TOC file instead of all the `lib/libname/libname.lua` entries.

Embedding LibStub

The next thing we need is `LibStub`. Take the file `LibStub.lua` from the download package and put it in the folder `SimpleTimingLibTest\libs\LibStub` to load it in your addon.

Building SimpleTimingLib-1.0

We can now create our library in the file `libs\SimpleTimingLib-1.0\SimpleTimingLib-1.0.lua`. The first thing we need to do in this file is create a new library, by calling the method `NewLibrary` of the library `LibStub`. The following code shows the beginning of our library. It tries to create the new library and cancels the execution if `LibStub` returns `nil` there. This happens when the same version or a newer one is already loaded.

The beginning of our file looks like this:

```
local MAJOR, MINOR = "SimpleTimingLib-1.0", 1
local SimpleTimingLib = LibStub:NewLibrary(MAJOR, MINOR)
```

```
if not SimpleTimingLib then
    return -- a greater or equal version is already loaded
end
```

The local variables MAJOR and MINOR hold the major and minor version of our library; they are visible in the whole file. We can now just copy and paste all the code from the old library, except for the following line:

```
SimpleTimingLib = {}
```

Our library will then just use the LibStub library (which is also just a table) instead of the old table in the global variable. The declarations of methods like the following work just fine:

```
function SimpleTimingLib:Schedule(time, func, ...)
    return schedule(time, func, self, ...)
end
```

In fact, the whole library works just fine with LibStub. We can even keep our two global functions we have left in for compatibility reasons. They will simply be overwritten when a new version of SimpleTimingLib is loaded over the current one.

Problems with Overwriting Old Versions

But there is also a problem when there is a new minor version that overwrites the old one. We currently keep all tasks in a local table, and there is no way to access this table from the outside. This also means that if our library has to overwrite an old version of itself, it would lose all old tasks. But it is easy to prevent this by storing this table in the library. The problem is this line:

```
local tasks = {}
```

Replace it with the following two lines to solve this issue:

```
SimpleTimingLib.tasks = SimpleTimingLib.tasks or {}
local tasks = SimpleTimingLib.tasks
```

This stores a reference to the task table in the field tasks of the library. The library will use the old table if there is already an older version of the library loaded or create a new one if it is being loaded for the first time. The local variable tasks also stores a reference to this table; I'm using this table here just so that we do not need to change anything else in the code.

But there is a second, similar problem: what happens to the frame if we upgrade the library during runtime? It is also simply stored in a local variable and is not accessible from the outside. Its OnUpdate script handler would continue to be called after the upgrade. This is actually no problem at all. But it comes with a small performance hit if the library is overwritten multiple times while loading the interface, so we want to recycle this frame.

Similar problem, similar solution: replace the line

```
local frame = CreateFrame("Frame")
```

with these lines:

```
SimpleTimingLib.frame = SimpleTimingLib.frame or CreateFrame("Frame")
local frame = SimpleTimingLib.frame
```

This creates the frame only if it doesn't already exist. `SimpleTimingLib.frame` holds the frame that was used by the old version of the library—the one that is about to be overwritten if there is such an old version.

That's it. Our library is now fully functional and can be embedded. But another nice feature would be to preserve its ability to act as a stand-alone library. Many people prefer stand-alone libraries over embedded libraries because using a lot of embedded libraries might slow down the loading process of the UI. It is easy to create a library that can be used as a stand-alone library as well as an embedded library. We just need to add a TOC file.

A TOC File for Our Library

Create a TOC file called `SimpleTimingLib-1.0.toc` in the folder `libs\SimpleTimingLib-1.0`. This TOC file will be ignored by the game if you use the library as an embedded library, as it is in a subfolder of an addon and not in an addon's main folder.

Suitable content for this TOC file looks like this:

```
## Interface: 30100
## Title: SimpleTimingLib-1.0 (Stand-alone)
LibStub\LibStub.lua
SimpleTimingLib-1.0.lua
```

Note that the stand-alone version of this library still needs to embed `LibStub`. This means you have to copy and paste the folder `LibStub` from `SimpleTimingLibTest\libs` to `SimpleTimingLibTest\libs\SimpleTimingLib-1.0`. This version of `LibStub` will not be loaded if you use the library as an embedded library, as the TOC file that references it will not be loaded in this case.

Our library can now be used as a stand-alone version; just move the folder `SimpleTimingLib-1.0` from `SimpleTimingLibTest\libs` to your addon folder. Thanks to our TOC file, World of Warcraft will recognize this folder as a separate addon and load it together with `LibStub`.

But how can we be sure that the library actually works? We wanted to write a small test addon that makes use of the library. Let's write that test code now.

Testing the Library

The place to put our test code is the file `SimpleTimingLibTest.lua`. The following code creates a new instance of our timing library and creates a simple slash command handler. This slash command is `/stltest <time> <lua code>` (for `SimpleTimingLibTest`); it is very similar to `/script`. It takes a number (*time*) as an argument, which is followed by Lua code to be executed after *time* seconds have passed.

In the `SimpleTimingLibTest.lua` file we use the Lua function `loadstring("lua code")`, which takes Lua code as a string and creates from it a function that can be executed. This function should always be used very carefully, as there might be a security issue if you execute a string (which might come from another player in the worst case) as code. It is also quite slow as it has to compile the string as Lua code. Because of these issues it should only be used if there is no other way to implement a given functionality.

```
local timingLib = LibStub("SimpleTimingLib-1.0"):New()

SLASH_STL_TEST1 = "/stltest"
SlashCmdList["STL_TEST"] = function(msg)
    local time, code = msg:match("(%d+) (.*)")
    if time and code then
        local func, errorMsg = loadstring(code)
        if func then
            timingLib:Schedule(tonumber(time), func)
        else
            error(errorMsg)
        end
    end
end
```

We can test whether our library is working properly by executing slash commands like this one:

```
/stltest 3 print("test")
```

This prints `test` to your default chat frame after three seconds. You can also test our library as a stand-alone library or you can embed the library in another addon with another minor version and confirm that the upgrading works. You will see that it is no problem and the library continues to work properly. This great flexibility is one of the main advantages of embedded libraries and `LibStub`.

We can now write our own libraries, but it is more interesting to use existing libraries. They allow you to add a lot of exciting functionality to your addon with little work. Let's look at a famous addon framework that can be included as an embedded library with `LibStub`: Ace3.

The Ace Framework

Ace3 is a framework that provides a lot of useful functionality for your addon. It is designed in a modular way, which means it consists of many small embeddable libraries. You only have to embed those libraries you need in your addon.

This section is not meant to be a reference for the whole Ace framework, so we will only look at a few particularly interesting and important parts of this framework. You can learn more about Ace3 at `http://www.wowace.com/projects/ace3/`.

Let's start creating a simple Hello, World addon.

A Simple Hello, World Addon with Ace3

Create a new folder with the name `HelloAce` in your addon folder and create the file `HelloAce.toc` with the following contents there:

```
## Interface: 30100
## Title: Hello, World with Ace3
embeds.xml
Core.lua
```

We are using the XML way of embedding the libraries here, as Ace addons often use many libraries because of the modular structure of Ace3. The main file of an Ace addon is usually called Core.lua, so let's use this name and create a file with the name Core.lua in our HelloAce folder.

We will make use of the following parts of Ace3 in our Hello, World mod: AceAddon-3.0, AceConsole-3.0, AceConfig-3.0, and AceDB-3.0. This means we have to download the latest version of Ace3 from http://www.wowace.com/projects/ace3/. This download contains all Ace3 libraries as well as LibStub, which is required by Ace3. You can either install the whole download package as a complete stand-alone version that bundles all libraries or copy and paste only certain libraries into your addon. We will only use a few libraries, so there is no need to install the whole Ace3 framework as a stand-alone package. We just copy the four subfolders we need into our addon and use them as embedded libraries.

Embedding Ace3 Libraries

Create the folder libs in your HelloAce folder and copy the following folders from the Ace3 download package there: AceAddon-3.0, AceConsole-3.0, AceConfig-3.0, and AceDB-3.0. You also need to copy the folder LibStub, which contains LibStub.lua, into your libs folder, as LibStub is required by the Ace libraries.

Libraries can also have dependencies. AceConfig-3.0 depends on CallbackHandler-1.0 and AceGUI-3.0. So we will also need to copy these two libraries into the libs folder of our addon.

We can now build our file embeds.xml. If you have peeked into a few folders that are included in Ace3.zip, you might have noticed that some Ace libraries consist of multiple Lua files, for example AceGUI-3.0 comes with many Lua files for the different widgets it can create. But we do not have to add them all by hand to our embeds.xml, as each one of the Ace libraries has its own XML file that includes all Lua and XML files it needs. We just have to add that XML file. Recall that you can use the element Include in an XML file to reference another XML file.

We can now build the file embeds.xml, which includes the four Ace libraries we want to use, the dependency LibStub, and the two dependencies of AceConfig-3.0:

```
<Ui xmlns="http://www.blizzard.com/wow/ui/"➡
xmlns:xsi="http://www.w3.org/2001/XMLSchema-instance"➡
xsi:schemaLocation="http://www.blizzard.com/wow/ui/..\FrameXML\UI.xsd">
    <Script file="libs\LibStub\LibStub.lua"/>
    <Include file="libs\AceAddon-3.0\AceAddon-3.0.xml"/>
    <Include file="libs\AceConsole-3.0\AceConsole-3.0.xml"/>
    <Include file="libs\AceDB-3.0\AceDB-3.0.xml"/>
    <Include file="libs\CallbackHandler-1.0\CallbackHandler-1.0.xml"/>
    <Include file="libs\AceGUI-3.0\AceGUI-3.0.xml"/>
    <Include file="libs\AceConfig-3.0\AceConfig-3.0.xml"/>
</Ui>
```

Note that the order here is important. The first included library line needs to be LibStub, as it is required by all other libraries. And it is also important to load CallbackHandler-1.0 and AceGUI before loading AceConfig.

Our next task is creating the real code of our addon in the file Core.lua.

First Steps with Ace3

All Ace3 addons follow an object-oriented model. Our addon is an instance of AceAddon-3.0, which means we call a constructor to create the object we will be working with. The constructor is the method NewAddon of the library AceAddon-3.0.

The first argument to that constructor is a string that is used as the identifier of our new addon; we will call our addon just HelloWorld. The following arguments can reference certain other Ace3 libraries, which will be used as what are called *mixins*. We will add AceConsole-3.0 as a mixin in our example but not AceDB-3.0 or AceConfig-3.0. You will see how to use these two libraries later.

A mixin adds the methods of the library that is mixed in to our AceAddon object. This means that these mixins basically just work like the multiple inheritance we saw in Chapter 6. We add AceConsole-3.0 as a mixin; it provides a few methods related to command line interfaces like registering slash commands or printing messages.

Our constructor then looks like this and can be added as the first line to Core.lua:

```
local HelloWorld = LibStub("AceAddon-3.0"):NewAddon("HelloWorld", "AceConsole-3.0")
```

HelloWorld now contains a normal table with an Ace3-specific metatable attached to it. There are a few important callback methods you can place in that table. One of these is OnInitialize; this method will be called after the addon and all its saved variables have been loaded. This is basically an event handler for the event ADDON_LOADED, with the first argument being the name of your addon. We can, for example, place our code that prints "Hello, World" there:

```
function HelloWorld:OnInitialize()
    print("Hello, World!")
end
```

There are two other callback methods: OnEnable and OnDisable; they are called when your addon is enabled or disabled, respectively. You can disable or enable an Ace3 addon by calling its methods Disable and Enable. A disabled Ace3 addon won't receive any events; you will see how we can add events to Ace3 addons later when we discuss AceEvent-3.0.

You might have asked why we are just using print in OnInitialize in our example. Isn't there an Ace3 method that deals with printing messages? Yes there is one. The print method is provided by AceConsole-3.0 and is just called Print. It prints a message to your default chat frame with your addon's identifier as a prefix. This allows us to create a fully functional Hello, World addon that uses Ace3 for everything if we change the line that says print("Hello, World") to the following:

```
HelloWorld:Print("Hello, World!")
```

The method Print is available only because we added AceConsole-3.0 as a mixin in our constructor. But you don't have to use these multiple-inheritance-style mixins here; you can also use the methods of AceConsole-3.0 directly, as in the following code:

```
LibStub("AceConsole-3.0"):Print("Hello, World!")
```

We don't get our addon's name as a prefix if we call Print directly, and it is easier to add all methods of AceConsole-3.0 to our AceAddon object. So you might want to add AceConsole-3.0 to almost all of your Ace3 addons as a mixin, as printing messages is always useful.

Our Hello, World addon in Ace3 is now complete. But that was too easy, and it seems pointless to use Ace3 here. So let's build a more complex addon.

Do you remember our first Hello, World addon we wrote in Chapter 3? It could do a lot more: we had a slash command that allowed us to add text that was saved in a table under a given key and another slash command allowed us to retrieve the stored text and send it to a chat channel. Let's build that with Ace3 so you can learn more about how Ace3 works.

Advanced "Hello, World" with Ace3

We will also place all the code of this advanced "Hello, World" addon in the file Core.lua. The constructor for the addon stays the same, so we can start the file with the following line:

```
local HelloWorld = LibStub("AceAddon-3.0"):NewAddon("HelloWorld", "AceConsole-3.0")
```

We now need to add slash commands. AceConsole-3.0 can be used to create slash commands.

Slash Commands with AceConsole

Our original advanced "Hello, World" addon had two slash commands: /hwadd to add text to the database and /hwshow to retrieve saved text and send it to a channel. Let's call our new slash commands /ahwadd and /ahwshow (ahw for Ace Hello World) to avoid compatibility issues with our old addon.

The method RegisterChatCommand(*cmd, func*) can be used to create a slash command in Ace. The first argument, *cmd*, is the slash command without the leading slash, and the second argument, *func*, can either be a function or the name of a method in your addon object that will be called when the user enters this slash command. Add the following lines to Core.lua to register our slash commands:

```
HelloWorld:RegisterChatCommand("ahwadd", "AddText")
HelloWorld:RegisterChatCommand("ahwshow", "ShowText")
```

Caution Do not add a leading slash when registering a slash command with AceConsole-3.0. If you do so, you will create a slash command that needs to be typed with two slashes in the game, and that's probably not what you expected to get.

Ace3 will now try to call the method AddText in the table HelloWorld when you type /ahwadd and ShowText when you type /ahwshow. It is possible to use the same method for multiple commands to add aliases. If you want to have the alias /ahelloworldadd for /ahwadd, you can add the following line:

```
HelloWorld:RegisterChatCommand("ahelloworldadd", "AddText")
```

We now need to implement the methods AddText and ShowText. They need to access saved variables. You might have guessed it—we can use AceDB-3.0 to handle saved variables in an Ace addon.

Saved Variables with AceDB-3.0

AceDB-3.0 is not added as a mixin to our addon like AceConsole-3.0, as it does not provide methods that can be used on AceAddon-3.0 objects. But it also follows an object-oriented design model and provides a constructor method that is called to initialize a new saved table. This saved table is usually stored in the field db of our addon object, but you can put it wherever you want. Note that the saved variables of an AceDB-3.0 instance are just normal saved variables; that means they are not available before the ADDON_LOADED event for our addon has occurred. So we cannot place the creation of our AceDB just anywhere in our code. We have to wait for this event.

We previously saw the callback method OnInitialize of the AceAddon-3.0 object; this method is called when our addon is fully initialized and its variables have been loaded. So this is a good place to create or load our AceDB.

Creating a New AceDB with Default Values

We create a new saved table by calling the method New of AceDB-3.0, which takes one mandatory argument that is used as a global variable in which the saved table will be stored. The AceDB constructor checks whether there is already a saved table from a previous session and restores it if such a table exists; otherwise, it creates a new, empty table in this global variable. Most Ace3 addons use the identifier of the addon (here HelloWorld) followed by DB for a global saved variable. Let's follow that convention and name our saved table HelloWorldDB.

The second argument to this constructor can optionally be a table that contains the default values for the table. We will use two fields in our saved table: the first one is called channel, and it stores the chat channel the messages will be sent to; the second one is texts, a table that stores our strings.

Such an AceDB-3.0 default table basically works like the default table we built in Chapter 7; it's just easier to use here, as this functionality is provided by the library. We don't need to worry about metatables and the recursive function to apply that metatable here. We can just use the provided methods of the library. You can read the source code of AceDB-3.0 if you are curious how it works internally.

We now have to create the defaults table somewhere and store it in a (preferably local) variable. The following code shows such a table and the call to the AceDB-3.0 constructor in the new OnInitialize method of our addon (you can delete the old Hello, World OnInitialize method):

```
local defaults = {
   global = {
      channel = "SAY",
      texts = {}
   }
}

function HelloWorld:OnInitialize()
   self.db = LibStub("AceDB-3.0"):New("HelloWorldDB", defaults)
end
```

Note that self is the hidden argument that is added by the colon notation. It will always be the addon object (here HelloWorld) when this method is called by Ace3.

You might have also wondered what the purpose of the subtable global is. If you try to add your options directly to the default table, you will get an error message saying that you tried to use an invalid data type. This error message does not refer to a normal Lua data type, it refers to the subtable global, which is one of eight AceDB data types. But what does global mean here, and what are the other seven data types? And will that subtable (or data type) also be present in the resulting AceDB?

AceDB Data Types

One might think that we can just use self.db.key = value to store a value and self.db.key to retrieve it. But AceDB-3.0 provides a more powerful way than accessing HelloWorld.db directly. The library provides eight subtables, which are called the data types (like the type global we saw in the defaults table earlier) in that table and are used for the actual data. These data types are always tables that hold the actual values we want to save.

Different data types store different sets of values based on the character the user is currently playing. For example, the data type class stores options based on the character's class. We could, for example, define a default value in the subtable class and, if the user changes it while playing a priest, she will see this change on all her alts that are also priests. But if she plays a hunter alt, she will still see the default value or her hunter-specific setting.

The following data types are provided by AceDB-3.0:

char: This table will be saved on a per-character basis and can be used instead of the TOC metadata SavedVariablesPerCharacter.

class: This allows you to save variables on a per-class basis. This is useful for mods that heavily depend on the class of the player.

faction: This allows you to save variables based on the faction of the character.

factionrealm: This saves options based on the realm and faction of the player; this means that a horde character will see a different factionrealm subtable than an alliance character on the same server.

global: This subtable stays the same for all characters on all servers of the user.

profile: This allows you to manage setting profiles in your addon. You can switch from one profile to another by calling the method addon.db:SetProfile(identifier), where identifier is a string that holds the name of that profile; this method will create a new, empty profile if identifier does not exist yet. Please read the API documentation of AceDB-3.0 on http://old.wowace.com/wiki/AceDB-3.0_API_Documentation for more information about managing profiles.

race: This subtable saves values based on the race of the player's character.

realm: This allows you to save variables based on the server of the character.

We just need the simplest data type of them, global. We don't want any per-character options and we also don't need profiles in a simple Hello, World addon. This means we are going to place all of our strings with their identifiers in HelloWorld.db.global.texts, and we save the channel the texts are sent to in HelloWorld.db.global.channel.

But we haven't told the game to actually save a variable yet; we have to add this global variable to our TOC file or AceDB-3.0 won't be able to save anything. Add this line to your TOC file to complete our persistent table:

```
## SavedVariables: HelloWorldDB
```

Don't forget that you always have to restart your game for it to recognize a change to your TOC file.

AceDB-3.0 provides more methods than those we looked at here; for example there are a few methods that are related to profiles, like copying or deleting profiles and listing all available profiles that the user can switch to. But this chapter is not meant to be a reference. Please refer to the AceDB-3.0 API documentation at http://old.wowace.com/wiki/AceDB-3.0_API_Documentation if you want to use these advanced features of AceDB in your addon.

Creating our Slash Command Handlers

We haven't implemented the methods that actually deal with our slash commands yet: AddText and ShowText. They receive, just like normal slash command handlers, the text the user typed in. We can recycle the code from the old non-Ace version of our addon for both methods. AddText looks like this:

```
function HelloWorld:AddText(msg)
    local identifier, text = msg:match("(%S+)%s+(.+)")
    if identifier and text then
        self.db.global.texts[identifier] = text
        self:Print(string.format("Added \"%s\" as \"%s\"", text, identifier))
    else
        self:Print("Usage: /ahwadd <identifier> <text>")
    end
end
```

The regular expression is the same pattern as we used in the old example: a word (everything except for spaces) followed by one or more spaces and one or more arbitrary characters at the end. The first word is our identifier, and the rest of the string minus the separating spaces is the text we want to store. If that pattern matches the entered text, the entry is added to our saved option; otherwise we print a short message that tells the user how to use this addon.

HelloWorld:ShowText(msg) is also easy. It reads the option from the saved table and sends it to the chat; otherwise it displays an error message:

```
function HelloWorld:ShowText(msg)
    local identifier = msg:trim()
    if self.db.global.texts[identifier] then
        SendChatMessage(self.db.global.texts[identifier], self.db.global.channel)
    else
        self:Print(string.format("Identifier \"%s\" doesn't exist yet.", identifier))
    end
end
```

Our old mod didn't have an option that stored the channel the message was sent to. The channel was a constant that was stored in a local variable, and there was no way to change it—except for editing the file. Our Ace version of this addon is designed better here: we saved this option, so we now need a way to modify it. We could, of course, just add another slash command handler and parse the string and set the option by hand. But there is a more powerful way to implement options in Ace3 addons: using AceConfig-3.0.

Configuration with AceConfig-3.0

There is an extremely powerful way to describe the options of your addons in Ace3, by using what is called an *AceOptions* table. This table contains an abstract description of each option your mod has; it is not just a slash command handler. AceConfig-3.0 can create either a slash command from that table or a graphical user interface. You will see how to build various GUIs from it later in this chapter.

A Simple AceOptions Table

An AceOptions table is a hierarchic structure. Each option table describes a single option, but certain option types may contain additional option tables. These additional tables can then also be of a type that contains even more subtables.

The field *type* in such a table contains a string that describes the type of the option. The simplest type is execute, which just executes a function when the slash command that corresponds to that option is entered. If an addon creates a GUI from such an option table, this will show up as a button. The function to execute has to be stored in the field *func* of the option table. The field *name* can be used to set the name of the option and the field *desc* for a longer description. The name would be shown on the button in a GUI while a description could, for example, be used as tooltip by an addon that builds a configuration GUI from such a table. But how your configuration menu will actually look is up to the addon that interprets the table and builds the GUI; we just describe our option here. Such a table could look like the following:

```
local myFirstAceOptionsTable = {
    name = "My first AceOption",
    type = "execute",
    func = function() print("hello, world!") end
}
```

func can also be a string here, and is then interpreted as the name of a method in your addon. Your AceConfig-3.0 doesn't know which addon this option table is related to, so it doesn't know in which table the method you are referring to is stored. You also have to add the table representing your AceAddon object (or any other table that holds the method you want to call) in the field handler of the option table.

The fields *name* and *desc* can be used by all option tables regardless of the type. But additional types can add additional fields that are required for that type. One particularly interesting type is group, which stands for a group of options that are visually grouped together in a GUI; for example, you might have a border around all options belonging to the same group or put all such options in a separate tab in a tab-based configuration menu. But that is also up to the configuration addon that creates the GUI.

Advanced AceOptions Tables with Groups

The type group needs the field args, which holds an arbitrary number of other option tables. args is a hash table; the key is used as short identifier for the option and the value is an AceOptions table. The identifier is used as sub-slash command in a command-line interface. A subtable of this field args of such a group can also be another table of the type group that also contains a third group, and so on.

The type of the first option table in almost all addons is group, as this type allows you to define many options in a single table. In a slash command, that first option group (or the root option if you think of the options as a tree) represents the slash command handler itself, all entries in arg are sub-slash commands. For example, let's assume we want to create the following slash command:

```
/myFirstAceOption subOption someNumericValue <x>
```

This command should accept a number between 1 and 100 and store this number somewhere. A useful option type for a numeric value is the type range. It would be displayed as a slider in a GUI. The corresponding AceOptions table could look like the following:

```
local mySecondAceOptionsTable = {
    type = "group",  -- /myFirstAceOption
    args = {
        subOption = {
            type = "group", -- /myFirstAceOption subOption
            args = {
                setting = {
                    type = "range",  -- /myFirstAceOption subOption someNumericValue <x>
                    min = 1,
                    max = 100,
                    set = function(info, value)
                        myAddon.db.global.someNumericValue = value
                    end,
                    get = function() return myAddon.db.global.someNumericValue end
                }
            }
        }
    }
}
```

The fields min and max store the minimum and maximum possible values; AceConfig will reject values outside this range and show a message that tells the user that the value needs to be between min and max. Values that are not numbers are also rejected with an appropriate error message.

The function stored in set is called the *setter* function of the option, which means it will be invoked by AceConfig-3.0 every time the user changes the option. It's up to this function to store the new value that is passed as second argument to it. The first argument is a table that contains additional information about how the option was set; we don't need this information here, so we just don't use it. The setter function could use this table, for example, to determine whether the user used a slash command or a specific GUI to set the option. You can later (when we use an AceOption table) try to add the following code to the setter function to see what information is stored in this info table:

```
for i, v in pairs(info) do
    print(i, v)
end
```

The function that is stored in get is the *getter* function, which is called every time the configuration front end needs to get the current value. This getter function also receives a table containing additional information in the same format as the first argument of the setter function. You can find full documentation of the fields of this table at http://old.wowace.com/wiki/AceConfig3.

Creating an AceConfig Table for our Hello, World Mod

Recall what we are actually trying to do here: we want to create the slash command /ahw channel <channel>. The whole slash command is our group, as shown in the next listing, and the subtable args just contains a single field: channel. This option will be invoked if the user types /ahw channel. A suitable type for the channel option is the type "select", which accepts only certain values. A GUI can display this as either a radio button or a dropdown menu. A smart GUI can decide which widget to use based on the number of possible values, but you can also help the GUI by providing the field style, which can either be "dropdown" or "radio".

The field values holds a table that defines all possible values for the selection. The index in this table is the actual value that will later be assigned to a table (here "SAY", "YELL", and so on); the value is the displayed text in a GUI or the text the user has to type in. We will use lowercase versions of the chat types here.

Our setter function receives this uppercase version of the string and assigns the variable HelloWorld.db.global.channel to it. The getter function returns the current value of this variable.

Our option table then looks like the following. Place it wherever you think it fits in file Core.lua, for example somewhere near the beginning.

```lua
local options = {
    name = "Hello, World!",
    type = "group",
    args = {
        channel = {
            name = "Channel",
            desc = "The chat channel the messages are sent to",
            type = "select",
            values = {
                SAY = "say",
                YELL = "yell",
                PARTY = "party",
                RAID = "raid",
                GUILD = "guild",
                BATTLEGROUND = "battleground",
            },
            set = function(info, value)
                HelloWorld.db.global.channel = value
            end,
            get = function()
                return HelloWorld.db.global.channel
            end
        }
    }
}
```

This describes the option we want to implement. We can now tell AceConfig-3.0 to create a slash command from it, so we can see if it is actually working.

Building Slash Commands from AceOption Tables

Creating a slash command is a really easy task. Just add the following line, which calls the method RegisterOptionsTable of AceConfig-3.0 to Core.lua somewhere after the option table:

```
LibStub("AceConfig-3.0"):RegisterOptionsTable("HelloWorld", options, "ahw")
```

The first argument is an identifier for the option table; we will use it later when we create a GUI from it. A good value for this is the ID of our addon. The second argument is our option table, and the third argument is the slash command we want to use (notice that it also lacks a leading slash). This third argument can also be an array of strings, which allows you to use more than one slash command. The whole slash command handler is created by Ace3; you don't need to do anything here.

You will now get the following message when you type /ahw in the game:

```
HelloWorld: Arguments to /ahw :
   channel - The chat channel the messages are sent to
```

You can now set the channel via /ahw channel <channel>; using invalid channels gives you an error message.

We could have easily implemented this functionality without using a library. But this way of creating slash commands comes in very handy as soon as you want to create more than one simple slash command. And we can also easily create a GUI based on the table options; this would certainly be more difficult without this neat library.

Building Graphical User Interfaces from AceOption Tables

The graphical user interface of AceConfig-3.0 is created dynamically when the user opens it for the first time. That means we just have to call a method that shows it. Execute the following slash command that calls the method Open of the library AceConfigDialog-3.0 in World of Warcraft to see what the automatically generated GUI looks like:

```
/script LibStub("AceConfigDialog-3.0"):Open("HelloWorld")
```

You might wonder where the library AceConfigDialog-3.0 comes from, as we did not include it in our embeds.xml. It is part of the AceConfig-3.0; you can find it in HelloAce\libs\ AceConfig-3.0\AceConfigDialog-3.0. The file AceConfig-3.0.xml includes this library; that's why it is already loaded and available. Figure 10-1 shows our configuration frame.

Figure 10-1. *An automatically generated AceConfig frame*

The frame looks good; it's just a little bit too big for just one option. We can set its default size by calling the method SetDefaultSize of AceConfigDialog-3.0. Add the following line after the call to RegisterOptionsTable to change the default size:

```
LibStub("AceConfigDialog-3.0"):SetDefaultSize("HelloWorld", 400, 200)
```

The first argument is the identifier of our AceOptions table, the second the width, and the third the height. These are the lowest possible values.

It is useful to create a slash command that opens the GUI, as your users certainly don't want to type that long /script command just to get an interface. The following function call creates the slash command /ahwgui, which opens the configuration menu:

```
HelloWorld:RegisterChatCommand("ahwgui", function()
   LibStub("AceConfigDialog-3.0"):Open("HelloWorld")
end)
```

Another interesting way to display an option table is using the interface options menu of the default UI. Blizzard added this menu to provide a central place where all addons can place their configuration menus. AceConfigDialog-3.0 can create a configuration page for your addon there.

Just add the following line to Core.lua:

```
LibStub("AceConfigDialog-3.0"):AddToBlizOptions("HelloWorld")
```

This method adds a tab for our Hello, World addon in the tab AddOns of the Interface Options menu.

But a real addon would certainly use more option types than just a dropdown menu. Let's look at the available types.

Option Types

Here is a list of all available option types:

color: Displays a color wheel; the setter function will receive four numbers between 0 and 1: red, green, blue, and alpha.

description: This is actually not an option; it adds an additional description in the GUI or slash command help text. The description has to be placed in the field name.

execute: You saw this option earlier; it just executes a given function. A GUI displays it as a button.

group: You also saw this option in the earlier example. It represents a group of options that belong together.

header: Like description, this is actually not an option. It displays a header in a GUI and in the slash command help text. name holds the displayed text.

input: Resembles a text option; it will create a text box in a GUI-based configuration menu. The field pattern can hold a regular expression that will be used to validate the user input. For example, %d+ will accept only numbers.

keybinding: Can be used to set key bindings in a GUI-based configuration menu. Not available in CLI-based menus.

multiselect: Works like the select option in our example, but the user can select multiple values here. The setter and getter functions will be called for every value in the field values. A value can either be selected or not.

range: We used this option in the example; it can be used for options that store numbers.

select: We also used this in the example mod. The field values holds all possible values, and the user can select one of them.

toggle: A simple boolean option, represented as a checkbox in a GUI.

These data types should cover all the options you need in an addon. But AceConfig-3.0 can do even more than in the few examples we tried out here; for example, it is possible to create confirmation dialogs when you change certain options, and there are a lot of option-type specific settings available. You can find the documentation for AceConfig-3.0 on http://old.wowace.com/wiki/AceConfig3.

You've seen different ways to visualize such an abstract AceOptions table, but it seems somewhat pointless to create all these GUIs for just one single option. However, we will encounter addons that require more than one option later in this chapter.

In the meantime, let's look at the FuBar plugin, which many addons use either for configuration or as a simple way to display data. Let's create such a FuBar plugin for our Ace3 Hello, World mod.

Creating FuBar Plugins

The first thing we need here is obviously FuBar. You can get the latest version of it on its project page on Curse if you don't have it already installed:

http://wow.curse.com/downloads/wow-addons/details/fubar.aspx

We now want to develop a simple plugin for it that is basically just a small Hello, World plugin.

FuBar is not an Ace3 addon. It is based on Rock, another addon creation framework that is similar to Ace. Like Ace, Rock consists of libraries that are embedded with LibStub, so it's not very different from the things you've seen in this chapter.

This chapter does not attempt to cover Rock completely, and we actually don't need to know much about Rock when developing a FuBar plugin. There is an embeddable library that provides the necessary API to write a FuBar plugin: LibFuBarPlugin-3.0. We just need to work with that library, which in turn communicates with Rock and FuBar. You can get the latest version of LibFuBarPlugin-3.0 on its WowAce project page: http://www.wowace.com/projects/libfubarplugin-3.0/.

Embedding LibFuBarPlugin-3.0

This library requires LibStub, FuBar, and Rock. But Rock is already provided by FuBar, and FuBar is required for LibFuBarPlugin-3.0 anyway, so we don't need to include Rock here. This means we can just embed it by copying the folder LibFuBarPlugin-3.0 from the downloaded zip archive to the folder libs of our Ace Hello World addon HelloAce.

Add the following line to your embeds.xml to load the library:

```
<Include file="libs\LibFuBarPlugin-3.0\lib.xml"/>
```

Note that the naming convention for libraries is not necessarily consistent between different libraries. The file that needs to be embedded here is simply called lib.xml. You can also figure out the file name that needs to be added by looking into the folder of the embedded library. It usually contains only one XML file or a single Lua file; this is the file that needs to be embedded.

Don't forget that you have to place this line after the line responsible for LibStub and between the opening and closing tags of the root element <Ui>. You must never add anything outside this element.

We also need to make a change to our TOC file. Our addon now depends on FuBar, so we add it as a dependency to ensure that FuBar is loaded before our addon is loaded. But simply adding FuBar as a required dependency creates two problems:

- What happens if our user does not have FuBar installed? A FuBar plugin should be an optional feature of an addon, not a required dependency.

- What if a user wants to use a FuBar-compatible addon (like FuBar2Broker) that displays a FuBar plugin in another addon (like TitanPanel)? There are, of course, fake-FuBar addons with the sole purpose of satisfying this dependency. Many FuBar2Broker users have such a fake-FuBar addon installed, but this is not a good solution.

A simple solution to both problems is using the TOC attribute `OptionalDeps`. But what happens if that optional dependency is not satisfied and we try to use `LibFuBarPlugin`, which needs `FuBar` and `Rock` (also provided by `FuBar` in our example)? We could include `Rock` as an embedded library, but it is a lot of overhead for a small FuBar plugin, as `Rock` is a really big addon framework. This library would then even be loaded if the user does not want the FuBar plugin at all. For this reason, most addons that come with a FuBar plugin don't include Rock and rely on the FuBar installation of the user to provide this library. We need to detect whether the user has FuBar (or a compatible addon) installed and create the plugin only if this is the case.

`LibFuBarPlugin` does not immediately throw an error message when we try to load it without having FuBar or Rock installed. This means you can add the following line to your TOC file to add the optional dependency:

```
## OptionalDeps: FuBar
```

Our embedded library loads properly, even if this optional dependency is not satisfied. We can now build our plugin. A good place to create this plugin is in a new file, as we can just use `return` there to cancel loading it if `FuBar` is not present. Create the file `FuBar.lua` and add it to the end of your TOC file. We can now start creating the actual FuBar plugin in this file.

■Tip Another possible solution is to put the FuBar plugin into a separate addon instead of a separate file. But I'm showing you here how to embed a FuBar plugin into an existing addon because outsourcing a tiny FuBar plugin into a separate addon is often not worth the effort.

Using LibFuBarPlugin-3.0

The following code first checks if Rock is present and cancels loading the file if that is not the case; place it in the file `FuBar.lua`.

```
if not Rock then -- check if Rock is present
   return -- cancel loading the file
end

-- create the plugin
local HelloFuBar = Rock:NewAddon("HelloFu", "LibFuBarPlugin-3.0")
```

You can now see an empty plugin with the text "Hello, World with Ace3" in your FuBar. This name is automatically taken from the field `Title` of your TOC file. We can use the method `SetFuBarText(text)` on our FuBar object `HelloFuBar` to change this text. At this point we already have a complete Hello, World plugin.

But that was too easy. FuBar can do a lot more: let's add some cool stuff here. Let's build a simple plugin that displays the zone you are currently in and your current position in that zone.

We can use the function GetRealZoneText() to get the name of the zone we are currently in and the function GetPlayerMapPosition(unitId) to get our current position. We will then create a string from these values and pass it to the method SetFuBarText. But where can we do this? LibFuBarPlugin-3.0 provides us a lot of callback methods we can define. One of them is OnUpdateFuBarText. This method is called every time FuBar requests the text to be displayed; for example, when the plugin is loaded. Let's create a function that sets the text to display:

```
function HelloFuBar:OnUpdateFuBarText()
    local zone = GetRealZoneText() -- the current zone
    local x, y = GetPlayerMapPosition("player") -- returns a value between 0 and 1...
    -- ...but the coordinates are usually displayed as a value between 0 and 100
    x, y = x * 100, y * 100 -- so multiply them by 100
    self:SetFuBarText(string.format("%s: %.1f, %.1f", zone, x, y)) -- display it
end
```

Our plugin now shows your current zone and position when you log in. But it never updates this position. We need to tell the plugin that it needs to update itself periodically. Such an update can be triggered by calling the method UpdateFuBarPlugin of the plugin object. We will have to do this ten times a second or so in order to keep the display updated. We can use a simple frame with an OnUpdate script handler for this; insert this frame and its script handler at the end of your file:

```
local frame = CreateFrame("Frame")
local t = 0
frame:SetScript("OnUpdate", function(self, elapsed)
    t = t + elapsed
    if t >= 0.1 then
        t = 0
        HelloFuBar:UpdateFuBarPlugin()
    end
end)
```

Another common FuBar plugin feature is displaying a tooltip when you place your mouse over the plugin. You can add additional information there. Let's add a tooltip that shows the name of the subzone that can be retrieved by calling the function GetSubZoneText() and the coordinates with a higher precision.

LibFuBarPlugin-3.0 calls the callback method OnUpdateFuBarTooltip every time it needs to update the text of the tooltip. The standard tooltip of the game that is stored in the global variable GameTooltip is also used by FuBar. FuBar takes care of displaying, hiding, and clearing that tooltip; we can just call the method AddDoubleLine on that tooltip in this callback method to set the contents we want:

```
function HelloFuBar:OnUpdateFuBarTooltip()
    local x, y = GetPlayerMapPosition("player")
    x, y = x * 100, y * 100
    GameTooltip:AddDoubleLine("Zone", GetRealZoneText())
    GameTooltip:AddDoubleLine("Subzone", GetSubZoneText())
    GameTooltip:AddDoubleLine("X", string.format("%.4f", x))
    GameTooltip:AddDoubleLine("Y", string.format("%.4f", y))
end
```

We now see a nice tooltip when we place our cursor over the plugin. The tooltip update method is called when the tooltip is shown or when we call the method UpdateFuBarPlugin. This means our tooltip is now also periodically updated.

Note For FuBar as for all the libraries presented here, this chapter is not a reference; we've looked at only a small part of what FuBar is capable of. The full documentation can be found on its wiki page on WowAce. com: http://old.wowace.com/wiki/LibFuBarPlugin-3.0.

You've now seen what embedded libraries are and how we can use them, and learned about the Ace3 framework. The next part of this chapter is more practically oriented. As promised in the last chapter, we will update the addon CooldownMonitor with a new fancy look. The timers that are created by our current status bar timer implementation do not look fancy at all. But there is a library that can help us with this: Deadly Bar Timers, a stand-alone library that is part of Deadly Boss Mods. This library is a status bar timer implementation that can display fancy bars with some eye-candy effects.

Improving CooldownMonitor with Deadly Bar Timers

Deadly Bar Timers (DBT) is a status bar timer library I wrote for Deadly Boss Mods. It is currently bundled with DBM and cannot be used as an embedded library in another addon. So you need to have DBM installed in order to use Deadly Bar Timers.

But DBT is completely independent from Deadly Boss Mods; you can use this library in any other addon you like. You only need the addon DBM-Core as a dependency; no other DBM modules are required. An addon that wants to use DBT does not need to interact with Deadly Boss Mods at all; it doesn't have to be a boss mod. Boss mods actually even don't use DBT directly; there is an abstraction layer on top of it in the API of DBM that is used by boss mod modules. You will learn more about creating boss mods with Deadly Boss Mods later in this chapter.

An obvious question that comes up here is: why didn't I design Deadly Bar Timers as an embedded library? Because it currently makes use of an XML template for the bars. XML files and templates are always problematic in an embedded library, because you can't just stop loading a XML file or updating an existing XML file. But converting DBT to an embeddable library is not impossible, and this is definitely something I plan to do in the near future after other priorities.

So there might be an embeddable version of DBT by the time you read this. Feel free to use it instead of the whole DBM installation if you want to. I will post additional information and revisions to the code here on the book's subforum on http://www.deadlybossmods.com/forum/ when there is such an embeddable library.

Let's continue working on CooldownMonitor now; we will add a brand-new look with Deadly Bar Timers and a lot of options with AceConfig-3.0.

Getting Started

The first thing you need is Deadly Boss Mods. You can download it at http://www. deadlybossmods.com. We will just need the addon DBM-Core for this section; you can delete all other folders from the download package if you don't want to use them. However, we are also going to use DBM-Gui later in the chapter, so you should not delete it. If there is an embeddable version of DBT by the time you are reading this, feel free to use it here. I will post details about it and how to use it in CooldownMonitor on the book's subforum on http://www.deadlybossmods.com/forum/.

Our addon now depends on DBM-Core, so you should modify the line RequiredDeps in its TOC file. It currently depends on the library SimpleTimingLib, which we just slightly modified to be an embeddable library. But we don't need this library any longer, as the only use for it was to trigger the end of the movable bar. Moving the bar is a function that is already provided by DBT, so we won't need to implement it by ourselves. So the RequiredDeps line looks like this:

```
## RequiredDeps: DBM-Core
```

Deadly Bar Timers is, like many libraries, object-oriented. This means that the first thing we do when we want to use it is create a new instance of it. The constructor is simply the method New of the library; it doesn't have any arguments. A good place to create our instance is at the beginning of the file, so add the following line to the beginning of the file CooldownBars.lua:

```
local bars = DBT:New()
```

We will now use this instance in the whole file. But what happens to the old code we wrote when we built the addon? We placed all code that was related to status bar timers in a separate file for a purpose: so we can just delete the whole file here without worrying about damaging an integral part of the addon. Delete the old code from CooldownBars.lua; we will entirely replace this file here. You can also keep the file and later add an option that allows the user to select one of the status bar timer implementations. You can then also easily add additional, different status bar timer implementations, such as LibCandyBars-2.0. This will not be covered here, but you can do it as an exercise after reading this chapter to get more practice with those libraries.

The main file of our addon calls exactly two functions, both of which are placed in CooldownBars.lua: CooldownMonitor.StartTimer(*timer*, *player*, *spell*, *texture*) and CooldownMonitor.Unlock(). This is our interface, connecting the part of the addon that deals with the combat log with the status bar timer implementation. We can just replace the status bar timer part of the addon as long as the arguments and functionality of these two functions remain unchanged.

If you want to keep the old timer implementation (or any additional implementation), you can add two wrapper functions to the main file; they should look like this:

```
function CooldownMonitor.StartTimer(...)
   if someOption == "old" then
      return CooldownMonitor.oldStyle.StartTimer(...)
   elseif someOption == "DBT" then
      return CooldownMonitor.newStyle.StartTimer(...)
   end
end
```

You would then just have to implement that option and place the `StartTimer` functions of the different status bar timer engines in these two tables. A similar function would be required for the `Unlock` function.

But we just deleted the old code, as these old timers looked really ugly. So we won't use that alternative here in this chapter. Let's build our new and improved `CooldownBars.lua` now. You've already seen the first line, which creates a new instance of DBT. Now, how can we start a timer?

First Steps with DBT

Let's examine how the most important functions of DBT work before we use them in our addon. Execute the following slash command in World of Warcraft to create a new instance of DBT and store it in a global variable. We will use this instance to try out the available methods from the command line without having to build an addon or reload the UI all the time.

```
/script bars = DBT:New()
```

Playing Around with DBT

The first thing we want to do is create a bar. There is a method that can be used to show a few test bars: `ShowTestBars`. The following instruction

```
/script bars:ShowTestBars()
```

creates five test bars. They start as small bars at their default position. When they are about to expire, they grow and move over to a second position, with smooth animation. This enlarge effect can be used to grab the user's attention, but it is too distracting for an addon like CooldownMonitor. We will disable it later.

Let's change the positions of our test bars by showing two draggable bars; we can do this by calling the method `ShowMovableBar(small, large)`. Both arguments are optional; they indicate whether to show a movable frame for the small/large bars. The default value of both arguments is `true`, so the following call shows two draggable bars:

```
/script bars:ShowMovableBar()
```

But we want to create our own bars and not use predefined dummy bars. We can start timers by calling the method `CreateBar` on our object.

Hello, World with DBT

Execute the following `/script` command to create a one-minute timer with the text `"Hello, World!"`:

```
/script bars:CreateBar(60, "Hello, World!")
```

Try to start the bar a second time while it is still running: it won't create a new one. Instead it resets the current one. The reason for this is that the second argument is actually not the displayed text; it is the identifier of the bar. It is used as the name if there is no actual name available; we will see how to set the name of a bar later. But using the identifier as the name is sufficient in almost all cases as you rarely want to have two timers with the same name at the same time.

Let's look at all the arguments that CreateBar takes when creating a bar:

DBT:CreateBar(*timer*, *id*, *icon*, *huge*, *small*, *color*)

Here *timer* is the time, *id* is the identifier and name, and *icon* is a texture that will be shown as small icon. The option *huge* can be set to true to enforce that the bar starts enlarged; *small* can be set to true to disable the enlarge effect and movement of the bar when it is about to expire. The last argument, color, is a table with the fields r, g, and b.

You might have guessed it: this function also creates and returns an object that resembles a single bar. But such a created object should only be used temporarily and not stored for later use. The reason for this is that it becomes invalid when the timer expires and it can easily lead to error messages and other bugs if you store a lot of invalid bar objects. It is better to use the method DBT:GetBar(*id*), which returns the bar object with a given ID if this bar exists; otherwise, it returns nil. A stored object wouldn't suddenly turn into a nil value; it would still be a table.

The Bar Object

The bar object can be used to modify certain settings of a bar; for example, there is the method bar:SetText(*text*), which can be used to change the displayed text. It is also possible to change the icon (SetIcon), color (SetColor), elapsed time (SetElapsed), and total time (SetTimer) of a running timer.

Execute the following code in-game while still having the DBT instance we created earlier in the global variable bars. It will create ten blue test bars with the same name:

```
for i = 1, 10 do
   local bar = bars:CreateBar(math.random(20, 60), "Test"..i)
   bar:SetColor{r = 0, g = 0, b = 1}
   bar:SetText("Test Bar :)")
end
```

Note that setting a custom color disables the default color gradient. We will later see a few options that are related to colors and dynamic color changing. But we actually don't want our bar to change its color, as the color is used to indicate the class of the player.

You've now learned the basics of DBT and we can create bars and move them around. We actually don't want to do more. Well, a little customization would be nice to have. We will see what options are available and how we can set them later when we add an AceConfig-3.0 configuration menu.

Let's build the basic functionality into CooldownBars.lua now.

Integrating DBT in CooldownMonitor

The function CooldownMonitor.StartTimer is very short and simple when using DBT. It calls CreateBar of the DBT instance we created in the first line. It then sets the color of the bar to the caster's class color:

```
function CooldownMonitor.StartTimer(timer, player, spell, texture)
    local bar = bars:CreateBar(timer, player..": "..spell, texture, nil, true)
    local class = CooldownMonitor.GetClassByName(player) -- the class of player
    if RAID_CLASS_COLORS[class] then
        -- we can use the table that is stored in RAID_CLASS_COLORS here directly
        -- as it uses the same format DBT does
        bar:SetColor(RAID_CLASS_COLORS[class])
    end
end
```

We use the fifth argument to disable the enlarge effect for all bars we create, as it is too distracting for a simple addon like ours. You can, if you want, make this optional by using a configurable option instead of true here.

The function CooldownMonitor.Unlock just needs to call the method ShowMovableBar. We set the second argument (show large movable bar) to false as there is no need to adjust the position of the enlarged bars if we don't have any:

```
function CooldownMonitor.Unlock()
    bars:ShowMovableBar(true, false)
end
```

Our slash command /cm unlock now works again and displays a movable bar for the small DBT bars. This position will be saved by DBT. But how can DBT tell all the addons that use it apart and load the correct position that belongs to our addon after we reload our interface? I've mentioned that there are other options that can be set to configure it; DBT must also be able to save and restore them.

Recall that we haven't defined any saved variables yet. We actually don't need to worry about saved variables here. DBT is a stand-alone library that manages its own saved variables. We just need to provide it with a specific identifier (a string) so it can assign our saved variables to our instance of it every time we load it. We can do this by calling the method LoadOptions(id), which creates and saves a new set of options when it is called for the first time with a specific identifier.

This method needs to be called after the variables are loaded. This means we have to create a frame and use it as an event listener to detect the ADDON_LOADED event where the first event argument equals CooldownMonitor:

```
local frame = CreateFrame("Frame")
frame:RegisterEvent("ADDON_LOADED")
frame:SetScript("OnEvent", function(self, event, addon)
    if addon == "CooldownMonitor" then
        bars:LoadOptions("CooldownMonitor")
    end
end)
```

The position of our bar is now saved, and we can also set other options. But we want to customize more than just the position of the bar. There are options available for almost everything, including the size, color, and texture of the bar. Let's add an AceConfig-3.0 based configuration menu.

Adding Options

We need the library AceConfig-3.0 and its dependencies AceConsole-3.0, AceGUI-3.0, and CallbackHandler-1.0. We also need LibStub, of course. Copy these libraries from the libs folder of our old Hello, World addon to the libs folder of CooldownMonitor. Create the file embeds.xml, add it as the first file to load to the TOC file, and embed our four libraries there by using the following XML:

```
<Ui xmlns="http://www.blizzard.com/wow/ui/"➥
xmlns:xsi="http://www.w3.org/2001/XMLSchema-instance"➥
xsi:schemaLocation="http://www.blizzard.com/wow/ui/ ..\FrameXML\UI.xsd">
    <Script file="libs\LibStub\LibStub.lua"/>
    <Include file="libs\AceConsole-3.0\AceConsole-3.0.xml"/>
    <Include file="libs\CallbackHandler-1.0\CallbackHandler-1.0.xml"/>
    <Include file="libs\AceGUI-3.0\AceGUI-3.0.xml"/>
    <Include file="libs\AceConfig-3.0\AceConfig-3.0.xml"/>
</Ui>
```

We will place our configuration menu in the file CooldownBars.lua, as all options are specific to DBT. To set DBT options, call its method DBT:SetOption(*optionName, value*). The first argument to this method is the option to set (a string); the second one is the new value. This method also checks whether the new value is valid and performs the necessary tasks to apply the changes by updating all currently visible bars.

A few important options we will use here are:

- IconLeft: Set this to true to show an icon on the left side.
- IconRight: Set this to true to show an icon on the right side.
- ExpandUpwards: Set this to true to expand the bars upwards; allows the user to place the bars on the bottom of the screen.
- Width: A number that defines the width of the frame.
- Scale: A number that defines the scale of the frame.

It is also a good idea to create a slash command handler for the options. This means we can delete our old slash command handler in CooldownMonitor.lua (or keep it, as the new one will simply overwrite it). The following code shows a skeleton configuration table, which should be placed at the end of CooldownBars.lua:

```
local options = {
    type = "group",
    args = {
        -- all following code will be placed here!
    }
}
LibStub("AceConfig-3.0"):RegisterOptionsTable("CooldownMonitor", options,➥
{"cm", "cooldownmonitor"})
```

We can now place our options in the table args. We could create additional suboptions of the type group there; this would create a tabbed GUI in which each subgroup is a tab. But that approach is not really worth the effort here, as we're just adding a few examples.

Basic Options

The first option we need is one to show the GUI. We can use the entry guiHidden here to hide the option from within the GUI, as we obviously just want it in the slash command. Place the following option in the table args to create the slash command /cm gui:

```
gui = {
   name = "Show the GUI",
   type = "execute",
   func = function() -- show the GUI
      LibStub("AceConfigDialog-3.0"):Open("CooldownMonitor")
   end,
   guiHidden = true, -- don't show this in the GUI
},
```

The next simple option we need is the one to unlock and move the bars, as we deleted that along with the old slash command handler:

```
unlock = {
   name = "Show movable bars",
   type = "execute",
   func = CooldownMonitor.Unlock,
},
```

Another useful and simple option is to show a few test bars, so users are able to test their changes. Note that DBT also enables you to create a dummy frame within a configuration menu. The options menu of DBM makes use of this technique, but it is rather complicated to include it in an automatically generated menu like the one from this example. Please refer to the documentation on http://www.deadlybossmods.com for details about this feature.

The following test function just calls the method ShowTestBars, which shows the five test bars we saw earlier in this section:

```
test = {
   name = "Show test bars",
   type = "execute",
   func = function() bars:ShowTestBars() end,
},
```

Let's add our first real DBT configuration option—an option of the type select to select the position of the icon that is displayed at the timer.

DBT Options

The DBT options IconLeft and IconRight control whether to show an icon on the left or the right side. This means we have four possible combinations, as shown in Table 10-1, for our select option.

Table 10-1. *Possible Combinations of the Options* IconLeft *and* IconRight

IconLeft	IconRight	Effect
false	false	No icon at all
true	false	Icon on the left side
false	true	Icon on the right side
true	true	Icons on both sides

The logic that translates these two boolean values into text that is then displayed can be implemented in the getter and setter functions. This makes these functions quite long (compared to the average one-line functions in our previous examples), as they require an if control structure that handles all four cases. This option should be placed, like all options we are creating here, in the subtable args of the root option we created earlier. Here's the code:

```
icon = {
    type = "select",
    name = "Icon position",
    values = { -- lookup table to get a name (used for output) from the ID
        none = "Don't show icon",
        left = "Show icon on the left side",
        right = "Show icon on the right side",
        both = "Show icon on both sides",
    },
    get = function() -- translates from the two booleans into an ID
        if bars:GetOption("IconLeft") and bars:GetOption("IconRight") then
            return "both"
        elseif bars:GetOption("IconLeft") then
            return "left"
        elseif bars:GetOption("IconRight") then
            return "right"
        else
            return "none"
        end
    end,
    set = function(info, value) -- translates an ID into the two booleans
        if value == "none" then
            bars:SetOption("IconLeft", false)
            bars:SetOption("IconRight", false)
        elseif value == "left" then
            bars:SetOption("IconLeft", true)
            bars:SetOption("IconRight", false)
        elseif value == "right" then
            bars:SetOption("IconLeft", false)
            bars:SetOption("IconRight", true)
```

```
        elseif value == "both" then
            bars:SetOption("IconLeft", true)
            bars:SetOption("IconRight", true)
        end
    end
},
```

The other DBT options we are going to use here are (as mentioned earlier) ExpandUpwards, Width, and Scale. Their getter and setter options are easier than in the previous example, as they just need to set a single option. For example, the setter for Width could look like this:

```
set = function(info, value)
    bars:SetOption("Width", value)
end
```

The functions to set the Scale and ExpandUpwards options differ in just a single string: the first argument that is passed to the method SetOption. This means we would have three very similar setters and also three very similar getters. There is often a better solution than writing a lot of similar functions in Lua, especially when dealing with such wrapper functions for options. We can create a function that creates and returns a closure that is used as a getter. The advantage of this is that we can easily modify all getter/setter functions that use this function just by modifying the template for the closure.

The function createSetter takes one argument, the option that will be modified in the created closure by calling SetOption on our DBT object. The createGetter function works in the same way; the closure just calls GetOption on the DBT object to get the current value instead of modifying it. Insert these two functions above the table options, as they need to be visible there.

```
local function createSetter(option)
    return function(info, value)
        bars:SetOption(option, value)
    end
end

local function createGetter(option)
    return function()
        return bars:GetOption(option)
    end
end
```

Building the actual options that are inserted into the subtable args of our option table is now really easy. The first option we want to implement is ExpandUpwards, which controls the direction our bars grow in when a new one is added. It is a simple boolean: false means that a new bar is added under the existing ones; true means that it is added on top of them. We just need to add an option of the type toggle and call the createGetter/createSetter functions to create the closures:

```
expandUpwards = {
    name = "Expand bars upwards",
    type = "toggle",
    get = createGetter("ExpandUpwards"),
    set = createSetter("ExpandUpwards")
},
```

The next two options are Width and Scale; these are numeric values that control the width and scale of our bar. Note that DBT currently does not allow you to change the height of a bar, because doing that comes with a few problems, like scaling the spark and text height properly. But you can still increase the height of bars by increasing the scale and reducing the width or vice versa. Future versions of DBT might include this pseudo-option directly.

The following code shows two options of the type range that represent width and scale sliders for our bars:

```
width = {
    name = "Bar width",
    type = "range",
    min = 100,
    max = 300,
    get = createGetter("Width"),
    set = createSetter("Width")
},
scale = {
    name = "Bar scale",
    type = "range",
    min = 0.2,
    max = 2.0,
    get = createGetter("Scale"),
    set = createSetter("Scale")
},
```

You can now use the slash command /cooldownmonitor gui in the game to see the automatically generated configuration menu. Note that the options are not in the order you might have expected, because args is a hash table and hash tables cannot be sorted. We will discuss hash tables and their internal structure further in Chapter 13. You can use the field order in the AceOptions tables here; this controls the position of the item in the GUI, where 0 is the first option, 1 the second, and so on.

DBT provides many additional options, like changing the bar's texture, its default colors, and so on. Please refer to the documentation at http://www.deadlybossmods.com for more details about available methods and options for DBT.

But DBM is obviously more than just this library that displays timers; it is a framework that allows you to write boss mods.

Deadly Boss Mods

You probably know this situation: you're fighting against a boss that has a special ability which turns a player of your raid into a living bomb. This player then needs to move away from all other players or you will all die. One player in your raid now gets this debuff and doesn't notice it. Half of your raid now screams "OMG, just run away!" in a frenzied chaos, and that player still doesn't move or moves too late. He explodes in your raid and everyone dies.

There are two ways to avoid such situations:

- Everyone in your raid pays attention all the time.

- Everyone has a mod installed that shows a really huge warning and plays a sound when they turn into a living bomb.

The first solution sounds simple, but you know that it is almost impossible to find a group where all 25 players are all paying attention all the time. This means that the second solution is the better one. Here comes Deadly Boss Mods into play; it is a framework that allows you to create boss mods.

Introduction to DBM

Deadly Boss Mods provides functions to create and show status bar timers based on DBT, and it can show warning messages in different colors and sizes to get the user's attention. It also helps you when working with combat log events by providing a simplified event handler that we will employ in just a bit.

The main purpose of DBM is obviously to write boss mods, but it is not limited to this. You can use it for every mod that needs the functionality of displaying timers and messages. For example, `DBM-Battlegrounds` is a DBM-based PvP mod that shows timers for captures and more in battlegrounds.

HISTORY OF DEADLY BOSS MODS

I came up with the idea of creating a framework for boss mods as early as my guild started raiding Molten Core in 2005. But I didn't create a whole framework at that point; instead, I wrote a few boss mods for some bosses in Molten Core.

The actual development of DBM started a year later, in 2006, when Blizzard released the instance Naxxramas. This instance featured 15 bosses, all of them extremely difficult to defeat. The boss fights were complicated and there was suddenly a need for a lot of boss mods. I then started to write the first version of my boss mod framework, which I simply named after my guild at that time: La Vendetta Boss Mods.

I quickly realized that it was a lot of work to write the whole framework and boss mods for all instances, so I asked for help in my guild. Martin "Nitram" Verges joined me and helped with this huge project. He wrote the whole graphical user interface and a lot of boss mods (most notable the Ulduar mods), while I developed the main part of the core of DBM. We then quickly developed the first stable version of DBM with boss mods for all relevant instances at this time.

La Vendetta Boss Mods was renamed to Deadly Boss Mods during The Burning Crusade in 2007, when our guild La Vendetta was disbanded and a few members formed a new guild called DeadlyMinds. Our guild master, Thomas "Nephilias" Holtermann, pestered us for a few months trying to convince us that renaming the addon was a good idea, and we finally agreed.

> The next big step was version 4.0 of Deadly Boss Mods, which was developed during the Wrath of the Lich King beta and released in late 2008. This version was a complete rewrite of Deadly Boss Mods and introduced a completely new boss mod API, which you will see in this section. This rewrite was needed because the old version had grown over time and become too complex. There was always constant development, and new features were added as Blizzard introduced new possibilities in their API over time. For example, the combat log was completely different when we started developing DBM. You had to parse strings to extract the necessary information; COMBAT_LOG_EVENT_UNFILTERED with all its arguments didn't exist. Loading addons on demand was not possible and addon communication with SendAddonMessage and CHAT_MSG_ADDON didn't exist in earlier days.
>
> The whole thing just became too complex as we added all these new features and updated existing features. We decided that the best solution was to make a clean cut and completely rewrite the addon. The only things we kept were the old boss mods; we wrote a compatibility layer that allows DBM 4.x to load older boss mods as the whole boss mod API was changed.

Let's write a simple example addon that demonstrates how DBM works. An addon that is based on DBM is usually written for a certain instance and consists of many boss mods that are then active only when you are in the instance the addon is for. The addon is usually load-on-demand and automatically loaded by DBM when you enter the corresponding instance. DBM makes use of the metadata stored in the TOC file to detect when to load the addon. Let's start by creating a TOC file for our simple example mod.

DBM TOC Files

Create an addon with the name DBM-HelloWorld by creating a folder DBM-HelloWorld with the file DBM-HelloWorld.toc in it; we will now start building this TOC file. You've actually seen a DBM TOC file already; I used one as an example when we first explored the TOC file, in Chapter 3. A suitable TOC file for our example addon looks like this:

```
## Interface: 30100
## Title: Hello, World with DBM
## LoadOnDemand: 1
## RequiredDeps: DBM-Core
## SavedVariablesPerCharacter: DBMHelloWorld_SavedVars, DBMHelloWorld_SavedStats
## X-DBM-Mod: 1
## X-DBM-Mod-Category: Other
## X-DBM-Mod-Name: Hello, World
## X-DBM-Mod-Sort: 1
## X-DBM-Mod-LoadZone: Ironforge,Orgrimmar
localization.en.lua
HelloWorld.lua
```

This creates a load-on-demand addon that depends on DBM-Core and registers two saved variables. DBM will use these variables to save the options of our boss mods and their boss kill statistics. All DBM-based addons must save these two variables, which consist of the addon's name without hyphens followed by _SavedVars and _SavedStats.

Our TOC file then defines the metadata attribute X-DBM-Mod, which is used by DBM to identify the addon as a DBM-addon; the value of this attribute can be anything (it just needs to be present). X-DBM-Mod-Category defines the category where the addon is placed in the DBM menu; other valid values are at the moment WotLK, BC, and Classic. X-DBM-Mod-Name is used as the name of the mod in the GUI, while X-DBM-Mod-Sort can be used to change the order in which the mods in a category are shown; 1 means that it is the first mod. The most important metadata attribute is always X-DBM-Mod-LoadZone, which specifies the zone in which the mod will be automatically loaded. You can specify multiple zones by separating them with commas. Add the city you are currently in for easier testing.

A full list of all available metadata attributes can be found in the documentation, at http://www.deadlybossmods.com.

■**Tip** Create the files HelloWorld.lua and localization.en.lua now to save a restart later.

You can now load the addon without even adding a single line of Lua code to it. It will show up in the DBM menu (/dbm) in the category "Other" and can be loaded there. It will also load automatically as soon as you enter one of the zones specified in the TOC file. Let's now add our first boss mod to this addon.

Boss Mods

You might have guessed it: DBM, just like most libraries, provides an object-oriented API for its boss mods. This means the very first line of code in a boss mod is always a call to the constructor:

```
DBM:NewMod(id, addon)
```

Creating a New Boss Mod

The first argument to the constructor is an identifier, which needs to be unique. This identifier is only used internally, for example when DBM needs to synchronize certain events with your raid group. The second argument is the name of the addon the boss mod belongs to; this can be omitted to hide the mod from the GUI.

```
local mod = DBM:NewMod("MyFirstBossMod", "DBM-HelloWorld")
```

We can now load the addon, and our new boss mod will show up as MyFirstBossMod in the subcategory Hello, World. Later we will change this to a localized name. The GUI also shows a few standard options: enabling the boss mod, enabling announce for it, and showing the default boss health frame. You will see the meaning of all these options later.

Our next step is registering a few test events and playing around with timers and announces. But there is one more thing that needs to be done before we can start. We need to tell the mod the zones in which it should be active and receive events. We can use the method mod:SetZone(...) for this; it takes a vararg of strings in which the boss mod will be enabled. But we already defined a list of zones in our TOC file, so why can't we just use that?

We can use the values from the TOC file by simply calling SetZone without arguments, but you sometimes want to define a mod that holds boss mods for multiple zones, and a boss mod should then be active in only one of them. So it can be useful to pass just one of the zones from the TOC here, but it is sufficient for us to use all of them. We can just add the following line to our file:

```
mod:SetZone()
```

If we don't call this method, our addon will be enabled in every zone. This isn't a problem, but it consumes unnecessary performance, especially as boss mods tend to use a lot of combat log events, which are fired very frequently.

Working with Events

We can now register a few events by calling the method RegisterEvents(...). This method takes a vararg of events that will all be registered. This differs from the normal RegisterEvent we know from frames by not only taking multiple arguments, it can also use subevents from COMBAT_LOG_EVENT_UNFILTERED events directly.

Let's register two events for testing, a real one and a combat log subevent, which is internally not a real event but a certain type of COMBAT_LOG_EVENT_UNFILTERED event.

```
mod:RegisterEvents(
    "CHAT_MSG_WHISPER", -- standard event
    "SPELL_CAST_FAILED" -- combat log pseudo-event
)
```

These events are automatically unregistered when the user disables the boss mod in the configuration menu. If the mod is enabled and one of the events occurs, DBM tries to call the method that corresponds to the name of the event in the mod object. Let's add a simple handler for the whisper event. The event handler receives the standard event arguments.

```
function mod:CHAT_MSG_WHISPER(msg, sender)
    if sender == UnitName("player") then
        print(msg)
    end
end
```

This method simply checks whether we whispered to ourselves and prints the message to the chat if that is the case.

The combat log event is more interesting, as DBM does not just pass the default combat log arguments here. Instead it passes only a single table that contains all the arguments under the argument's standard names. The names of the arguments are taken from the names of local variables used by Blizzard; you can find them all in Appendix B in the section about the combat log events. These tables make working with combat log events easier, as you don't have to mess around with 10 or more arguments when you just need a single one. Let's look at a simple event handler for the event SPELL_CAST_FAILED. I chose this event because it is easy to produce for testing; just try to cast a damage spell without having a target or a spell with cast time while moving. This method prints the spell's name, its ID, and the reason why it failed:

```
function mod:SPELL_CAST_FAILED(args)
    print(args.spellName, args.spellId, args.missType)
end
```

You can now test these two methods in the zone you specified in the TOC file; they simply print information to your chat frame. But we wanted to play around with real DBM warnings; let's see how we can create them.

Warnings and Announces

There are two types of warnings: normal announces and what are called special warnings. The former are normal messages that are shown in the raid warning frame and the chat frame. The latter consist of a huge blue text in the middle of the screen and a sound effect; they should be used only for critical events.

Both warning types are also objects; the constructor for normal announces is mod:NewAnnounce(*id*, *color*, *icon*). The first argument is a unique identifier for the warning, and the second is a number between 1 and 4 that specifies the color. 1 (light blue) should be used for unimportant messages, while 4 (red) is for extremely important messages. These four colors can be set by the user in the DBM configuration menu. The third argument is the icon to use; this can either be the path of a texture or a spell ID. You can create special warnings by calling mod:NewSpecialWarning(*id*), where *id* is also a unique identifier; we will explore its purpose later.

Let's now create such warning objects. Place the following code above your event handler, as we are going to store the warning objects in local variables. They need to be available in the event handler.

```
-- 42921 = Arcane Explosion, just a dummy icon
local warnHelloWorld = mod:NewAnnounce("WarnHelloWorld", 2, 42921)
local specWarnHelloWorld = mod:NewSpecialWarning("SpecWarnHelloWorld")
```

It is a good idea to prefix the variables (and IDs) for normal warnings with warn and those for special warnings with specWarn. The advantage of this naming convention is that you avoid problems with possible name collisions when you have different warnings for the same event; it also makes your code more readable.

We can now use the method Show on these objects to show the actual warning. Another useful method is Schedule(*x*), which calls Show after *x* seconds. Remove the old CHAT_MSG_WHISPER handler and replace it with this one in order to test our two warnings. Normal announces are sent to the raid warning chat if the user is authorized to do so (that is, either a raid leader or an assistant) and has the announce option of this boss mod enabled.

```
function mod:CHAT_MSG_WHISPER(msg, sender)
    if sender == UnitName("player") and msg:lower() == "hello" then
        warnHelloWorld:Show()
        specWarnHelloWorld:Schedule(5)
    end
end
```

Try to whisper "hello" to yourself now; this triggers the normal warning and the special warning five seconds later. A scheduled warning can be canceled by calling its method Cancel.

Note that we haven't specified any text for these warnings yet, so DBM just uses the ID. You will see how we can add text later.

You might wonder why we need to incur the overhead of creating all these objects; wouldn't it be easier to just provide a method like ShowWarning(*text*, *color*, *icon*) in the boss mod object? DBM 3 and earlier had such methods, but creating objects for every single warning has a big advantage: DBM knows which warnings belong to a boss mod at the time the mod is created. This information is used to create options to enable or disable these warnings. For example, look at the configuration menu of our boss mod; it has two new options that can easily be used to disable the warnings.

Timers

Timers are very similar to warnings; every timer in a boss mod is represented as an object. The constructor is mod:NewTimer(*time, id, icon*). The first argument is the time for the timer, the second one a unique identifier (a string) that is required to identify the timer. This ID will be used if, for example, you disconnect during a boss fight and log in again while the fight is still ongoing. DBM will then send a combat status request to the raid, and another DBM user will tell you the IDs and status of all currently running timers. The third argument is the icon of the timer; this can either be the path of a texture or a spell ID.

Let's build an example timer that will be started by our SPELL_CAST_FAILED handler. Insert the following line above that handler, because it needs to be visible in the event handler:

```
local timerHelloWorld = mod:NewTimer(60, "TimerHelloWorld", 42921)
```

We can now start this timer by calling its method Start (or its alias Show). This method takes an optional argument *time*, which changes the time of the timer; the default value is the time specified in the constructor. This argument can be negative to subtract a time from the default time. But it is sufficient in most cases to specify the time in the constructor just once when the timer object is created. The method Stop can be used to stop a currently running timer, the method Schedule to schedule the Start method, and Cancel to cancel this scheduled task.

Replace our old SPELL_CAST_FAILED handler with this one, which just starts the timer with its default time of 60 seconds every time this event occurs:

```
function mod:SPELL_CAST_FAILED(args)
    timerHelloWorld:Start()
end
```

The timer now starts when the SPELL_CAST_FAILED event occurs and restarts itself if it is already running while this event occurs. But it also doesn't have a name yet, as we haven't added any localization yet. Let's see how we can localize boss mods in DBM.

Localizing Boss Mods

Localization also works in an object-oriented way; Deadly Boss Mods provides a localization object that stores all localizations of a boss mod. Let's create such an object for our example boss mod in the file localization.en.lua:

```
local L = DBM:GetModLocalization("MyFirstBossMod")
```

This creates a new localization object for the boss mod MyFirstBossMod. Note that this boss mod doesn't exist yet, because localization.en.lua is loaded before the boss mod. DBM saves this localization object and attaches it to our boss mod when we create it later.

The created object L now provides a few methods that can be used to store localizations in different categories. All of these methods take as an argument a table that contains key-value pairs for localized strings. The key is the identifier for the localized string; the value is the localized text.

General Localization

One of these methods is SetGeneralLocalization, which is used to set general localizations of a mod, such as the name of the boss mod, in the field name. Add the following line to your localization file to set the name of our boss mod.

```
L:SetGeneralLocalization{
    name = "Hello, World with DBM"
}
```

This localization category is also the place to store all general-purpose localized variables that are not used in timers, warnings, or options. Later we will read them from this table.

SetOptionLocalization sets the localized texts that are used in the GUI; the key here is the ID of a warning or timer. Add the following code to your localization file to get a fully localized GUI for our example addon:

```
L:SetOptionLocalization{
    WarnHelloWorld = "Show Hello, World announce",
    SpecWarnHelloWorld = "Show Hello, World special warning",
    TimerHelloWorld = "Show Hello, World timer",
}
```

Timer Localization

The next category is Timer, which contains all localized strings for timers. We have just one single timer here, so we need just one entry:

```
L:SetTimerLocalization{
    TimerHelloWorld = "Hello, World",
}
```

All localized strings in this table will be processed by string.format when the timer is created. The methods Show(timer, ...), Schedule(x, timer, ...), and Stop(...) of the timer object take additional arguments, which will be passed to string.format. A timer can be started multiple times if different arguments are passed to it, as the ID and all additional arguments are used as identifiers for the created DBT bar. DBM catches all error messages caused by invalid format strings and replaces invalid format directives and missing arguments with "unknown". This robustness is necessary in a boss mod as it can happen that an argument is nil. For example, imagine a function that tries to get the target of a boss. It might fail because of lag or the target being out of range, resulting in a nil value in the format string. It's better to get a timer or warning that says "Evil spell on unknown!" than no warning, or even worse an error message in the middle of a fight.

Warning Localization

The last localization category is Warning, which is used for both announces and special warnings. Add the following function call to our localization file to complete the localization of our boss mod:

```
L:SetWarningLocalization{
    WarnHelloWorld = "Hello, World",
    SpecWarnHelloWorld = "Special Warning",
}
```

We now have a fully localized boss mod. Warning localizations are also processed by `string.format`, just as for timers. The arguments passed to the method `Show` are used to format it and everything that would cause an error is replaced by `"unknown"`.

It is often important in boss mods that the user is able to identify a player quickly in a warning, so coloring player names by their class color in warnings is a useful feature. DBM can do this automatically; you just need to highlight all player names in a string, or DBM won't be able to identify them. The marker characters are the greater than and less than signs. Change the line saying `WarnHelloWorld = "Hello, World"` in our warning localization to the following code:

```
WarnHelloWorld = ">%s< said Hello, World!",
```

We now need to update our event handler in the boss mods file; replace the old CHAT_MSG_ WHISPER handler with the following one, which displays our warning every time someone whispers "hello". The sender's name is passed to `Show` and DBM automatically adds corresponding colors codes there if this player is a member of your party or raid.

```
function mod:CHAT_MSG_WHISPER(msg, sender)
    if msg:lower() == "hello" then
        warnHelloWorld:Show(sender)
    end
end
```

You now get a properly colored warning every time someone whispers "hello" to you. We only localized options, timers, and warnings but it is also possible to create general purpose localized strings that can be accessed from the boss mod.

■**Caution** The color feature works only if the sender is in the same party or raid group as you are. This also means that it does not work at all if you are not in a group.

Accessing Localized Variables

The method `mod:GetLocalizedStrings()` returns an object that can be used to access all localized strings available in a boss mod. This object is often stored in the local variable `L` inside a boss mod file and is created right after the call to the boss mod's constructor. Thus the second line of a boss mod often looks like this:

```
local L = mod:GetLocalizedStrings()
```

`L` can be used like a normal table; trying to retrieve a value from it looks up the value in all localization categories of a mod, starting in the general category. If the requested key does not reference a localized string, it returns the string itself. This means the table never returns `nil` for any field, so it can safely be used without checking for missing localizations. This allows you to write boss mod prototypes quickly (for example, while raiding) and add all the localizations later.

Adding More Languages

We've added only English localizations here. But the purpose of this localization system is to support multiple languages. This doesn't work any different than in other localizations you've seen thus far. Just add a new file like, for example `localization.de.lua` for a German localization and place it right under the English localization file in the TOC file. Add the following line to the very first lines of this new localization files to ensure that it is loaded only on German clients.

```
if GetLocale() ~= "deDE" then
    return
end
```

The rest of this file then just looks like the English localization files. It is no problem if a localization key is missing here; DBM will then just use the value from the English file. The first few lines of a German localization file could look like this:

```
local L = DBM:GetModLocalization("MyFirstBossMod")

L:SetGeneralLocalization{
    name = "Hallo, Welt mit DBM"
}
```

This was just a brief overview of a few features that are provided by DBM. It can do a lot more, like detecting boss pulls, kills, and wipes or creating automatically localized timers and warnings based on spell IDs. Please refer to the documentation at `http://www.deadlybossmods.com` to learn more.

Summary

In this chapter you learned to make use of libraries and how we can use other libraries in our addons. The most important library we used here was `LibStub`, a tiny library that allowed us to embed other libraries into our addons. We then rewrote our library `SimpleTimingLib` for the third time; it can now be used as both a stand-alone library as well as an embedded library using `LibStub`.

The next example mod in the chapter showed us how we can write simple mods by using the very powerful framework Ace3 that consists of many embedded libraries. It was really easy to write that example mod thanks to the functions provided by Ace3.

Our next topic in this chapter was extending our CooldownMonitor from the last chapter by using my implementation of status bar timers that is included in Deadly Boss Mods. These new status bar timers gave CooldownMonitor a brand-new and fancy look. We also included `AceConfig-3.0` to create a basic configuration menu to style our timers.

The last topic in this chapter was Deadly Boss Mods, a framework that allows you to create boss mods. You learned how we can work with the combat log in this framework and which combat-related features and predefined functions are provided by it.

■ ■ ■

## CHAPTER 11

Working with Secure Templates

Did you ever wonder what keeps you from developing an addon that completely automates your game? Well, such an addon would break the EULA, and you don't want to do that because you don't want to lose your World of Warcraft account. But what keeps you technically from developing such an addon?

The whole UI is written in Lua and XML, so there are functions that allow you to move your character and to cast spells. For example, there is the function CastSpellByName("*name*"), which allows you to cast a spell. But try to do this with a simple spell like Attack:

```
/script CastSpellByName("Attack")
```

You will get an error message saying that your action has been blocked because it is only available to the Blizzard UI. In this chapter we will explore how the game determines what belongs to the default UI and what does not. We will also discuss the circumstances under which we are able to cast spells and execute certain restricted actions from an addon.

Secure and Tainted Code

All Lua values and references are always either *secure* or *tainted* in World of Warcraft. Everything that is created from an addon or via slash commands will be tainted, and everything that is created by the game is secure. The current *execution path* (an execution path is the currently running code, which is started by the game and ends as soon as all called functions have returned) can also be either secure or tainted, but it always starts as secure. It will become tainted as soon as it encounters anything that is tainted.

The game uses digital signatures to check the integrity of the default UI when it is loaded, and only code that has been digitally signed by Blizzard will be flagged as secure upon loading, so every value created by the Blizzard UI is flagged as secure. This also means that all of your addons are automatically tainted and all values you create are also tainted.

What does this mean for you? There are certain functions, known as *restricted functions*, that can only be called from a nontainted execution path. One of these restricted functions is CastSpellByName. But we don't need to discuss all of these functions here, as we will never be able to call any of them. Let's see an example demonstrating tainted and secure code.

Restricted Functions

Before the taint system was introduced in patch 2.0, I once wrote an addon that prevented certain spell casts in certain situations. Why would I want to do this? The addon was a boss mod for Nefarian in Blackwing Lair. Just in case you don't know, this really old boss, Nefarian, places a debuff on a certain class from time to time that corrupts some of the class's spells and abilities. For holy priests like me, this debuff turns all healing spells into damaging spells, so it is a really bad idea to continue healing the tank when you've got this debuff. The addon detected this and blocked all healing spells while the debuff was active.

Blocking spells worked with hooks in a few functions in this addon; one of these hooks was in the function CastSpellByName. Let's try to write a simple hook for this function. Note that this function is invoked only when you use the /cast slash command (for example in a macro) but not when you click a button in your action bar. Action bars work slightly differently (we will see them later in this chapter), and I will only show you the hook into CastSpellByName to keep it simple.

The following code can easily be executed in the game with an addon like TinyPad:

```
local old = CastSpellByName
CastSpellByName = function(...)
   print(...)
   return old(...)
end
```

This should print all arguments passed to CastSpellByName and then call it. The actual addon had a simple check for a variable that was set if the debuff was active. Now try to execute the following slash command or to use a macro that casts a spell:

```
/cast Attack
```

You will get the same error message as if you had called CastSpellByName directly, even though the actual call to it comes from the default UI. Our simple hook just broke all slash commands that can cast spells; /castrandom and /castsequence are also affected.

Let's see what happened by tracing the call. The execution path starts in the OnEnterPressed event of your chat frame as a secure execution. It then goes through a lot of code in the file FrameXML\ChatFrame.lua that identifies your command as a slash command until it finally reaches its slash command handler in the table SecureCmdList. This works just like normal slash command handlers; don't worry about the different name. The handler parses the slash command, determines whether you are trying to use an item or a spell, and gets the optional target argument. The execution is still secure when Lua reaches the following handler, which is also defined in the file FrameXML\ChatFrame.lua:

```
SecureCmdList["CAST"] = function(msg)
   local action, target = SecureCmdOptionParse(msg);
   if ( action ) then
      local name, bag, slot = SecureCmdItemParse(action);
      if ( slot or GetItemInfo(name) ) then
         SecureCmdUseItem(name, bag, slot, target);
      else
         CastSpellByName(action, target);
      end
   end
end
```

It now calls the function stored in the global variable `CastSpellByName`, which is normally secure. But we overwrote it with our custom hook function, which is not secure.

The execution path now becomes tainted the moment it enters our function. This tainted execution now calls the real function `CastSpellByName`, which is still secure (but the reference stored in the local variable `old` is tainted; you will see how exactly the spreading of taint works in just a bit). It doesn't help us that the function is still secure—it is called from a tainted execution path and therefore fails. The only way to get rid of this taint is to reload your user interface.

We can use the function `issecurevariable(tbl, key)` to check whether a value that is stored in a table is tainted. The first argument is optional and is by default the global environment `_G`. We can thus use the following code to check the integrity of `CastSpellByName`:

```
print(issecurevariable("CastSpellByName"))
```

It will print `nil` followed by the empty string. This second return value is the addon that caused the taint; the empty string means that it was tainted by a `/script` command entered by the user. As you can see, it is not possible to hook a protected function using the traditional way of hooking it. But there is another way to hook functions.

Hooking Secure Functions

The interface API provides the function `hooksecurefunc(tbl, key, hook)`, which can be used to hook a secure function without affecting its taint. Again, the first argument `tbl` is optional and is by default the global environment. The last argument is the function that will be executed every time after the hooked function was called. The hook receives the same arguments as the original function.

It is actually not a "real" hook, as it's not possible either to modify arguments passed to the original function or to change its return values. So it is not possible to write an addon like the one I described earlier. But such post-hooks are often sufficient, especially when you want to make minor changes to default UI elements. An example of an addon using such a hook is the Battleground mod of Deadly Boss Mods. It hooks into the function that updates the score frame, and the hook sets the color of the players in the frame to each one's respective class color.

Reload your UI if you haven't already done this to get rid of our old hook and the taint so we can play around with this function. Let's test if `CastSpellByName` is now secure:

```
print(issecurevariable("CastSpellByName"))
```

It now prints 1 followed by `nil` (the mod that tainted the variable if it was tainted), meaning everything is fine. We now apply our new hook, which also just prints the arguments it receives:

```
hooksecurefunc("CastSpellByName", function(...)
   print(...)
end)
```

We can now again check whether it is still secure:

```
print(issecurevariable("CastSpellByName"))
```

We still see 1 and `nil` as the result, so it's not tainted. You can now test your spell-cast macros or a simple slash command like /cast Attack; it works properly and the hook function is called.

Note that this way of hooking functions works only if the function is stored in a table or global variable (which is technically an entry in a table). You obviously won't encounter a secure function that is stored in a local variable, as this local variable would only be visible in the file it was created in; this file is digitally signed, and you therefore cannot write your code in it. But you may run into a situation where you need to hook an event handler of a frame without tainting it. You can use the method `frame:SetHook(`*handler,* *hook*`)` on this frame to add a secure hook to one of its event handlers. We saw this method earlier when we discussed event handlers.

You should always use `hooksecurefunc` or `frame:SetHook` if you want to hook functions defined by Blizzard that are not tainted yet. The reason for this is that the taint can quickly spread over the whole default UI. A single tainted value can quickly infect other functions and values. Let's see how taint spreads and how we can trace it.

How Taint Spreads

A secure execution loses its secure status and becomes tainted when it executes a tainted function or accesses a tainted value. A value is tainted when it is created or modified in a tainted execution path. Note that just accessing a secure value from a tainted execution path does not taint it. You always create a copy of a value when you access it (note that the value of a variable that holds a complex object like a table is always a reference to that table, so you get a tainted reference to a secure table and not a tainted copy of the table), and it is this copy that will be tainted. The original value stays secure if it was secure before.

A single tainted variable can thus quickly spread over the whole default UI as it taints the execution path from the time it's accessed. All values that are created by this code after the taint occurred will then also be tainted. Other code then accesses these values and also becomes tainted, and so on. You can quickly break something you did not expect to break by tainting a single value.

So far we have used a lot of code that was directly called by Lua code of the default UI, like slash command handlers or dropdown menus. But they didn't break anything, because Blizzard took care of the taint issue in its code. This code either makes sure that no important values can become tainted or uses the function `securecall(`*func,* `...)`. This function takes another function and executes it with the given arguments, and the old taint status of the execution path is restored after the function returns. That means using this function in your own code is pointless, as the taint status would revert to tainted, and that doesn't help you.

Spreading taint was a big issue in earlier versions of the game, especially in the months after the taint system was introduced. However, Blizzard now takes many precautions to prevent addons from breaking the default UI by hooking random functions that do not handle functionality related to protected functions. All critical parts of the default UI make sure that they do not access variables that might be tainted by addons. Hooking functions that do not handle anything related to protected functions directly without using `hooksecurefunc` is pretty safe.

But you should still use `hooksecurefunc` when you want to post-hook a secure function. It can still happen that tainting an innocent-looking variable or function breaks parts of the default UI. But Blizzard notices and fixes such issues quite fast. I had an example where tainting the function `WorldMapFrame_Update` of the world frame could break the Set Focus option, which is certainly an unexpected result. However, this issue was fixed with patch 3.1.1, and it is now safe to taint WorldMapFrame_Update.

However, if you ever notice that your code has broken the default UI, you should run the following command and reload your UI to get more debugging information:

```
/console taintLog 1
```

You can then execute the function being blocked because of your addon, and you will get the file taint.log in your Logs folder after logging out. This file contains additional information about the failed protected call and the call that caused the taint.

For example, the following hook into the function UnitHealth taints critical parts of the unit frames, and you must never use such a hook in an addon:

```
local old = UnitHealth
UnitHealth = function(...)
    return old(...)
end
```

■**Caution** Taint issues can be very hard to reproduce with different addon constellations. This means that any addon you have can break this example, even if it seems to be completely unrelated to the actual issue. Keep this in mind when you receive an error report regarding taint from one of your users. and always ask for a list of installed addons and a taint log when trying to debug a taint issue.

Now try to engage a mob and kill it. You will see a message in your chat frame saying that a default UI action was blocked due to an addon. The broken functionality is the target's target frame of the default UI; it won't be able to update properly if your target changes its target. This was logged in the taint.log file:

```
5/21 02:37:11.252  Global variable UnitHealth tainted by MACRO_TAINT -
local old = UnitHealth
UnitHealth = function(...)
    return old(...)
end:4
5/21 02:37:11.252       RunScript()
5/21 02:37:11.252       Interface\AddOns\TinyPad\TinyPad.lua:199 OnClick()
5/21 02:37:11.252       TinyPadRun:OnClick()
5/21 02:37:11.252  Execution tainted by MACRO_TAINT while reading UnitHealth - ➡
Interface\FrameXML\TargetFrame.lua:620 TargetofTarget_Update()
5/21 02:37:11.252       Interface\FrameXML\TargetFrame.lua:229 TargetFrame_OnUpdate()
5/21 02:37:11.252       TargetFrame:OnUpdate()
5/21 02:37:11.252  An action was blocked in combat because of taint➡
from MACRO_TAINT - TargetofTargetFrame:Show()
5/21 02:37:11.252       Interface\FrameXML\TargetFrame.lua:632 TargetofTarget_Update()
5/21 02:37:11.252       Interface\FrameXML\TargetFrame.lua:229 TargetFrame_OnUpdate()
5/21 02:37:11.252       TargetFrame:OnUpdate()
```

The log file first tells you which addon caused the taint; the addon is `MACRO_TAINT` in this case, because I ran the hook from TinyPad, which uses `RunScript(str)` to execute the entered text as Lua code. Code loaded through `RunScript` is considered to be a macro by World of Warcraft, as the command `/script` also uses `RunScript` internally. The next few lines show the call stack of the execution path that tainted the variable.

The next lines in the log tell you about the actual problem that occurred. The function `TargetofTarget_Update()` tried to perform a protected action but it was blocked as the execution became tainted while accessing the global variable `UnitHealth`. The next lines show the call stack of the failed call and the actual call that failed: `TargetofTargetFrame:Show()`. The `Show` method of certain frames that deal with protected actions, like targeting or casting spells, is what is called a *protected* method, which cannot be called from tainted code while you are in combat. Trying to perform such a call results in a notification in your chat frame and an entry in the taint log. We will discuss protected methods and frames in the next section. We now know what we can't do; let's see what we can do. It is still possible to create an addon that casts spells or targets units under certain circumstances.

Using Secure Templates for a Unit Frame Mod

A secure template is a normal XML template that can be used for your frames. These templates already have certain functionality that can normally only be called from secure code, like targeting a party member or casting a spell. Possible uses for these templates are unit frames and action buttons. But they are also considered *protected* frames, and you cannot call certain methods while you are in combat. Let's write a simple example mod that shows unit frames for you and your current target.

The game provides a secure template that can be used for this: `SecureUnitButtonTemplate`. As noted, every frame you create from this template will be a protected frame, and a protected frame cannot do certain actions while you are in combat. Let's look at the restrictions on protected frames before reviewing the available templates.

Restrictions on Protected Frames

The following methods of protected frames cannot be called from tainted code while you are in combat. All of these methods still work as they work for normal frames when you are not in combat.

- `frame:Show()`
- `frame:Hide()`
- `frame:SetPoint(point, relativeTo, relativePoint, x, y)`
- `frame:SetWidth(width)`
- `frame:SetHeight(height)`
- `frame:SetAttribute(attribute, name)` (you will see the purpose of this method in just a bit)

Children of a protected frame are not necessarily also protected, so you can add normal frames as children to your secure frame. But all parents and frames you anchor your secure frame to automatically become protected, because if they were not, you could simply show

/hide or move the parent or anchor to bypass these restrictions. This can sometimes lead to unexpected problems, as frames might suddenly become protected. So be careful when choosing the parent and anchors of a protected frame. You can use the method `frame:IsProtected()` to check whether a frame is currently protected.

The purpose of these restrictions is to prevent addons like CT-HealMonitor, which existed in 2006 before secure templates were introduced in World of Warcraft 2.0. This addon showed a few unit frames, which were sorted by their missing health; that is, the player with the lowest health was ranked highest. Healers could simply always click on the top player in that list and heal him all the time. You can, of course, still create a mod that displays players sorted by their health, but you can no longer target these players by clicking on them while you are in combat. There was also an addon that automatically chose the best heal spell to cast and the best target for it. Such addons are no longer possible; you can only execute a predefined protected action with an explicit click on a protected frame that was created from a secure template.

Protected frames do not have special methods assigned to them, but the secure templates are not tainted and can therefore call protected functions. The different available secure templates provide different predefined functionality that is related to protected functions. Let's see all available templates to get an overview over the whole system before we start with the example mod.

Available Secure Templates

There are basically two types of addons that need to make extensive use of secure templates: unit frame mods and action bar mods. Action buttons just require a simple template that allows you to execute actions that would otherwise be blocked when you click them while unit frames require a lot of different templates. The following list shows all available secure templates:

- `SecureActionButtonTemplate`: Can be used to implement buttons that execute restricted functions when they are clicked.

- `SecureUnitButtonTemplate`: A template for unit frames, it is tied to a specific unit that will be targeted when you click on the frame. It can also be shown and hidden automatically if the unit comes into existence or vanishes.

- `SecureGroupHeaderTemplate`: An abstract header for a list of unit buttons, as for displaying a raid group. This frame should not be used directly; it is a template for the following templates:

  - `SecurePartyHeaderTemplate`: A template that can contain `SecureUnitButtonTemplate` to display your whole group; this template inherits from `SecureGroupHeaderTemplate`.

  - `SecureRaidGroupHeaderTemplate`: A template that can be used for subgroups of a raid; it works similarly to the party header.

  - `SecureGroupPetHeaderTemplate`: An abstract header for a list of pets, it should not be used directly; it acts as a template for the following templates.

    - `SecurePartyPetHeaderTemplate`: A template for pets in your party.

- `SecureRaidButtonTemplate`: A template for pets in your raid group.

All of these secure templates just provide functionality and no design. You are completely free to style them according to your needs. You can add normal frames as children to these secure templates, and there are no restrictions on these children.

Let's now create our simple example mod that just displays two unit frames: one for yourself and one for your target. We need to inherit these two frames from SecureUnitButtonTemplate, but how do we tie that to a specific unit and how can we tell the frame anything about the restricted actions it should do? Just using a simple variable or function call would taint important code of the template and break it. There is another way to communicate with this frame—through *attributes* of the secure frame.

Building Unit Frames with Attributes

Attributes of secure frames are set by calling the method SetAttribute(*attribute, value*), where *attribute* is a string that identifies the attribute and *value* the new value. GetAttribute(*attribute*) can be used to retrieve the current value of the attribute. SetAttribute is one of the protected methods of protected frames, which means we cannot change the attributes while we are in combat. The most important attribute we are going to need for our example mod is the attribute unit of the unit button template. This sets the unit the frame is tied to.

We now know enough about templates to make use of them, so let's start building our example mod here. Create a new folder for our addon and call it MyUnitFrames or something similar; then add an appropriate TOC file and add an XML to that TOC file. We now build a template that inherits from SecureUnitButtonTemplate for our two unit frames.

Building a Template for Our Unit Frames

It's no problem to create a template from a secure template; the created template will then, of course, also be protected. This protection is actually also an XML attribute and it is set in the template SecureFrameTemplate in the file FrameXML\SecureTemplates.xml, which is used for all secure frames. And XML attributes are always inherited from the template. The XML looks like this:

```
<Frame name="SecureFrameTemplate" protected="true" virtual="true"/>
```

You cannot change this to false in your template, because there is no way for you to remove the protection attribute of a frame or template after it has been protected. Add the standard root element to your XML before we start creating our frame:

```
<Ui xmlns="http://www.blizzard.com/wow/ui/"➡
xmlns:xsi="http://www.w3.org/2001/XMLSchema-instance"➡
xsi:schemaLocation="http://www.blizzard.com/wow/ui/..\FrameXML\UI.xsd">
</Ui>
```

Add the following to your XML file (between the <Ui> tags) to create a simple template that resembles a simple unit frame. It consists only of a portrait, a font string for the name, and a health bar:

```
<Button name="MyUnitFrameTemplate" virtual="true" movable="true"➡
inherits="SecureUnitButtonTemplate">
    <Size>
        <AbsDimension x="96" y="32"/>
    </Size>
```

```
    <Layers>
      <Layer level="ARTWORK">
         <Texture name="$parentPortrait">
            <Size>
               <AbsDimension x="32" y="32"/>
            </Size>
            <Anchors>
               <Anchor point="LEFT"/>
            </Anchors>
         </Texture>
         <FontString name="$parentName" inherits="GameFontNormal">
            <Anchors>
               <Anchor point="TOPLEFT" relativePoint="TOPRIGHT"➥
relativeTo="$parentPortrait"/>
            </Anchors>
         </FontString>
      </Layer>
   </Layers>
   <Frames>
      <StatusBar name="$parentHealth" minValue="0" maxValue="1">
         <Size>
            <AbsDimension x="64" y="16"/>
         </Size>
         <Anchors>
            <Anchor point="BOTTOMLEFT" relativePoint="BOTTOMRIGHT"➥
relativeTo="$parentPortrait"/>
         </Anchors>
         <BarTexture file="Interface\TargetingFrame\UI-StatusBar"/>
      </StatusBar>
   </Frames>
   <Scripts>
      <OnDragStart>
         self:StartMoving()
      </OnDragStart>
      <OnDragStop>
         self:StopMovingOrSizing()
      </OnDragStop>
   </Scripts>
</Button>
```

We defined only two script handlers in the template; these handlers deal with dragging the frame. Note that StartMoving and StopMovingOrSizing are not protected functions; this means that moving the frame with your mouse while you are in combat is no problem. But moving it via calls to SetPoint does not work in combat.

We will also need an OnLoad handler that initializes the frame by calling a few functions; for example, we need to call the method RegisterForDrags there. We also need an event handler for the event UNIT_HEALTH that is fired every time the health of a unit changes; we will update the health bar there.

But defining these two handlers in the template is actually not smart, as the two frames we are going to create from this template are too different. But defining these handlers later in the frames would generate some duplicate code, and as I've said, duplicate code is bad. It would certainly be possible to define parts of the handlers in the OnLoad handler and use a Lua file with a few initialization functions to avoid a few lines of duplicate code. But the purpose of this example is to demonstrate a simple unit frame in XML with a few lines of Lua code. These few lines of duplicate code are not worth the additional complexity that avoiding them would add.

Using the Template

We've now discussed the essentials of secure unit button templates, and we are ready to create the actual two frames from our template. Note that the frames are very simple; they just show a portrait, the unit's name and level, and a simple health bar. Both frames start by default in the middle of the screen but they can be dragged at any time. You can add your own art as textures and an additional mana bar to get a fully featured unit frame mod. Adding this to the example would have added unnecessary complexity, as we would need to take care of a lot of tasks like coloring it correctly according to the mana type (mana/energy/rage and so on).

Let's start with the player frame. It needs to perform the following tasks in the OnLoad handler: register click and drag events, set the $parentName to the player's name, and set $parentPortrait to a texture of the player's portrait. It also needs to call an initialization function that is provided by the secure template: SecureUnitButton_OnLoad(*self*, *unit*, menuFunc). Here, *unit* is the unit ID the frame is for; this method will then call self:SetAttribute("*unit*", *unit*) so we don't have to do this. menuFunc is a function that will be called when the player right-clicks the player frame. We will use the default player dropdown menu here.

The event handler uses the API function SetPortraitTexture(*texture, unit*), which takes a texture as its first argument and a unit ID as its second argument. This function creates a portrait of the unit and sets it as the texture; it also updates this portrait if the appearance of the unit changes (for example, when you equip a new helmet).

We also need the event UNIT_HEALTH and an event handler that updates the status bar if the event is called with arg1 == "player". Here's the code:

```
<Button name="MyPlayerFrame" parent="UIParent" inherits="MyUnitFrameTemplate">
    <Anchors>
        <Anchor point="RIGHT" relativePoint="CENTER"/>
    </Anchors>
    <Scripts>
        <OnLoad>
            self:RegisterForClicks("AnyUp")
            self:RegisterForDrag("LeftButton")
            self:RegisterEvent("UNIT_HEALTH")
            _G[self:GetName().."Name"]:SetText(UnitName("player"))
            SetPortraitTexture(_G[self:GetName().."Portrait"], "player")
            SecureUnitButton_OnLoad(self, "player", function()
                ToggleDropDownMenu(1, nil, PlayerFrameDropDown, self, 106, 27)
            end)
        </OnLoad>
```

```
    <OnEvent>
        local arg1 = ...
        if arg1 == "player" then
            _G[self:GetName().."Health"]:SetValue(
                UnitHealth(arg1)/UnitHealthMax(arg1)
            )
        end
    </OnEvent>
    </Scripts>
</Button>
```

We now have a fully functional player frame that works just fine. Let's add a target frame; this is slightly more complicated because we need to deal with changing the target. We can use the event PLAYER_TARGET_CHANGED here and update the target's portrait, name, and health in the event handler. But what happens if we select no target at all? We can't just call the method self:Hide() on our frame, because hiding a protected frame is not allowed in combat.

The game provides what is called a *secure state driver* to do this. We can call the function RegisterUnitWatch(*frame*) for our frame to tell the secure template API to take care of hiding the frame. It will then hide the frame when the unit that is set in the attribute unit no longer exists and show it when it comes into existence.

Add the following button to your XML to create a target frame. Both the OnLoad and OnEvent handlers are very similar to those of the player frame, so this code should be quite easy to understand. Note that there is no need to set a target's portrait and name with OnLoad, as you never have a target selected when logging in.

```
<Button name="MyTargetFrame" parent="UIParent" inherits="MyUnitFrameTemplate">
    <Anchors>
        <Anchor point="LEFT" relativePoint="CENTER"/>
    </Anchors>
    <Attributes>
        <Attribute name="unit" type="string" value="target"/>
    </Attributes>
    <Scripts>
        <OnLoad>
            self:RegisterForClicks("AnyUp")
            self:RegisterForDrag("LeftButton")
            self:RegisterEvent("UNIT_HEALTH")
            self:RegisterEvent("PLAYER_TARGET_CHANGED")
            SecureUnitButton_OnLoad(self, "target", function()
                ToggleDropDownMenu(1, nil, TargetFrameDropDown, self, 120, 10)
            end)
            RegisterUnitWatch(self)
        </OnLoad>
        <OnEvent>
            if event == "UNIT_HEALTH" then
                local arg1 = ...
```

```
            if arg1 == "target" then
              _G[self:GetName().."Health"]:SetValue(
                UnitHealth(arg1)/UnitHealthMax(arg1)
              )
            end
          elseif event == "PLAYER_TARGET_CHANGED" then
            _G[self:GetName().."Health"]:SetValue(
                UnitHealth("target")/UnitHealthMax("target")
            )
            SetPortraitTexture(_G[self:GetName().."Portrait"], "target")
            _G[self:GetName().."Name"]:SetText(UnitName("target"))
          end
        </OnEvent>
      </Scripts>
    </Button>
```

■**Caution** Our addon breaks the Set Focus option of the default target dropdown menu. The reason for this is that the default UI function that handles this dropdown menu relies on being secure code and we taint it by creating a tainted wrapper function that calls it. Blizzard did not implement Set Focus as a secure button. In a real addon, you would have to create your own dropdown menu that uses a secure action button template; you will see later in this chapter how secure templates can change the focus target.

Both frames are now fully functional (except for the mentioned focus issue). But what happens internally when we click on our frame? We never implemented an OnClick handler here, but the frames still behave like normal unit frames. Let's take a look at the single predefined handler our frame has: the OnClick handler, which calls the function SecureUnitButton_OnClick.

The Code Behind the OnClick Handler

The function SecureUnitButton_OnClick is, like all other predefined script handlers and helper functions, defined in the file FrameXML\SecureTemplates.lua.

```
function SecureUnitButton_OnClick(self, button)
   local type = SecureButton_GetModifiedAttribute(self, "type",➥
button);
   if ( type == "menu" ) then
      if ( SpellIsTargeting() ) then
         SpellStopTargeting();
         return;
      end
   end
   SecureActionButton_OnClick(self, button);
end
```

Don't forget that this function is part of the default UI and it is therefore considered secure code. So it is allowed to call all the protected functions we may not call.

The helper function SecureButton_GetModifiedAttribute is used to get the action you want to do based on the mouse button you pressed and modifier keys on the keyboard like Ctrl. This action is defined in the attribute **mod**-type*X* where *X* is the button (1 = left button, 2 = right button, 3 = middle button), and *mod* can be a modifier key on the keyboard like alt, shift, or ctrl. It is possible to use * instead of mod- to ignore modifier keys. Possible values for this attribute are "target" and "menu". The default values are *type1 = "target" and *type2 = "menu", meaning that a left-click targets the unit and a right-click opens the menu. The asterisk at the beginning means that modifier keys are ignored. These default values are suitable for our purpose, so let's keep them.

The function then checks whether we want to open the menu and, if so, whether we currently have an active spell cast that is waiting for a target selection. If that is the case, the spell cast is canceled and the function returns at this point. Otherwise it forwards the call to the OnClick handler of the SecureActionButtonTemplate, as a unit frame shares the basic functionality of an action button; that is, something happens when you click on it. This OnClick handler is quite long and boring, as it covers all possible button actions, like casting spells based on certain conditions, and so on. We will return to action buttons later.

You may be wondering if we can't bypass the restriction that you always need a user input to execute a protected function simply by calling the OnClick handler by hand. You could execute the following function call to fake a mouse click:

```
protectedFrame:GetScript("OnClick")(protectedFrame, "LeftButton")
```

There would normally be no way for an addon to tell if this was a real click or faked. But recall that the whole handler is defined in the template by Blizzard, and it is secure code. An execution path always starts secure and it stays secure if it goes right into this predefined handler. But your call that fakes the click starts from tainted code, as your code is always tainted, and so the whole execution path is tainted. This causes the action to fail.

The next step in creating a complete unit frame addon would be implementing party and raid frames; for those we need the templates that are inherited from SecureGroupHeaderTemplate.

Using Group Header Templates

Group header templates control a group of unit frames like your party or a raid subgroup. They manage everything automatically, like removing players who leave the group or sorting the displayed frames by their name or other criteria. I will not show you a complete example of using these templates here, as it is actually quite hard to test them because you need a raid group that is willing to help you with the testing. It is also not very likely that you are ever going to need these templates, as they are only useful for party and raid frame mods. There are already a lot of different raid frame mods out there, and they are highly customizable. The main actions are restricted by the template anyway, so it's quite unlikely that there is the need to write a new one as all possible features are already implemented by the ones that currently exist.

But let's still see how they work in theory. You simply create a new template from this template and add a simple header like a text to it that shows the raid subgroup or class the header belongs to. You can then use Table 11-1 to set the attributes of this secure template to define how it is displayed.

Table 11-1. *Attributes of Header Templates*

Attribute	Type	Description
showRaid	boolean	Show the header while you are in a raid group.
showParty	boolean	Show the header while you are in a party.
showPlayer	boolean	Show a unit frame for yourself if you are not in a raid.
showSolo	boolean	Show if you are not in a group. (Requires showPlayer to be set.)
nameList	string	A comma-separated list of players in your group that will be shown under this header. (This causes the template to ignore the attribute groupFilter.)
groupFilter	string	A comma-separated list of raid subgroups (1–8), classes (class name in uppercase like the second return value of UnitClass(*uId*); for example, PRIEST) or raid role (MAINTANK or MAINASSIST) that will be shown under this header.
strictFiltering	boolean	Defines how the groupFilter setting is applied; if strictFiltering is set, a player must match both a raid subgroup and a class from the filter (default: false).
point	string	The anchor point where the unit frames will be anchored to (default: "TOP").
xOffset	number	The x offset for the anchor of all unit frames (default: 0).
yOffset	number	The y offset for the anchor (default: 0).
sortMethod	string	Defines how the group of unit frames will be sorted; can either be "INDEX" or "NAME".
sortDir	string	Defines the sort order; can either be "ASC" or "DESC".
template	string	The name of the XML template that will be used for the unit frames.
templateType	string	The frame type of the unit frame template (default: "Button").
groupBy	string	Groups the units by their "GROUP", "CLASS", or "ROLE" before the sorting is applied. nil disables this grouping (default: nil).
groupingOrder	string	A comma-separated list of groups, classes, or raid roles that specifies how the groups of groupBy will be ordered. For example, this could be "WARRIOR,PRIEST" if groupBy is set to "CLASS" to ensure that warriors are shown before priests.
maxColumns	number	The maximum number of columns that will be created by the header to display the unit frames (default: 1).
unitsPerColumn	number	The maximum number of units per column; nil means infinite (default: nil).
startingIndex	number	Hides the first $x - 1$ units from the group header. This is done after the sorting is applied (default: 1, all units are shown).
columnSpacing	number	The space between two columns (default: 0).
columnAnchorPoint	string	The anchor point for new columns.

The template does all the hard work; you just define an XML template for a unit button and set it as the *template* attribute of the header. The header manages the unit buttons; it creates them from your template and does all the positioning. You also don't need to worry about dealing with events like players joining and leaving the group; this is all taken care of by the header template. The template does this for you because you would not be able to. You can't show, hide, or move your unit frames while you are in combat, but players can join and leave your raid while you are in combat. The whole template is secure code and can perform all these actions you are not allowed to do in combat.

Table 11-1 just lists the attributes for raid or party frames; pet frames have two additional attributes: useOwnerUnit and filterOnPet. Both are boolean attributes. useOwnerUnit displays a unit frame for the owner of the pet instead of a unit frame for the pet itself, and filterOnPet can be set to use the pet's name for filtering and sorting instead of the owner's name.

The next important type of secure frame is the action button, which is basically just a button that executes a protected function when you click it.

Using Secure Action Button Templates

Action buttons make extensive use of attributes to define the actions that are taken when the button is clicked. The attribute type controls which action will be executed when the button is clicked. Table 11-2 shows all possible values for type. All of these actions refer to protected functions, which could normally not be called from tainted code, but the template is secure code.

Table 11-2. *Secure Action Button Types*

Type	Description
actionbar	Changes the currently active action bar based on the value stored in the attribute action. The attribute *action* can be "increment", "decrement", or two numbers separated by a space to swap between these two action bar pages.
action	Executes the action that is stored in the action button of the frame's ID (ID in the sense of frame:SetID() and frame:GetID()). This means that if your frame has the ID 1, it will execute the action stored in your leftmost action button on the first action bar page.
assist	Assists the unit that is stored in the attribute *unit*.
attribute	Sets the attribute *attribute-name* of the frame *attribute-frame* to *attribute-value*. This is the only way to change attributes of protected frames while you are in combat. It can be used to create a configuration menu that can set protected settings while you are in combat.
cancelaura	This cancels the buff with the ID that is stored in the attribute *index*. It is alternatively possible to store the name of the buff in the attribute *spell* and the rank in the attribute *rank*.
click	Executes the click action of the button that is stored in the attribute *clickbutton*.
focus	Sets the focus target to the unit stored in the attribute *unit*.
item	Uses or equips the item that is stored in the attribute *action*.
macro	Executes the string that is stored in the attribute *macrotext* as a normal macro. This string may exceed the 255-character limit of normal macros.
mainassist	Sets the raid role of the unit stored in the attribute *unit* to "mainassist".

Continued

Table 11-2. *Continued*

Type	Description
maintank	Sets the raid role of the unit stored in the attribute *unit* to "maintank".
pet	Casts the pet spell that is stored in the attribute *action*.
spell	Casts the spell that is stored in the attribute *action*.
stop	Simply calls SpellStopTargeting(). This function cancels the target selection of a spell.
target	Targets the unit that is set in the attribute *unit*.

These are a lot of possible options for our button, but they are all really simple. Most of them just call a protected function when the button is clicked. Let's see an example of a secure action button.

A Simple Secure Action Button

A simple example of a secure action button is the Warsong Gulch battleground mod in Deadly Boss Mods. It adds to the score display a small frame that shows the name of the current flag carrier. This frame is a secure action button, and it targets the flag carrier when you click on it. Let's see how this is done in this DBM module. You can find this mod in the file DBM-Battlegrounds\Warsong.lua of the DBM.

The first thing the mod obviously must do is create a frame from the secure template. This is done in the method CreateFlagCarrierButton, which is called when you join Warsong Gulch:

```
function Warsong:CreateFlagCarrierButton()
    if not Warsong.Options.ShowFlagCarrier then return end
    if not self.FlagCarrierFrame1Button then
        self.FlagCarrierFrame1Button = CreateFrame("Button", nil, nil,➥
"SecureActionButtonTemplate")
        self.FlagCarrierFrame1Button:SetHeight(15)
        self.FlagCarrierFrame1Button:SetWidth(150)
        self.FlagCarrierFrame1Button:SetAttribute("type", "macro")
        self.FlagCarrierFrame1Button:SetPoint("LEFT", "AlwaysUpFrame1", "RIGHT", 28,4)
    end
    if not self.FlagCarrierFrame2Button then
        self.FlagCarrierFrame2Button = CreateFrame("Button", nil, nil,➥
"SecureActionButtonTemplate")
        self.FlagCarrierFrame2Button:SetHeight(15)
        self.FlagCarrierFrame2Button:SetWidth(150)
        self.FlagCarrierFrame2Button:SetAttribute("type", "macro")
        self.FlagCarrierFrame2Button:SetPoint("LEFT", "AlwaysUpFrame2", "RIGHT", 28,4)
    end
    self.FlagCarrierFrame1Button:Show()
    self.FlagCarrierFrame2Button:Show()
end
```

The code creates two frames of the type `Button` that inherit from `SecureActionButtonTemplate`. It then sets their *type* attributes to `macro`. You might have expected the type `target` here, but `target` can only target a specific unit ID, and there are no fixed unit IDs for your enemies in a battleground. By contrast, `macro` can execute an arbitrary macro text like `/targetexact somePlayer`, which means `macro` provides a greater flexibility.

The frames are then anchored to `AlwaysUpFrame1` and `AlwaysUpFrame2`, which are the small score display frames at the top of the default UI. The actual macro text is set by the method `CheckFlagCarrier`. This method is called when the flag carrier changes while the player is not in combat and every time the player leaves combat in Warsong Gulch. The local variable `FlagCarrier` holds a table with the flag carrier of the Alliance (1) and Horde (2):

```
function Warsong:CheckFlagCarrier()
    if not UnitAffectingCombat("player") then
        if FlagCarrier[1] and self.FlagCarrierFrame1 then
            self.FlagCarrierFrame1Button:SetAttribute("macrotext",➥
"/targetexact " .. FlagCarrier[1])
        end
        if FlagCarrier[2] and self.FlagCarrierFrame2 then
            self.FlagCarrierFrame2Button:SetAttribute("macrotext",➥
"/targetexact " .. FlagCarrier[2])
        end
    end
end
```

This method ensures that the flag carrier button targets the correct player if that is possible. The text of the frame is changed outside this function, because this strategy works fine while you are in combat, so the targeted unit might differ from the displayed text if the flag is picked up by someone else while you are in combat. But there is no way for us to update the target in combat, because of the restrictions on protected frames.

I'm not printing the function that determines the current flag carrier and sets the string. The function is quite long, with about 70 lines, because it needs to parse system chat messages to determine the carrier with `string.match` as there is no good usable event. The code that sets the text of the frame is also long and complicated, as it needs to determine the class of an enemy player that picks up the flag. You can't just call `UnitClass` on enemies that are out of your range, so the function uses a workaround and accesses the battleground scoreboard, which contains the classes of all enemies. You can read the function that is stored in the local variable `updateflagcarrier` at the end of the file if you want to know how this works.

But an action button can do more than just targeting someone when you click on it.

An Advanced Secure Action Button

Let's create a simple example action button to see what this feature is capable of. Create a new addon with an appropriate TOC file and add a new XML file to it. You can also recycle the example unit frame mod we created earlier in this chapter if you don't want to restart the game for the new addon.

Creating a Secure Button with XML

We will create a simple action button for testing here; this button will just show up in the center of your screen and use the default style from OptionsButtonTemplate. We can then use an in-game editor like TinyPad to execute short Lua scripts to set attributes to test our button.

Creating a secure button with the style of a default action button is really easy thanks to multiple inheritance. We can just add both SecureActionButtonTemplate and OptionsButtonTemplate to the *inherits* attribute. Or more generally, you can always just add a secure template to your *inherits* attribute if you need the functionality of a secure template. The XML file then looks like this:

```
<Ui xmlns="http://www.blizzard.com/wow/ui/"➥
xmlns:xsi="http://www.w3.org/2001/XMLSchema-instance"➥
xsi:schemaLocation="http://www.blizzard.com/wow/ui/ ..\FrameXML\UI.xsd">
    <Button name="SecureTestButton" text="Secure Button"➥
parent="UIParent" inherits="SecureActionButtonTemplate,OptionsButtonTemplate">
        <Anchors>
            <Anchor point="CENTER"/>
        </Anchors>
        <Size>
            <AbsDimension x="128" y="24"/>
        </Size>
        <Scripts>
            <OnLoad>
                self:RegisterForClicks("AnyUp")
            </OnLoad>
        </Scripts>
    </Button>
</Ui>
```

This code displays a small button in the center of your screen with the text "Secure Button." Feel free to place the button wherever you want to. The call to RegisterForClicks in the OnLoad handler is important because by default the button listens only to clicks with the left mouse button, and we want to use the right button later in this example.

We will now use advanced attributes to do something with this button. We can access it under the global variable SecureTestButton, so let's add the first few more advanced attributes to it.

Playing Around with Attributes

In the unit frame example, you've seen that attributes can contain modifiers that allow you to execute different actions based on the mouse button that was pressed. A modifier of an attribute consists of a prefix and a suffix, where the prefix holds modifier keys on the keyboard while the suffix defines the mouse button. Both the prefix and suffix are optional; the default value matches all keys.

A good button type for testing is always macro, as you can just assign something like /say hello, world as the macrotext attribute. Execute the following code to set the button's type to macro:

```
SecureTestButton:SetAttribute("type", "macro")
```

Let's now add macro texts depending on the mouse button used. Earlier we saw the prefix * in the default values from the unit frame template; this is actually not always necessary. Omitting the prefix and suffix has the same effect as using an asterisk for both. However, omitting just the prefix or the suffix means that none of the modifier keys or mouse buttons may be pressed. It is obviously not possible to click an onscreen button without using a mouse button (using another button with the type "click" to fake a click sends the mouse button the screen button was clicked with), so you don't want to omit the suffix when you use a prefix.

The following code sets the macrotext attribute that is used if the button is clicked with the left mouse button (recall that we can append 1 to the attribute name to tie it to the left mouse button); we don't need the asterisk for the prefix here:

```
SecureTestButton:SetAttribute("macrotext1", "/say hello")
```

Your character now says "hello" when you left-click the button. A real example mod would say "hello, world," so let's add "world" as right-click text:

```
SecureTestButton:SetAttribute("macrotext2", "/say world")
```

We can now also add a keyboard modifier. We need to use the asterisk as a suffix here, or the action would match no mouse button:

```
SecureTestButton:SetAttribute("shift-macrotext*", "/say hello world")
```

Our character now says "hello world" when we shift-click the button with any mouse button. Note that the old functionality didn't break; we can still use just the left or right button to get "hello" or "world" respectively.

It is also possible to remove a specific modifier combination by setting its value to the value of the variable ATTRIBUTE_NOOP (noop is short for "no operation"; the variable actually just holds the empty string). Using Shift and the middle mouse button currently results in "hello world"; let's remove that.

```
SecureTestButton:SetAttribute("shift-macrotext3", ATTRIBUTE_NOOP)
```

It is possible to use these modifiers for all attributes including the type attribute. A button can then execute completely different actions based on the used mouse button and modifier keys. Let's try this by changing the type to target when you right-click the button with the Alt key down:

```
SecureTestButton:SetAttribute("alt-type2", "target")
```

A good target unit for testing is player, so let's set this as the unit attribute:

```
SecureTestButton:SetAttribute("unit", "player")
```

You can now target yourself by alt-right-clicking the button. Note that the secure templates will always evaluate the type attribute with all its modifiers before it gets the required additional templates. This means that adding the attribute alt-macrotext2 is pointless now as it would never be used because the type will always be target when you right-click the button with the Alt key down.

The whole example seems to be highly artificial, as you certainly never need a button that sends text based on the mouse button used. And sending chat messages can also be implemented without using secure frames at all. We will see more useful and powerful commands related to secure actions in the next chapter when we discuss macros. Macros can be used to implement functionality very similar to secure buttons; they can even execute the OnClick handlers of existing secure buttons.

Summary

This chapter first showed how the game prevents addons from automating the gameplay with the code taint system. This taint system makes sure that unmodified code of the default UI has more permissions than code that is provided by the user. We learned about protected functions, which cannot be called by our code. But we also saw how addons may circumvent these restrictions in certain situations by using secure templates.

The last part of the chapter was about implementing advanced secure button actions by using modifiers in attributes. You saw how we can create a single button that executes completely different actions based on the used mouse button and keyboard modifiers. Note that everything behind the secure templates, including the modifiers in attributes, is implemented in Lua. You can read the file FrameXML\SecureTemplates.lua of the default UI if you are curious how these templates work internally. This file is one of the more complicated in the default UI, but it is also one of the best commented, so it should be understandable.

■ ■ ■

## CHAPTER 12

Macros

For anyone learning Lua to get the most out of WoW, it's a safe bet you already have a few macros in your action bars. They can be incredibly useful when you want to perform complex tasks like casting different spells on different targets based on conditions, with just one button. Such conditions can also be quite complex; for example, you can detect whether your current target is hostile or friendly, alive or dead.

If you currently do have any macros in your action bars, did you create them yourself or did you copy and paste them from somewhere? If you created them yourself, did you know exactly what you were doing? Many players think that macros just consist of a simple list of simple slash commands, but they are extremely powerful. Certain slash commands can contain powerful conditions and have a variety of options that can be used.

A macro is always executed line by line, which means you have to insert a new line after every slash command you want to use. For example, a macro that sends two messages to the say chat looks like this:

```
/say Hello...
/say ...World!
```

You can add every slash command that is available in the game to a macro, from game-provided slash commands like /say <text>, through small Lua scripts via /script <Lua code>, to complex Lua functions in slash commands created by addons. The only restriction is that the number of characters per macro is limited to 255. But we will find ways to circumvent this restriction here.

This chapter is about creating macros, so we will explore how macros work and how we can create extremely powerful macros. We will start with an overview of the available commands for macros.

Available Commands

You probably know the basic slash commands, like /cast <spell>, /use <item> (which are internally actually the same command), or /castsequence <spell1>, <spell2>, ... But there are many more commands; for example, did you know about the command /petautocasttoggle <pet spell>?

Secure and Normal Slash Commands

Most of the important slash commands we are going to use for macros are described as *secure slash commands* because they often simply execute a single protected function. All of these slash commands are stored in a table that is accessible only from the file FrameXML\ChatFrame. lua; the name of the local variable holding the table is SecureCmdList. Recall that normal slash commands like the ones created by an addon are stored in the globally accessible table SlashCmdList.

These normal commands are quite boring from our point of view, as everything they can do can also be done by a Lua script. You also already know all the important normal slash commands that are provided by the game, as you use them every day. For example, /raid <text> sends a message to the raid, and that's something you type in your chat frame all the time. And there is the command /random for loot distribution. Other commonly used normal slash commands are emotes; for example, /facepalm <some guy who just wiped the raid> can be incredibly useful sometimes.

However, this chapter does not cover these provided normal commands. You already know the most important ones, as you are using them every day. All other less commonly used normal slash commands deal with managing the guild or the raid, and these functions are often also available in the GUI. Also, these slash commands are often very simple; they often accept just one argument like a text or a target. We want to write powerful macros you can use in boss fights or in the arena.

■**Note** Blizzard has a list of all available normal slash commands on its web page if you need additional information about a game-provided normal slash command: http://www.worldofwarcraft.com/info/ basics/slashcommands.html.

Let's now focus on secure commands, which are more complicated than they seem at first glance. Adding complexity are the conditions and options you can add to a slash command. Conditions are checked before the command is executed; the slash command is ignored if the conditions are not met. You will see more about conditions later.

We will first explore which slash commands are available and the options they provide. There is one option that is somewhat special as it is available for all slash commands and is internally actually a condition—the `target` option.

The Target Option

Let's use a slash command you all know as an example: `/cast <spell>`. This seems to be a simple command; it casts a spell on your current target. But you can also use `/cast [target=focus] <spell>` to cast a spell on your focus target. The value of this option is `focus` in the example, but it can be any valid unit ID or the name of a nearby player or NPC.

`target` is an option that is available for all secure commands. The option obviously doesn't make sense for all commands but it is syntactically valid in every secure command; it just doesn't have an effect in every command.

Note Only secure commands support the `target` option; normal slash commands do not. But many normal slash commands, like emotes, take a target for the action as an argument.

This option leads to our first useful macro, casting a spell on our target's target. This can, for example, be used by healers to target a mob like a boss and automatically heal its current target. Just insert a healing spell of your class to use this macro:

`/cast [target=targettarget] <healing spell>`

Another useful macro for hunters or warlocks is targeting a spell on the target of the pet. This can be done with the following slash command:

`/cast [target=pettarget] <spell>`

List of Secure Commands

Table 12-1 lists all available secure commands that deal with casting spells or using and equipping items. Some more advanced slash commands, like `/castsequence`, are explained in detail later.

Tip All secure slash commands are written in Lua. You can find them in the file `FrameXML\ChatFrame.lua` (search for `SecureCmdList` there). Reading the code behind a slash command can help you understand it.

Table 12-1. *Available Secure Slash Commands for Spells and Items*

Command	Description
/startattack <target>	Your character starts attacking <target> or your current target if it is omitted. It is also possible to use the target option instead.
/stopattack	Stops the auto attack.
/cast <spell or item>	Casts <spell> or uses <item>. Alias: /spell.
/use <spell or item>	Equal to /cast.
/castrandom <spell1>,<spell2>,...	Randomly selects one of the spells or items from the comma-separated list and casts or uses it.
/userandom <item1>,<item2>	Equal to /castrandom.
/castsequence <spell1>,<spell2>,...	Casts <spell1> when it is executed for the first time, <spell2> when it's clicked for the second time, and so on. Its arguments may also be items. This command is even more powerful with its additional reset option, which is explained in detail later in this chapter.
/stopcasting	Cancels a spell cast.
/cancelaura <buff>	Cancels the buff <buff>.
/cancelform	Leaves your current shapeshift form.
/equip <itemName>	Equips the item <itemName> from your inventory. Alias: /eq
/equipslot <slot> <item>	Equips <item> in the slot with the ID <slot>. Slot IDs are explained later.
/changeactionbar <page>	Changes your current action bar page to <page>.
/swapactionbar <page1> <page2>	Swaps between the action bar pages <page1> and <page2>. This selects <page1> if you currently have neither <page1> nor <page2> selected.

These few commands that mainly deal with spells and items are the most important ones for macros. Note that you can usually cast just one spell per macro because of the global cooldown. However, there are a few spells that do not activate the global cooldown, like the Shaman and Druid spell Nature's Swiftness. The following macro casts an instant Healing Wave if Nature's Swiftness is ready. It casts a normal Healing Wave if you have cooldown on Nature's Swiftness.

```
/cast Nature's Swiftness
/cast Healing Wave
```

You can also use this macro with a Druid; just replace Healing Wave with a Druid healing spell like Healing Touch. Examples of other spells that also do not activate the global cooldown are Inner Focus (Priest) and Presence of Mind (Mage). You can build similar macros with these two spells.

But there are more slash commands that do more than cast spells. Table 12-2 lists all the secure commands that deal with your target and focus target; these commands can also come in handy.

Table 12-2. *Available Secure Slash Commands for Your (Focus) Target*

Command	Description
/target <name>	Targets <name>. This also targets nearby players or NPCs starting with <name>; you can use /targetexact <name> to avoid this behavior. It is also possible to use the target option instead of the argument. Alias: /tar
/targetexact <name>	Targets the nearest unit with the exact name <name>. You can use the target option instead of the argument.
/targetenemy	Targets the nearest hostile unit.
/targetenemyplayer	Targets the nearest hostile unit that is a player.
/targetfriend	Targets the nearest friendly unit.
/targetfriendplayer	Targets the nearest friendly player.
/targetraid	Targets the nearest raid member.
/cleartarget	Clears your target.
/targetlasttarget	Targets your last target.
/targetlastenemy	Targets your last hostile target.
/targetlastfriend	Targets your last friendly target.
/assist <target>	Assists <target>, it is also possible to use the target option instead of the argument. Alias: /a <target>
/focus <target>	Focuses <target>; you can also use the target option.
/clearfocus	Clears your focus target.

Table 12-3 lists slash commands that are especially important for hunters and warlocks, as they deal with commanding your pet.

Table 12-3. *Available Secure Slash Commands for Pets*

Command	Description
/petattack <target>	Causes your pet to start attacking <target>. It is also possible to use the target option instead.
/petfollow	Sets your pet to Follow.
/petstay	Sets your pet to Stay.
/petpassive	Sets your pet to Passive.
/petdefensive	Sets your pet to Defensive.
/petautocaston <spell>	Enables auto casting of your pet's spell <spell>.
/petautocastoff <spell>	Disables auto casting of your pet's spell <spell>.
/petautocasttoggles <spell>	Toggles auto casting of your pet's spell <spell>.

Table 12-4 lists all slash commands that deal with raid roles, like main tank or main assist assignments. You might wonder why the following functions are protected, as they don't seem to deal with functionality that could automate the game. The reason is that if they were not protected, you could write an addon that always sets the player with the lowest health in your raid as main tank. A unit frame addon could then use a secure group header that shows all of your main tanks. This would always display the player with the lowest health, and the purpose of the secure/tainted code system is to prevent such addons.

Table 12-4. *Available Secure Slash Commands for Raid Roles*

Command	Description
/clearmaintank	Clears the main tank assignments. Alias: /clearmt
/maintank <target>	Sets <target> as the new main tank. It is also possible to use the target option instead. Alias: /mt
/maintankoff <target>	Removes the main tank role from <target>. Alias: /mtoff
/clearmainassist	Clears the main assist assignments. Alias: /clearma
/mainassist <target>	Sets <target> as new main assist. Alias: /ma
/mainassistoff <target>	Removes the main assist status from <target>. Alias: /maoff

These were the four main categories of secure slash commands. But there are a few more miscellaneous commands available. Table 12-5 lists all remaining secure commands.

Table 12-5. *Available Miscellaneous Secure Slash Commands*

Command	Description
/duel <target>	Requests a duel with <target>. It is not possible to use the target option here.
/forfeit	Cancels a duel. Aliases: /yield and /concede
/stopmacro	Stops the execution of the macro.
/click <secure frame> <mouseButton>	Executes the OnClick handler of the secure frame stored in the global variable <secure frame> with <mouseButton>. This is an extremely powerful command as it allows us to click on arbitrary secure button templates; you will see how we can use this later.

Two commands in the tables in this section were not fully explained there: /castsequence and /equipslot. Let's take a closer look at each.

Cast Sequences

There is an additional option for the cast sequence command: the reset option, which defines criteria that determine when to reset to the first spell in the cast sequence. This option is not required; by default, a cast sequence restarts when it reaches the last spell in the list. You might expect that the reset option, like the target option, is added in square brackets to the beginning of the command's arguments, but that is not the case. The reset option must be placed between the optional conditions (that is, the target option) and the list of spells. The following example illustrates this:

```
/castsequence [target=focus] reset=30 <spell1>,<spell2>,...
```

This starts a 30-second timer every time the macro is executed and resets to the first spell when the timer expires. This means that it resets if you don't use the cast sequence for 30 seconds. But reset accepts more values than just numbers; it can also be a string that defines a trigger that resets the action. The following triggers are available:

- target resets the sequence when you change your target.

- combat triggers when you leave combat.

- The keyboard modifiers ctrl, alt, and shift reset the sequence when you hold the key while executing the macro.

The code behind the slash command handler simply uses string.find on this option and resets the sequence if it finds a matching trigger, so you can just concatenate multiple triggers to reset it when one of them occurs. For example, reset=ctrltarget30 resets it when you Ctrl-click the macro, when you change your target, or when you haven't used the macro for 30 seconds.

Item Slot IDs

The secure command /equipslot <slot> <item> takes an item slot ID the item will be equipped in. The commands /use <item> and /cast <item> also accept such an ID instead of the name of an item.

There are two types of inventory IDs: strings (such as HeadSlot for your head) and numbers (such as 1 for your head). Macros can only use the numeric identifiers, while addons can (and should) also use the string identifiers in API functions like this:

```
id, texture = GetInventorySlotInfo(slotName)
```

Figure 12-1 shows the character frame with all slot identifiers.

Figure 12-1. *Inventory slot IDs*

The numbers are important for us here because we cannot use the strings in macro commands. We can now write simple, yet powerful macros that make use of items. Imagine you have two of these fancy "activate to do x extra damage for y seconds" trinkets equipped. They usually share a short cooldown, so you can't activate both of them at the same time. It can be useful to have a macro that activates the trinket that is currently not on cooldown.

This is easy with the /use (or /cast) command; we can just try to activate both trinkets in the same macro:

```
/use 13
/use 14
```

If one of them is on cooldown it will be skipped with the usual "this item is not ready yet" message. Later you will see how to suppress this error message.

The macros we've tried thus far are quite simple, and you probably already knew how to use most of the commands. So let's create a few more advanced macros with conditions.

Conditions

Conditions are added in square brackets to a macro, just like the target option (which is syntactically actually a condition). A good example of a simple condition is exists, which evaluates to true if the command's target exists or to false if the target doesn't exist. The following slash command casts <spell> on your target if you have a target and does nothing otherwise:

```
/cast [exists] <spell>
```

You can also use the target option to modify the command's target. The exists condition then also refers to the unit that is referenced by the target option. The following command casts <spell> on your focus target if you have one:

```
/cast [target=focus,exists] <spell>
```

Multiple conditions are always separated with commas in a single command. We could now add other conditions to this macro, but let's get an overview of the existing conditions first.

■**Tip** Use the red question mark as icon for your macros, as it automatically chooses an appropriate icon based on the conditions.

Available Conditions

Table 12-6 lists all available conditions with a short description. Some more complicated conditions, like equipped, are explained in detail later in this section.

Table 12-6. *Available Conditions*

Condition	Description
bar:*x*	true if action bar *x* is currently selected.
btn:*x*	true if the macro was clicked with mouse button *x*, works just like the button suffix for attributes of secure templates. *x* can also be any string that can be passed as a button to the /click command.
channeling:*<spell>*	true if you are currently channeling *<spell>*. The spell is optional, just using channeling without a spell evaluates to true if you are currently channeling any spell.
combat	true if you are in combat.
dead	true if the command's target is dead.
equipped:*<itemType>*	true if you have an item of the type *<itemType>* equipped. The argument is slightly more complicated and explained in detail later. Alias: worn:*<itemType>*.
exists	true if the target exists.
flyable	true if you are in Outlands or Northrend and it is possible to mount. Caution: this condition evaluates to true in zones like Wintergrasp or Dalaran (a bug that renders this condition almost completely useless).
flying	true if you are currently flying.
group:*<type>*	Valid group types are party and raid, evaluates to true if you are in such a group.
harm	true if your target is hostile.
help	true if your target is friendly.
indoors	true if mounting is not possible.
mod:<modifier>	true if the macro was clicked with the given modifier key. Valid values for <modifier> are ctrl, alt, and shift.
mounted	true if you are on a mount.
outdoors	true if mounting is possible.
party	true if your target is in your party.
pet:*<name>*	true if your currently active pet is *<name>*. The argument is optional, it is also possible to just use pet to check for any pet.
stance:*x*	true if you are currently in the stance or shapeshift form with the ID *x*. Stance IDs are explained in detail later. The ID is optional, you can use just stance to check if any stance or shapeshift form is active. Alias: form:*x*
stealth	true if you are being stealthed.
swimming	true if you are currently swimming.

These conditions can be used with all secure commands except the duel commands, /duel and /forfeit.

One of the more complicated conditions from this list was equipped, which takes the type of an item instead of its name. Every item has a type and a subtype, which can be used, for example, to categorize an item within an auction house. The identifier that can be used in this macro condition is the localized string of the item type as it is shown in the auction house. For example, you can use the condition equipped:Cloth to check whether you are currently wearing a cloth item. It doesn't make much sense to use the armor type here; the interesting option is using a weapon type. For example, rogues can use the following macro to combine Backstab (which requires a dagger) and Sinister Strike in a single macro depending on the currently equipped weapon:

```
/cast [equipped:Daggers] Backstab
/stopmacro [equipped:Daggers]
/cast Sinister Strike
```

This casts Backstab and cancels the macro if you are wielding a dagger; otherwise, it casts Sinister Strike. You will see a way to write such a macro with a single cast command in the next section.

Caution Item categories are always plural, so using [equipped:Dagger] does not work.

Two other important categories are One-Hand and Two-Hand; they evaluate to true if you are wielding any one-handed or two-handed weapon.

The other condition that is not fully explained in the table is stance:x. Stances are the different battle stances of warriors, as well as druid shapeshift forms, the shadowform and Spirit of Redemption of priests, rogue stealth, the shaman's ghost wolf, and the warlock's demon form. The stance ID 1 refers to the first stance or shapeshift that is visible in your shapeshift/stance bar, 2 to the second, and so on. For example stance:1 refers to the warrior's battle stance or the druid's bear form.

The stance ID can refer to different forms/stances depending on the talent specialization (spec) of a druid or priest. For druids, stance:5 refers to the Moonkin form if they have the Balance spec and to Tree of Life if they have the Restoration spec. Priests are slightly more complicated; stance:1 refers to Shadowform if it is available and to Spirit of Redemption if this is available but Shadowform is not. Spirit of Redemption is stance:2 if both talents are specced.

Caution Auras of paladins and aspects of hunters are not stances, even though they show up on the shapeshift/stance bar. This means you cannot use the stance condition to check which aura or aspect is currently active.

We've now discussed all the conditions that can be used. Let's combine them to build complex expressions.

Combining Conditions

The simplest way of checking two conditions doesn't actually combine two different conditions. All conditions in the form `condition:argument` accept multiple arguments separated with slashes which will be combined with a logical OR. The following command casts *<spell>* if you have Shift or Alt pressed:

```
/cast [mod:shift/alt] <spell>
```

But we can also combine two different conditions in a single command. The simplest combination is the conjunction (combining the conditions with the logical AND).

The Logical AND

You've already seen an example of this in the last section, as the `target` option is syntactically a condition:

```
/cast [target=focus,exists] <spell>
```

We can just add another condition separated with a comma to check both of them. The following example casts Resurrection on your target if it exists and is dead:

```
/cast [exists,dead] Resurrection
```

It is also useful to have conditions that check whether your target exists and is not dead. We need the logical NOT to do this.

The Logical NOT

The negation of a condition can also be done easily. Just add the prefix `no` to a condition to negate it (apply the logical NOT). Thus, `nodead` means your target is alive. The following macro casts *<spell>* on your target if it exists and is alive:

```
/cast [exists,nodead] <spell>
```

The logical NOT is restricted to a single condition; you cannot add brackets in a macro condition. Let's try to negate the condition from the last example. Imagine you were writing this negated expression as a Lua expression; it would look like this:

```
not (exists and not dead)
```

In a macro it is not possible to use a condition like `[no(exists,nodead)]`. We need to transform this expression into an equivalent expression that can be represented in a macro. We can do this in a simple case like this just by analyzing the meaning of the condition. It means that our target either does not exist or is dead. This can be written as `(not exists) or dead` in Lua syntax. You will see how we can use a logical OR in a macro in just a bit.

The transformation between these two forms is not always that obvious, especially if you have more complex expressions. But there is a simple law in boolean algebra that can be used to do this transformation. De Morgan's Law looks like this:

```
not (A and B) = (not A) or (not B)
```

If we apply this to our expression not (exists and not dead) we get (not exists) or (not not dead). Obviously, not not dead means the same as dead, so we get (not exists) or dead.

This law also applies to terms with or instead of and:

```
not (A or B) = (not A) and (not B)
```

But we still can't use the expression in a macro, as we haven't discussed the logical OR yet; let's see how this works.

The Logical OR

To combine two conditions with a logical OR, add another block of expressions in square brackets. The example from the last section then looks like this:

```
/cast [noexists][dead] <spell>
```

This casts <spell> if your target doesn't exist or is dead. The OR operator is also somewhat restricted. Imagine you have an expression in the form (A or B) and (C or D). You might think it is possible to write the macro condition as [[A][B],[C][D]], but that is not possible. You also have to transform your expressions into the *disjunctive normal form*, breaking the expression down into multiple subexpressions, which can be as simple as normal conditions and are combined with logical OR.

There is also a useful law for transforming such expressions—the distributive law:

```
A and (B or C) = (A and B) or (A and C)
A or (B and C) = (A or B) and (A or C)
```

Let's try to apply this law to the expression (A or B) and (C or D) to transform it into a form that is suitable for a macro:

```
(A or B) and (C or D)
= ((A or B) and C) or ((A or B) and D)
= ((A and C) or (B and C)) or ((A and D) or (B and D))
= (A and C) or (B and C) or (A and D) or (B and D)
```

This form of the expression has the same meaning as the original form and can be used as a macro condition that looks like this:

```
[A,C] [B,C] [A,D] [B,D]
```

That was a highly abstract process. Fortunately, it is rarely needed, as you rarely have such complex expressions in a macro. But it's still good to know how you can transform logical expressions. You can also apply these laws to expressions in Lua to shorten or clarify them. However, let's get to something more practical now: useful macros that incorporate a logical or in their expression.

What happens when we add multiple target options to the different blocks in a single slash command? The answer is that the game always starts parsing an expression with the first block and checks whether it evaluates to true. If this is the case, it runs the command and skips the remaining square bracket blocks. Otherwise it runs the next block, and so on. Every time it encounters a new target option, it overwrites the old target setting for the command (which is target by default) and saves the new setting. The following command casts <spell> on yourself, as the second target option is never executed:

```
/cast [target=player] [target=focus] <spell>
```

The first block always evaluates to true as it doesn't contain a condition, so the second block is never executed and its target option has no effect. But we can also add conditions to the block to set the target option depending on these conditions. We can use this technique to extend one of our first macros in this chapter, the one that casts a healing spell on your target's target:

```
/cast [target=targettarget] <healing spell>
```

You can target a mob and heal the player that is currently tanking it with this macro, but it is useless when we have a friendly player targeted. The following macro checks whether our current target is friendly and casts a heal on it if so; otherwise it casts the heal on the target's target:

```
/cast [target=target,help] [target=targettarget] <healing spell>
```

Note that the first target option is actually not required, as target is set to target by default.

We can extend the macro even further by first checking for the unit ID mouseover. This unit ID works with secure unit templates that allow you to heal players by hovering your raid frames with your mouse. The next check can then be the target followed by the target's target. It may happen that help fails on all of these unit IDs, but we can still cast the spell on ourselves in this case. The following is the ultimate macro for lazy healers; it performs all of the checks mentioned earlier and selects a target that can be healed:

```
/cast [target=mouseover,help] [target=target,help]➡
[target=targettarget,help] [target=player] <healing spell>
```

Note that target=target is required in the second block, as the first block changed the target setting to mouseover. Just using [help] as the second would be pointless, as it would check whether the mouseover target is friendly, which is not the case. We know that because if it were friendly, the second block would never be reached.

■Note It is not necessary to add checks to see if the targets are alive here, because the condition help does a little more than just check whether the target is friendly; it checks whether the target is a valid target for a beneficial spell, and dead targets are not valid targets for such spells (except for resurrection spells which cannot be used together with a help check).

We can now build complex expressions with the conditions, but the form of the whole command is still quite simple: an if <expression> then do something end construct. Having an elseif or else block would be a nice addition.

Simple Control Structures

The only control structure that is available in a macro is an if-else-elseif block. There is no such thing as a loop in a macro.

An else or elseif block is started with a semicolon in a macro. This is then followed by a condition and the macro arguments to use. I previously presented a macro that casts Backstab if you have a dagger equipped and Sinister Strike otherwise:

```
/cast [equipped:Daggers] Backstab
/stopmacro [equipped:Daggers]
/cast Sinister Strike
```

This macro uses the stopmacro command, and as I said, we are going to try another version of it that consists of just one line. We just need to add a semicolon followed by the contents of the else-block, which is here simply using Sinister Strike as the argument to cast:

```
/cast [equipped:Daggers] Backstab; Sinister Strike
```

An elseif-block uses an additional condition after the semicolon, like the following macro, which casts a damage spell if you have a hostile target and a healing spell if your target is friendly:

```
/cast [harm] <damage spell>; [help] <healing spell>
```

Another interesting use of this control structure is using the btn or mod condition to execute different actions based on the mouse button or keyboard modifier used. The following macro can be used by rogues to apply a poison to both weapons by clicking it first with the left and then with the right mouse button:

```
/cast Wound Poison VII
/cast [button:1] 16; [button:2] 17
```

The first command uses the poison, which then expects you to choose a target. The second command then uses the pending spell on your main hand if you left-click the macro and on the off hand if you right-click the macro.

Another really powerful macro is one for warriors that tries to interrupt a spell. Warriors can interrupt spells in Battle and Defensive Stance with Shield Bash (which requires a shield). Pummel can be used in Berserker Stance; this spell doesn't need a specific weapon type. The following macro casts Pummel if you are in Berserker Stance; otherwise it checks if you have a shield equipped and then casts Shield Bash. If this check also fails, meaning that you are in Battle or Defense Stance and do not have a shield equipped, it casts Berserker Stance so you can just execute the macro a second time:

```
/cast [stance:3] Pummel; [equipped:Shields] Shield Bash; Berserker Stance
```

Note that it is not possible to cast Berserker Stance and Pummel with just one click, as Berserker Stance triggers your global cooldown.

One thing you might have noticed in this and most of the earlier macros is that they automatically show the correct spell if you chose the red question mark as macro icon. But we can also control which spell and tooltip are displayed.

Macro Feedback

A macro always uses the icon and cooldown of the spell it casts when you execute it under the current circumstances. But this is not always sufficient, and it is possible to control this behavior by using the commands #show and #showtooltip at the beginning of the macro. These two commands also require the question mark icon for your macro.

Both commands are quite simple. They take a single argument, which is then shown in your action bar for this macro. The following macro shows up as Attack in your action bar and behaves just as if you had the normal Attack and not a macro in the action bar. But it casts Flash Heal when you click on it:

```
#show Attack
/cast Flash Heal
```

The command #showtooltip follows exactly the same syntax; the only difference is that you also get a tooltip for the spell when you place your mouse over the macro. It also sets the icon. The #show command just sets the icon, and the tooltip shows the name of the macro.

It is also possible to use the conditions known from secure commands here, and semicolons are used for simple if-then-else constructs. The following macro creates a button that shows Backstab if you have a dagger and Sinister Strike otherwise:

```
#showtooltip [equipped:Daggers] Backstab; Sinister Strike
```

But the macro that used the same conditions earlier already had this functionality (except for the tooltip, which just showed the macro's name). The icon of the macro was already correct, and you rarely need a tooltip for an action button. So you might wonder what the real use for these commands is. The answer is that you cannot always use simple slash commands with conditions in your macro. For example, you need this functionality when the actual work is done by Lua code, as /script commands are not parsed to determine the icon to display. You will see an example of this when we create a mount macro at the end of this chapter.

You will also need to use #showtooltip if you have a stopmacro command in your macro and you want to show a different icon if the command's condition is met, as the game does not check the stop conditions when determining the icon/tooltip to display. However, you will rarely need to display a different icon based on a stopmacro condition, as you can usually avoid using stopmacro altogether by using control structures.

Another possible use for #showtooltip is when your macro calls other macros or executes the click actions of secure buttons. For example, let's assume you have two macros in your first action two action bar slots, ActionButton1 and ActionButton2. You now want to create a macro that executes macro 1 if you have a hostile target and macro 2 otherwise:

```
#showtooltip [harm] <damage spell>; <heal spell>
/click [harm] ActionButton1; ActionButton2
```

The button would show no icon at all if we didn't use #showtooltip here, as WoW does not parse the buttons referenced by /click when determining the icon to display. But why would we want to write such a macro that simply calls another macro? Because both of the other macros can also be up to 255 characters long, which means we have just successfully circumvented the 255-character limit of a macro. But there are other ways to do this without having to split up your macro into many small parts. Let's see how we can use this combination with /click and secure action button templates to create really long macros.

Circumventing the 255-Character Limit

You rarely need more than 255 characters in a macro, but one case where you do is when you want to do the "kill all rare mobs" achievement. It can be really useful to have a macro that tries to target all rare spawns and displays a message when it manages to target one. You can then fly around in the spawn areas of the rare mobs and click the macro all the time.

We need to create a secure action button with Lua code and set its type to macro and its attribute macrotext to something like the following:

```
/targetexact Loque'nahak
/targetexact High Thane Jorfus
...etc with all 23 Northrend rare spawns
/stopmacro [noexists]
/script ChatFrame1:AddMessage("Found a rare spawn: "..UnitName("target"))
```

This would obviously not fit in a normal macro, so let's build a secure action button for it. The best place to create such a button to use in a macro is in a separate addon. I have a small addon called RandomCrap, which just consists of an XML and a Lua file that hold some functions and templates I use regularly. But you can also enter the following code in an addon like TinyPad if you just want to test it.

The simplest way to create such a macro is to write a string with the 23 /targetexact commands. Note that delimiting the string with square brackets allows you to use new lines in the string, so you can just write your long macro literally in your code. But it is smarter here to create a table with all the names of all the bosses and automatically generate the macro text from this string. It is shorter and more flexible, for example; you can later easily change the target command from /targetexact to /target if you want to allow partial matches:

```
local rarespawns = {"Loque'nahak", "Hildana Deathstealer", "Fumblub Gearwind",
"Perobas the Bloodthirster", "King Ping", "Crazed Indu'le Survivor",
"Grocklar", "Syreian the Bonecarver", "Griegen", "Aotona", "Vyragosa",
"Putridus the Ancient", "High Thane Jorfus", "Old Crystalbark", "Icehorn",
"Vigdis the War Maiden", "Tukemuth", "Scarlet Highlord Daion", "Seething Hate",
"Zul'drak Sentinel", "Terror Spinner", "King Krush", "Dirkee"}
local targets = ""
for i, v in ipairs(rarespawns) do
   targets= targets.."/targetexact "..v.."\n"
end

local frame = CreateFrame("Button", "RareSpawns", nil, "SecureActionButtonTemplate")
frame:SetAttribute("type", "macro")
frame:SetAttribute("macrotext", targets..[[
/stopmacro [noexists]
/script ChatFrame1:AddMessage("Found a rare spawn: "..UnitName("target"))]])
```

The code first generates the /targetexact part of the macro text and then creates a secure action button and sets its type to macro. The attribute macrotext is then set to the string generated earlier, followed by the stop condition and the code that displays a message.

This technique works with every macro that requires more than 255 characters, but it also has a small disadvantage: you have to use the #show (or #showtooltip) command to get an icon and tooltip in your action bar. We can now build a macro that clicks on our invisible secure action button with the long macro attribute. The macro is quite simple as the /click command expects a global variable containing a button.

```
/click RareSpawns
```

This has the same effect as clicking the secure button we created.

Using Lua in Macros

One last topic remains, and it actually has little to do with traditional macros—using Lua in a macro. Doing this is quite simple: just use the slash command /script <lua code>. But what Lua could be of use in a macro? Remember that it is not possible to cast a spell or use an item from Lua, as these functions are protected and can therefore only be called from secure code. Code from a macro can never be secure.

Sending Chat Messages

You saw a simple chat message example for Lua in a macro in the last section. We called ChatFrame1:AddMessage(msg) to display a notification in our chat frame. Another similar use is sending a chat message, but this does not necessarily require Lua code. Simple chat messages can be sent with the usual slash commands like /say and /raid. It is even possible to include the target in a chat message by using %t in the message; it will be replaced with the name of your current target. This is not a function specific to macros, and you can always use %t in your chat messages to refer to your target in World of Warcraft. The following macro is useful for druids; it casts Rebirth and sends the name of the resurrected player to the raid chat:

```
/cast Rebirth
/raid Battle res on %t!
```

The macro doesn't use any Lua at all. But another useful functionality in such a macro is sending a whisper to the player who will be resurrected so he can prepare himself to get back in the fight. You might think it was possible to use /w %t Battle res incoming! here. But %t only works in chat messages, not as the target of a whisper. This means we need Lua code to send a whisper to our current target:

```
/cast Rebirth
/raid Battle res on %t!
/script SendChatMessage("Battle res incoming!", "WHISPER", nil, UnitName("target"))
```

An obvious disadvantage of using Lua in macros is that you quickly hit the 255-character limit. The solution to this is outsourcing the actual Lua code in a small addon, which then provides a simple slash command or Lua function that is called from a macro. The following code creates the slash command /wtarget <msg>, which sends <msg> to your current target:

```
SLASH_WHISPERTARGET1 = "/wtarget"
SLASH_WHISPERTARGET2 = "/wtar" -- alias /wtar <msg>
SlashCmdList["WHISPERTARGET"] = function(msg)
    if UnitName("target") then
        SendChatMessage( msg, "WHISPER", nil, UnitName("target"))
    end
end
```

You can now simply use the following command in a macro:

```
/wtar Battle res incoming!
```

Besides being shorter and simpler to use, this doesn't generate an error message when you have no target.

Another good function would be one to schedule messages to be sent after a specific time. This allows you to create countdown macros, which can be very useful, so let's see how to do it.

Timers in Macros

The simplest way to implement this is just using `SimpleTimingLib` from your macro. But it's easier to create a slash command that takes a time in seconds and another slash command that will be executed after this time. The following code creates a slash command that executes another slash command after a given time. It requires the library `SimpleTimingLib` to be installed, either as a stand-alone version or embedded in the addon:

```
local function runCmd(cmd)
    local old = ChatFrameEditBox:GetText()
    ChatFrameEditBox:SetText(cmd)
    ChatEdit_SendText(ChatFrameEditBox)
    ChatFrameEditBox:SetText(old)
end

SLASH_IN1 = "/in"
SlashCmdList["IN"] = function(msg)
    local time, cmd = msg:match("(%d+) (.+)")
    if cmd:sub(1, 1) ~= "/" then
        cmd = "/"..cmd
    end
    SimpleTimingLib_Schedule(time, runCmd, cmd)
end
```

The function `runCmd` executes the actual command by using a trick—it modifies the text contained in the default chat edit box and calls the function `ChatEdit_SendText(editBox)`, which is defined in the file `FrameXML\ChatFrame.lua`. It would also be possible to parse the command here and find the slash command handler or emote that is associated with it, but that would be quite an effort (requiring about 30 lines of code). You can read the function `ChatEdit_ParseText(editBox, send)` in the file `frameXML\ChatFrame.lua` if you are curious to see how slash commands are handled in the default UI.

We can now use the /in command in macros like this:

```
/raid Pull in 3 seconds!
/in 1 /raid Pull in 2 seconds!
/in 2 /raid Pull in 1 second!
/in 3 /raid Pull now!
```

It is also possible to omit the leading slash in the command to be scheduled, as the /in handler adds a slash if the command doesn't start with a slash. The syntax /in 3 raid Pull now! would also work.

■**Caution** It is not possible to execute any secure command with the /in command, because the execution path is tainted by the addon that provides the slash command.

Another timer slash command that comes with Deadly Boss Mods is the so-called pizza timer, which can be started with the slash command /dbm timer xx:yy <text>. This shows a DBT timer with the name <text>. You can use this in a macro to track the cooldown of an ability or spell locally. But there is also another, more powerful slash command: /dbm broadcast timer xx:yy <text>, which broadcasts a DBM timer to your party or raid group. This command requires raid assistant or leader status.

Raid leaders can use a macro like the following to announce short breaks with a timer to the raid group:

```
/rw Have a short break! (5 min)
/dbm broadcast timer 5:00 Break
```

Suppressing Errors

Why would anyone want to suppress an error message? The answer is that there are macros which always generate error messages, even if they are executed successfully. An example of this is the trinket macro we used earlier:

```
/use 13
/use 14
```

This macro tries to activate both trinkets, and this always generates an error message. The second /use command fails because of the global cooldown if the first succeeds. A simple way to get rid of the small red "Item is not ready yet" message is to clear the frame that displays it. This frame is stored in the global variable UIErrorsFrame; its type is MessageFrame. Such a message frame basically works like a chat frame (which is a ScrollingMessageFrame), but without the ability to scroll. You can add messages to such a frame with its method frame:AddMessage(msg) and, most important for us here, clear it with the method frame:Clear(). A full reference for this frame type (and all other frame types) is available in Appendix A.

The following macro clears the `UIErrorsFrame` after trying to execute the two `/use` commands:

```
/use 13
/use 14
/script UIErrorsFrame:Clear()
```

It is of course also possible to place this code in an addon. But the Lua code here is relatively short, so it is not really worth the effort.

Tuning Options

A few commonly used macros are unlike other macros, as they are basically just Lua scripts you execute once. These "macros" simply set a so-called *cvar* (console variable, a variable that stores game settings like your video options), and this can also be done by editing the file `World of Warcraft\WTF\config.wtf`. Such an option can be set by calling `SetCVar("option", "value")` and retrieved with `GetCVar("option")`.

One popular example of such a macro is the following one, which allows you to zoom out further by setting the option `cameraDistanceMaxFactor` to 2.5. The distance slider in the interface options menu ends at 2.0.

```
/script SetCVar("cameraDistanceMaxFactor", "2.5")
```

Note that the value of the option is saved in your `config.wtf`; this means you only have to execute this "macro" once, and you will probably not store this simple Lua script in a macro at all.

There are many other options available that can be set to higher values than allowed by the options menu. The video options that control the "Ground Clutter" density and distance are a good example of this. The following macro sets these two options to values beyond the sliders in the video effects menu:

```
/script SetCVar("groundEffectDensity", "256")
/script SetCVar("groundEffectDist", "140")
```

This increases the amount of grass and other vegetation and the range on which it is visible. However, this can decrease your FPS drastically if you don't have a high-end system; remember that the options in the configuration menu are limited to lower values for a reason.

Circumventing the [flyable] Bug

Another really useful macro is one that uses your flying mount if you are in a zone where flying mounts are allowed or your normal mount otherwise. This would seem to be a really simple macro if the condition `flyable` worked properly. You could then simply use the following macro to do this:

```
/cast [flyable] <flying mount>
/cast [noflyable] <normal mount>
```

But flyable does not work properly. This condition evaluates to true if you are in an area in Outlands or Northrend where mounting is allowed. This worked just fine before Wrath of the Lich King, as flying mounts were allowed everywhere in Outlands that normal mounts were allowed. This is no longer true with Wrath of the Lich King, as you cannot use your flying mount in Dalaran (except for the subzone Krasus' Landing) or Wintergrasp, but the condition still evaluates to true there. This means the macro fails in these zones.

But using a mount is not a protected action, even though it can be done with the secure slash command /cast. The function CallCompanion(type, id), which was introduced in patch 3.0 (the same patch that broke flyable), can be used to summon a non-combat pet or a mount. Type can either be "CRITTER" to summon a non-combat pet or "MOUNT" to use a normal mount. The ID of a mount can be acquired from the default pet and mount menu; the first mount (or pet) that is displayed there has the ID 1, the second the ID 2, and so on.

The following code creates a slash command /mount, which uses a random flying or normal mount from a list of available mounts based on the zone you are currently in.

```
local groundMounts = {1, 16, 26}
local flyingMounts = {5, 10, 22}

SLASH_MOUNT1 = "/mount"
SlashCmdList["MOUNT"] = function(msg)
   local zone = GetRealZoneText()
   local subZone = GetSubZoneText()
   if IsMounted() then
      Dismount()
   elseif IsFlyableArea() and zone ~= "Wintergrasp"
   and (zone ~= "Dalaran" or subZone == "Krasus' Landing") then
      CallCompanion("MOUNT", flyingMounts[math.random(#flyingMounts)])
   else
      CallCompanion("MOUNT", groundMounts[math.random(#groundMounts)])
   end
end
```

Note that it is necessary here to check whether we are already mounted, and dismount if so because CallCompanion(type, id), unlike the /cast command, does not dismount you. The slash command then uses a good condition to check whether flying in the zone is really allowed and uses a random mount from the table flyingMounts if this is the case. Otherwise it uses a random mount from the table groundMounts. You have to fill these tables with the IDs of your favorite mounts if you want to use a macro based on this script.

A possible macro that makes use of an addon providing this slash command might look like this:

```
#showtooltip [flyable] <flying mount>; <normal mount>
/mount
```

#showtooltip is just to get an icon and tooltip for the macro, and it doesn't really matter that this icon is wrong in Dalaran and Wintergrasp.

Summary

This chapter demonstrated a different way of interacting with the World of Warcraft API: through slash commands, which seem to be quite simple at first glance. But these secure slash commands can be combined with complex conditions that make them very powerful. We looked at all available secure slash commands, which can execute actions that can normally only be done from secure code (that is, from the default UI) or by using secure templates.

We discussed how we can combine multiple conditions to build complex expressions by using logical operators. We then saw how we can use these expressions in simple if-then-else-end blocks in slash commands.

The next main topic in this chapter was using Lua in macros, and we tried out a lot of useful Lua scripts you can use in your macros. You also saw how to combine macros with secure templates to circumvent the 255-character limit, a workaround that can be important if you want to use long macros.

Secure slash commands and secure templates are the only ways of executing certain actions like casting spells. You saw in this chapter how to combine these two techniques to create extremely powerful macros that help you in your raids or PvP matches.

Make sure to check the WoWWiki page http://www.wowwiki.com/Useful_macros if you are looking for macros. This page has a quite large compilation of macros for every purpose; you will probably find whatever you are looking for there. You probably already know this list of macros and have copied a few macros from there. But you now know how these macros work and you can customize them to fit your needs. It's always better to understand a chunk of code and be able to customize it than just to copy and paste it.

CHAPTER 13

■ ■ ■

Tips, Tricks, and Optimization

This is the third and last chapter that is entirely focused on Lua and uses only a few functions of the World of Warcraft API. I will show you a few useful tips and tricks you can use in your addons. This chapter also covers the coroutine standard library, which hasn't been discussed yet as it is quite complicated and rarely used in addons (but it is still very powerful).

I will also show you how a few things in Lua work internally, including strings and tables. It is important to understand how these elements work if you want to use them in a smart way. Every data structure has its strengths and weaknesses, so it is important that you choose the right one in your addon. Choosing the right data structure also allows you to optimize your code to run faster or with less memory usage. However, optimization is a really overhyped topic in World of Warcraft addons. You will see a lot of completely unnecessary or wrong (meaning the resulting code is actually slower) optimizations when reading addon code.

Memory usage especially is a completely overhyped topic. Many people claim that addons with high memory usage slow down their game and cause lag spikes. What they describe as "high memory usage" often means 1 megabyte or more, which is ridiculous to worry about, as you probably have 2 GB of memory or more, and World of Warcraft alone rarely needs more than a gigabyte. This leaves you with 1 gigabyte for your OS, background applications, and your addons. I mentioned this topic in Chapter 6, when we discussed the garbage collectors of Lua 5.0 and Lua 5.1. World of Warcraft used Lua 5.0 before the Burning Crusade, and it had a really bad garbage collector for an application like a game. Such a garbage collector is described as a "stop the world" collector; it stops the execution of the script while it collects garbage. But the new Lua 5.1 garbage collector is really fast, and you should not worry about it too much.

As you begin writing WoW addons in Lua, you won't need many of the optimization tips and tricks I'm showing you here. However, you will need a deeper understanding of Lua as your coding skills develop and you write bigger and more complex addons.

This chapter shows you when you should think about performance, how you can measure it, and what can be optimized. I'm also showing you a lot of small tricks that can make your life easier. The first thing we need to discuss is measuring the performance of an addon or any Lua script.

Measuring Performance

Lua provides only a few functions that allow you to measure its performance, while World of Warcraft has several advanced profiling functions.

Measuring Performance in Lua

There are basically two resources that can be used by a Lua script: CPU time and memory. However, saving CPU cycles and saving memory are often two mutually exclusive aims. Many optimizations that reduce the required CPU time do so by using more memory, for example as a cache. You will have to trade off CPU usage against memory usage. But in most cases you should opt for less CPU usage and more memory usage, as memory is cheap and you usually have enough of it.

Measuring CPU Time

You can get the CPU time that was used by a specific Lua script by calling the function `os.clock()`, which is not available in World of Warcraft. This function returns the CPU time used by the currently executing Lua script, and you can use it to quickly get the time required to execute a certain script outside the game. The following example illustrates this:

```
for i = 1, 10^8 do end
print(os.clock())
```

The result depends on the speed of your computer.

Another way to get the execution time is to use an external program that starts the Lua script and prints the time required to run it. This can be done with the simple program `time` in Linux and Unix by calling `time lua5.1 myScript.lua`. Windows does not come with such a program, but that is not a problem, as `os.clock()` is sufficient for us here.

The `os.clock()` function always returns the total execution time of the whole script. You can use the following idiom around a block of code to measure its execution time independently from the rest of your script:

```
local t = os.clock()
-- code here
print(os.clock() - t)
```

■**Note** Although I will not include the line `print(os.clock())` at the end of every example in this chapter; you can add it wherever you want to measure the speed.

Measuring Memory Usage

The other important resource you have to work with is the available memory. You've already seen how we can track the memory usage of a Lua script, when we discussed the garbage collector in Chapter 6. The function `collectgarbage(option)` returns the amount of memory (in KB) currently in use by Lua if *option* is set to `"count"`.

The following code prints the size of an empty table in bytes by comparing the memory usage before and after creating the table. The resulting value is multiplied by 1024 to get a value in bytes, which is more meaningful here, as an empty table is relatively small:

```
local mem = collectgarbage("count")
local x = {}
print((collectgarbage("count") - mem) * 1024) --> 32
```

Profiling Addons in World of Warcraft

World of Warcraft provides a few advanced features that can be used to profile the performance of your addon. There are advanced functions available for memory and CPU profiling.

■**Note** Most of the examples in this chapter can be tested with a normal Lua interpreter without using World of Warcraft. I will note when an example works only in World of Warcraft because it uses WoW-specific functions.

CPU Profiling in WoW

The CPU profiling functions of World of Warcraft are quite powerful; they track almost everything. They can tell you the amount of CPU time used by a specific function or by all event handlers of a given frame. These profiling features are disabled by default because they come with a significant performance hit. Execute the following slash command to enable the profiling:

```
/console set scriptProfile "1"
```

You have to reload your UI before this change takes effect. But don't forget to disable this feature by executing the following command after you are done with profiling:

```
/console set scriptProfile "0"
```

Once profiling is enabled, there are a few functions you can call to profile your code:

ResetCPUUsage(): Resets the profiling statistics.

UpdateAddOnCPUUsage(): Updates the data that is retrieved by all of the following functions. You have to call this function before retrieving statistics with the functions that follow in this list.

GetAddOnCPUUsage(*addon*): Gets the CPU time used by *addon* in milliseconds until the last call to UpdateAddOnCPUUsage(). The *addon* argument can represent the name of the addon as either a string or a number.

GetFunctionCPUUsage(*func, includeSubs*): Retrieves the CPU time in milliseconds that was used by *func*. The *includeSubs* argument can be set to false to ignore the time needed by functions called by *func*; the default value is true, meaning that all following function calls are included in the statistics.

GetFrameCPUUsage(*frame, includeChildren*): Returns the CPU time in milliseconds used by all event handlers of frame. The includeChildren argument can be set to false to ignore the script handlers of the frame's children; the default value is true, meaning that the CPU usage of the children is included in the result.

GetEventCPUUsage(*event*): Gets the CPU time used by all event handlers that handle *event*.

Memory Profiling in WoW

Memory profiling functions in WoW are similar to the CPU profiling functions. However, you don't need to enable them explicitly, as these functions do not come with a performance hit.

UpdateAddOnMemoryUsage(): Updates the data that is retrieved by the following function.

GetAddOnMemoryUsage(*addon*): Gets the memory that was used by *addon* (string or number) by the last call to UpdateAddOnMemoryUsage().

Some Conventions

Throughout this chapter you will see a lot of short examples that compare the performance of different solutions for the same problem. I will often tell you the time required by the scripts on my computer (a laptop with a Core 2 Duo with 2.00 GHz CPU). You can then easily see which script is faster. But I will also use percentage values from time to time, which can cause a lot of confusion.

For example, what does "100% faster" mean? Let's say we have two scripts, A and B, and the former runs faster than the latter. I will say that script A runs x% faster than script B if script A runs in x% less time than B. 100% faster would thus mean that script A runs in no time at all.

Another important convention I'll use in this chapter is the *big O notation*. This notation provides us with a way to describe the resource usage (CPU or memory) of an algorithm based on the size of the input value. I'll spare you the definition as it is highly mathematical, but let's see how this works without too much math.

The big O notation looks like this: $O(f(n))$, where $f(n)$ is replaced with a function that describes the growth of the required CPU time or memory usage, and n is the size of the input, for example the size of a table or the length of a string. This means that an O(1) function does not become slower (requiring more memory) when you use it on larger input values. A simple example of this is the following function:

```
function foo(t, key)
    return t[key]
end
```

This function does not become slower if you use a larger table t, because accessing a key is internally an O(1) operation (you will see how table indexing works in detail later). The following function goes through a table and looks for a specific value; it is therefore O(n) as it grows in line with the size of the table t (because it has to iterate over the whole table):

```
function foo(t, val)
    for k, v in pairs(t) do
        if v == val then
            return k
        end
    end
end
```

Note that an O(*n*) operation is not necessarily slower than an O(1) operation on certain input values. For example, the following completely pointless function runs in O(1) but is still very slow:

```
function foo(t)
    for i = 1, 10^9 do
    end
    return t
end
```

The performance of this function is obviously poor. But it does not get worse when you use a bigger table *t*, which means it is O(1). The O(*n*) function earlier is probably faster for all input values you ever might use, but it is slower than this O(1) for really huge tables. And it keeps getting slower as the table grows. This illustrates that the big O notation only tells us how fast the required time grows, not how much time is actually required.

Also interesting is the following function, which takes a sorted array filled with numbers. It checks whether a given number is in this array but it is faster than the previous O(*n*) function as it uses the so-called *binary search* algorithm, which runs in O(log *n*):

```
function binSearch(t, val) -- t: sorted (ascending) array
    local start, last = 1, #t
    while start <= last do
        local middle = math.floor(start + (last - start) / 2)
        if t[middle] > val then
            last = middle - 1
        elseif t[middle] < val then
            start = start + 1
        else -- t[i] == val, found it
            return middle
        end
    end
end
```

The function is more complicated than iterating over the table, but it is faster. Feel free to test it with the techniques I mentioned earlier. The binSearch function first looks at the element in the middle of the array and continues looking for the value in the left part of the array if the value in the middle is larger than val. Otherwise it looks in the right part of the array, as we assume that the array is sorted. The function continues doing this until the searched interval is empty or the value is found.

Another example that will help you get a feeling for the meaning of the big O notation is the following function. It implements the *bubble sort* algorithm, which sorts a table in the time $O(n^2)$:

```
function bubbleSort(t)
   for i = 1, #t do
      for i2 = 1, #t do
         if t[i] < t[i2] then
            t[i], t[i2] = t[i2], t[i]
         end
      end
   end
end
```

You might have guessed that $O(n \log n)$ lies between $O(n)$ and $O(n^2)$. An example of such a function is `table.sort(t, compare)`. It can sort a table in $O(n \log n)$, as it internally uses *quicksort*. It is actually not strictly $O(n \log n)$; it might run in $O(n^2)$ in the worst case, but it is very unlikely that this happens for huge tables. $O(n \log n)$ is the average required time for quicksort. There is another sorting algorithm that guarantees to run in $O(n \log n)$: *merge sort*. But it is still slower than quicksort for almost all tables, as a single step is more expensive than in quicksort. Most programming languages thus use quicksort. I'm not showing quicksort here, as you don't need to worry about sorting tables in Lua; you can just use `table.sort`.

You now know how you can measure the performance of your code, and we've discussed the necessary conventions. But what should be optimized and what not?

The Main Rules of Optimization

There are two basic rules of optimizations one should always obey:

- Don't do it.

- Don't do it yet (for experts only).

The results of optimizing your code without thinking about it first are that you'll probably waste your time, you'll make your code harder to understand, and you might do it wrong and lose performance in the end. This means that you should always measure the performance of your script to see if it needs optimization; 99% of all addons simply don't need to be optimized.

All of the following optimization tips should only be applied to code that is crucial for the performance of your addon. An example of this would be an OnUpdate handler that is used by more than one frame (like the OnUpdate handler of the bar objects in our first version of CooldownMonitor). Another example is the COMBAT_LOG_EVENT_UNFILTERED event, which can be called really often. I measured peaks of up to 800 events per second in certain boss fights; this means your event handler is called even more often than an OnUpdate handler. Do not waste your time with optimizing a function that is called only occasionally. Always measure performance before and after optimization to see if the optimization really works.

Let's see what can be optimized in an addon. A good example of something that can be a real performance hog is the string.

Strings

Strings seem to be innocuous, and you probably didn't expect that a simple operation like the concatenation of two strings can slow down your script. You need to know how strings work internally in order to understand the problems you can run into.

Understanding Strings

Strings seem to be a value type, meaning that they seem to be passed as values (rather than references) to a function. The function can then modify the string, and the caller doesn't notice it. The following example illustrates this behavior:

```
function test(s)
   s = s.."foo"
end

local s = "test"
test(s)
print(s) --> test
```

This prints test because strings behave as if they were passed as values, which means the modification of the string in test does not affect the original string.

But a string is internally always passed as a reference; you just don't notice this implementation detail because strings are immutable. There is no way to change an existing string; you can only generate new strings. This means that the statement t = t.."foo" creates a new string that consists of the concatenation of t and "foo" and stores it in the local variable t.

Every string is internally kept in the *string pool* (think of it as a huge hash table with all strings), and every string is unique. The following happens when you try to create a new string: Lua builds the string, checks to see if it is already in the string pool, and inserts it if it doesn't exist. You then get a reference to this string in the string pool.

There is nothing new so far; I described this behavior in Chapter 2. But what does it mean for us? Strings are subject to garbage collection, which means an unused string doesn't vanish immediately when you remove the last reference to it. So if you have an extremely long string (let's say 50 million characters long, or 50 MB memory usage) and append a short string (for example, "\n" for a new line), you will have this string twice in your memory until the original string is collected.

Example: Concatenation in Addon Communication

Let's start with an example. Imagine you have a function that accepts CHAT_MSG_ADDON events with strings sent by other players. But the message you want to receive may exceed the 255-character limit of chat messages, so your sender function splits the outgoing message into multiple strings and the receiver function concatenates them.

A Simple Event Handler

The following code shows two functions that could be used in such an addon, syncHandler and receive. The receive function is called every time the addon receives a part of a multipart message; the prefix "Foo-End" indicates the end of the message. The function concatenates and stores all partial messages in the table received with the sending player as key, to prevent problems when multiple players send you messages at the same time. Then receive calls syncHandler with the fully concatenated message as its argument when the last part of a message is received.

```
local function syncHandler(msg)
    -- do stuff here
    -- adding print(msg) here is a bad idea as msg will be really long
    print("Received a sync message!")
end
```

```
local received = {}
local function receive(player, prefix, msg)
    received[player] = received[player] or ""
    received[player] = received[player]..msg
    if prefix == "Foo-End" then
        return syncHandler(received[player])
    end
end
```

It is very unlikely that you will ever need to send a lot of data through to another player, so let's say the maximum number of messages you expect to receive here is 10 and each one has a size of 245 characters, which gives us 10 characters for the prefix to identify the addon.

Fake Events for the Event Handler

Add the following code after the functions to simulate the CHAT_MSG_ADDON events with test data:

```
local testMsgs = {}
local player = "TestPlayer"
local msg = string.rep("x", 245)
for i = 1, 10 do
    table.insert(testMsgs, {player, "Foo", msg})
end
table.insert(testMsgs, {player, "Foo-End", msg})

for i, v in ipairs(testMsgs) do
    receive(unpack(v))
end
```

This code simply creates 10 messages and passes them to receive. Try to execute the code and you will see that it runs extremely fast, and you probably don't expect it to be a problem. But let's examine what happens when you run the code.

It concatenates the first message with the second one, so that you now have the original message (245 bytes) and the concatenated message (490 bytes) in your memory. It then concatenates this 490-byte message again with the 24-byte message; you now have three strings: the original string, the first two strings concatenated, and the first three strings concatenated (735 bytes).

The overall size of the generated strings is now already 1470 bytes, and it gets worse and worse with each additional message. The memory that is moved around if we concatenate n messages is $245 \times (1 + 2 + \ldots + n) = 245 \times n \times (n + 1) / 2$ bytes. Thus the example code that simply concatenates ten messages already uses 13 MB of memory. A real addon would even require slightly more memory, as the received sync messages would differ. Our example uses the same content for every test message, so it doesn't generate a new 245-byte string in every step. But this is only a small amount of memory required compared to the concatenation.

Note that the garbage collector will collect unused strings during the concatenation so that the whole memory isn't allocated at the same time. But this can really slow your script down, especially because the required memory grows by $O(n^2)$.

Memory Usage If Something Goes Wrong

Imagine that something goes wrong and you receive a lot of synchronization messages without a Foo-End message. Or even worse, what happens if a malicious player in your raid sends you faked messages all the time to crash your game?

Sending 10,000 messages can be done relatively quickly. Let's test what would happen if someone tries to do this. Change the line saying for i = 1, 10 do to the following to simulate 10,000 messages:

```
for i = 1, 10000 do
```

We can calculate the memory that is moved around during this concatenation with the formula from earlier: $245 \times 10{,}000 \times (10{,}000 + 1) / 2 = 12{,}251{,}225{,}000$ bytes. That is over 12 gigabytes. Running this script now takes about 30 seconds on my laptop as Lua requires a tremendous amount of memory and the garbage collector is working all the time. You can watch the process lua5.1.exe in your Task Manager while you execute the script. This will give you an impression of how Lua has to shuffle memory around to concatenate all those strings.

Figure 13-1 shows the memory graph in my Task Manager while executing the script with 10,000 messages. You can clearly see that the garbage collector runs interleaved with your script; it is started every few execution steps and collects a few objects that are considered to be garbage.

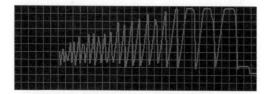

Figure 13-1. *Graph of memory usage while concatenating 10,000 strings*

This problem with string concatenation is not restricted to Lua; many languages (most notably Java and C#) have a similar way of dealing with strings and thus the same problems. The solution in many languages is a StringBuilder object that internally uses a smarter way of concatenating the strings. Lua doesn't have such an object, but there is still a simple solution to this problem.

The Solution

There is one function that can be used to concatenate multiple strings without quadratically increasing memory usage: table.concat(*tbl*, *delimiter*). This function takes a table that has only strings in its array parts and concatenates them (separated by *delimiter*, which is optional). The World of Warcraft API provides a similar function that can also be used: string.join(*delimiter*, ...). It works on multiple string arguments instead of a table, but we will use table.concat as it is more convenient for our example.

We can modify the function receive to build a table containing all received strings; this table is then concatenated when the last message is received:

```
local received = {}
local function receive(player, prefix, msg)
   received[player] = received[player] or {}
   table.insert(received[player], msg)
   if prefix == "Foo-End" then
      return syncHandler(table.concat(received[player]))
   end
end
```

You can test it with 10,000 or even 100,000 messages; it runs extremely fast. Table 13-1 compares the performance of the old version, which simply concatenated the strings, with the new receive function, which uses table.concat.

Table 13-1. *Comparison of String Concatenation and* table.concat

Number of Messages	Time in seconds (concatenation)	Time in seconds (table.concat)
1,000	0.16	0.01
5,000	5.3	0.04
10,000	29	0.06
15,000	80	0.09
20,000	•	0.12
100,000	•	0.6

The asterisks mean that concatenating strings fails with a "not enough memory" error message on my laptop (32 bit OS with 2 GB memory) when I try to use 20,000 or more messages. You might go farther with more memory or with a 64-bit version of Lua, but the required time still grows extremely fast. Tuning the garbage collector settings to be more aggressive will also help, but it does not solve the actual problem.

What we learn from this is that one should be careful with string concatenations. Using a concentration operator in a loop is a particularly bad idea in most cases; try to use table.concat or string.join whenever possible.

Optimizing `string.format`

This optimization is specific to World of Warcraft and helps you to avoid string garbage. Imagine you have a `FontString` object in a unit frame that displays the health of the unit. You now register the `UNIT_HEALTH` event and use an event handler like the following:

```
local healthString = "Health: %d/%d"
function myFrame:UNIT_HEALTH(uId)
    if uId == myFrame.unit then
        local txt = healthString:format(UnitHealth(uId), UnitHealthMax(uId))
        myFrame.fntStrHealth:SetText(txt)
    end
end
```

The handler is now called every time the health of the watched unit changes, which can be as often as every frame. Imagine you use this handler in a raid frame mod and you are in a 40-man battleground like Alterac Valley. The handler is probably called about 20 to 40 times every frame if the group is currently in combat. Every call creates a new string from the format string with about 20 characters.

What happens to these strings? They are passed to the `SetText` method and never used again by Lua, only internally by the frame. This means that they are now garbage and will be collected sooner or later. It seems to be not much; only about 600 bytes of garbage if 30 raid frames are updated. But every font string that is often updated (think of your combat log or the text displayed on timers) generates these garbage strings, which are passed to a function and then dropped. All of these frames together can quickly generate a lot of garbage, which keeps the garbage collector busy and slows down the game.

You actually already know the solution to this problem, as I mentioned it earlier in this book when we wrote the addon CooldownMonitor. All frames that display text like `FontStrings` have the method `SetFormattedText`, which basically has the following functionality:

```
function frame:SetFormattedText(str, ...)
    return frame:SetText(str:format(...))
end
```

The only difference is that it does not call `string.format` in Lua; it formats the string internally and displays it without generating a Lua string. This can save a lot of garbage if it is used consistently.

This simple trick can safely be used every time you have to format a string and then display it. It is one of the easiest optimizations in World of Warcraft. Another really easy optimization is using local variables instead of global variables.

Local Variables

I have already mentioned several times that one should prefer local variables over global ones. But why? Well, one obvious reason is that your code will be more readable if a variable is only accessed and changed in a specific block of code. Moreover, a global variable can be accessed and changed from anywhere, so you can never be sure what other file or addon also modifies a given global variable.

Global Variables vs. Local Variables

But there is another reason you should prefer local variables over global ones: accessing a local variable is about 30% faster. We can test this with a *tight loop* (a loop with a single instruction to measure the performance of this instruction) that counts from 1 to 10^8. The following code uses a global variable to do this:

```
i = 0
while true do
   i = i + 1
   if i >= 10^8 then
      break
   end
end
```

It runs quite slowly; Lua needs 13.1 seconds on my laptop for this loop. Recall how global variables work in Lua: all global variables are stored in a huge hash table called the global environment, _G. You will see how tables work in detail later in this chapter. A local variable is a "real" variable, which means that its name is just an identifier for the compiler and not a string. Lua knows where a local variable is stored in your memory, while it needs to calculate the position of a global variable.

The following version uses a local variable instead of a global one, so it should be faster:

```
local i = 0
while true do
   i = i + 1
   if i >= 10^8 then
      break
   end
end
```

The simple change of adding the keyword local makes the code about 78% faster (so that it takes only about 2.8 seconds). Note that the results can vary slightly for you, as they depend on a lot of factors.

Another interesting test is to declare the used local variable outside of the function that uses it. This means we create a closure of a function that references this local variable. Such a local variable is also called an *upvalue* in Lua. Here's an example:

```
local i = 0
function test()
   while true do
      i = i + 1
      if i >= 10^8 then
         break
      end
   end
end
test()
```

One might expect that there is no difference between a local variable and an upvalue. But there is a huge difference; this code runs in 4.6 seconds. It is still 65% faster than using a global variable. But using a "real" local variable is 39% faster than an upvalue.

What Does It Mean?

Accessing a global variable is still incredibly fast. The huge speed gains we saw in the last section are not so huge in a real application. They were so high in the previous examples simply because the only thing the examples did was access variables. Let's see an example that calls the functions math.cos and math.sin.

Accessing these two functions takes even longer than accessing a simple global variable, as each call first gets the global variable math, which is a table. Lua then needs to get the fields cos and sin from this hash table; the time needed for this is comparable to accessing a global variable, as global variables are technically also entries in a hash table. Note that the size of a hash table does not affect the time needed to get an entry from it (we will see how this works later in this chapter).

```
for i = 1, 10^8 do
   math.sin(math.cos(5))
end
```

This runs in 31.5 seconds on my computer. Let's store the functions in local variables. This reduces the four table/global variable accesses to two local variable accesses:

```
local sin = math.sin
local cos = math.cos

for i = 1, 10^8 do
   sin(cos(5))
end
```

The code now runs in 23 seconds, only 27% faster. You can also test upvalues, and you'll find that there is barely a difference.

But there is a difference, and this optimization can be applied easily. It is always a good idea to save references to functions or tables that are used in frequently called code in local variables. You will see this optimization in a lot of files; they often begin with code looking like the following. This optimization technique is often called *caching*, as the local variables basically act as cache for the global functions.

```
local pairs, ipairs = pairs, ipairs
local tremove = table.remove
-- and so on with all frequently called functions
```

But one important question is left unanswered: why is accessing a global variable so slow? Global variables are stored in a table (_G), so we need to understand how tables work in order to understand what happens when we access a global variable.

Tables

Tables are divided into two parts: the array part and the hash part. The array part is relatively simple, so we will start with it.

Understanding Arrays

An array is a very simple data structure that uses positive integers as indices; these indices are used to calculate the position of an entry in your memory. This means we first need to look at how the memory is organized internally.

What Arrays Look Like Internally

Your memory is divided into many small cells, each of which is 8 bits (1 byte) wide, and you can only access these cells. The cells are numbered, and the number of a cell is its address. The size of your memory on 32-bit systems is limited to 2^{32} bytes, or 4 gigabytes, as the maximum number of bits that can be used for an address is 32.

We luckily don't need to worry about this when programming in Lua, as Lua already does all the hard work for us. We cannot tell Lua to read the memory at a given address. But we can get the memory address of some Lua objects, like tables, as the default __tostring() method prints it:

```
local t = {}
print(t) --> table: 0059AC90
```

Here, 0059AC90 is the base memory address of t on my system; you will probably get a different memory address. Lua internally stores various items of information about the table at this memory address. One of these items is the memory address of the array part of the table, which can be in a completely different part of your memory (the same applies to the hash part). I will refer to this address as the array base address from now on.

The interesting question is what happens when we now try to access a field in the table, like t[1]. Lua first checks whether the index is in the range of the array, as arrays internally have a fixed size, even though they seem to be dynamically sized. (We will further discuss sizes of arrays later in this section.) Lua checks the hash table part of the array if the requested index is not in the range of the array part.

If it is in the array part, Lua first subtracts one from the index to get a zero-based index, which is used internally. This zero-based index is now multiplied by 16 and added to the array base address. The calculated memory address holds an object that represents an array entry, which is always 16 bytes wide.

The following illustration shows how such an array t looks in your memory. The table header is at the memory address that is returned by tostring(t); it is slightly simplified here, as it is internally 32 bytes wide and consists of more than just its array and hash address. Discussing everything that is stored in a table header would go too far here and is not important for understanding how tables work. The array address holds the position of t[1], the first entry in the array part. A short calculation shows that this is correct:

arrayAddress + 16 × (1 - 1) = arrayAddress + 16 × 0 = arrayAddress

t[2] is then at arrayAddress + 16, t[3] at arrayAddress + 32, and so on.

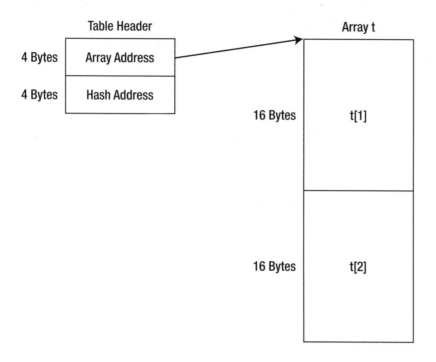

This explains why accessing an array is comparatively fast and does not get slower as you add more elements to it. Lua can always calculate the position of every element in the array. One obvious conclusion we can draw from this behavior is that the size of an array must be fixed internally. Imagine what would happen if it was not fixed and you tried to insert a value somewhere. The memory at the calculated position is not necessarily part of the array, and you might overwrite something important, causing your script to crash. This is not the case, so we can see that the size of the array is fixed.

Array Size

The initial size of an array depends on the table constructor used. A simple {} creates an empty array part, while {1} creates an array with one slot. You might have guessed that {1, 2} creates two slots, but you probably didn't guess that {1, 2, 3} creates an array part with four entries, of which one will stay empty.

The reason for this is that arrays always double their size once they reach their limits (powers of two). The following code illustrates this behavior:

```
local t = {} -- 0 entries
t[1] = 1 -- 1 entry
t[2] = 1 -- 2 entries
t[3] = 1 -- 4 entries
t[4] = 1 -- 4 entries
t[5] = 1 -- 8 entries
t[6] = 1 -- 8 entries
-- and so on...
```

Resizing an array is with O(n) a comparatively expensive operation, compared to accessing or changing a value. Lua needs to find a new place in your memory with enough consecutive free space for all entries and then copy the old array to it. You don't want to do this all the time when you have a large array and add new values to it. We can test the performance of different table constructors with a simple loop:

```
for i = 1, 10^7 do
   local t = {1, 2, 3, 4, 5}
end
```

This code runs in 8 seconds on my laptop as the table is initially created with 8 entries. The following code creates an empty table and adds the entries afterward:

```
for i = 1, 10^7 do
   local t = {}
   t[1], t[2], t[3], t[4], t[5] = 1, 2, 3, 4, 5
end
```

This code, which does the same thing, requires 31 seconds to run, as it resizes the table three times in every execution of the loop's body.

There is a third way to create such a table, by explicitly using the integer indices in the table expression:

```
for i = 1, 10^7 do
   local t = {[1] = 1, [2] = 2, [3] = 3, [4] = 4, [5] = 5}
end
```

You might expect this to run as fast as the first version, but it takes 13 seconds. The reason for this is that Lua does not recognize it as an array in the first place. It mistakes the indices for hash table entries and generates a table with an eight-slot hash table part. However, it is still faster than adding the entries outside of the constructor, as Lua internally fills and resizes the array without the overhead of switching between Lua code and the internal C code.

This discussion of array size leads us to an old issue we encountered in the Chapter 4 example SimpleTimingLib, which used arrays to store arguments that were later passed a function with unpack(). The problem was that one might pass nil as an argument to a function, which raised the question of whether arrays can store nil values. The answer I gave you there was yes, but only under certain circumstances.

It depends on the size of the array and the number of nil values. Lua tries to balance memory usage and access speed when using integer indices. Having an array with 128 entries just because you want to use the entries 1 and 65 obviously doesn't make sense at all. But having a 4-slot array when you want to use the entries 1 and 3 does make sense and is possible.

Lua uses the array part if we explicitly tell the compiler to do so in the table constructor. The following example illustrates this:

```
print(unpack{nil, nil})
print(unpack{nil, nil, nil, 4}) --> nil nil nil 4
print(unpack{nil, nil, nil, 4, 5, 6}) --> nil nil nil 4 5 6
```

Note that an array can never have trailing nil values; they will always be cut off. This also works when creating arrays from the vararg parameter . . . .

You might wonder why SimpleTimingLib sometimes failed with relatively few `nil` values even though it used the vararg to create the table. The reason is that modifying the table, for example by using the hash table part of it, causes Lua to optimize the array by moving values into the hash table part.

The array part will then be used only if more than 50% of the slots in the array part are occupied. We can test it with a simple function that adds a dummy field to the hash table part of the array. Our SimpleTimingLib used the hash table to store the function to be called and the time when the task is due:

```
function foo(...)
   local t = {...}
   t.x = 5
   return unpack(t)
end
```

```
-- use 3 of 4 fields works
print(foo(1, nil, 3, 4)) --> 1 nil 3 4
-- 2 of 4 fields is not enough
print(foo(1, nil, nil, 4)) --> 1 (4 is in the hash table)
-- 5 of 8 is enough
print(foo(nil, nil, 3, 4, 5, 6, 7)) --> nil nil 3 4 5 6 7
-- 4 of 8 is not enough
print(foo(nil, nil, 3, 4, 5, 6)) --> (everything in the hash table part)
```

This illustrates the "more than 50%" restriction that applies as soon as you start using the hash table part. However, this restriction is not really a problem for our timing library, as you rarely need to pass multiple `nil` values to a function. And even if you have to do so, most functions also accept `false` instead, which can be used without problems in an array.

Understanding Hash Tables

A hash table is a more sophisticated data structure than a simple array. It has the ability to associate arbitrary values like strings with other values and is therefore also called an *associative array*. What makes hash tables especially interesting is that reading or setting a value in them is an O(1) operation. One might think that an associative array internally simply iterates over all entries until it finds the requested one, which would be an O(n) operation. But that is not the case. Lua can calculate the memory address of a given entry in the hash table, and you will see how this works as we build our own hash table.

I'll outline how a hash table works before we create the example table.

Hash Table Basics

Arrays simply store values; hash tables also have to store the key, which can also be an arbitrary Lua value. Hash table entries are also called *key/value pairs*. You might have guessed the memory usage of such a key/value pair: 32 bytes, as arrays use 16 bytes.

A hash table internally uses an array with a fixed size to store its key/value pairs. The array starts with no slots for key/value pairs and grows by the same rules as the array part of the table.

The position of a key/value pair in this array can be calculated from the key by using a *hash function*, which converts an arbitrary object into a number called the *hash code* (or simply *hash*) of the object. This hash is then used as the index for the key/value pair in the array. The simple calculation hash % #*array* (with *array* being the array used for the key/value pairs) ensures that this index is guaranteed to be inside the bounds of the array.

Note that this hash is not unique; there might be multiple different objects with the same hash, which leads to a *collision* in the hash table. A good hash function ensures that the number of collisions in the table is kept low, but you cannot avoid them completely. This means that we need a way to resolve these conflicts.

There are several ways of resolving conflicts; one of the simplest is using a linked list of key/value pairs in the slot where multiple keys collide. New colliding keys will simply be appended to the list, and the get operation that retrieves a key/value pair from the hash table will iterate over the list and check if the requested key is in one of the key/value pairs.

The worst case is that all keys in your table have the same hash code, which degrades the hash table. It is then a linked list that is traversed every time you add a new entry or read an entry from it which is an O(*n*) operation. But it is extremely unlikely that this will happen when using a good hash function like the Lua hash function.

That was the theory; let's now create a simple hash table.

Creating a Hash Table

We will create a hash table object in Lua to get a better understanding of hash tables. Note that the performance of the hash table we create here will be very poor compared to the original Lua hash tables, especially because we are using Lua hash tables with two entries (three entries in case of a collision) to represent key/value pairs in Lua. The only purpose of this example is to demonstrate how hash tables work.

Our hash table object will behave like a normal Lua hash table. We can do this by using metamethods to overload the table-access operations. The only difference is the performance, which as noted will be very bad; one reason for this is that it is written in Lua and not in C, like the hash tables provided by the language. Another reason is that the hash table will even internally use Lua hash tables to represent key/value pairs. Our example also uses a very simple hash function; this will lead to a lot of collisions, as a good hash function is somewhat complicated. You can read the Lua source code (file ltable.c) if you understand C and want to see how the Lua hash tables work in detail.

Let's start with creating a simple hash function. We will be using a function that simply uses tostring on the value and then calculates the sum of all characters' byte values in the string. This can be done with two simple functions:

```lua
local function sum(...)
    local result = 0
    for i = 1, select("#", ...) do
        result = result + select(i, ...)
    end
    return result
end

local function hash(k)
    k = tostring(k)
    return sum(k:byte(1, #k))
end
```

You might be tempted to use a recursive function for sum, but recursion is usually slower than a loop. Let's assume for a second that we really want to use this hash table in an addon; that means the hash function is a performance-critical part of the implementation. So using recursion to sum up a few numbers is off the table here.

Let's now build the actual hash table, which usually defines three operations: a get operation to retrieve the value that is associated with a given key, put to store a new key/value pair in the table or to update an existing one, and delete to remove an existing key. We don't have to define methods for this; we can use the metamethods __index for the get operation and __newindex for put and delete.

Let's start by creating the __index method. We will use the field size to store the current maximum size of the array to emulate a static sized array. kvPairs holds the array with all the key/value pairs that are currently stored in our hash table. The method calculates the position of the requested key and then checks all key/value pairs stored in this *bucket* (an entry in the array holding the key/value pairs) which is just one pair unless there have been collisions. We have to add 1 to the calculated position because Lua arrays are 1-based; the position 0 would be in the hash table part of the array, and we don't want that.

```
HashTableMT = {}
HashTableMT.__index = function(self, k)
    local pos = hash(k) % self.size + 1 -- calculate the position
    if not self.kvPairs[pos] then -- doesn't exist...
        return nil -- ...return nil
    else
        local pair = self.kvPairs[pos]
        while pair do -- traverse the list to find it
            if pair.key == k then -- found the key
                return pair.value -- return the associated value
            end
            pair = pair.next -- check next item in list
        end
        return nil -- requested key didn't exist in this bucket
    end
end
```

This function demonstrates why retrieving a value from the hash table is an O(1) operation if the hash function is good. The position is calculated and the operation is then a simple array access, which is an O(1) operation because the actual memory address can be calculated.

The __newindex method is slightly more complicated than __index as it needs to check for collisions and resolve them. We also need an additional attribute in our hash table object: usedSlots, which holds the number of currently occupied slots. The put operation calls the function resize, which doubles the size of the hash table if we use more slots than we have.

```
HashTableMT.__newindex = function(self, k, v)
    local pos = hash(k) % self.size + 1 -- calculate the position
    if not self.kvPairs[pos] then -- entry doesn't exist yet
        if v == nil then
            return -- inserting a new nil value is pointless
        end
```

```
        self.kvPairs[pos] = {key = k, value = v} -- just add a new key/value pair
        self.usedSlots = self.usedSlots + 1 -- increment the number of used slots
    else
        -- we either have a collision or we are trying to update an existing handler
        -- let's check if the key already exists in this bucket
        local pair = self.kvPairs[pos]
        while pair do
            if pair.key == k then -- found it, let's update it
                pair.value = v -- update...
                return -- ...and return, no need to update the size or resize the array
            end
            pair = pair.next
        end
        -- the entry does exist but our key is not in the bucket
        -- this means we've got a collision :(
        -- --> insert the new element at the beginning of the linked list
        self.kvPairs[pos] = {key = k, value = v, next = self.kvPairs[pos]}
        self.usedSlots = self.usedSlots + 1
    end
    -- check if we reached the limit
    if self.usedSlots > self.size then
        resize(self) -- double the size
    end
end
```

One thing you might notice is that setting a field to nil does not remove it from the table. It just sets its value to nil, but the key/value pair still exists and the table doesn't shrink. Regular Lua hash tables show the same behavior; the only way to really remove something from them is to trigger a resize. This resize operation has to calculate the new positions (*rehash* the table); this means it has to loop over all entries in the array, so this is a good place to drop the nil values from it. Place the following function above the __newindex metamethod, as it is required there:

```
local function resize(self)
    self.size = self.size * 2
    self.usedSlots = 0
    local oldArray = self.kvPairs
    self.kvPairs = {}
    -- rehash the table by inserting all non-nil entries into the new re-sized array
    for i, v in pairs(oldArray) do
        local pair = v
        while pair do
            if pair.value ~= nil then
                self[pair.key] = pair.value
            end
            pair = pair.next
        end
    end
end
```

Note that our table can never actually shrink, only grow. Real Lua tables can also shrink when a rehash is triggered, but a rehash can only be triggered by adding entries, not by deleting them.

Our hash table is nearly finished. The last thing we need before we can test it is a constructor:

```
function CreateHashTable()
    return setmetatable({size = 1, usedSlots = 0, kvPairs = {}}, HashTableMT)
end
```

Testing Our Hash Table

The simplest test we can run is using a few keys that do not collide and check to confirm that we can read them:

```
local t = CreateHashTable()
t.a = 1
t.b = 2
t.c = 3
t.d = 4
print(t.a, t.b, t.c, t.d) --> 1 2 3 4
```

The hash code of a is 97, b is 98, and so on. This means that consecutive characters do not collide with our hash algorithm. We know that t behaves like a normal table, so let's test whether it is really using our hash table implementation, by adding the following code:

```
print(rawget(t, "a"), rawget(t, "b")) --> nil nil
print(rawget(t, "c"), rawget(t, "d")) --> nil nil
```

The rawget function performs a raw table access without invoking the metamethod __index. We can now try to read the key/value pairs from the subtable kvPairs. Note that accessing t.kvPairs does not invoke __index, as this metamethod is only called if rawget returns nil. (The same is true for __newindex.)

```
print(t.kvPairs[1].key, t.kvPairs[1].value) --> d 4
print(t.kvPairs[2].key, t.kvPairs[2].value) --> a 1
print(t.kvPairs[3].key, t.kvPairs[3].value) --> b 2
print(t.kvPairs[4].key, t.kvPairs[4].value) --> c 3
```

The first entry contains the key d as:

```
hash("d") % 4 + 1 = 100 % 4 + 1 = 1
```

One might expect "a" to be the first entry in this hash table because it was the first one we added to it, but you cannot control the order of elements in a hash table and you cannot sort a hash table. We already know that from normal Lua hash tables, where the iterator function next returned the key/value pairs in an order that seemed to be random. We can now explain why: next just iterates over the array that holds the key/value pairs and follows all linked lists in case of collisions, so the order of hash entries might even change when the table is resized.

Another interesting test is provoking a collision, which is really easy with our bad hash function. For example, the keys 1 and "1" collide as the hash calls tostring on the key:

```
local t = CreateHashTable()
t[1] = "number"
t["1"] = "string"
print(t[1], t["1"]) --> number string
```

We can also see the collision by looking into the array kvPairs, where both entries are stored in the second bucket:

```
print(t.kvPairs[2].key, t.kvPairs[2].value) --> 1 number
print(t.kvPairs[2].next.key, t.kvPairs[2].next.value) --> 1 string
```

One last test for our hash table is checking if the rehash works properly. Let's start with a hash table with the two colliding entries "a" and "c":

```
local t = CreateHashTable()
t.a = 1
t.c = 2
print(t.kvPairs[2].key, t.kvPairs[2].value) --> a 1
print(t.kvPairs[2].next.key, t.kvPairs[2].next.value) --> c 2
```

This actually already triggers the first rehash when the second entry is added. This is why "c" is in the second entry of the list and not in the first, as you might expect, because colliding entries are added to the beginning of the list. But let's test what happens if we add another entry, which resizes the table to 4. We see that "a" and "c" no longer collide if the table is resized to 4:

```
t.b = 3
print(t.kvPairs[2].key, t.kvPairs[2].value) --> a 1
print(t.kvPairs[3].key, t.kvPairs[3].value) --> b 3
print(t.kvPairs[4].key, t.kvPairs[4].value) --> c 2
```

Everything seems to work just fine in our hash table. We can now use this knowledge to see what we can optimize when using tables.

Basic Table Optimizations

The simplest way to optimize tables is to avoid creating them unnecessarily. A good example of this is a typical constructor for an object:

```
function CreateSomeObject()
    return setmetatable({}, {__index = someObjectPrototype})
end
```

This creates a new metatable for each object that is created. That is not necessary, as all objects have the same metatable. It is better to define the metatable outside the function as we have done throughout the book:

```
local someObjectMT = {__index = someObjectPrototype}
function CreateSomeObject()
   return setmetatable({}, someObjectMT)
end
```

This was a very obvious optimization. But there are more sophisticated tricks that do require understanding the internal details of hash tables. One of them is creating tables with the appropriate size. Imagine you have a table storing an object that starts with four entries, but you know that there will be a fifth entry added later. Let's write a simple demonstration of this:

```
for i = 1, 10^7 do
   local obj = {a = 1, b = 2, c = 3, d = 4}
   obj.e = 5
end
```

The problem is that the fifth entry triggers a rehash of the table, and the code therefore runs quite slowly, taking 18 seconds on my laptop. We can create a table with a hash table of the size 8 by adding a dummy entry and setting it to `nil` in the table constructor:

```
for i = 1, 10^7 do
   local obj = {a = 1, b = 2, c = 3, d = 4, e = nil}
   obj.e = 5
end
```

This avoids the rehash and is 33% faster, as it runs in only 12 seconds.

Let's see more optimization with a real-world example: our library SimpleTimingLib desperately needs optimization, as we did not consider performance in its current version.

Optimizing SimpleTimingLib

The current implementation of SimpleTimingLib is not very smart. The `OnUpdate` handler performs a task that runs in $O(n)$, which is not acceptable if you want to use this library in addons that schedule a lot of tasks.

Using Another Data Structure

Those of you who are familiar with this topic might suggest using a so-called *priority queue* as the data structure. You're probably already thinking of a binary search tree like an AVL tree or a heap such as a binary heap or a Fibonacci heap; these are theoretically extremely efficient solutions for our problem. However, such a data structure is very sophisticated and difficult for beginning programmers to understand. So we are not going to see it here. I did consider explaining a simple priority queue (a *binary heap*); it would be relatively short with about 50 lines of code. However, the explanation would certainly be very long and complicated. I therefore decided to skip this here as it would be beyond the scope of the book. If you are interested in this topic, you might want to read a book about algorithms and data structures. However, we can still improve SimpleTimingLib here; the difference in performance between the solution I'll present here and a proper priority queue is minimal for most use cases.

We will see a very simple but effective solution here: a linked list that stores all entries. This seems to be very similar to our current solution using an array. But we will use a simple trick to speed the code up: we will keep the array sorted when inserting new values. The OnUpdate handler only needs to look at the first entry in this list if it is sorted. Thus it runs in O(1), while the new insert operation runs in O(n).

I've tested all of the data structures just mentioned for the scheduler used in Deadly Boss Mods. A proper priority queue, which does both the schedule (*insert*) operation and the *extract min* operation (removing the timer with the lowest time value) in O(log n), provides a clear advantage over a simple linked list. But I used millions of simultaneous timers in this test, which is not a realistic scenario for either DBM or SimpleTimingLib. For example, Deadly Boss Mods makes extensive use of its scheduling library, but there are usually only four to eight timers running at a given time in a complex boss fight. The advantage is then extremely small as a lot of the time is not wasted in the O(n) insert operation but in tasks like building the table that holds the function arguments.

But a small advantage is still an advantage, and DBM therefore uses a binary heap as the priority queue for its scheduling. You can read the well-commented code in the file DBM-Core.lua (search for "Scheduler" to find it) if you are curious about how such a data structure works. But beware: it is not discussed here for the reason that it is beyond the scope of a beginner's book so the code might seem to be very sophisticated.

Enough theory; let's get started with implementing our linked list in SimpleTimingLib.

Building SimpleTimingLib-1.1

We basically moved the hard work from the OnUpdate handler to the function that inserts the entry, which is quite a smart solution. OnUpdate is called very frequently, while the insert function is only called from time to time by another addon.

All of the following code blocks are updates for the embedded library SimpleTimingLib-1.0, which means you must replace the respective functions. It might also be a good idea to increase the major version of this library to SimpleTimingLib-1.1.

The first thing we change is the array that currently stores all entries; we will replace it with a linked list and therefore initialize the variable tasks with nil instead of an empty table. Replace this:

```
SimpleTimingLib.tasks = SimpleTimingLib.tasks or {}
```

with this:

```
SimpleTimingLib.tasks = SimpleTimingLib.tasks or nil
```

The schedule function now creates an ascending sorted linked list of all scheduled tasks:

```
local function schedule(time, func, obj, ...)
   local t = {...}
   t.func = func
   t.time = GetTime() + time
   t.obj = obj
   if not tasks then
      -- list is empty or the new is due before the first one
      -- insert the new element at the very beginning
      t.next = tasks
      tasks = t
```

```
    else -- list is not empty, find last entry which is < time
        local node = tasks
        while node.next and node.next.time < time do
            node = node.next
        end
        t.next = node
        node.next = t
    end
end
```

You can easily see from the code that this operation is now O(n), as it might iterate over the whole linked list to find the right place to insert it. The following code shows the new OnUpdate handler:

```
local function onUpdate()
    local node = tasks
    while node do
        if node.time <= GetTime() then
            tasks = node.next
            node.func(unpack(node))
        else
            break
        end
        node = node.next
    end
end
```

It looks like a typical O(n) operation, as it seems to loop over the whole array. It might run in O(n) when all scheduled tasks are due in the current frame. However, we have to look at the overall performance, and even in worst case, that all tasks are executed in this frame, you will have an empty linked list in the next call to OnUpdate. In almost all calls, the function will look only at the first element, because it cancels the loop as soon as it encounters a task that is not due yet.

The unschedule function also needs to be adjusted, but we can't really optimize it. The reason for this is that we have to look at all tasks to check whether they match the provided arguments:

```
local function unschedule(func, obj, ...)
    local node = tasks
    local prev -- previous node required for the removal operation
    while node do
        if node.obj == obj and (not func or node.func == func) then
            local matches = true
            for i = 1, select("#", ...) do
                if select(i, ...) ~= node[i] then
                    matches = false
                    break
                end
            end
```

```
            if matches then
                if not prev then -- trying to remove first node
                    tasks = node.next
                else
                    prev.next = node.next
                end
            else -- set prev to the current node if it was not removed
                prev = node
            end
            node = node.next
        end
    end
end
```

SimpleTimingLib now looks slightly more complicated, but it will be faster if used by a lot of addons. The purpose of a library is to be used by multiple addons, and you have to assume that a library is used extensively by another addon. You don't want to waste unnecessary performance here.

Another optimization that can easily be applied is recycling tables.

Recycling Tables?

Recycling tables is often not worth the effort in Lua. The garbage collector works very efficiently and collecting tables is usually faster than emptying tables and refilling them. But World of Warcraft provides the function table.wipe(t), which quickly deletes all entries from a given table.

We could do the following: create a stack and push all tables that are no longer required on this stack after wiping them. The scheduling function could then try to pop a table from this stack or create a new one if that is not possible. However, there are a few problems:

- We have to use a loop to insert all arguments into a recycled table. We are currently using simply {...}, and we earlier saw that this is faster than a loop.

- Imagine that there are a lot of timers required for a short period of time. You would then have a lot of dead timer objects on your recycle stack, and it would never shrink back. On possible solution for this would be using a weak table to store all the recycled timers; the garbage collector would then collect all tables that are not recycled. But this comes with another disadvantage, discussed next.

- It would not be possible to use a stack as a data structure, because the garbage collector would destroy it by collecting elements in the middle of it. The only solution is using a hash table and next to get the first element from it. But recall that in our hash table implementation, next would simply look for the first spot in the table that is not free, and this might take some time. This is especially problematic as the hash table can become comparatively big if there are a lot of timers started; recall that a hash table can only shrink if you add even more nil elements to it. You will see more about the performance of next on almost empty big tables in just a bit.

- It would be very hard to track the number of tables that are currently available for recycling, as the garbage collector will delete them in an unpredictable order and point in time. However, it would still be possible to track the number by using a *finalizer* metamethod, a function that is called when the object is collected. But this creates an even bigger overhead, as objects with finalizers require special treatment. I will tell you more about finalizers in the next section when we discuss userdata values.

The weak hash table solution still seems to be attractive in spite of the disadvantages, as you probably didn't expect next to be such a performance hog. Let's see how much worse next can be. The following code creates a simple example hash table with 50,000 entries:

```
local t = {}
for i = 1, 50000 do
   t[-i] = i -- negative entries are always in the hash part
end
```

Let's test a simple loop that removes all entries from the table:

```
for k, v in pairs(t) do
   t[k] = nil
end
```

It is as fast as one might expect it to be, about 0.03 seconds on my laptop. Now let's try to use the following code instead. It also deletes all the entries from the table, but it uses a while loop and next(t, nil) to retrieve the first entry of the table until the table is completely empty:

```
local k, v = next(t, nil)
while k and v do
   t[k] = nil
   k, v = next(t, nil)
end
```

This loop requires 5 seconds of CPU time on my laptop because next has to go over the whole table to find an entry at the end. This takes some time on a huge table with only a few entries, and our hash table that stores recycled tables can become such a table if there are a lot of timers in a short period (the hash table grows) followed by a period with only a few timers (the garbage collector removes most of them).

Recycling tables is in this case not worth doing, because of these disadvantages. You would increase the CPU usage to save a few kilobytes of memory. But your CPU is usually overloaded with work when playing World of Warcraft, while a few kilobytes of memory won't make any difference.

We now have optimized a lot of tables, and we worked with strings earlier. But there are two more interesting data types we have not discussed at all yet: userdata values and threads Let's first see how we can use userdata.

Utilizing Userdata

I told you in Chapter 2 that you cannot create userdata values from Lua, but this doesn't mean we can't use them. Now, what could we do with a userdata object? The most common use of this object is to represent an object that is provided by the Lua host, like World of Warcraft frames. All frames are represented by a table holding a userdata object. But the only thing we can do with this object is to pass it to functions provided by the API that know what this userdata object actually represents. This means we currently can't do anything with userdata objects except use them as identifiers.

But userdata values can have metatables, and they even define two additional metamethods: __len is called when you use the length operator # on the userdata object, and __gc is a finalizer, executed when the userdata object is collected by the garbage collector. But there are still two problems: how can we create a userdata object, and how do we apply a metatable to it? setmetatable does not work on userdata values. There is no way to create a userdata value and apply a metatable to it according to the official documentation.

However, there is an undocumented function in Lua that creates a new userdata value (without any data attached to it) and a metatable attached to it. The name of this function is newproxy(mt), which already suggests its purpose: using it as a proxy.

Using Userdata as a Proxy

A proxy object wraps a table and can track, modify, or block accesses to it. You saw a proxy table in Chapter 6, where I showed you a few useful tricks for debugging by using a proxy for the environment of your file. This proxy tracked and forwarded all accesses to the global environment; that is, all global variables.

The first argument *mt* of newproxy(*mt*) can be true to create a new, empty metatable for the new userdata value, or false to create it without a metatable. The third possible value for *mt* is another userdata object that already has a metatable, which will then be used for the new userdata object.

The following example shows a userdata proxy to track accesses to another table:

```
local myTable = {}
local p = newproxy(true)
getmetatable(p).__index = function(self, k)
    print("Accessing "..tostring(k))
    return myTable[k]
end

getmetatable(p).__newindex = function(self, k, v)
    print("Setting "..tostring(k).." to "..tostring(v))
    myTable[k] = v
end

p.test = "123"
p.foo = 1
p.foo = p.foo + 1
print(myTable.test)
```

You might wonder where the advantage over using normal tables is. Well, the only difference is the memory usage. A table allocates 32 bytes of memory that is wasted if the only purpose of the table is forwarding accesses through a metatable. The userdata object does not allocate any unnecessary memory, but the advantage is still very minimal and often not worth the effort.

However, the default UI makes use of newproxy in a similar way in a lot of code related to secure templates and restricted frames. It is used there as a proxy that wraps frames in order to protect them from becoming tainted. The comments in the files suggest that the only reason they use userdata objects instead of tables is memory usage.

Userdata Metamethods

There are two additional metamethods available, as mentioned earlier. First, __len is invoked when you use the length operator # on a userdata value. We can use this to create a wrapper for a hash table object that keeps track of the hash table's size. We will use the metatable of the userdata object as storage for the contents of the hash table. The field __size in the metatable will store the size of the hash table. Here's the code:

```
local function index(self, k)
   return getmetatable(self)[k]
end

local function newindex(self, k, v)
   local mt = getmetatable(self)
   local old = mt[k]
   mt[k] = v
   if old and v == nil then -- deleting an existing entry
      mt.__size = mt.__size - 1
   elseif not old and v ~= nil then
      mt.__size = mt.__size + 1 -- adding a new entry
   end
end

local function len(self)
   return getmetatable(self).__size
end

function NewHashTable()
   local obj = newproxy(true)
   getmetatable(obj).__index = index
   getmetatable(obj).__newindex = newindex
   getmetatable(obj).__len = len
   getmetatable(obj).__size = 0
   return obj
end
```

We can test our hash table object by adding the following code:

```
local t = NewHashTable()
print(#t) --> 0
t.foo = "bar"
print(#t) --> 1
t.x = 1
t.y = 2
t.z = 3
print(#t) --> 4
t.foo = nil
print(#t) --> 3
t[1] = 4 -- also counts entries in the array part
print(#t) --> 4
```

One disadvantage of using such a table is that accessing and setting values in it is slower than in a regular table. That is because you have an additional function call every time you access or change a value.

The second metamethod is the finalizer __gc, which is invoked when the userdata value is deleted by the garbage collector. The reason such a metamethod exists is that a userdata value often stores data that cannot be accessed by Lua, and the garbage collector cannot clean up regular userdata values. A finalizer is usually not a Lua function but a function provided by the underlying API that cleans up the userdata value.

The use of this metamethod is somewhat limited for us, as we can only add Lua functions here. The following example simply prints a message, as I can't think of a useful application for this metamethod:

```
local p = newproxy(true)
getmetatable(p).__gc = function(self)
   print("Collected "..tostring(self))
end
```

There is no need to trigger the garbage collector by calling collectgarbage("collect") as the garbage collector also collects all objects with finalizers when the scripts ends. The reason for this behavior is that the userdata objects might have opened system resources like files, and the finalizer closes them. Lua therefore has to ensure that all finalizers are called, even if the script terminates with an error.

There is another feature of Lua we haven't discussed yet, as you will rarely need it in World of Warcraft: the coroutine library.

The Coroutine Library

This library is one of the Lua standard libraries, and I mentioned it at the beginning of the book. The library allows you to create coroutine objects, which are basically functions with one difference: they can *yield* and they can be resumed. Yielding in a coroutine is similar to returning in a function, but a coroutine will continue executing at the point where it yielded when it is resumed. A function cannot store the point where it returned and resume there.

Coroutine Basics

There can only be one coroutine running at a given time, as coroutines do not implement multithreading. A coroutine can therefore not be stopped from the outside; it has to yield and can then be resumed from the outside.

Let's get an overview of the available functions that work with coroutines:

coroutine.create(*func*): Creates a new coroutine object from the given function *func*. This function is executed when the coroutine is resumed for the first time (that is, when started).

coroutine.resume(*co*, ...): Resumes the coroutine *co* and passes the arguments ... to it. This function returns true followed by the values passed to the yield function or return statement if the coroutine runs without errors, false followed by the error message otherwise.

coroutine.yield(...): Yields and activates the coroutine that called the currently active coroutine. All arguments passed to this function are returned as additional return values of the coroutine.resume call that resumed the currently active coroutine. yield returns the additional values that are passed to the resume function when the coroutine is resumed the next time.

coroutine.running(): Returns the coroutine that is currently running or nil if no coroutine is running.

coroutine.status(*co*): Returns the status of the coroutine *co*, which has the following possible values: running means that it is currently running; suspended means that it yielded or was not started yet; normal means that the coroutine is currently stopped because it resumed another coroutine; dead means the function the coroutine was created from has returned or an error occurred.

coroutine.wrap(*func*): Creates a coroutine from *func* and returns a wrapper function that calls coroutine.resume on the created coroutine every time the wrapper function is called. This wrapper function strips the first return value (which indicates occurred errors) and generates an error message if this value was false.

It looks quite complicated, so let's see a simple example.

A Coroutine Example

The following example creates a coroutine that wraps a function which basically consists of an infinite loop. This function yields in the body of the loop and passes a counter to the calling function:

```
local function foo()
   for i = 1, math.huge do
      coroutine.yield(i)
   end
end

local co = coroutine.wrap(foo)
print(co())   --> 1
print(co())   --> 2
print(co())   --> 3
```

This example was quite simple but you can imagine that coroutines can quickly become very complicated, especially when you have multiple coroutines that resume each other and pass arguments around.

However, it is very unlikely that you are ever going to need such complicated coroutine constructs in a World of Warcraft addon. But simple loops like in this example can be used if you need to execute a longer task and you want to distribute it over multiple frames to avoid a lag spike. You can simply define an OnUpdate handler that checks whether a given coroutine is still alive and executes it in this case. The coroutine then executes a few steps of the task and yields.

Summary

This chapter was one of the toughest in this book, as it goes really deep into detail. Don't worry if you didn't understand every single detail. You might want to read this chapter a second time after you have written your first addon by yourself. You can then apply a few of the tips and tricks I presented here to improve your addon.

You learned how we can measure and improve the performance of our addons with a lot of small tricks, and you also learned a lot of details about how Lua internally works. We discussed in detail how strings and tables work, with examples for optimizing them.

We then improved our library SimpleTimingLib by applying the discussed optimization techniques. The insertion is now an O(n) operation and the OnUpdate handler is O(1); the older version was the other way around. This is better because the OnUpdate handler is called every frame, while the insertion is only called from time to time.

I then showed you two parts of the Lua API we hadn't discussed earlier. One of them was the function newproxy(), a completely undocumented feature that can be quite useful as it allows you to create a userdata object. The last trick I showed you here was how we can use the coroutine standard library, which is rarely used in World of Warcraft addons. This library can be incredibly useful and powerful, but it is quite hard to use.

■ ■ ■

## CHAPTER 14

Other Uses for Lua

You now know pretty much everything needed to program great World of Warcraft addons, but you have learned more than just how to write addons for World of Warcraft. You've learned the programming language Lua, which is used by far more applications and games than just WoW. An incomplete list of applications that use Lua can be found on Wikipedia: http://en.wikipedia.org/wiki/Lua_(programming_language)#Applications.

There are many games, like Warhammer Online, Crysis, Far Cry, and S.T.A.L.K.E.R, that use Lua in a similar way to World of Warcraft. Besides WoW, the most interesting game that uses Lua for its interface is Warhammer Online, as it also supports addons that are very similar to WoW addons. I'll show you a simple Hello, World addon for Warhammer Online here.

Another particularly interesting application is SciTE, the editor I presented at the beginning of the book. You can use Lua to customize it to your needs, as I will show how to do in this chapter. We are going to write a function that fixes the indention of Lua code in the editor, which can be useful when you copy and paste Lua code from somewhere like a WoWWiki article or forum post.

And there is yet another project I'm going to show you here in this chapter. Lugre is a Lua binding for the graphics engine OGRE 3D, a fully featured 3D graphics engine that can be used to write your very own game. Lugre allows you to use all of its features from Lua. I'll show you a simple example of this here because I think it's one of the coolest projects using Lua out there.

Customizing SciTE with Lua

You are probably already using this editor as an IDE for your addons. You can find my customized version of it in the code download if you have been using another IDE or editor. The editor is based on Scintilla, an open-source editor engine used by many editors, most notably SciTE, Notepad++, and Code::Blocks. SciTE is highly customizable; you can change almost everything by modifying the config files, and almost the whole Scintilla API is exposed to user-provided Lua scripts.

Let's start with a look at the config file. You can open this file by clicking Open Global Options File in the Options menu. I've already added two user-defined commands there: a simple Hello, World script and a script that inserts the current time. You can find the definitions of these two commands at the end of the config file:

```
## Hello, World
command.name.1.*=Hello World from SciTE
command.1.*=HelloWorld
command.subsystem.1.*=3
command.mode.1.*=savebefore:no

## Insert Timestamp
command.name.2.*=Insert Timestamp
command.2.*=Timestamp
command.subsystem.1.*=3
command.mode.1.*=savebefore:no
command.shortcut.2.*=Ctrl+I
```

I'm not going into detail on the SciTE config commands here, but you can find the full documentation at http://www.scintilla.org/SciTEDoc.html. The code basically creates two commands that show up in the Tools menu. The second one uses Ctrl-1 as a shortcut, while the first has no shortcut defined. It will automatically use Ctrl-1, as that is the first custom command. These two commands then call the global Lua functions HelloWorld and Timestamp, which are created in the startup script startup.lua. Let's start with a simple Hello, World script.

Hello, World with SciTE

The file startup.lua is in the SciTE installation directory, but you can also open it by clicking Open Lua Startup Script under Options. We can create the function HelloWorld there:

```
function HelloWorld()
    print("Hello, World")
end
```

You can now press Ctrl-1 (or select Hello, World from the Tools menu) to execute it; there is no need to restart SciTE. It automatically detects when you modify the startup script and reloads it the moment you save the file. The output we get is simply "Hello, World" in the default output area of SciTE.

But printing to the standard output is trivial; it would be more interesting to insert text into the currently opened document. SciTE provides a few objects in the global namespace of this startup script. One of these objects is editor. It provides numerous methods that can be used to insert text, read text, or modify existing text. For example, we can use the method editor:AddText(text) to insert something at the current caret position:

```
function HelloWorld()
    editor:AddText("Hello, World")
end
```

SciTE now inserts "Hello, World" into our file when we press Ctrl-1 or select the command from the menu. There are, of course, all the usual Lua functions available, so it is easy to write the command that inserts the current date and time into the document:

```
function Timestamp()
   editor:AddText(os.date())
end
```

But you don't have to click a command in a menu to execute a Lua function; you can also define event handlers that are called on events like file saves.

Event Handlers

You can create a function that acts as an event handler by naming a global function after the event. For example, the event OnDoubleClick occurs when you double-click in the editor or output pane. Add the following function to your startup script to display a message every time the user double-clicks:

```
function OnDoubleClick()
   print("OnDoubleClick")
end
```

It prints OnDoubleClick every time you double-click, an effective demonstration but not a really useful application. Other event handlers may be more valuable, such as OnBeforeSave, which is executed before a file is saved and receives the name of the file being saved as an argument. You could use it to do a few checks or fixes before writing the file to disk.

For example, we can insert a "last modified" time stamp before the file is saved. The following OnBeforeSave handler does this by iterating over all lines, using editor.LineCount to determine the number of lines and editor:GetLine(i) to retrieve a line. It looks for the pattern $Modified.-$ and replaces it with $Modified: timestamp$ by using the methods editor:SetSel(selStart, selEnd) and editor:ReplaceSel(newText).

■**Note** The strings in this function must not use $Modified...$, because the event handler would otherwise modify itself while editing the file, which would be really annoying. The following code therefore uses \36 (the ASCII code for $) instead of $ to prevent this.

The event handler uses the attribute editor.CurrentPos to save the caret position before doing the selection and the method editor:GotoPos(pos) to restore it after updating the file. This prevents the script from changing the caret position and scrolling to the occurrence of $Modified$.

```
function OnBeforeSave(file)
   local oldPos = editor.CurrentPos -- save the old position to prevent scrolling
   -- lines are zero-based in SciTE
   for i = 0, editor.LineCount - 1 do
     local line = editor:GetLine(i)
```

```
      if line then -- line is sometimes nil in large files
          local startPos, endPos = line:find("\36Modified.-%\36")
          if startPos and endPos then -- text in current line?
              -- get the absolute position of the line in the document
              local lineStart = editor:PositionFromLine(i)
              -- select text and replace it, the editor position is 0-based
              -- but the result from string.find is 1-based
              editor:SetSel(lineStart + startPos - 1, lineStart + endPos)
              editor:ReplaceSel(string.format("\36Modified: %s\36", os.date()))
          end
      end
  end
  editor:GotoPos(oldPos) -- restore old position
end
```

This simple event handler allows you to place $Modified$ anywhere in your files; it will automatically add and update a time stamp there every time you save the file.

SciTE Documentation

There is a lot of good documentation available for SciTE:

http://scintilla.sourceforge.net/SciTELua.html: The official documentation, it only covers the basics.

http://lua-users.org/wiki/UsingLuaWithScite: A very good tutorial and documentation.

http://lua-users.org/wiki/SciteScripts: A lot of useful Lua scripts that can be used in SciTE.

http://scite-interest.googlegroups.com/web/ScintillaSciteDoc.html: Full documentation of all available objects and their methods/attributes.

Our next topic is another MMORPG (Massively Multiplayer Online Role-Playing Game), Warhammer Online (WAR). Its interface is written in Lua and can be extended with addons.

Lua in Warhammer Online

In this section you will see how a simple Hello, World addon works in Warhammer Online (http://www.warhammeronline.com). There are many similarities between the user interfaces of WoW and WAR; it is easy for a World of Warcraft addon programmer to get started in WAR. The WAR Interface API looks to me like a very unpolished version of the World of Warcraft API; many features are similar to World of Warcraft but more difficult to use or unnecessarily complicated.

Hello, World in Warhammer Online

Addons are placed in the folder Interface\AddOns\<addon name>; you will have to create this folder by hand for your first addon. Create a folder called HelloWorld for our Hello, World addon there. If we were programming for WoW now, the next step would be creating a .toc file. Warhammer Online uses .mod files instead.

The .mod File

The main difference between a WoW .toc file and a WAR .mod file is that the .mod file is written in XML. Create a file called HelloWorld.mod in the HelloWorld folder and place the following XML in it:

```xml
<?xml version="1.0" encoding="UTF-8"?>
<ModuleFile xmlns:xsi="http://www.w3.org/2001/XMLSchema-instance">
    <UiMod name="HelloWorld" version="1.2.1" autoenabled="true">
        <Description text="A Hello, World AddOn"/>
        <Author name="You!"/>
        <Files>
            <File name="HelloWorld.lua"/>
        </Files>
    </UiMod>
</ModuleFile>
```

The XML should be pretty self-explanatory. The version of the game the addon is created for is stored in the version attribute of the UiMod element. This attribute is equivalent to the Interface attribute of World of Warcraft. The game will complain that the addon is outdated if this version number is lower than the current version of the game (which is currently 1.2.1).

The XML also contains metadata like the description and author of the addon. It then loads the file HelloWorld.lua, which we are going to write next.

■**Tip** It is not necessary to restart the game when you change the .mod file in WAR. It is sufficient to reload the UI by typing /reload.

The Lua File

The simplest way to create a Hello, World addon is just to write the code that displays "Hello, World" in this file. You might be tempted to write print("Hello, World") there, but print is not available. We have to use the method EA_ChatWindow.Print(*msg*) to print a message.

But this function doesn't accept a normal Lua string; we have to convert it to a UCS-2 encoded string. This is the character encoding that is used by WAR, and it basically means that every character consists of two bytes. There is a simple function available that takes a normal string and converts it to UCS-2 so it can be displayed: L. Recall that you don't need parentheses for a function call that only takes a single string or table. We can therefore simply write the following line into our Lua file and reload the interface with /reload:

```lua
EA_ChatWindow.Print(L"Hello, World!")
```

We now see "Hello, World" in the chat frame after reloading the UI.

■**Tip** Use the command /debug and enable logging in the opened menu to see Lua errors in WAR.

You might now expect the next step in the Hello, World addon to be adding a slash command. But slash commands are really complicated in Warhammer Online. The only way to add a slash command is by hooking a function provided by the game. There is a library available that does the hook and provides a function to register slash commands: LibSlash, which can be downloaded on war.curse.com. It is easy to use and it comes with its own documentation, so I'm skipping slash commands here. Event handlers are more interesting.

Event Handlers

There are two types of event handlers in Warhammer Online: events that are defined in the .mod file of an addon and game events. The former event type is the equivalent of script handlers in World of Warcraft, while the latter is similar to WoW game event handlers.

Let's start with the events in the .mod file. There are only three event handlers available:

OnInitialize: Called when the addon is loaded.

OnShutdown: Called before you leave the game or reload your interface.

OnUpdate: Called every frame.

To test the OnInitialize handler, add the following element to the UiMod element of your .mod file:

```
<OnInitialize>
  <CallFunction name="HelloWorld_Initialize"/>
</OnInitialize>
```

This simply calls the function stored in the global variable HelloWorld_Initialize. Let's create this function in our Lua file.

```
function HelloWorld_Initialize()
  EA_ChatWindow.Print(L"Hello, World from OnInitialize!")
end
```

This produces a message in your chat when you reload your interface.

The second type of event handler can be registered with the function RegisterEventHandler(event, func). The event argument is not a string but a number that identifies the event. All events with their corresponding IDs are stored in the table SystemData.Events. Similarly, func is not a function but a string that holds the name of a global variable that contains a function, which will then be called when the event occurs. It is also possible to pass a string in the format "someTable.key" to call the function stored under key in the table in the global variable someTable.

Let's use the event CHAT_TEXT_ARRIVED for testing; it is fired every time you receive a chat message. A full list of events is available at http://www.thewarwiki.com/wiki/Event_List. We can't pass the event's name as a string, so we need to get the ID of the event from the table SystemData.Events, Our function call then looks like this:

```
RegisterEventHandler(SystemData.Events.CHAT_TEXT_ARRIVED, "HelloWorld_OnChat")
```

We can now create the function HelloWorld_OnChat, which is called every time the event occurs. One might expect this function to receive arguments that contain the sender of the chat message and the text, but this is not the case. The event arguments are stored in GameData. ChatData. The *name* argument stores the player (or NPC) who sent the message, and *text* stores the actual message. Let's write a function that simply displays a message in your chat saying *<sender> message*.

This sounds easy, but the *name* and *text* fields from this table are not strings, they are wstrings. A wstring is a data type introduced by WAR; it is one of the multi-byte UCS-2 encoded strings that we also needed for the function Print. The problem is that you can't mix normal strings with wstrings in concatenations. A possible solution to this seems to be using string.format, but this does not work with wstrings at all.

A properly working function that displays a message looks like this:

```
function HelloWorld_OnChat()
    local name = GameData.ChatData.name
    local msg = GameData.ChatData.text
    EA_ChatWindow.Print(L"<"..name..L"> "..msg)
end
```

The game never automatically converts between wstrings and normal strings; you will always have to do this by hand. You can use WStringToString to convert a wstring to a normal string, but you risk losing information if the string contains special characters.

Those are the basics of using Lua for Warhammer Online addons. It is slightly more complicated than the World of Warcraft API; in particular, having two different data types for strings can be extremely confusing and annoying. But it's still Lua and therefore not too hard to understand and learn the API.

Documentation

There are many very good web sites out there if you want to learn more about addons in Warhammer Online:

http://www.thewarwiki.com: This wiki is the equivalent to WoWWiki in Warhammer Online.

http://war.curse.com/: Curse is not only for World of Warcraft addons; you can also find many Warhammer Online addons there.

You now know how you can use Lua in two different games, but wouldn't it be even cooler to write your very own game? You can do this with Lua by using the engine Lugre.

Lua and Lugre

Lugre (http://lugre.schattenkind.net) provides a Lua API for OGRE 3D and can be used to write a whole game just with Lua. This section is a little more advanced and requires basic knowledge of 3D graphics. I'm not explaining every single term here, because the whole topic is very complex and can literally fill books. There is in fact a good book about OGRE 3D available: *Pro OGRE 3D Programming,* by Gregory Junker (Apress, 2006). It doesn't cover Lugre, but you need to know how OGRE 3D works in order to use Lugre, which simply forwards most of your function and method calls to the corresponding OGRE functions and methods.

Setting Up Lugre

The simplest way to install Lugre is to get the precompiled binary version with a small example project from the SVN repository: svn://zwischenwelt.org/lugre/trunk/example. In case you don't know what Subversion (SVN) is for, it is a version control system, managing the source code of a project. It allows you to switch between different versions of a project and have multiple programmers working on the same project as it synchronizes the files.

What this means for you is that you will need a client that uses the Subversion command checkout to get all the latest versions of all the code that is stored in this repository. A very good client for Windows is TortoiseSVN, which can be obtained on http://tortoisesvn.tigris.org/. You will have a few new commands in your context menu in your Explorer; one of them is SVN Checkout. Create a new folder for Lugre and run this command. Enter svn://zwischenwelt.org/lugre/trunk/example when it asks you for a repository.

■**Note** Subversion is not only useful for relatively big projects like Lugre. I use it for every addon that is longer than a Hello, World example, as it is an incredibly useful tool to have. Curse.com offers free Subversion repositories for addons. There are also tutorials available on setting it up, but this is fairly easy with TortoiseSVN.

Lugre comes with a small example project: you can run the file example.exe in the folder bin to start it. It shows a tree in a skybox, nothing really impressive. But consider that the whole code that is responsible for creating and managing this scene is written in Lua. The next example shows how this works.

Creating a Simple 3D Application

The code responsible for this application can be found in the file main.lua in the folder Lua. We will not delete the whole file, as it also contains a lot of boring initialization code that we are going to reuse for our example.

Open the file and navigate to the function Main, the main function that is called by Lugre when the program is started. Find the following two lines at the beginning of the function:

```
----- your init code here ----
Bind("v",function(state) Client_TakeScreenshot(gMainWorkingDir.."screenshots/") end
```

Now delete everything between these lines (keep the call to Bind so that you can take a screenshot by pressing V) and the following lines:

```
-- mainloop
while (Client_IsAlive()) do MainStep() end
```

It is important that you do not delete these two lines, as this is the main loop of the program. It calls the function MainStep repeatedly until you close the program; MainStep can be found right below the function Main. This function calls other functions, which handle user input and draw frames. We will not change anything in this function; we will only replace the code we deleted earlier.

We will now create a simple scene that is similar to the original example, showing a few trees with different parameters and a simple skybox.

Creating Trees

A tree is created from a CaduneTreeParameters object, an object that stores various attributes of our tree. Multiple trees can use the same CaduneTreeParameters object to create multiple trees that look alike. These objects are not directly part of OGRE 3D; they are provided by an addon for OGRE, Cadune Tree. But Lugre already includes a lot of extensions and addons for OGRE to make your life easier.

The tree itself consists of two different GFX objects, one for the stem and another one for its leaves. These two objects need to be placed at a specific position within our scene. We will place the tree-creation in a small auxiliary function so we can quickly create different trees without having to copy and paste a lot of code. Create the following function above the main function, as it needs to be visible there:

```
local function CreateTree(leaves, leafScale, leafMaterial, x, y, z)
    local p = CreateCaduneTreeParameters()
    p:SetNumLeaves(leaves)
    p:SetLeafScale(leafScale)
    p:SetLeafMaterial(leafMaterial)
    local s = CreateCaduneTreeStem(p)
    s:Grow()
    local gfx_stem = s:CreateGeometry()
    local gfx_leav = s:CreateLeaves()
    gfx_stem:SetPosition(x, y, z)
    gfx_leav:SetPosition(x, y, z)
    return s
end
```

The function takes three parameters that determine the look of the leaves, followed by three parameters that define the position of the tree in our small scene. We can now create our first tree by placing the following line into the main function at the point where we previously deleted the old example code:

```
local s1 = CreateTree(10, 3, "Leaves/Ivylite", -10, -10, 10)
```

This creates a nice-looking tree in the left area of our scene. You can play around with the parameters to modify how the tree looks. Add the following line to create a second tree in the right half of the screen:

```
local s2 = CreateTree(3, 5, "Leaves/Orange", 10, -10, 10)
```

This creates a tree with a different type of leaves and different parameters. We now need a sky with a sun and moon for our scene.

The Sky

The object we are going to use here is, like the tree object, not directly a part of OGRE 3D but of an additional library included in Lugre, in this case Caelum. It does more than simply display a skybox with a sun and a few clouds; it provides an entire universe for our small scene. It displays a sun and a few clouds or a moon and stars depending on the time. The time can be set and it automatically moves forward with a specified multiplier, so we can easily achieve a day and night effect without writing a lot of code.

Place the following lines right under the code that creates the two trees:

```
local caelum = CreateCaelumCaelumSystem(
    CAELUM_COMPONENT_SKY_DOME +
    CAELUM_COMPONENT_SUN +
    CAELUM_COMPONENT_CLOUDS +
    CAELUM_COMPONENT_MOON +
    CAELUM_COMPONENT_IMAGE_STARFIELD
)
```

We now have a simple sky in our scene, but our trees have lost their color: they are gray now. We need to set a few parameters that define how the Caelum object can control the ambient light and fog in our scene. Add the following code to get realistic colors for our trees:

```
caelum:SetManageSceneFog(true)
caelum:SetSceneFogDensityMultiplier(0.0001)
caelum:SetManageAmbientLight(true)
```

The scene still looks static, because we haven't defined a time scale yet. This means that the time runs in real-time, so you'd need to wait a few hours until it turns night in our little universe. But we can speed this up by calling `SetTimeScale` on the `UniversalClock` object that is tied to the Caelum:

```
caelum:GetUniversalClock():SetTimeScale(1000)
```

You can play around with the parameters to achieve different effects. We have created a simple scene, but you can now see that it is possible to create a whole game with this engine.

Documentation

There are many very good web sites out there if you want to learn more about Lugre and OGRE:

http://lugre.schattenkind.net/index.php/Main_Page: The official Lugre wiki with a tutorial that covers creating a simple Pong game with Lugre.

http://www.ogre3d.org: The web site of the OGRE 3D project, the 3D engine used by Lugre. There are many exciting tutorials, along with documentation for the API and its addons.

Summary

In this chapter you saw that Lua can be used for more than just World of Warcraft. It is embedded as a scripting language in many games and applications. The language is the same in all of the platforms; only the provided API that consists of functions, variables, and objects differs.

But Lua can not only be used inside another application; there are frameworks available that allow you to write a full stand-alone application in Lua. We saw the framework Lugre here, which allows you to write a complete game with just Lua. But there are hundreds of other frameworks out there that add exciting functionality to a Lua program. There are many possible ways to use Lua, if writing World of Warcraft addons ever becomes boring. A list with numerous libraries and bindings that allow you to use other libraries or frameworks can be found at `http://lua-users.org/wiki/LibrariesAndBindings`.

Frame Reference

This appendix contains information on all the frame types that you can create in World of Warcraft, with all the XML attributes and elements as well as all Lua methods and available script handlers. Frame types follow an object-oriented model, meaning that a frame type can inherit attributes and methods from another frame type. You can find an introduction to object-oriented programming in Chapter 6 if you are not familiar with this topic.

You may wonder why there is such an appendix in this book, as you can probably find most of the information covered here on the Internet. WoWWiki has a few good pages that deal with exactly the same topic as this appendix. However, the information there is scattered over multiple pages and many of the articles are outdated or incomplete. This appendix is up to date as of patch 3.1 (the next patches probably won't change anything important in the frame API) and contains everything you need to know about a particular frame type in one place.

Object

Object is an abstract frame type; that is, you cannot create frames from this type. But this type is the base class for all other frame types as every other type inherits from Object. This means that all of the methods, XML attributes, and XML elements listed here are available for all frames.

This frame type is sometimes also called UIObject, which is probably the type's internal name used in the C++ code of the game.

XML Attributes

The Object type has the following XML attributes.

alpha

Defines the frame's transparency (0 – 1). Default: 1.

parent

Defines the frame's parent.

name

Defines the frame's name.

inherits

The template to use.

virtual

Creates a template. Default: `false`.

Lua Methods

The `Object` type has the following Lua methods.

object:GetAlpha()

Returns the frame's alpha value.

object:GetEffectiveAlpha()

Returns the frame's effective alpha value by multiplying its alpha value with the parent's effective alpha.

object:GetName()

Returns the name of the frame.

object:GetObjectType()

Returns the type of the `object`.

object:GetParent()

Returns the parent of the frame.

object:IsObjectType(objType)

Returns 1 if `object` is of the type `objType`, or of a type that inherits from `objType`. For example, `CreateFrame("CheckButton"):IsObjectType("Button")` returns 1 because the type `CheckButton` inherits from the type `Button`.

object:SetAlpha()

Sets the frame's transparency (0 – 1).

object:SetParent(obj)

Sets the frame's parent.

Font

Font is an object that inherits from Object and represents a font that can be used by FontStrings or Buttons.

XML Attributes

The Font type has the following XML attributes.

font

The path to the font file you want to use.

justifyH

Sets the horizontal justification setting. This can either be LEFT, RIGHT, or CENTER. Default: CENTER.

justifyV

Sets the vertical justification setting. This can either be BOTTOM, TOP, or MIDDLE. Default: MIDDLE.

monochrome

Uses a monochrome font. Default: false.

outline

The outline to use; can be NONE, NORMAL, or THICK. Default: NONE.

spacing

The spacing between characters. Default: 0.

XML Elements

The Font type has the following XML elements.

FontHeight

Controls the height of the font with its Value attribute.

Color

Controls the color of the font with its r, g, b, and a attributes.

Shadow

Contains the two elements Color and Offset. Color controls the color with the attributes r, g, b, and a, and Offset controls the shadow offset with one of the elements AbsDimension or RelDimension.

Lua Methods

The Font type has the following Lua methods.

font:CopyFontObject(*otherObject*)

Copies all settings from *otherObject*.

font:GetFont()

Returns the font file used.

font:GetFontObject()

Returns the font object itself. This method makes sense when called from a frame that inherits from Font.

font:GetJustifyH()

Returns the horizontal alignment of the text.

font:GetJustifyV()

Returns the vertical alignment of the text.

font:GetMultilineIndent()

Returns the multiline indention setting.

font:GetShadowColor()

Returns the color of the font's shadow.

font:GetShadowOffset()

Returns the offset of the shadow.

font:GetSpacing()

Returns the spacing between characters.

font:GetTextColor()

Returns the color of the text.

`font:SetFont(`*path*`)`

Sets the font file to use.

`font:SetFontObject(`*font*`)`

This method makes sense only when called from a frame (such as a `MessageFrame`) that inherits from a `Font`. This method can then set or change the used font object for the text of the frame.

`font:SetJustifyH(`*align*`)`

Sets the horizontal justification setting. The *align* argument can be `LEFT`, `RIGHT`, or `CENTER`.

`font:SetJustifyV(`*align*`)`

Sets the vertical justification setting. The *align* argument can be `TOP`, `BOTTOM`, or `MIDDLE`.

`font:SetMultilineIndent(`*indent*`)`

Controls whether to indent the continuation of a string that does not fit in a single line.

`font:SetShadowColor(`*r, g, b, a*`)`

Sets the color of the shadow.

`font:SetShadowOffset(`*x, y*`)`

Sets the offset of the shadow.

`font:SetSpacing(`*n*`)`

Sets the spacing between characters.

`font:SetTextColor(`*r, g, b, a*`)`

Sets the color of the text.

Region

`Region` inherits from `Object`. The only way to create a `Region` is by calling `frame:CreateTitleRegion()` or using the XML element `TitleRegion` of a frame; you cannot use `CreateFrame` to create a `Region`. It is the base class for everything that is visible on your screen (`Frame`, `Texture`, and so on), as it defines sizes and anchors.

XML Attributes

The `Region` type has the following XML attributes.

setAllPoints

Fits the frame into its parent. Default: `false`.

hidden

Defines whether the frame starts visible or hidden. Default: `false`.

XML Elements

The `Region` type has the following XML elements.

Size

`Size` consists of either the element `AbsDimension` or `RelDimension`. The former refers to an absolute size that depends only on the effective scale of the frame, while the latter refers to a size relative to the whole screen. Both have the attributes *x* and *y* that specify the actual size. A detailed description can be found in Chapter 5.

Anchors

Consists of one or more Anchor elements. An anchor has the attributes `Point`, `RelativePoint`, and `RelativeTo` and the element `Offset` which, like `Size`, consists of `AbsDimension` or `RelDimension` and specifies the offset. A detailed description can be found in Chapter 5.

Lua Methods

The `Region` type has the following Lua methods.

region:ClearAllPoints()

Removes all points but does not change the position. You have to set a new point in order to move the frame.

region:GetBottom()

Returns the *y* coordinate of the frame's bottom.

region:GetCenter()

Returns the *x* and *y* coordinates of the frame's center.

region:GetHeight()

Retrieves the frame's height.

region:GetLeft()

Returns the *x* coordinate of the frame's left border.

region:GetNumPoints()

Returns the number of anchor points.

region:GetPoint(*n*)

Retrieves the *n*th point of the frame. The return values are equivalent to the arguments passed to SetPoint when creating the anchor.

region:GetRect()

Returns the frame's bottom left *x* and *y* coordinates followed by the width and height.

region:GetTop()

Returns the *y* coordinate of the frame's top.

region:GetWidth()

Returns the width of the frame.

region:Hide()

Hides the frame.

region:IsProtected()

Returns 1 if the frame is a protected frame.

region:IsShown()

Determines whether the frame is shown. This does not take the frame's parent into account; see IsVisible.

region:IsVisible()

Determines whether the frame and all of its parents (and grandparents, and so on) are shown.

region:SetAllPoints(*frame*)

Stretches the frame to fit into *frame*.

region:SetHeight(*height*)

Sets the frame's height.

region:SetPoint(*point, relativeFrame, relativePoint, x, y*)

Adds an anchor point. See Chapter 5 for a detailed description.

region:SetWidth(*width*)

Sets the frame's width.

`region:StopAnimating()`

Stops all currently playing animations.

`region:GetAnimationGroups()`

Returns all animation groups of the frame.

`region:CreateAnimationGroup(`*`name, inherits`*`)`

Creates a new animation group for the frame.

`region:IsDragging()`

Determines whether the user is currently dragging the frame or its parent.

`region:CanChangeProtectedState()`

Determines whether you are allowed to call a protected method from tainted code at the moment.

Frame

`Frame` inherits from `Region`, which means it has all the methods and attributes of `Object` and `Region`.

XML Attributes

The `Frame` type has the following XML attributes.

`toplevel`

Fits the frame into its parent. Default: `false`.

`movable`

Defines whether the frame starts visible or hidden. Default: `false`.

`resizable`

Makes the frame resizable. Default: `false`.

`frameStrata`

Defines the frame strata. Frame strata are described in Chapter 5.

`framelevel`

Defines the level of the frame.

enableMouse

Enables mouse input. Default: `false`.

enableKeyboard

Enables keyboard input. Default: `false`.

clampedToScreen

Prevents the frame from being dragged off the screen. Default: `false`.

jumpNavigateEnabled

Allows the element to be selected with a gamepad or joystick.

jumpNavigateStart

Sets the frame as first frame to be selected when using a gamepad or joystick. Default: `false`.

XML Elements

The `Frame` type has the following XML elements.

TitleRegion

A frame of the type `Region`, which is used as the title region of the frame.

ResizeBounds

Consists of the two elements `MinResize` and `MaxResize`, which can contain an `AbsDimension` or a `RelDimension` element defining the minimum and maximum size of the frame.

Backdrop

Defines the backdrop. A detailed description is available in Chapter 5.

HitRectInsets

Sets the rectangle in which the frame accepts mouse clicks via the attributes left, right, top, and bottom.

Layers

Contains multiple `Layer` elements, which in turn may contain multiple `Textures` or `FontStrings`. A detailed description is available in Chapter 5.

Frames

Contains multiple frames of any type that inherits from `Frame`.

Scripts

Contains the script handlers.

Lua Methods

The Frame type has the following Lua methods.

frame:AllowAttributeChanges()

A protected method. Allows tainted code to change attributes in the current execution path while in combat.

frame:CreateFontString(*name, layer, inheritsFrom*)

Creates a new FontString object in the layer layer as child of the frame.

frame:CreateTexture()

Creates a new Texture object in the layer as child of the frame.

frame:CreateTitleRegion()

Creates a new TitleRegion, a frame of the type Region. A title region comes with predefined script handlers (unchangeable, because SetScript doesn't exist for Regions) for OnDragStart and OnDragStop; these handlers call StartMoving and StopMovingOrSizing respectively on the Region's parent if it is movable.

frame:DisableDrawLayer(*layerLevel*)

Hides the given layer level.

frame:EnableDrawLayer(*layerLevel*)

Displays the given layer level.

frame:EnableJoystick()

Enables joystick and gamepad input for the frame.

frame:EnableKeyboard()

Enables keyboard events.

frame:EnableMouse()

Enables mouse events.

frame:EnableMouseWheel()

Enables mouse wheel events.

`frame:GetAttribute(`*`attr`*`)`

Returns the value of *attr*.

`frame:GetBackdrop()`

Returns the frame's backdrop as a table in the same format as `SetBackdrop` expects it.

`frame:GetBackdropBorderColor()`

Returns the color of the backdrop's border.

`frame:GetBackdropColor()`

Returns the color of the backdrop.

`frame:GetBoundsRect()`

Like `GetRect` but takes the frame's layers into account.

`frame:GetChildren()`

Returns how many children the frame has.

`frame:GetClampRectInsets()`

Returns all children of the frame.

`frame:GetDepth()`

Get the frame's depth on 3D monitors.

`frame:GetEffectiveDepth()`

Returns the frame's effective depth by taking the parent's depth into account.

`frame:GetEffectiveScale()`

Returns the effective scale of the frame.

`frame:GetFrameLevel()`

Returns the frame level, which determines whether a frame is in front of or behind another frame in the same stratum.

`frame:GetFrameStrata()`

Returns the stratum the frame is in.

`frame:GetHitRectInsets()`

Returns the rectangle that defines where the frame can be clicked.

frame:GetMaxResize()

Returns the maximum width and height the frame can be resized to by the user.

frame:GetMinResize()

Returns the minimum width and height.

frame:GetNumChildren()

Returns all children of the frame.

frame:GetNumRegions()

Returns the number of regions in the frame.

frame:GetRegions()

Returns all regions (Textures and FontStrings) of the frame.

frame:GetScale()

Returns the frame's scale.

frame:GetScript(*script*)

Returns the function assigned to ScriptHandler.

frame:GetTitleRegion()

Returns the title region of the frame.

frame:HasScript(*script*)

Determines whether the frame can have the script handler *script*.

frame:HookScript(*script, func*)

Hooks the script handler *script* with the function *func*.

frame:IgnoreDepth(ignore)

Displays the frame in the default depth if ignore is true.

frame:IsClampedToScreen()

Determines whether the frame is clamped to the screen.

frame:IsEventRegistered(*event*)

Determines whether *event* is registered.

`frame:IsIgnoringDepth()`

Returns true if IgnoreDepth was called with true.

`frame:IsJoystickEnabled()`

Returns true if the frame accepts joystick and gamepad input.

`frame:IsJumpNavigateEnabled()`

Determines whether the frame can be selected with a joystick or gamepad.

`frame:IsJumpNavigateStart()`

Returns 1 if the frame is the first frame that is selected in an environment with a gamepad or joystick instead of a mouse.

`frame:IsKeyboardEnabled()`

Returns 1 if the frame receives keyboard events.

`frame:IsMouseEnabled()`

Returns 1 if the frame receives mouse events.

`frame:IsMouseWheelEnabled()`

Returns 1 if the frame receives mouse wheel events.

`frame:IsMovable()`

Returns 1 if the frame is movable.

`frame:IsResizable()`

Returns 1 if the frame is resizable.

`frame:IsToplevel()`

Returns 1 if the frame is a top-level frame.

`frame:IsUserPlaced()`

Returns 1 if the userplaced attribute is set.

`frame:Lower()`

Reduces the frame's level.

`frame:Raise()`

Increases the frame's level.

frame:RegisterAllEvents()

Registers all available events for debugging purposes.

frame:RegisterEvent(*event*)

Registers the given event.

frame:RegisterForDrag(*btn1*, ...)

Enables the OnDragStart/Stop handlers for the given mouse buttons.

frame:SetAttribute(*attribute*, *value*)

Sets *attribute* to *value*.

frame:SetBackdrop(*backDrop*)

Sets the frame's backdrop; *backDrop* is a table in the following format:

```
{
    bgFile = "bgFile", edgeFile = "edgeFile", tile = false,
    tileSize = 16, edgeSize = 32,
    insets = {left = 0, right = 0, top = 0, bottom = 0}
}
```

A description of backdrops can be found in Chapter 5.

frame:SetBackdropBorderColor(*r*, *g*, *b*, *a*)

Sets the border color of the backdrop.

frame:SetBackdropColor(*r*, *g*, *b*, *a*)

Sets the background color of the background.

frame:SetClampRectInsets(*x*, *y*, *width*, *height*)

Sets the rectangle that is used to determine whether the frame is on or off the screen.

frame:SetClampedToScreen(*clamped*)

Prevents the user from dragging the frame off the screen.

frame:SetDepth(*depth*)

Sets the frame's depth on 3D monitors.

frame:SetFrameLevel(*level*)

Sets the frame's level.

`frame:SetFrameStrata(strata)`

Sets the frame's strata.

`frame:SetHitRectInsets(x, y, width, height)`

Sets the rectangle in which the frame accepts mouse clicks.

`frame:SetID(id)`

Sets the ID of the frame.

`frame:SetJumpNavigateEnabled(enabled)`

Makes the frame selectable with a gamepad or joystick.

`frame:SetMaxResize(width, height)`

Sets the maximum size of the frame.

`frame:SetMinResize(width, height)`

Sets the minimum size of the frame.

`frame:SetMovable(movable)`

Makes the frame movable with `StartMoving`.

`frame:SetResizable(movable)`

Makes the frame resizable.

`frame:SetScale(scale)`

Sets the scale of the frame.

`frame:SetScript(script, func)`

Sets the script handler for *script* to *func*.

`frame:SetToplevel(topLevel)`

Makes the frame a top-level frame.

`frame:SetUserPlaced(userPlaced)`

Saves the position of the frame.

`frame:StartMoving()`

Attaches the frame to your mouse cursor.

frame:StartSizing()

Starts to resize the frame.

frame:StopMovingOrSizing()

Stops resizing or moving the frame.

frame:UnregisterAllEvents()

Unregisters all events.

frame:UnregisterEvent(event)

Unregisters the given event.

Script Handlers

The Frame type has the following script handlers.

OnAnimFinished(*self*)

OnAttributeChanged(*self, attributeName, value*)

OnCursorChanged(*self, x, y, w, h*)

OnDoubleClick(*self, button*)

OnDragStart(*self, button*)

OnDragStop(*self*)

OnEnter(*self, motion*)

OnEnterPressed(*self*)

OnEscapePressed(*self*)

OnEvent(*self, event, ...*)

OnHide(*self*)

OnKeyDown(*self, key*)

OnKeyUp(*self, key*)

OnLeave(*self, motion*)

OnLoad(*self*)

OnMouseDown(*self, button*)

OnMouseUp(*self, button*)

OnMouseWheel(*self, delta*)

OnReceiveDrag(*self*)

OnShow(*self*)

OnSizeChanged(*self, width, height*)

OnSpacePressed(*self*)

OnTabPressed(*self*)

OnUpdate(*self, elapsed*)

FontString

FontString inherits from Region. You cannot create a FontString via CreateFrame; you have to create it by calling the method CreateFontString of a frame object or by defining it in the <Layers> element in the XML description of a frame.

FontStrings have all methods of Fonts except for CopyFontObject. However, FontStrings do not inherit from Font; fontstring:IsObjectType("Font") returns nil.

XML Attribute

The FontString type has only one XML attribute.

text

The text on the button.

Lua Methods

The FontString type has the following Lua methods.

fontString:CanNonSpaceWrap()

Returns 1 if the font string is set to wrap in the middle of a word.

fontString:GetDrawLayer()

Returns the layer the font string is in. Layers are explained in detail in Chapter 5.

fontString:GetStringHeight()

Returns the height needed by the font string.

fontString:GetStringWidth()

Returns the width of the font string.

fontString:GetText()

Returns the displayed text.

fontString:SetAlphaGradient(*start, length*)

Creates an alpha gradient starting at start over length pixels.

fontString:SetDrawLayer(*layer*)

Changes the draw layer.

fontString:SetFormattedText(*fmtStr*, ...)

Sets formatted text.

fontString:SetNonSpaceWrap(*nonSpace*)

Controls whether the font string is allowed to wrap in the middle of a string.

fontString:SetText(*text*)

Sets the text.

fontString:SetTextHeight(*height*)

Sets the text height.

fontString:SetVertexColor(*r*, *g*, *b*, *a*)

Sets the vertex color of the font string.

Texture

Texture inherits from Region. You cannot create a Texture via CreateFrame; you have to create it by calling the method CreateTexture of a frame object or by defining it in the <Layers> element in the XML description of a frame.

XML Attributes

The Texture type has the following XML attributes.

alphaMode

Controls the effect of the texture's alpha channel. This can be one of the following values: DISABLE, BLEND (default), ALPHAKEY, ADD, or MOD.

file

The file containing the texture to display.

XML Elements

The Texture type has the following XML elements.

Color

Sets the texture to a solid color, with the attributes *r*, *g*, *b*, and *a*.

Gradient

Creates a gradient on the texture; the attribute *orientation* of this element controls the orientation and can either be HORIZONTAL (default) or VERTICAL. The two elements MinColor and MaxColor of the Gradient element set the start and end color.

TexCoords

Controls the texture coordinates with the attributes *left*, *right*, *top*, and *bottom*.

Lua Methods

The Texture type has the following Lua methods.

texture:GetBlendMode()

Returns the blend mode.

texture:GetDrawLayer()

Returns the draw layer.

texture:GetTexCoordModifiesRect()

Returns 1 if texture coordinates modify the display rectangle and nil if they stretch the texture.

texture:GetTexture()

Returns the path of the texture used.

texture:GetVertexColor()

Returns the vertex color.

texture:IsDesaturated()

Returns 1 if the texture is desaturated.

texture:SetBlendMode()

Sets the blend mode.

texture:SetDesaturated(*desaturated*)

Changes the desaturation state of the texture.

texture:SetDrawLayer(*layer*)

Changes the draw layer.

texture:SetGradient(*orientation, startR, startG, startB, endR, endG, endB*)

Creates a gradient over the whole texture. The *orientation* argument can be either HORIZONTAL or VERTICAL.

texture:SetGradientAlpha(*orientation, startR, startG, startB, startA, endR, endG, endB, endA*)

Same as SetGradient but with an additional alpha value.

texture:SetRotation(*angle, cx, cy*)

Rotates the texture *angle* degrees around the center point *cx*/*cy*, which is relative to the center of the texture. Default values for *cx* and *cy* are 0.

texture:SetTexCoord(*left, right, bottom, top*)

Sets texture coordinates. Chapter 8 contains a detailed description.

texture:SetTexCoordModifiesRect(*modifies*)

Sets whether texture coordinates change the displayed part of the texture or stretch the texture.

texture:SetTexture(*file* or *r, g, b, a*)

Loads and displays the provided files or fills the texture with a solid color.

texture:SetVertexColor(*r, g, b, a*)

Sets the vertex color of the texture. You can think of the vertex color as a colored light shining on the texture.

Button

Button inherits from Frame; it can be used to create clickable buttons.

XML Attributes

The Button type has only one XML attribute.

text

The text on the button.

XML Elements

The Button type has the following XML elements.

ButtonText

The font string that is used for the button's text.

DisabledColor

A color object (uses r, g, b, and a attributes); sets the vertex color for the disabled texture.

DisabledFont

Sets the font for the disabled button in its *style* attribute (expects the name of a Font object).

DisabledTexture

A texture object; sets the disabled button texture.

HighlightColor

A color object; sets the vertex color for the highlight texture.

HighlightFont

Sets the font for the highlighted button in its *style* attribute (expects the name of a Font object).

HighlightTexture

A texture object. The highlight button texture.

NormalFont

Sets the font for the normal button in its *style* attribute (expects the name of a Font object).

NormalTexture

A texture object; sets the normal button texture.

PushedTextOffset

A dimension object that defines the text offset when the button is pushed.

PushedTexture

A texture object; sets the pushed button texture.

Lua Methods

The Button type has the following Lua methods.

button:Click()

Executes the button's OnClick handler.

button:Disable()

Disables the button.

button:Enable()

Enables the button.

button:GetButtonState()

"PUSHED" or "NORMAL".

button:GetDisabledFontObject()

Returns the disabled font object.

button:GetDisabledTexture()

Returns the disabled texture.

button:GetFontString()

Returns the used font string.

button:GetHighlightFontObject()

Returns the highlight font object.

button:GetHighlightTexture()

Returns the highlight texture.

button:GetNormalFontObject()

Returns the normal font object.

button:GetNormalTexture()

Returns the normal texture.

button:GetPushedTextOffset()

Returns the x and y offsets of the pushed text.

button:GetPushedTexture()

Returns the pushed texture.

button:GetText()

Returns the displayed text.

button:GetTextHeight()

Returns the text's height.

button:GetTextWidth()

Returns the text's width.

button:IsEnabled()

Checks whether the button is enabled.

button:LockHighlight()

Shows the highlight texture.

button:RegisterForClicks(*btn1*, ...)

Registers the given mouse buttons for click events.

button:SetButtonState()

Sets the button's state ("NORMAL" or "PUSHED").

button:SetDisabledFontObject(*font*)

Sets the disabled font object.

button:SetDisabledTexture(*texture*)

Sets the disabled texture.

button:SetFontString(*fntStr*)

Sets the FontString object used.

button:SetFormattedText(*formatStr*, ...)

Sets formatted text.

button:SetHighlightFontObject(*font*)

Sets the highlight font object.

button:SetHighlightTexture(*texture*)

Sets the highlight texture.

button:SetNormalFontObject(*font*)

Sets the normal font object.

button:SetNormalTexture(*texture*)

Sets the normal texture.

button:SetPushedTextOffset(*x*, *y*)

Sets the pushed text's offsets.

button:SetPushedTexture(*texture*)

Sets the pushed texture.

button:SetText(*text*)

Sets the displayed text.

button:UnlockHighlight()

Hides the highlight texture.

Script Handlers

The Button type has the following script handlers.

```
PostClick(self, button)
PreClick(self, button)
OnClick(self, button, down)
```

CheckButton

CheckButton inherits from Button and represents a check box.

XML Attributes

The CheckButton type has only one XML attribute.

checked

Can be set to true to check the button by default.

XML Elements

The CheckButton type has the following XML elements.

DisabledCheckedTexture

A texture object; sets the texture that is shown on disabled checked buttons.

CheckedTexture

A texture object; sets the texture that is shown on normal checked buttons.

Lua Methods

The CheckButton type has the following Lua methods.

checkButton:GetChecked()

Returns 1 if the button is checked.

checkButton:GetCheckedTexture()

Returns the texture object of checked buttons.

checkButton:GetDisabledCheckedTexture()

Returns the texture object of disabled checked buttons.

checkButton:SetChecked(checked)

Sets the check button to checked.

checkButton:SetCheckedTexture(*texture*)

Sets the normal checked texture.

checkButton:SetDisabledCheckedTexture(*texture*)

Sets the disabled checked texture.

Cooldown

Cooldown is the cooldown display that can be seen on action bars. It inherits from Frame.

XML Attributes

The Cooldown type has the following XML attributes.

reverse

Set this to true for a reverse cooldown. Default: false.

drawEdge

Set this to true to draw edges around the cooldown display. Default: false.

Lua Methods

The Cooldown type has the following Lua methods.

cooldown:SetCooldown(*start, duration*)

Displays a cooldown that started at start (timestamp as returned by GetTime() and GetSpellCooldown(*spellName*)) with the given duration in seconds.

cooldown:SetReverse(reverse)

Set this to true for a reverse cooldown.

ColorSelect

ColorSelect is a frame that allows the user to pick a color. This frame type inherits from Frame.

XML Elements

The ColorSelect type has the following XML attributes.

ColorWheelTexture

A texture object that is used for the color wheel.

ColorWheelThumbTexture

A texture object that is used for the color wheel thumbnail.

ColorValueTexture

A texture object that is used for the color selector.

ColorValueThumbTexture

A texture object that is used for the color selector thumbnail.

Lua Methods

The ColorSelect type has the following Lua methods.

colorSelect:GetColorHSV()

Returns the selected color as HSV (hue, saturation, value) values.

colorSelect:GetColorRGB()

Returns the selected color as RGB.

colorSelect:GetColorValueTexture()

Returns the color value texture object.

`colorSelect:GetColorValueThumbTexture()`

Returns the color value thumbnail texture object.

`colorSelect:GetColorWheelTexture()`

Returns the color wheel texture.

`colorSelect:GetColorWheelThumbTexture()`

Returns the color wheel thumbnail texture.

`colorSelect:SetColorHSV(h, s, v)`

Sets the selected color to the given HSV value.

`colorSelect:SetColorRGB(r, g, b)`

Sets the selected color to the given RGB value.

`colorSelect:SetColorValueTexture(texture)`

Sets the color value texture.

`colorSelect:SetColorValueThumbTexture()`

Sets the color value thumb texture.

`colorSelect:SetColorWheelTexture()`

Sets the color wheel texture.

`colorSelect:SetColorWheelThumbTexture()`

Sets the color wheel thumb texture.

Script Handlers

The `ColorSelect` type has only one script handler.

`OnColorSelect(self, r, g, b)`

EditBox

`EditBox` is a frame that allows the user to enter text. It inherits from `Frame`. `EditBox`es have all methods of `Fonts` except for `CopyFontObject`. However, `EditBox`es do not inherit from `Font`; `editBox:IsObjectType("Font")` returns `nil`.

XML Attributes

The EditBox type has the following XML attributes.

autofocus

Automatically grabs the focus when it is shown. Default: false.

blinkSpeed

The blink speed of the cursor. Default: 0.5.

historyLines

Determines how many history lines will be saved. Default: 0.

ignoreArrows

Ignores the arrow keys so you can still move with them while the edit box has the focus. Default: false.

letters

The maximum number of allowed letters. Default 0: (meaning no limit).

multiLine

Creates a multiple-line edit box. Default: false.

numeric

Accepts only numbers. Default: false.

XML Elements

The EditBox type has the following two XML attributes.

HighlightColor

A color element that sets the color of highlighted text with its r, g, and b attributes.

TextInsets

Controls the padding between the text and border with its left, right, top, and bottom attributes.

Lua Methods

The EditBox type has the following Lua methods.

editBox:AddHistoryLine(*text*)

Adds *text* to the history.

editBox:ClearFocus()

Removes the focus from the edit box.

editBox:GetAltArrowKeyMode()

Returns 1 if the edit box ignores the arrow keys.

editBox:GetBlinkSpeed()

Returns the blink speed.

editBox:GetCursorPosition()

Returns the cursor position.

editBox:GetHistoryLines()

Returns the maximum number of history lines.

editBox:GetIndentedWordWrap()

Returns the indented word wrap setting.

editBox:GetInputLanguage()

Returns the input language; "ROMAN" for non-Asian clients.

editBox:GetMaxBytes()

Returns the maximum number of bytes the edit box can store.

editBox:GetMaxLetters()

Returns the maximum number of letters the edit box can store.

editBox:GetNumLetters()

Returns the current number of letters.

editBox:GetNumber()

Tries to interpret the entered text as a number.

editBox:GetTextInsets()

Returns the text insets.

editBox:HasFocus()

Returns 1 if the edit box currently has the focus.

editBox:HighlightText(*start, end*)

Highlights the text from *start* to *end*. Omit the arguments to highlight the whole text.

editBox:Insert(*text*)

Inserts *text* at the current position.

editBox:IsAutoFocus()

Returns 1 if the edit box automatically grabs the focus.

editBox:IsInIMECompositionMode()

Returns 1 if the IME mode is enabled. This is a feature for Asian clients.

editBox:IsMultiLine()

Returns 1 for multiple-line edit boxes.

editBox:IsNumeric()

Returns 1 for numeric edit boxes.

editBox:IsPassword()

Returns 1 for password edit boxes.

editBox:SetAltArrowKeyMode(*ignoreArrows*)

Sets the option whether to ignore arrow keys.

editBox:SetAutoFocus(*autoFocus*)

Sets the auto focus option.

editBox:SetBlinkSpeed(*blinkSpeed*)

Sets the cursor blink speed.

editBox:SetCursorPosition(*pos*)

Sets the cursor position.

editBox:SetFocus()

Grabs the focus.

editBox:SetHistoryLines(*n*)

Sets the maximum number of history lines.

editBox:SetIndentedWordWrap(*wrap*)

Sets the word wrap setting.

editBox:SetMaxBytes(*n*)

Sets the maximum number of bytes accepted by the edit box.

editBox:SetMaxLetters(*n*)

Sets the maximum number of letters accepted by the edit box.

editBox:SetMultiLine(*multiLines*)

Creates a multiple-line edit box.

editBox:SetNumber(*n*)

Sets a numeric edit box to *n*.

editBox:SetNumeric()

Makes the edit box accept only numbers.

editBox:SetPassword()

Hides entered characters.

editBox:SetTextInsets(*left, right, top, bottom*)

Sets the padding between the text and the border of the edit box.

editBox:ToggleInputLanguage(*language*)

Uses another input language; only important for Asian clients.

Script Handlers

The EditBox type has the following script handlers.

```
OnChar(self, char)
OnCharComposition(self, char)
OnCursorChanged(self, x, y, width, height)
OnEditFocusGained(self)
OnEditFocusLost(self)
OnInputLanguageChanged(self, language)
OnTextChanged(self)
OnTextSet(self)
```

GameTooltip

GameTooltip frames can be used as tooltips. This type inherits from Frame. Tooltips are automatically resized as you add more lines with their methods.

Lua Methods

The GameTooltip method has the following Lua methods.

gameTooltip:AddDoubleLine(*left, right, lR, lG, lB, rR, rG, rB*)

Adds a line with two font strings to the tooltip. lR, lG, and lB control the color of the left text *left* and *rR, rG*, and *rB* the color of the right text code inline.

gameTooltip:AddFontStrings(*left, right*)

Adds a double line consisting of two font string objects to the tooltip.

gameTooltip:AddLine(*text, r, g, b*)

Adds a new single line.

gameTooltip:AddTexture(*texturePath*)

Adds the given texture file.

gameTooltip:AppendText(*text*)

Appends *text* to the end of the last line.

gameTooltip:FadeOut()

Fades the tooltip and hides it.

gameTooltip:ClearLines()

Removes all content from the tooltip.

gameTooltip:GetAnchorType()

Returns the current anchor type. These types are explained in Chapter 4.

gameTooltip:GetItem()

Returns the name and link of the currently displayed item.

gameTooltip:GetMinimumWidth()

Returns the minimum width of the tooltip.

gameTooltip:GetOwner()

Returns the tooltip's owner.

gameTooltip:GetPadding()

Returns the padding to other objects.

gameTooltip:GetSpell()

Returns the currently displayed spell.

gameTooltip:GetUnit()

Returns the currently displayed unit.

gameTooltip:IsEquippedItem()

Returns 1 if the tooltip displays a currently equipped item.

gameTooltip:IsOwned()

Returns 1 if the tooltip has an owner.

gameTooltip:IsUnit()

Returns 1 if the tooltip displays a unit.

gameTooltip:NumLines()

Returns the maximum number of lines.

gameTooltip:SetAction(*slotId*)

Shows the tooltip of a given action button slot.

gameTooltip:SetAnchorType(*anchorType, xOffset, yOffset*)

Sets an anchor type.

Setting Tooltip Contents

The following methods deal with setting the tooltip to specific items or spells. There is no description of these methods, as the names and arguments are self-explanatory and the functions are rarely needed.

```
gameTooltip:SetAuctionItem(index)

gameTooltip:SetAuctionSellItem()

gameTooltip:SetBackpackToken(id)

gameTooltip:SetBagItem(bad, slot)
```

```
gameTooltip:SetBuybackItem(id)

gameTooltip:SetCurrencyToken(id)

gameTooltip:SetEquipmentSet(id)

gameTooltip:SetExistingSocketGem(id)

gameTooltip:SetGlyph(id)

gameTooltip:SetGuildBankItem(id)

gameTooltip:SetHyperlink(link)

gameTooltip:SetHyperlinkCompareItem(link)

gameTooltip:SetInboxItem(id)

gameTooltip:SetInventoryItem(id)

gameTooltip:SetLootItem(id)

gameTooltip:SetLootRollItem(id)

gameTooltip:SetMerchantCostItem(id)

gameTooltip:SetMerchantItem(id)

gameTooltip:SetPetAction(id)

gameTooltip:SetQuestItem(quest, id)

gameTooltip:SetQuestLogItem(id)

gameTooltip:SetQuestLogRewardSpell(id)

gameTooltip:SetQuestLogSpecialItem(id)

gameTooltip:SetQuestRewardSpell(id)

gameTooltip:SetSendMailItem(id)

gameTooltip:SetShapeshift(id)

gameTooltip:SetSocketGem(id)

gameTooltip:SetSocketedItem(id)

gameTooltip:SetSpell(spellId)

gameTooltip:SetTalent(id)

gameTooltip:SetTotem(id)

gameTooltip:SetTracking(id)

gameTooltip:SetTradePlayerItem(id)

gameTooltip:SetTradeSkillItem(id)

gameTooltip:SetTradeTargetItem(id)

gameTooltip:SetTrainerService(id)

gameTooltip:SetUnit(uId)
```

gameTooltip:SetUnitAura(*uId, i, filter*)

gameTooltip:SetUnitBuff(*uId, i, filter*)

gameTooltip:SetUnitDebuff(*uId, i, filter*)

gameTooltip:SetMinimumWidth(*width*)
Sets the minimum width.

gameTooltip:SetOwner(*frame*)
Sets the owner of the tooltip. A tooltip is hidden when its owner is hidden.

gameTooltip:SetPadding()
Sets the padding.

MessageFrame

MessageFrame is a frame that displays a few font strings; older font strings are hidden as you append new strings. It looks like a chat frame but without the scroll bars.

MessageFrame has all methods of Fonts except for CopyFontObject. However, MessageFrame does not inherit from Font; messageFrame:IsObjectType("Font") returns nil.

XML Attributes

The MessageFrame method has the following XML attributes.

displayDuration
The time after which an element is removed.

fade
Enables the fade out effect. Default: true.

fadeDuration
Duration of the fade effect. Default: 3.0.

font
The font used.

insertMode
Where to insert new messages; TOP or BOTTOM. Default: BOTTOM.

XML Elements

The MessageFrame type has one available XML element.

textInsets

Controls the padding of the displayed text with the attributes *left*, *right*, *top*, and *bottom*.

Lua Methods

The MessageFrame type has the following Lua methods.

messageFrame:AddMessage(*msg*, *r*, *g*, *b*)

Adds a message in the given color.

messageFrame:Clear()

Clears the frame.

messageFrame:GetFadeDuration()

Returns the fade duration.

messageFrame:GetFading()

Returns the duration of the fade effect.

messageFrame:GetInsertMode()

Returns the insert mode.

messageFrame:GetTimeVisible()

Returns the time after which a message is hidden.

messageFrame:SetFadeDuration(*fadeDuration*)

Sets the duration of the fade effect.

messageFrame:SetFading(*fadeOut*)

Enables or disables the fade effect.

messageFrame:SetInsertMode(*insertMode*)

Sets the insert mode (TOP or BOTTOM).

messageFrame:SetTimeVisible(*t*)

Sets the time after which a message is hidden.

Model

Model is a frame that inherits from Frame and displays a 3D model.

XML Attributes

The Model type has the following XML attributes.

file

The path of the model to display.

fogNear

The near fog distance. Default: 0.0.

fogFar

The far fog distance. Default: 1.0.

glow

The glow intensity. Default: 1.0.

scale

The scale of the model. This is a different value than the SetScale/GetScale scale.

XML Elements

The Model type has only one XML attribute.

FogColor

Controls the color of the fog with its r, g, b, and a attributes.

Lua Methods

The Model type has the following Lua methods.

model:AdvanceTime()

This must be called by the OnUpdate handler if you want to play animations in the model.

model:ClearFog()

Removes the fog.

model:ClearModel()

Removes the model.

`model:GetFacing()`

Returns the direction the model is looking in.

`model:GetFogColor()`

Returns the color of the fog.

`model:GetFogFar()`

Returns the maximum fog distance.

`model:GetFogNear()`

Returns the minimum fog distance.

`model:GetLight()`

Returns the current light situation. The return values are the same as the arguments to `SetLight`.

`model:GetModel()`

Returns the model used.

`model:GetModelScale()`

Returns the scale of the model.

`model:GetPosition()`

Returns the position of the model inside the displayed scene.

`model:ReplaceIconTexture()`

Unknown.

`model:SetCamera(id)`

Sets the camera to a camera that is defined in the model file.

`model:SetFacing(facing)`

Sets the facing to a radian value.

`model:SetFogColor(r, g, b, a)`

Sets the color of the fog.

`model:SetFogFar()`

Sets the fog's far clip distance.

`model:SetFogNear()`

Sets the fog's near clip distance.

`model:SetGlow(`*n*`)`

Sets the glow intensity.

`model:SetLight(`*enabled, omni, dirX, dirY, dirZ, ambIntensity,*➥
ambR, ambB, dirIntensity, dirR, dirG, dirB`)`

Sets the light to use; all arguments except the first are optional. You will rarely have to call this as the default light is fine.

`model:SetModel(`*path*`)`

Sets the model file to use.

`model:SetModelScale(`*scale*`)`

Scales the model.

`model:SetPosition(`*x, y, z*`)`

Places the model at position *x*, *y*, and *z* in the displayed scene.

`model:SetSequence(`*id*`)`

Sets the animation ID that will be played. This ID is defined in the model file.

`model:SetSequenceTime(`*id, time*`)`

Sets the model to a specific point in time of a specific sequence ID.

PlayerModel

`PlayerModel` is derived from `Model` and can be used to display players and NPCs.

Lua Methods

The `PlayerModel` type has the following Lua methods.

`playerModel:RefreshUnit()`

Refreshes the currently displayed unit; for example, to update the worn equipment.

`playerModel:SetCreature(`*creatureId*`)`

Sets the model to display the given creature. This only works on creatures in your local cache, meaning creatures you have already seen.

`playerModel:SetRotation(`*`rotation`*`)`

Rotates the model.

`playerModel:SetUnit(`*`unitID`*`)`

Displays the model of the given unit ID.

DressUpModel

`DressUpModel` inherits from `PlayerModel` and is a specialized version of it that provides functions to preview items.

Lua Methods

The `DressUpModel` type has the following Lua methods.

`playerModel:Dress()`

Equips the player's default equipment.

`playerModel:TryOn(`*`item`*`)`

Equips the given item link or item ID.

`playerModel:Undress()`

Undresses the displayed player.

TabardModel

`TabardModel` inherits from `PlayerModel` and is a specialized version of it that provides functions to preview guild tabards.

Lua Methods

The `TabardModel` type has the following Lua methods.

`tabardModel:CanSaveTabardNow()`

Returns 1 if the tabard can be saved.

`tabardModel:CycleVariation(`*`variationType, index`*`)`

Cycles through the different available options.

`tabardModel:GetLowerBackgroundFileName()`

Returns the filename of the lower background texture.

tabardModel:GetLowerEmblemFileName()

Returns the filename of the lower emblem texture.

tabardModel:GetLowerEmblemTexture()

Returns the lower emblem texture.

tabardModel:GetUpperBackgroundFileName()

Returns the filename of the upper background texture.

tabardModel:GetUpperEmblemFileName()

Returns the filename of the upper emblem texture.

tabardModel:GetUpperEmblemTexture()

Returns the upper emblem texture.

tabardModel:InitializeTabardColors()

Initializes the tabard frame.

tabardModel:Save()

Saves the tabard.

ScrollFrame

ScrollFrame inherits from Frame and represents a scroll bar that can be used to scroll another frame.

XML Elements

The ScrollFrame type has only one XML element.

ScrollChild

An arbitrary frame that is scrolled by the scroll bar.

Lua Methods

The ScrollFrame type has the following Lua methods.

scrollFrame:GetHorizontalScroll()

Returns the current scroll offset.

`scrollFrame:GetHorizontalScrollRange()`

Returns the maximum scroll range.

`scrollFrame:GetScrollChild()`

Returns the frame that is being scrolled by the scroll frame.

`scrollFrame:GetVerticalScroll()`

Returns the vertical scroll offset.

`scrollFrame:GetVerticalScrollRange()`

Returns the maximum vertical scroll range.

`scrollFrame:SetHorizontalScroll(offset)`

Sets the current horizontal scroll position.

`scrollFrame:SetScrollChild(frame)`

Sets `frame` as the scroll child, that is, the frame that is being scrolled.

`scrollFrame:SetVerticalScroll(offset)`

Sets the current vertical scroll position.

`scrollFrame:UpdateScrollChildRect()`

Updates the displayed area of the scroll child. This method is called automatically when the user scrolls in your frame.

Script Handlers

The `ScrollFrame` type has the following script handlers.

```
OnHorizontalScroll(self, offset)
OnScrollRangeChanged(self, xRange, yRange)
OnVerticalScroll(self, offset)
```

ScrollingMessageFrame

`ScrollingMessageFrame` is a frame type that is derived from `Frame`; it can be used to display multiple messages with a scroll bar, as in a chat frame.

ScrollingMessageFrame has all XML attributes and elements and Lua methods of `MessageFrame`. However, it is technically not a message frame, as `scrollingMessageFrame:IsObjectType("Font")` returns `nil`. The methods and attributes of `MessageFrame` are not listed here.

XML Attributes

The `ScrollingMessageFrame` type has only one XML attribute.

maxLines

The maximum number of lines that can be added to the scroll frame. Default: 8.

Lua Methods

The `ScrollingMessageFrame` type has the following Lua methods.

scrollingMessageFrame:AddMessage(*text, r, g, b, id, addToStart*)

Adds a message with the given color and ID. The ID can later be used to change the color of the message with `UpdateColorByID`. The *addToStart* argument can be used to insert the message at the opposite side from the default insert position.

scrollingMessageFrame:AtBottom()

Determines whether the frame is scrolled to the very bottom.

scrollingMessageFrame:AtTop()

Determines whether the frame is currently scrolled to the very top.

scrollingMessageFrame:GetCurrentLine()

Returns the line number of the last added message. Lines are zero-based; the first line has the line ID 0. Note that a message can consist of multiple lines.

scrollingMessageFrame:GetCurrentScroll()

Returns the number of messages that are currently not visible at the bottom.

scrollingMessageFrame:GetHyperlinksEnabled()

Determines whether hyperlinks are enabled or disabled in the scrolling message frame.

scrollingMessageFrame:GetMaxLines()

Returns the maximum number of lines that can be displayed.

scrollingMessageFrame:GetNumLinesDisplayed()

Returns the number of lines that are currently visible in the frame.

scrollingMessageFrame:GetNumMessages()

Returns the number of messages that were added to the scrolling message frame.

`scrollingMessageFrame:PageDown()`

Scrolls down by one page.

`scrollingMessageFrame:PageUp()`

Scrolls up by one page.

`scrollingMessageFrame:ScrollDown()`

Scrolls down.

`scrollingMessageFrame:ScrollUp()`

Scrolls up.

`scrollingMessageFrame:ScrollToBottom()`

Scrolls to the bottom.

`scrollingMessageFrame:ScrollToTop()`

Scrolls to the top.

`scrollingMessageFrame:SetHyperlinksEnabled(enabled)`

Enables or disables hyperlinks in the frame.

`scrollingMessageFrame:SetScrollOffset(offset)`

Scrolls to a given position from the bottom. Negative offsets will scroll to a position relative to the top.

`scrollingMessageFrame:UpdateColorByID(id, r, g, b)`

Changes the color of all messages inserted with the given *id*.

SimpleHTML

SimpleHTML is a frame type that is derived from Frame; it allows you to display simple HTML. You can read the Wikipedia article `http://en.wikipedia.org/wiki/HTML` if you are not familiar with HTML. The following elements are allowed in a SimpleHTML frame.

- `<a href="hyperlink">text</a>` to create links. Clicking on the link calls the OnHyperlinkClicked handler with the usual arguments. It is not possible to use URLs here.
- `<br/>` to start a new line.

- `<h1>`, `<h2>`, `<h3>`, and `<p>` for normal text. The attribute `align` can be used to control the text alignment and can be `left`, `right`, or `center`.

- `<img src="texturePath" align="left/right/center" width="x" height="y"/>` to embed images. All attributes except for `src` are optional.

You also need the obligatory `<html>` and `<body>` tags or World of Warcraft won't recognize your code as HTML. Your text should look like this:

```
<html>
   <body>
      <!-- your code here -->
   </body>
</html>
```

SimpleHTML has all the methods of `Font` except for `CopyFontObject`. But there is a small difference: all `Font` methods take an optional first parameter that can be either `"p"`, `"h1"`, `"h2"`, or `"h3"` to change the styles of the different available text types. The default value for this optional parameter is `"p"`.

All XML attributes and elements of `Font` are also available; they control the style of `<p>` tags. The elements `FontStringHeader1 – 3` can be used to set the style of `<h1> – <h3>` tags from XML.

XML Attributes

The `SimpleHTML` type has the following XML attributes.

file

An HTML file to load.

hyperlinkFormat

Defines how HTML links are displayed; this will be processed by `string.format` with the first argument being the target of your link and the second the text. The default value is `"|H%s|h%s|h"`, which means your link is displayed like a regular in-game link.

text

The HTML text to display.

XML Elements

The `SimpleHTML` type has only one XML element.

FontStringHeader1 – 3

`FontString` objects that are used for h1 – h3 styled texts.

Lua Methods

The `SimpleHTML` type has the following Lua methods.

simpleHTML:GetHyperlinkFormat()

Returns the hyperlink format.

simpleHTML:GetHyperlinksEnabled()

Returns whether hyperlinks are enabled.

simpleHTML:SetHyperlinkFormat(*fmt*)

Sets the hyperlink format.

simpleHTML:SetHyperlinksEnabled(*enabled*)

Enables or disables hyperlinks.

simpleHTML:SetText(html)

Sets the HTML to display.

Slider

Slider inherits from Frame and is a frame type to input numeric values.

XML Attributes

The Slider type has the following XML attributes.

defaultValue

The default value of the slider. Caution: this triggers the script handler OnValueChanged before OnLoad is called.

drawLayer

The layer in which the slider's textures will be drawn. Default: OVERLAY.

maxValue

The maximum value of the slider.

minValue

The minimum value of the slider.

orientation

HORIZONTAL or VERTICAL (default).

valueStep

The step size.

XML Elements

The Slider type has the following XML elements.

ThumbTexture

A texture object. This texture is used as a thumb (small draggable dot).

Lua Methods

The Slider type has the following Lua methods.

slider:Dislabe()

Disables the slider.

slider:Enable()

Enables the slider.

slider:GetMinMaxValues()

Returns the minimum and maximum values that can be set by the user.

slider:GetOrientation()

Returns the orientation; can be either HORIZONTAL or VERTICAL.

slider:GetThumbTexture()

Returns the thumb texture.

slider:GetValue()

Returns the current value.

slider:GetValueStep()

Returns the step size.

slider:IsEnabled()

Returns 1 if the slider is enabled.

slider:SetMinMaxValues(*min, max*)

Sets the minimum and maximum values.

slider:SetOrientation(*orientation*)

Sets the orientation; can be HORIZONTAL or VERTICAL.

slider:SetThumbTexture(*texture*)

Sets the thumb texture.

slider:SetValue(*val*)

Sets the current value.

slider:SetValueStep()

Sets the step size.

Script Handlers

The Slider type has only one script handler.

OnValueChanged(*self, value*)

StatusBar

StatusBar inherits from Frame and can be used to display progress, like a timer.

XML Attributes

The StatusBar type has the following XML attributes.

defaultValue

The default value of the slider.

drawLayer

The layer in which the bar's textures will be drawn. Default: ARTWORK.

maxValue

The maximum value of the bar.

minValue

The minimum value of the bar.

orientation

HORIZONTAL or VERTICAL (default).

rotatesTexture

Can be set to `true` to rotate the texture to fit the status bar. Allows you to use horizontal textures for vertical bars. Default: `false`.

XML Elements

The `StatusBar` type has the following XML elements.

BarColor

Controls the color of the status bar with its r, g, b, and a attributes.

BarTexture

A texture object that is used for the status bar.

Lua Methods

The `StatusBar` type has the following Lua methods.

statusBar:GetMinMaxValues()

Returns the minimum and maximum values of the bar.

statusBar:GetOrientation()

Returns the orientation.

statusBar:GetRotatesTexture()

Returns the rotate texture setting.

statusBar:GetStatusBarTexture()

Returns the texture.

statusBar:GetValue()

Returns the current value.

statusBar:SetMinMaxValues(*min, max*)

Sets the minimum and maximum values.

statusBar:SetOrientation(*orientation*)

Sets the orientation to either `HORIZONTAL` or `VERTICAL`.

statusBar:SetRotatesTexture()

Changes the texture rotation setting.

statusBar:SetStatusBarColor(*r, g, b, a*)

Changes the color of the bar.

statusBar:SetStatusBarTexture(*texture*)

Changes the bar's texture.

statusBar:SetValue(*value*)

Sets the value.

Combat Log and Unit Reference

This appendix contains all the information you are ever going to need about the combat log and combat-related functions. You can probably find all the information presented here on the Internet (for example on WoWWiki), but it is scattered. It can be useful to have all the combat-related events and units in a single place.

Combat Log Events

The two combat log events `COMBAT_LOG_EVENT` and `COMBAT_LOG_EVENT_UNFILTERED` have the same arguments; the only difference is that the unfiltered event is called for all combat log events, while the normal event is fired only for events that pass through your currently active combat log filter. You should always use the unfiltered event in your addon unless you are writing a combat log replacement that uses the combat log filter settings.

These events receive numerous arguments (up to 20) based on the subevent. The basic event arguments are also covered in Chapter 9, which deals with the combat log.

Standard Arguments

As listed in Table B-1, there are eight standard arguments, which are always available.

Table B-1. *The First Eight Combat Log Arguments*

Argument Name	Description
timestamp	A timestamp that contains the exact time when the event occurred. This can be used as the second argument to date(*fmt*, *time*).
event	The subevent.
sourceGUID	The GUID (globally unique identifier) of the entity that generated the event.
sourceName	The name of the entity that generated the event. For example, if you cast a spell this is your name.
sourceFlags	Flags that contain additional information about the entity that generated this event. Table B-11 later in this appendix shows how we can extract information from this bit field.
destGUID	The GUID of the target.
destName	The target's name.
destFlags	Flags of the target.

Additional Arguments for the Prefixes SPELL_ and RANGE_

Table B-2 lists the arguments appended to all SPELL_* and RANGE_* subevents.

Table B-2. *Additional Arguments of SPELL and RANGE Events*

Argument Name	Description
spellId	The ID of the spell. This is the same ID that is also used by many WoW database sites, like Wowhead. You can build a URL with the following pattern to retrieve additional information about a spell ID from such a site: http://www.wowhead.com/?spell=<spellId>
spellName	The name of the spell.
spellSchool	The school of the spell. This is a bit field.

Additional Argument for the Prefix ENVIRONMENTAL_

The ENVIRONMENTAL_* events define only one additional argument, the string *environmentalType*. This value is one of the following strings:

- DROWNING
- FALLING
- FATIGUE
- FIRE
- LAVA
- SLIME

Additional Arguments for the Suffix _DAMAGE

All subevents that end in _DAMAGE receive the additional arguments listed in Table B-3.

Table B-3. *Additional Arguments of Events with the Suffix _DAMAGE*

Argument Name	Description
amount	The amount of damage the attack did.
overkill	The overkill damage if the target died from the attack.
school	The school of the damage; like the spell's school, this is a bit field.
resisted	The amount of damage that was resisted.
blocked	The amount of blocked damage.
absorbed	The amount of absorbed damage.
critical	1 if the hit was critical, nil otherwise.
glancing	1 if it was a glancing strike, nil otherwise.
crushing	1 if it was a crushing blow, nil otherwise.

Additional Arguments for the Suffix _HEAL

All subevents that end in _HEAL receive the additional arguments listed in Table B-4.

Table B-4. *Additional Arguments of Events with the Suffix _HEAL*

Argument Name	Description
amount	The amount of damage the attack did
overhealing	The overheal
critical	1 if the hit was critical, nil otherwise

Additional Arguments for the Suffix _MISSED

All subevents that end in _MISSED receive the additional arguments listed in Table B-5.

Table B-5. *Additional Arguments of Events with the Suffix _MISSED*

Argument Name	Description
missType	The reason the spell or attack missed
amount	The amount of damage that missed

The missType is one of the following strings:

- ABSORB
- BLOCK
- REFLECT
- RESIST (amount is nil if the whole spell was resisted)
- VULNERABILITY (amount will be negative, as a vulnerability results in more damage dealt)

Additional Argument for the Suffix _FAILED

There is only one additional argument for failed spells or attacks: missType. Don't confuse this suffix with the suffix _MISSED and its argument with the same name. A failed spell was not cast at all, for example because of insufficient mana. A missed spell or attack was cast but resisted or parried, for example.

missType is here already a localized string that is displayed as it is in your UI and not an identifier.

Additional Argument for the Suffix _EXTRA_ATTACKS

There is only one additional argument for actions that cause extra attacks: amount, the number of additional attacks granted. All of the extra attacks will generate the usual SWING_DAMAGE events.

Additional Arguments for the Suffixes _ENERGIZE, _DRAIN, and _LEECH

Subevents that end in _ENERGIZE, _DRAIN, or _LEECH receive the additional arguments listed in Table B-6.

Table B-6. *Additional Arguments of Events with the Suffixes _ENERGIZE, _DRAIN, and _LEECH*

Argument Name	Description
amount	The amount of power gained.
powerType	The power type (mana, energy, health, and so on).
extraAmount	Only available for _LEECH. The additional power that was drained from the affected target but was not transferred to the caster (for example, when using Drain Life with full health).

The argument powerType is a number that identifies the power type. There are global variables available that should be used instead of the numeric identifiers as it makes your code more readable and resilient to API changes. Table B-7 lists all global variables with their respective values.

Table B-7. *Possible Values for powerType*

Variable	Value
SPELL_POWER_MANA	0
SPELL_POWER_RAGE	1
SPELL_POWER_FOCUS	2
SPELL_POWER_ENERGY	3
SPELL_POWER_HAPPINESS	4
SPELL_POWER_RUNES	5
SPELL_POWER_RUNIC_POWER	6

Additional Arguments for Dispels and Interrupts

There are four events used when buffs are canceled prematurely: SPELL_DISPEL if it was dispelled, SPELL_DISPEL_FAILED if a display attempt was resisted, SPELL_STOLEN if a buff was stolen (for example by Steal Magic), and SPELL_AURA_BROKEN_SPELL if a damage-sensitive debuff (like Polymorph) was broken by an attack on the target.

The event SPELL_INTERRUPT is fired when a spell is interrupted; it uses the same arguments as the dispel events, so it's listed here. Table B-8 lists the additional arguments of these events.

Table B-8. *Additional Arguments of Dispel and Interrupt Events*

Argument Name	Description
extraSpellId	The ID of the spell that was interrupted or dispelled.
extraSpellName	The name of the interrupted/dispelled spell.
extraSchool	The school (bit field) of the interrupted/dispelled spell.
auraType	Only available for SPELL_DISPEL, SPELL_AURA_BROKEN_SPELL, and SPELL_STOLEN; this value is either BUFF or DEBUFF.

Additional Arguments for Buff Events

There are six buff-related events:

- SPELL_AURA_APPLIED
- SPELL_AURA_REMOVED
- SPELL_AURA_APPLIED_DOSE
- SPELL_AURA_REMOVED_DOSE
- SPELL_AURA_REFRESH
- SPELL_AURA_BROKEN

All of them receive the additional argument *auraType*, which is either BUFF or DEBUFF. The events ending with _DOSE also receive the argument *amount*, which indicates the value of buff stacks on the affected unit after the event.

Note that the event SPELL_AURA_BROKEN_SPELL is, despite the name, a dispel event and uses different arguments.

Additional Arguments for Damage Shield Events

There are three events related to damage shields: DAMAGE_SHIELD is fired when an attacker is damaged by the effect of a shield (such as Fire Shield). This event behaves like a SPELL_DAMAGE event and receives the same arguments as such an event. DAMAGE_SHIELD_MISSED uses the same arguments as SPELL_MISSED.

Another shield type is one that splits the damage among multiple persons; it uses the event DAMAGE_SPLIT, which takes the same arguments as DAMAGE_SHIELD.

Additional Arguments for Enchant Events

Applying enchants or temporary effects like poisons or Shaman weapon buffs generates the event ENCHANT_APPLIED. The event ENCHANT_REMOVED is fired when the effect wears off. Both events use the arguments listed in Table B-9.

Table B-9. *Additional Arguments of Events with the Prefix ENCHANT_*

Argument Name	Description
spellName	The name of the spell or poison used
itemId	The ID of the targeted item
itemName	The name of the targeted item

The Spell School Bit Field

The default UI provides bit masks to extract flags from this bit field. Table B-10 shows all global variables that hold bit masks for spell bit fields.

Table B-10. *Bit Masks for Spell Schools*

Variable	Bit Mask
SCHOOL_MASK_NONE	0x0
SCHOOL_MASK_PHYSICAL	0x1
SCHOOL_MASK_HOLY	0x2
SCHOOL_MASK_FIRE	0x4
SCHOOL_MASK_NATURE	0x8
SCHOOL_MASK_FROST	0x10
SCHOOL_MASK_SHADOW	0x20
SCHOOL_MASK_ARCANE	0x40

The Unit Flags Bit Field

Table B-11 shows the global variables that can be used as bit masks on the sourceFlags and destFlags arguments.

Table B-11. *Bit Masks for Unit Flags*

Variable	Bit Mask
COMBATLOG_OBJECT_AFFILIATION_MINE	0x00000001
COMBATLOG_OBJECT_AFFILIATION_PARTY	0x00000002
COMBATLOG_OBJECT_AFFILIATION_RAID	0x00000004
COMBATLOG_OBJECT_AFFILIATION_OUTSIDER	0x00000008
COMBATLOG_OBJECT_REACTION_FRIENDLY	0x00000010
COMBATLOG_OBJECT_REACTION_NEUTRAL	0x00000020
COMBATLOG_OBJECT_REACTION_HOSTILE	0x00000040
COMBATLOG_OBJECT_CONTROL_PLAYER	0x00000100
COMBATLOG_OBJECT_CONTROL_NPC	0x00000200
COMBATLOG_OBJECT_TYPE_PLAYER	0x00000400
COMBATLOG_OBJECT_TYPE_NPC	0x00000800
COMBATLOG_OBJECT_TYPE_PET	0x00001000

Variable	Bit Mask
COMBATLOG_OBJECT_TYPE_GUARDIAN	0x00002000
COMBATLOG_OBJECT_TYPE_OBJECT	0x00004000
COMBATLOG_OBJECT_TARGET	0x00010000
COMBATLOG_OBJECT_FOCUS	0x00020000
COMBATLOG_OBJECT_MAINTANK	0x00040000
COMBATLOG_OBJECT_MAINASSIST	0x00080000
COMBATLOG_OBJECT_RAIDTARGET1	0x00100000
COMBATLOG_OBJECT_RAIDTARGET2	0x00200000
COMBATLOG_OBJECT_RAIDTARGET3	0x00400000
COMBATLOG_OBJECT_RAIDTARGET4	0x00800000
COMBATLOG_OBJECT_RAIDTARGET5	0x01000000
COMBATLOG_OBJECT_RAIDTARGET6	0x02000000
COMBATLOG_OBJECT_RAIDTARGET7	0x04000000
COMBATLOG_OBJECT_RAIDTARGET8	0x08000000
COMBATLOG_OBJECT_NONE	0x80000000

Unit IDs

A unit ID is a string that identifies a player or NPC. What are called *primary* unit IDs that consist of single identifier (for example player); secondary (as well as tertiary, and so on) unit IDs can be built by appending suffixes to primary IDs. Table B-12 lists all primary unit IDs.

Table B-12. *Primary Unit IDs*

Prefix	Description
focus	Your focus target.
player	You.
pet	Your pet.
partyn	The nth party member. Note that you are not your own party member, meaning that you cannot refer to yourself by using such a unit ID. $0 < n < 5$.
partypetn	The pet of the nth party member. $0 < n < 5$; you cannot refer to your own pet with this unit ID.
raidn	The nth raid member. This can, unlike partyn, be you.
raidpetn	The pet of the nth raid member. This can, unlike raidpetn, be you.
arenan	The enemy players in arena matches. $0 < n < 6$.
target	Your current target.
mouseover	The unit your mouse is currently over.
none	Refers to no unit.
npc	The NPC you are currently interacting with. Interacting means that you have a window like the flight map or quest dialog of the NPC opened.

The two suffixes `target` and `pet` can be appended to any unit ID to refer to the target or pet of a unit. Note that there is no difference between `partypetn` and `partynpet` when using the unit ID in a unit function like `UnitName(uId)`. But `partypetn` is a primary unit ID, while `partynpet` is secondary. There are some events that are only fired for primary IDs; for example, `UNIT_TARGET` is fired every time a unit with a primary ID changes its target. You will therefore see the `partypetn` and `raidpetn` IDs as arguments in many `UNIT_*` events.

Unit Functions

There are several functions available that retrieve information about the unit identified by a given unit ID:

- `UnitAffectingCombat(uId)`: Checks if the unit is in combat.

- `UnitArmor(uId)`: Returns the armor of the unit ID. This can only be used on yourself.

- `UnitAttackBothHands(uId)`: Returns 1 if the unit wields two weapons.

- `UnitAttackPower(uId)`: Returns the melee attack power. This can only be used on yourself.

- `UnitAttackSpeed(uId)`: Returns the attack speed of the unit in seconds.

- `UnitAura(uId, buffId, filter)`: Returns information about a specific buff on the unit. The first buff on a unit has the ID 1, the second 2, and so on. The third operational argument is a string that sets a filter. Possible values for the filter are the following:

  - `CANCELABLE`: Matches buffs that can be canceled.

  - `NOT_CANCELABLE`: Matches buffs that cannot be canceled.

  - `HARMFUL`: Matches spells that do harm.

  - `HELPFUL`: Matches helpful spells.

  - `PLAYER`: Matches buffs cast by you.

  - `RAID`: Matches buffs that you can cast on other raid members.

  You can combine multiple filters in the filter string. The default value for *filter* is `"HELPFUL"`, meaning that it only returns buffs. For example, `"HARMFUL PLAYER"` matches all harmful spells that have been cast by you.

  The return values of this function are `name`, `rank`, `icon`, `count`, `debuffType`, `duration`, `expirationTime`, `unitCaster`, and `isStealable`.

- `UnitCanAssist(uId1, uId2)`: Determines whether a unit can assist another unit.

- `UnitCanAttack(uId1, uId2)`: Determines whether a unit can attack another unit.

- `UnitCanCooperate(uId1, uId2)`: Determines whether two units can cooperate; that is, whether both units are players of the same faction. The difference between this function and `UnitCanAssist` is that a player can assist an NPC but not cooperate with one.

- `UnitCharacterPoints(uId)`: Returns the number of unspent talent points of a unit.

- `UnitClass(uId)`: Returns the localized class of a player followed by the English name of the class in capital letters.

- UnitClassification(*uId*): Gets the classification of a unit; this can be normal, trivial ("gray" mobs), elite, rare, rareelite, or worldboss.

- UnitCreatureFamily(*uId*): Gets the creature family of a beast (for example, Cat or Spider).

- UnitCreatureType(*uId*): Gets the creature type of a unit (for example, Beast or Giant).

- UnitDefense(*uId*): Gets the defense skill of a unit.

- UnitDetailedThreatSituation(*uId1*, *uId2*): Returns the threat situation between two units. The return values are isTanking, status, threatpct, rawthreatpct, threatvalue.

- UnitExists(*uId*): Determines whether a unit ID references an existing unit.

- UnitFactionGroup(*uId*): Returns the faction of a unit (for example, Sons of Hodir or Alliance).

- UnitGUID(*uId*): Returns the GUID of a unit.

- UnitHasRelicSlot(*uId*): Determines whether a unit has a relic slot.

- UnitHealth(*uId*): Returns the current health of a unit.

- UnitHealthMax(*uId*): Returns the maximum health of a unit.

- UnitInParty(*uId*): Determines whether a unit is in your party.

- UnitInRaid(*uId*): Determines whether a unit is in your raid.

- UnitInRange(*uId*): Returns 1 if *uId* is less than 30 yards away from you.

- UnitIsAFK(*uId*): Determines whether a player is AFK.

- UnitIsCharmed(*uId*): Checks whether a unit is mind-controlled.

- UnitIsConnected(*uId*): Checks whether a player is online.

- UnitIsCorpse(*uId*): Determines whether a unit is a corpse.

- UnitIsDead(*uId*): Determines whether a unit is dead.

- UnitIsDeadOrGhost(*uId*): Determines whether a unit is dead or in ghost forms.

- UnitIsDND(*uId*): Checks whether a unit has DND enabled.

- UnitIsEnemy(*uId1*, *uId2*): Checks whether two units can attack each other.

- UnitIsFeignDeath(*uId*): Determines whether a unit is feigning death. This only works on units in your party or raid.

- UnitIsFriend(*uId1*, *uId2*): Returns 1 if two units are friendly towards each other.

- UnitIsGhost(*uId*): Checks whether a unit is in ghost form.

- UnitIsPVP(*uId*): Checks whether a unit is flagged for PvP.

- UnitIsPVPFreeForAll(*uId*): Checks whether a unit is flagged for FFA PvP (for example in the Stranglethorn Arena).

- UnitIsPartyLeader(*uId*): Determines whether a unit is the leader of a party.

- UnitIsPlayer(*uId*): Determines whether a unit is a player.

- `UnitIsPlusMob(uId)`: Returns 1 for elite mobs.

- `UnitIsTapped(uId)`: Checks whether a mob is tapped by someone else.

- `UnitIsTappedByPlayer(uId)`: Checks whether a mob is tapped by you.

- `UnitIsTrivial(uId)`: Checks whether a mob is trivial ("gray").

- `UnitIsUnit(uId1, uId2)`: Checks whether two unit IDs reference the same unit.

- `UnitIsVisible(uId1)`: Checks whether a unit is in your range (about 100 yards).

- `UnitLevel(uId)`: Gets the level of a unit.

- `UnitName(uId)`: Returns the name and server (in battlegrounds) of a player.

- `UnitOnTaxi(uId)`: Checks whether a unit is on a taxi service.

- `UnitPlayerControlled(uId)`: Checks whether a unit is controlled by a player.

- `UnitPlayerOrPetInParty(uId)`: Determines whether the unit is a member of your party or a pet of a party member.

- `UnitPlayerOrPetInRaid(uId)`: Works like `UnitPlayerOrPetInParty` but for raid groups.

- `UnitPower(uId, powerType)`: Gets the current amount of *powerType* (mana, energy, and so on) of a unit. *powerType* uses the same values as mentioned in the combat log event above.

- `UnitPowerMax(uId, powerType)`: Gets the maximum amount of *powerType* of a unit.

- `UnitPowerType(uId)`: Gets the current power type of a unit.

- `UnitRace(uId)`: Gets the localized race of a unit followed by a non-localized capitalized string.

- `UnitRangedAttackPower(uId)`: Returns the ranged attack power. This only works on yourself.

- `UnitReaction(uId1, uId2)`: Determines the reaction of *uId1* towards *uId2*. Possible values are `friendly`, `neutral`, and `hostile`.

- `UnitXP(uId)`: Gets the current XP of *uId1*. This only works on yourself.

- `UnitXPMax(uId)`: Gets the maximum XP of *uId1*. This only works on yourself.

Index

You Need the Companion eBook